MBA、MEM、MPAcc、MPA 等管理类联考与经济类联考

英语（二）新教材

主编 都学课堂学术中心 副主编 查国生 薛冰等

教材配套课程开通说明

输入激活码，此码仅限用一次，
如有问题联系客服：400-600-0270

北京理工大学出版社
BEIJING INSTITUTE OF TECHNOLOGY PRESS

版权专有　侵权必究

图书在版编目（CIP）数据

MBA、MEM、MPAcc、MPA 等管理类联考与经济类联考英语（二）新教材 / 都学课堂学术中心主编 . —北京：北京理工大学出版社，2019.2（2020.3 重印）

ISBN 978 – 7 – 5682 – 6751 – 9

Ⅰ. ①M… Ⅱ. ①都… Ⅲ. ①英语 – 词汇 – 研究生 – 入学考试 – 自学参考资料 Ⅳ. ① H310.421

中国版本图书馆 CIP 数据核字（2019）第 032744 号

出版发行 / 北京理工大学出版社有限责任公司	
社　　址 / 北京市海淀区中关村南大街 5 号	
邮　　编 / 100081	
电　　话 /（010）68914775（总编室）	
（010）82562903（教材售后服务热线）	
（010）68948351（其他图书服务热线）	
网　　址 / http://www.bitpress.com.cn	
经　　销 / 全国各地新华书店	
印　　刷 / 三河市鑫鑫科达彩色印刷包装有限公司	
开　　本 / 787 毫米 ×1092 毫米　1/16	责任编辑 / 高　芳
印　　张 / 31.75	文案编辑 / 胡　莹
字　　数 / 792 千字	责任校对 / 杜　枝
版　　次 / 2019 年 2 月第 1 版　2020 年 3 月第 6 次印刷	责任印制 / 李志强
定　　价 / 84.80 元	

图书出现印装质量问题，请拨打售后服务热线，本社负责调换

都学课堂管理类联考学术委员会

数学委员 陈　剑　孙华明　刘　智　朱　曦　刘　沛　王　宁
逻辑委员 饶思中　陈慕泽　孙江媛　刘强伟　孙　勇　史先进
写作委员 陈君华　田　然　刘连帆　李　诚　王　莹
英语委员 查国生　陈　鹏　唐名龙　颜贤斌　顾　越　薛　冰
　　　　　　韩　健　杨红宇
面试复试 张诗华　许焕琛　王　亮　蔺雪飞

满足全部需求的贴心学习备考服务

一、在线题库——考研必备工具

极简的用户界面,给考生带来近乎完美的刷题体验;原题录入,三重校验,试题质量有保障;配套名师讲评,考生可边刷题边学习,高效提分;桌面与移动多屏覆盖,数据云端同步;全国各大院校官方推荐。

在线题库链接:https://ktiku.doxue.com/doxue/exam

下载APP,立即做题

二、单词小程序——大数据算法,科学记忆

都学课堂独家研发单词小程序,采用计算机大数据算法科学筛选考研核心词汇,依据艾宾浩斯遗忘曲线分频分组科学记忆单词,智能区分已学与未学词汇,从而实现高效复习、全面掌握英语核心词汇的学习效果,是管理类、经济类联考考生专属背单词工具。

扫码,开始背单词

三、公益大模考——百所院校联合承办

自2015年以来,都学课堂与各大院校共同发起万人公益大模考,为考生提供优质的模考服务,真实的考试环境,帮助了数以万计的考生完成考前的模拟考试演练,被考生视为检验复习成果的试金石。

36个城市同步开考;150余所院校联合发起;专业评分名师讲评;全真模拟实战演练。

扫码,快速报名模考

查老寄语

考生朋友们：

大家好！通过这本书认识彼此，我们就算是结下了不解的师生之缘。我们都知道升学难，最难是考研；考研难，最难在英语。对那些离开校园已久且长期不用英语的在职人员来说更是如此。根据《全国硕士研究生入学统一考试英语（二）考试大纲》（以下简写为"大纲"），报考 MBA、MEM、MPAcc、MPA 等专业硕士研究生招生考试的考生需要参加英语（二）考试，英语（二）考试的试卷内容包括英语知识应用（10%）、阅读理解（40%+10%）、翻译（15%）和写作（10%+15%）四大部分。各项试题均以语篇形式呈现，不仅包含了一定数量的词汇和短语，而且还涉及英语语法、语篇结构和文化背景等知识。如何通过考试并取得优异的成绩是我们共同面对的问题。我是一名普通的大学教师，曾多次主持英语（二）考试的命题和阅卷工作，而且至今依旧奋战在考研辅导第一线。根据本人与全体编委同事的经验，特对考生朋友们提出以下建议：

一、必须研读大纲

要想攻克考研英语，首先得从了解考研英语开始，而大纲是最好的研读资料。通过研读大纲，考生才能充分了解考试要求、考点范围、命题规律和试题特点。也只有在充分了解上述信息后，备考才有目标，复习才有实效。本书最显著的特点就是没有直接将整个大纲摆在考生面前，而是将其合理分解，并与具体题型紧密结合起来，再经过资深辅导教师深入浅出的分析和总结，从而确保考生备考有的放矢，复习切实有效。

二、备考必有规划

凡事预则立，不预则废！但凡决定参加考研，就必须制定一个系统、周密、切实可行的复习规划。复习规划可以根据个人的具体情况而定，但必须落实到以下四个方面：

（一）打好词汇基础

要顺利通过考研英语考试，尤其是取得优异成绩，词汇基础过硬才是第一保障。但需要郑重声明：除熟记考研词汇（约 5 500 个）外，考生还应该熟悉并掌握构词的基本元素（词根、前缀和后缀）以及构词的基本原理。

（二）掌握语法核心

语法包括词法和句法两个方面。就考研英语而言，测试语法不再采用传统的"点对点"的形式，而是将语法测试与四大题型紧密结合，"间接"地测试语法。提倡"核心语法"，就是建议考生在考纲制定的考点范围内，将各考点主次分明，难易相分，再将精力进行合理的分配。无论现有的英语语法基础如何，考生都应该将复习重心放在句法部分，尤其是句子成分、基本句型、复杂句式、特殊结构等方面。只有掌握了这些基本的知识要点，考生才能够快速地攻克考试中的长难句。

（三）熟知应试技巧

就英语知识而言，基本内容包括词汇、语法、常识以及常识背后的常理。但考研毕竟是选拔性考试，这意味着在规定的时间内准确快速地呈现最佳答案才是备考目标的重心。因此，在掌握考纲规定的知识之余，考生必须熟悉各考试题型的试题特征，并掌握对应的解题技巧。一言以蔽之：应试技巧不是万能的，没有应试技巧是万万不能的。这是国内考研的现状，更是应试选拔的实情。

（四）展开系统模拟

考场就是没有硝烟的战场！系统模拟是考场获胜的必要环节。坦率地讲，广大考生并不缺乏练习，他们真正缺乏的是系统的练习。所谓系统的练习，就是指严格模拟真实考场，切实展开水平检测。通过系统的实战练习，考生可以实现以下目标：

1. 检测水平，查漏洞补短板；
2. 积累知识，提升阅读语感；
3. 管控时间，夯实心理素质；
4. 积累心得，熟悉解题技巧。

三、复习必备资料

系统的备考规划必须依托完整的复习资料才能收获实效。当下考生面临的问题不是资料的稀缺，而是如何选择资料。打开网页，踏入书店，都不难找到与考研相关的资料。但对于考生来说，最重要的是找到适合自己的考研资料。这本书是一个不错的选择！因为它有如下特点：

（一）创作阵容强大，值得点赞

参与本书编写的学术委员有命题专家、阅卷专家，还有长期坚持在考研辅导第一线的资深教师。他们有丰富的教学经验，对考试大纲的透彻理解，还有对命题规律的精准把握。

（二）结构设计合理，内容全面

本书以词汇记忆和核心语法为开篇内容，然后紧扣考试四大题型从试题特征与解题技巧等方面逐一展开阐述。应试技巧以考试大纲分析和命题趋势剖析为基础，结合真题进行讲解。此外，在真题同源训练环节，也严格遵循命题规律科学地进行选材。这使得巩固练习不仅具有实战性，而且具有预测性。

（三）知识呈现有序，表达生动

任何知识都须以合理的方式呈现给读者，否则将增加读者理解的时间成本。此外，简洁、形象、生动的表达也大大有利于提高掌握知识的效率。为了避免文字信息超载给读者带来阅读压力，本书改变了昔日的风格，通过植入大量的图示、图标并辅以简单明了的阐述来使考试要点一目了然，使知识难点迎刃而解。

我坚信：只要考生听取了上述三条建议，按照既定复习计划潜心备考，英语（二）考试将不再是考生步入研究生阶段的绊脚石，而是行之有效的敲门砖。

衷心希望广大考生能够实现自己的梦想。让我们携手共勉，共创美好明天！

前 言

英语（二）新教材升级版终于和广大考研朋友见面了。与旧版相比较，升级版更加凸显了复习规划、基础积累、方法实效、能力培养和配套服务。本书是由都学课堂集全体辅导名师和资深教研人员的知识、阅历和智慧为一体，呈现给考生的考研复习宝典。

新教材升级版主要由必备基础篇、技巧提高篇、真题实战篇三个部分组成。必备基础篇，从科学备考规划入手，在词汇和语法上立足。在词汇学习方面，新教材升级版一改"死记硬背"的背词气息，转而强调单词的内在逻辑和外在联系，积极引导考生从内外两面着手掌握或创造适合自身的记忆逻辑。对于非英语专业的考生来说，学习单词就要不择手段。无论什么方法，只有适合自己的才是最好的！在语法学习方面，紧扣考研英语的命题规律和试题特征，从运用的角度着重讲解句法，进而为突破长难句打下坚实的基础。技巧提高篇，同样立足于命题规律，以考点为中心，注重题型认知、特点分析和对应性解题策略。在题材选取方面，新教材升级版特别重视预测性，各题型的配套练习，除节选部分真题作为例题讲解外，均设置了充足的真题同源素材。毋庸置疑，同源素材比真题更具有预测性，因为考过的真题永远不会再考。此外，在真题同源练习精讲环节，特别注重长难句的讲解和核心单词的拓展。

任何教材，如果脱离了同步配套服务，就好比向考生扔出一颗炮仗，而教师在一旁听响声。为了确保考生学好，考场考好，新教材升级版特地配备了同步精品视频课程，通过名师引导讲解学习，真正实现线上线下联动，教师学生互动。

梦想付诸行动才能成真，行动依赖方法才有实效。为了考生的梦想，英语（二）新教材一直在行动，在努力！

都学课堂

Part A　必备基础篇

第一章　词汇必备 2
　第一节　复习规划 2
　第二节　学习方法 4

第二章　核心语法 8
　第一节　语法概述 8
　第二节　要点详解 11

Part B　技巧提高篇

第三章　英语知识运用 62
　第一节　最新大纲解读与应试策略 62
　第二节　英语知识运用精讲 67

第四章　阅读理解（A 部分）...................................... 117
　第一节　最新大纲解读与命题趋势 117
　第二节　题型分类与解题技巧 120
　第三节　真题同源实战 128

第五章　阅读理解（B 部分）...................................... 228
　第一节　最新大纲解读与命题趋势 228

I

第二节	题型分类与解题技巧	230
第三节	真题同源实战	239

第六章　英译汉...278

第一节	大纲解读与应试策略	278
第二节	英译汉技巧	282
第三节	精讲精练	307

第七章　英文写作...323

第一节	英文写作大纲解读与应试策略	323
第二节	写作高分要素与谋篇布局原则	327
第三节	应用文（小作文）高分指南	346
第四节	图表作文（大作文）高分指南	361
第五节	高分范文与热点话题预测	390
第六节	提纲作文或图表作文句型	405
第七节	作文修改	443

Part C　真题实战篇

2018 年全国硕士研究生招生考试英语（二）试题	448
2018 年全国硕士研究生招生考试英语（二）参考答案	462
2019 年全国硕士研究生招生考试英语（二）试题	463
2019 年全国硕士研究生招生考试英语（二）参考答案	477
2020 年全国硕士研究生招生考试英语（二）试题	478
2020 年全国硕士研究生招生考试英语（二）参考答案	492

附录

全国专业硕士培养单位	494

Part A　必备基础篇

- 第一章　词汇必备
- 第二章　核心语法

考点分析　该部分是全书的基础篇，主要讲述考研英语（二）大纲中规定的词汇以及语法知识。该部分分为两章：第一章词汇必备，主要讲述相关词汇的学习；第二章核心语法，主要讲述语法的要点。

时间安排　该部分是整个备考规划中的基础部分，建议考生用5天时间精读。在精读过程中，考生须重点掌握词汇及语法知识。

第一章 词汇必备

第一节 复习规划

大纲明确表明：考生应能较熟练地掌握约5 500个常用词汇以及相关常用词组；应能根据具体语境、句子结构和前后文逻辑关系理解一些非常用词汇的词义。这充分表明考研英语在词汇方面不仅有数量要求，还有难易层次之分。为了便于考生高效备考，特做如下归纳：

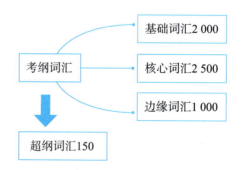

基础词汇：约2 000个。全为初中、高中词汇。基础相对薄弱的考生应率先完成对该部分单词的学习和记忆。

核心词汇：约2 500个。考生需要重点学习和记忆这部分单词。

边缘词汇：约1 000个。英语基础相对扎实的考生需要了解记忆该部分单词；基础相对薄弱的考生可酌情而定。

超纲词汇：每年考试都会涉及约150个（约3%）超纲词汇。对这些非常用词汇的测试目的在于考核考生对具体语境、句子结构和前后文逻辑关系的理解。因此对付这一部分单词主要是靠自身的阅读理解能力，而不是对于这些单词的记忆。

除了掌握词汇之外，考生还必须对构词的基本元素（词根、前缀和后缀）以及构词的基本原理有相应的掌握。这不仅可以提高单词学习的效果和效率，而且还有利于理解一些非常用词汇。例如2019年英语（二）试题第25题（阅读Text 1）考查词汇"transgression"的词义。虽然通过上下文语境可以推断出该词的含义，但是如果直接从构词基本元素和基本规则入手，似乎更加简单，分析如下：

前缀trans-表示转移或跨越，常见单词transport（*n.&vt.*运输），translate（*v.*翻译）均可以验证。

词根-gress-表示行走或走动，基础词汇progress（*n.*进步；提示：pro-作为单词前缀，表示向前，向上）同样可以验证。

名词后缀-ion仅仅表示单词词性。

综上所述，transgression就表示跨越某个界限，延伸为违反某种规定，即僭越。所以可以理解为"犯错，违反"。尽管是一个非常用词汇，但是其构词基本元素都可以在基础词汇中找到。这也提醒考生，学习单词不要死记硬背，而要活学活用。

单词学习是一场持久性攻坚战，最忌讳"一时兴起，心血来潮""三天打鱼，两天晒网""投机取巧，急功近利"。但现实往往就是如此！上述现象不仅普遍，而且通常是考生考研英语成绩不过关的罪魁祸首。要赢得胜利，学习单词就必须要有一个详细的规划。结合备考周期，通常采用如下方案：

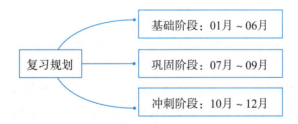

基础阶段：本阶段持续半年，建议在备考进入系统复习阶段（即6月底）前完成。在此期间，学习重心就是背单词！无论采用什么方法或借助什么资料，目标就是——搞定单词。因为没有单词基础，任何应试方法、秒杀技巧都是"自编自导自演式的自圆其说"！

巩固阶段：参加持久战，贵在坚持！巩固阶段的学习不是对基础阶段学习过程的机械重复，而是全面升级。何为升级？升级就是以"新高度"审视单词学习，以"新方式"巩固记忆成果。所谓"新高度"就是在掌握单词的基础上，从"知其然"转移到"知其所以然"；所谓"新方式"就是敢于从结构拆解入手，充分掌握构词的基本元素和基本原理。

以学习单词appreciate为例：

学习进度	学习模式	学习任务
基础阶段	直接记忆	拼写appreciate；vt.欣赏，感激；vi.增值，涨价
巩固阶段	全面升级	拆解ap+preci+ate；ap-为前缀（前缀ad-的变形）；-ate表示动词后缀；词根-preci-（=price），表示价值；认为事物有价值，就是欣赏，认为他人的所作所为对你有价值，就要感激。从发音角度掌握词根，preci=price=praise，进而进一步巩固单词： praise（n.&vt.赞扬） appraise=ap+praise（vt.估价，评价，鉴定） depreciate=de+preci+ate（v.轻视，贬低）

在新的备考阶段只有全面升级对单词的学习，才能永葆学习激情直至取得最后的胜利。据调查显示：在进入巩固阶段后，很多考生由于没有找到明确的目标和方式，导致学习单词的激情锐减，甚至还出现了遗忘现象。

冲刺阶段： 复习进入冲刺阶段，单词学习也不能放弃。不可否认，冲刺阶段的主要任务就是系统模拟练习。因此学习单词的模式也需要相应调整。在冲刺阶段，单词方面的学习任务是：提升与拓展。也就是说在做题的过程中要敢于运用各种方法突破对陌生单词的理解，并对这些词汇进行总结与归纳。

第二节　学习方法

由于学习内容、学习目标、学习主体的不同，相应地，采用的方式方法也应有所不同。就考研英语单词学习而言，大多数考生通常采用"自然拼读记忆"，即依托单词的拼读和拼写来达到记忆词义的目的。但结合考研的实情，本书特别推荐：结构拆解记忆法。结构拆解记忆法是将重心放在单词拼写与词义的关联上，更适合成年人学习。结构拆解记忆法包括的具体内容如下：

一、单词分类

由于分类标准不同，分类结果也会有所不同。结构拆解记忆法从视觉入手，将单词分为四大类，即独体词、合成词、会意词、派生词（特别声明：如此分类，虽不够严谨，有些许牵强，但确实有效）。具体诠释如下：

1. 独体词→类比汉语独体字的概念。特指一类单词，从发音、拼读乃至语义角度都很难被有机切分，比如：calm，dip，work，ozone等。

2. 合成词→源自英语单词基本构词法。特指一类单词可以被切分为独立的基础单词，比如：underscore（under+score），outline（out+line），football（foot+ball）等。

3. 会意词→类比汉语会意字的概念。会意词的准确定位应该是"前缀派生词"，因其构词原理与会意字相同，为便于符合中国人的习惯，且突出对逻辑推理能力的培养，就此牵强运用一回。比如单词：concentrate=con+centr+ate（前缀con-表示共同或顺势加强；词根-centr-（=center）表示中心；动词后缀-ate表示使……；综合得出：使……到一个中心点→集中）；比如汉字：休=人+木→人靠在树上→休息。

4. 派生词→源自英语单词基本构词法。派生词专指"后缀派生词"这一类，不要和"前缀派生词"（会意词）相互混淆。需要提示的是：派生词也不是简单地在单词尾部添加后缀而成，有时候在派生过程中也会发生变化，甚至会变得面目全非，比如：clear→clarify，wide→width，broad→breadth等。

划分单词类别对记忆单词非常重要。因为单词归类本身就是根据对单词背后逻辑进行的判断而得出的结论。这个结论代表了不同的思维角度，也体现了不同的思维方式，更是创造性地将单词学习与各种能力联系了起来。（参阅下图）

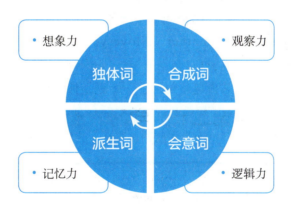

二、记忆逻辑

考场上，阅读的过程就是建立"拼写"（词形）与"理解"（词义）之间的关系的过程。对应到单词学习环节，就是如何构建"单词记忆逻辑"。有了记忆逻辑，单词学习就可以实现：

1.记忆精准，不会张冠李戴，似懂非懂

2.记忆快捷，不会事倍功半，裹足不前

3. 记忆持久，不会稍纵即逝，昙花一现
4. 过程快乐，不再死气沉沉，萎靡不振

构建单词记忆逻辑首先要发现"记忆逻辑"。结合四大单词类别的结构特征，可以得出如下结论：

> 1. 合成词，会意词（前缀派生词）和派生词（后缀派生词）的构词原理就是记忆逻辑，例如：
>
> upset=up+set（合成词。up表示向上；set表示安置；（把底）向上放→vt.打翻→心情被打翻→vt.使烦恼，扰乱；adj.心烦的）
>
> disaster=dis+aster（会意词。前缀dis-表示否定；词根aster=astr=star表示星星；星星掉下来，占星术认为"星星陨落"就是灾难降临→n.灾难）
>
> clarify=clari+fy（派生词。词根clari=clare=clear表示清楚；动词后缀-fy表示使……；把事情弄清楚→vt.澄清）
>
> 2. 独体词，由于在结构上无法拆解，因此不存在内在逻辑。但为了避免"死记硬背"，应积极运用"创新思维"从词形、读音、词义角度创造记忆逻辑，例如：
>
> pest的发音似"拍死它"，于是联想到"害虫"（谐音记忆）；
>
> ozone是由o+z+one组成，O字母代表氧元素，z字母看似数字"2"，one表示1，则O(2+1)=O_3，这是臭氧分子式，所以ozone表示臭氧；
>
> family，句子"Father and mother, I love you!"各单词取首字母，则组成了"family"，所以family表示家庭。
>
> 当然，不是每个单词都能从内部结构入手。对此，我们可以退而求其次，寻求外部联系，构建词汇与词汇间的联系，即采用联想记忆法。例如：
>
> ripe & reap：ripe表示成熟的；reap表示收割，收获。关联逻辑：庄稼成熟，然后收割。

三、记忆元素

结构拆解记忆法的基本元素主要包括：前缀，后缀和词根。掌握常见的基本构词元素是单词记忆的前提。构词的基本元素诠释如下：

1. 后缀：后缀是最常见的单词构词元素，主要有两个功能，即"定词性"和"定词义"功能。比如：trainer=train+er，后缀-er从"定性"角度表明单词是一个名词；从"定义"的角度表明单词是动作的发出者（施动者，而非受动者）。又如trainee=train+ee，后缀-ee一方面表示单词是一个名词,另一方面表示单词是动作的接受者(受动者,而非施动者)。推而广之,就很容易掌握以下单词:employer(n.雇主)→employ(vt.雇佣)→employee(n.雇员);interviewer(n.采访者,面试官)→interview(vt.采访,面试)→interviewee(n.受访者,参加面试者)。后缀还包括形容词后缀、动词后缀和副词后缀,鉴于篇幅有限,不再一一介绍。(备注:有些后缀对单词词义没有任何影响)

2. 前缀:如果说后缀的主要功能是改变词性,那么前缀的主要功能则是改变词义。一个单词,必须要将前缀含义与接在其后的单词构成词素(或单词)的含义结合起来,经过推理之后才能得出具体的含义。比如:

dislike=dis+like,dis-为否定前缀;like表示喜欢;综合推理可知:dislike表示不喜欢;
unlike=un+like,un-为否定前缀;like表示像;综合推理可知:unlike表示不像。

3. 词根:如果说前缀、后缀是单词的装饰点缀之物,那词根则是单词的主心骨。词根表达了单词词义的根源,但不一定表示单词的最终含义。大多数词根都是黏着词素(不能独立存在),必须与后缀、前缀结合后才能构成单词。由于是黏着词素(不是独立的单词),因此不便于记忆。例如:

progress=pro+gress(前缀pro-表示向前或向上;词根-gress-表示走;向前走,即进步)
opportunity=op+port+unity(前缀op-表示顺势加强;词根-port-表示搬运;unity表示统一;(把天时,地利,人和三个要素)搬在一起,从而形成机会)

在方法介绍结束之余,本着对考生负责、对学术严谨的态度,特作出以下声明:

第一,结构拆解记忆法适合成年人记忆单词,虽然适用于大多数单词,但是不能满足所有单词记忆要求。因此,考生也要结合具体情况,展开具体分析。无论白猫黑猫,能抓住老鼠的猫就是好猫。

第二,鉴于本书章节限制,结构拆解记忆法只能介绍其梗概。如果要结合更多具体单词示例,建议考生阅读《考研英语(二)命题人单词解密》一书。

第三,无论多好的记忆方法,都不能确保所有记忆效果持久。因此建议考生在背诵单词的同时,要大胆实践,积极探索,认真总结。简而言之就是一句话:只有通过运用,对单词的印象才会深刻!

第二章 核心语法

第一节 语法概述

英语知识体系共有两大基础，其一为单词，其二为语法。二者支撑起"听、说、读、写、译"五大技能。没有这两大基础，考生在考场上不是"高奏凯歌"，而是"四面楚歌"。

每年考试大纲都会对语法考核范围和考核要求做出明确界定，但是对其考查形式却没有具体说明。分析真题试卷可知：语法考核不再沿袭"点对点"形式，而是采用间接形式，即在运用中考查语法。总之，考研英语语法测试的特点是：处处无语法，处处考语法。攻克考研语法，需要解决以下四个问题：

一、语法是什么？

语法分为词法和句法两个部分。词法是在单词范畴内研究语言知识和使用规则。句法则是扩大到句子层面（甚至篇章）研究语言知识和使用规则。为了使考生便捷、高效地学习语法，先将语法知识体系梳理如下：

第二章 核心语法

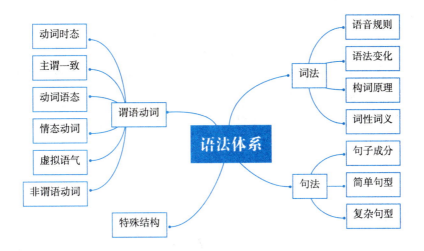

二、语法怎么考？

根据卷面试题形式可知，考研不再就语法单独命题（不再设置传统的语法单选题），而是在综合运用中测试语法。尤其在英语知识应用（完形）、阅读理解、翻译中，对长难句的理解在很大程度上都必须基于较好的语法基础，否则句子结构无法拆解，前后逻辑无法理顺，上下文语境无法把握，自然得不出正确答案。写作带有很强的主观能动性，灵活地运用基本句型、植入复杂句式、穿插特殊结构都能为写作增光添彩，也是取得高分的重要手段。

三、语法考什么？

语法知识内容丰富，体系庞杂。虽然方方面面都很重要，但根据对考研英语试题特征的分析可知，语法测试主要考查句法范畴。建议考生掌握的语法核心要点如下：

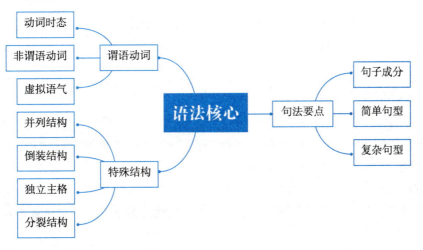

说明： 备考尚有余力的考生应该突破上述要点范畴，并将其他领域的内容逐一掌握。

四、语法怎么学？

在了解考试形式和考试重点之后，最重要的就是如何落实学习任务。对如何学习语法本书给出的建议可以概括为：扫盲点，建体系，重实践。具体阐述如下：

（1）扫盲点：对每个语法核心要点都逐一理解透彻，并熟练掌握，直到彻底消除知识盲区。

（2）建体系：掌握语法的困难之处在于知识点较多，容易混淆。破局之道就在于构建知识体系。用知识体系将相互关联的知识要点串联起来，从而可以避免顾此失彼。

（3）重实践：由于没有直接的语法知识的测试，因此很多考生不太重视语法学习，有的甚至把语法学习当作是累赘，浪费宝贵的复习时间和精力，此点需要引起考生们的警惕。在理解语法知识点后，重要的是积极运用，在实践中加深对语法要点的认知，同时运用语法要点帮助理解句意。考研英语最大的特点就是长难句特别多。在长难句中，不仅成分多样，而且结构复杂。例如2017年真题阅读理解Text 4，第一段就由一个句子构成，详情如下：

> Though often viewed as a problem for western states, the growing frequency of wildfires is a national concern because of its impact on federal tax dollars, says Professor Max Moritz, a specialist in fire ecology and management.
>
> **结构拆解：**
>
> Step 1<抓主句>: says Professor...
>
> Step 2<找从句>: Though... tax dollars
>
> **要点识别：**
>
> ①主句中，a specialist...是前面Professor Max Moritz的同位语；
>
> ②Though... tax dollars整个句子作says的宾语，该从句中又包括一个由though引导的让步状语从句。
>
> 如此，整个句子则可以调整为"普通"形式，即
>
> Professor Max Moritz, a specialist in fire ecology and management, says though often viewed as a problem for western states, the growing frequency of wildfires is a national concern because of its impact on federal tax dollars.
>
> 〖**参考译文**〗火灾生态和管理专家马克斯·莫里茨教授表示，尽管越来越频繁的野火经常被西部州视为一个问题，但由于其对联邦税收的影响，这个问题成为一个全国关注的问题。

第二节 要点详解

这本书是备战考研英语（二）的综合性优选辅导用书，内容涉及词汇、语法、解题技巧和附录等内容，且讲解重心放在了四大题型上。就语法核心要点而言，本书因为篇幅有限而主要集中在以下几个方面：

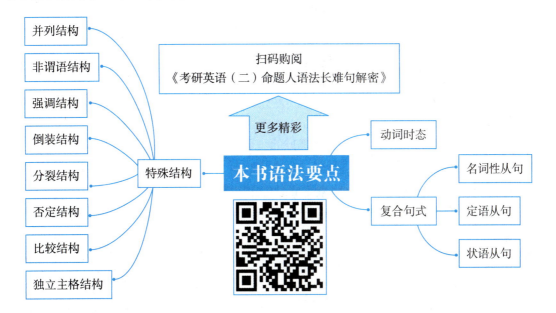

一、动词的时态

时态是"时"与"体"的组合。做有关时态的试题时首先要学会定"时"，即根据题干内容判断要填的动词所对应的动作是什么时候发生的。是现在，过去，将来，还是过去将来？当题干中出现一个过去的动作，而我们要表达的动作晚于题干中的动作时，那么要用过去将来时。定完"时"后。要学会定"体"。"体"分为：一般体、进行体、完成体、完成进行体。

此外，一般过去时和现在完成时的区别是一大难点。首先要搞清现在完成时是现在时，不是过去时，即现在完成时说的是现在的情况。现在完成时有几种用法，但是最不容易掌握的是"过去的事情对现在产生的影响"。虽然动作发生在过去，但说话者如果用现在完成时，表明说话者的重心已经不在过去的动作本身，而是那个动作对现在产生的影响。

需要多加关注的动词时态有八种：一般现在时、一般过去时、一般将来时、现在进行时、过去进行时、现在完成时、过去完成时、过去将来时。

容易混淆的三组动词时态是：一般过去时和现在完成时；一般过去时和过去完成时；过去完成时与现在完成时。

学习动词的时态时，切不可脱离实际运用的语境，一味死记硬背语法规则的条条框框。了解了八种常用时态的一些常用规则后，要留心以英语为母语者在实际生活中如何使用各种时态和语态。

建立时态的时、体概念（"时"即现在时、过去时、将来时、过去将来时；每个时又分为四个"体"，即一般体、进行体、完成体、完成进行体）。

解决动词的时态问题，要遵循如下思路：

（1）这件事情说的是什么时候的事情或情况（定"时"）；

（2）这个动作处于什么状态，是完成了，还是未完成，还是既不表完成又不表进行（定"体"）。

英语中动词共有十六种时态，要求掌握的一般只有八种：一般现在时、一般过去时、一般将来时、现在进行时、过去进行时、现在完成时、过去完成时，过去将来时。另外现在完成进行时、过去完成进行时和将来完成时也比较常用。

时态＼体	现在	过去	将来	过去将来
一般	一般现在时	一般过去时	一般将来时	一般过去将来时
进行	现在进行时	过去进行时	将来进行时	过去将来进行时
完成	现在完成时	过去完成时	将来完成时	过去将来完成时
完成进行	现在完成进行时	过去完成进行时	将来完成进行时	过去将来完成进行时

动词时态的基本用法

➡ 一般体 ⬅

一般体中的一般现在时和一般过去时分别表示现在和过去的经常性、习惯性动作或状态。所谓一般体，表示既不"进行"，又不"完成"。如：

We have meals three times a day.

我们一日吃三餐。（现在的习惯）

He is always ready to help others.

他总是乐于助人。（现在的状态）

When I was a boy, I often went to play in that park.

我小时候，常去那个公园玩。（过去的习惯）

1. 一般现在时

（1）一般现在时还可表示客观真理、科学事实。如：

The sun rises in the east.

太阳从东方升起。

（2）一般现在时还可用在if，unless，even if引导的条件状语从句中，由when，before，until (till)，as soon as，the moment，once引导的时间状语从句中，由no matter what/who/which/when/where/how或whatever，whoever，whichever，whenever，wherever，however引导的让步状语从句中，这时主句往往表将来发生的动作（will/shall/can/must）或主句是祈使句。如：

I'll go with you as soon as I finish my work.

我一完成工作就跟你走。

If city noises are not kept from increasing, people will have to shout to be heard even at the dinner table 20 years from now.

如果不阻止城市噪音继续增加的话，20年后人们同在饭桌旁也得大喊着才能被听到。

Whatever you say, I will not change my mind.

无论你说什么，我都不会改变主意。

2. 一般过去时

该时态往往表示"刚才，在过去"之意，暗示现在已经"不再这样"。

— Come in, Peter. I want to show you something.

— Oh, how nice of you! I never thought you were going to bring me a gift.

——彼得，进来。我想给你看点东西。

——噢，你真是太好了！我从没想过你会给我带礼物。

Your phone number again? I didn't quite catch it.

再说一遍你的电话号码好吗？我刚才没听见。

3. 一般将来时

（1）现在看来以后要发生的动作或存在的状态以及事物的固有属性或必然趋势。如：

Tom will come back next week. 汤姆下周回来。

Fish will die without water. 离开水，鱼就会死。

（2）"be going to +动词原形"多用在口语中，表示"计划、打算要做某事"，此外，be going to 还可表示根据现在的迹象，对未来进行推断。如：

He is going to speak on TV this evening.

他计划今晚在电视上讲话。

Look at the dark clouds, and it is going to rain.

看这乌云，马上要下雨了。

（3）"be about to +动词原形"表示"最近的将来（immediate future）"，因此，该句型很少与表示将来的具体时间状语连用，但可以和when引导的状语从句连用。如：

The train is about to start when I arrive at the station.

当我到火车站时，火车就要开了。

（4）有些动词如come，go，stay，arrive，leave，begin，start等，其一般现在时、现在进行时亦可表示按计划、安排将来要发生的动作或存在的状态。如：

He comes here tonight.

今晚他打算来这儿。

I arrive in Beijing at 3:00 p.m. tomorrow.

我明天下午3点到北京。

What are you going to do next week?

下周你打算做什么？

（5）"be to +动词原形"的用法较多。

①表示"按计划或安排要做的事"。如：

When are you to leave for home?

你什么时候回家？

She is to be married next month.

她将于下个月结婚。

The Queen is to visit Japan in a week's time.

女王将于一周后访问日本。

这种结构也可用于过去时。was/were to do sth.表示曾经计划要做的事，但不表明计划是否被执行，或表示"命运（即命中注定要发生的事）"，而非计划；was/were to have done sth.表示未曾实现的计划。如：

I felt nervous because I was soon to leave home for the first time.

我感到很紧张，因为我很快就要第一次离开家了。

They said good-bye, little knowing that they were never to meet again。

他们互相告别，不知道以后再也不会见面了。

We were to have told you, but you were not in.

我们本来想告诉你的，但是你不在家。

②表示"应该"，相当于should，ought to。如：

You are to report to the police.

你应该报警。

What is to be done?

应该怎么办呢？

③表示"想，打算"，相当于intend，want。如：

If we are to be there before ten, we'll have to go now.

如果我们要在10点前到，我们现在就得走。

④用于第一人称疑问句，表示征求对方意见。如：

Am I to go on with the work?

要我继续完成这项工作吗？

What are we to do next?

我们下一步该怎么办？

⑤用于否定句，表示"禁止"，相当于mustn't。如：

The books in this room are not to be taken outside.

这个房间里的书不能带出去。

You are not to smoke in the reading room.

你不可以在阅览室里吸烟。

⑥表示"可以，可能"，相当于may，can。如：

The news is to be found in the evening Paper.

这条消息可以在晚报上看到。

Such people are to be found everywhere.

这种人到处都有。

She is nowhere to be found.

在哪里也找不到她。

⑦were to do sth.用于if或even if/even though从句中，表示对未来的假设。如：

If I were to tell you that I admired him, would you believe me?

要是我告诉你我羡慕他，你会相信吗？

Even if the sun were to rise in the west, I would never do such a thing.

即使太阳从西边出来，我也决不做这种事。

⑧be to blame（该受责备，对某件坏事应负责任）与be to let（待出租）两种结构中，用不定式的主动形式表示被动含义。如：

Which driver is to blame for the accident?

这次事故是哪个司机的责任？

This house is to let.

这个房子要出租。

进行体

（1）一个长动作作为背景，被一个短动作打断，长动作往往用进行体，短动作用一般体。如：

My brother fell while he was riding his bicycle and hurt himself.

我弟弟骑自行车时从车子上掉了下来，伤了自己。

The students were busy writing when Miss Brown went to get a book she had left in the office.

同学们在忙着写作，这时布朗老师去取她忘在办公室的书。

Tom slipped into the house when no one was looking.

当没人注意的时候，汤姆溜进了房子。

The reporter said that the UFO was traveling east to west when he saw it.

那位记者说，当他看到那个不明飞行物时，它正在自东向西飞行。

（2）表示动作的未完性、暂时性。如：

— Have you moved into the new house?

— Not yet. The rooms are being painted.

——你搬进新房子了吗？

——还没呢。房间还正在粉刷呢。（未完性）

I don't really work here; I am just helping out until the new secretary arrives.

我不在这上班，我只是来帮忙，直到新秘书来了（我就走）。（暂时性）

Selecting a mobile phone for personal use is no easy task because technology is changing so rapidly.

选一部供个人使用的手机不是一件容易的事，因为技术变化太快。（"变化"尚未完成）

（3）表示计划、安排要做的事。如：

I've won a holiday for two days to Florida. I am taking my Mum.

我获得了一次去佛罗里达度假两天的机会。我计划带着我妈妈去。（计划）

（4）表示现在或当时发展中的或正在进行的情况。如：

I first met Lily 3 years ago. She was working at a clothes shop at the time.

三年前我第一次遇到了莉莉，当时她正在一家服装店工作。

— Is this coat yours?

— No. My coat is hanging there behind the door.

——这是你的外套吗？

——不是，我的在门后挂着呢。

（5）表示反复出现的或习惯性的动作，往往含有赞赏、厌恶、遗憾等情绪，常与always，continually，constantly连用。如：

He is always thinking of others first.

他总是先想到他人。

He is always making the same mistake.

他总是犯同样的错误。

（6）瞬间动词的进行体可以表示将来。（见一般将来时的用法部分）

完成体

1. 现在完成时

（1）一个动作开始于过去，持续到现在（也许还将持续下去）。表示从过去延续到现在并包括现在在内的一段时间的状语有：lately，recently，in the last/past few days/years（在过去的这几天/年里），since then，up to now，so far（至今）等。如：

In the past few years, great changes have taken place in my hometown.

在过去的几年里，我的家乡发生了巨大变化。

He has been busy writing a book recently.

最近他一直在忙着写书。

He has written 8 books so far.

到现在为止，他一共写了8本书。

（2）一件发生在过去的事情对现在产生的影响，注意这时说话者说话的重心在"过去的事情对现在产生的影响"。常用的状语有already，just（刚刚），yet，never，before等。如：

He has turned off the light. (= The light is off now.)

他关掉了灯。

The concert has started. (= The concert is on now.)

音乐会开始了。

I have already seen the film. (= I know the film now.)

我看过那部电影了。

（3）This/It is the first/second... time + that 从句，that 从句的谓语要用现在完成时。如：

This is the first time (that) I have come here.

这是我第一次来这里。

（4）在条件、时间、让步状语从句中，表示将来某时间以前已完成的动作。如：

I will not believe you unless I have seen it with my own eyes.

除非我亲眼看到，否则我不会相信你的。（强调"看完"）

I will go with you as soon as I have finished my work.

我干完了工作就和你一起去。（强调"干完"）

（5）瞬间动词又叫非延续性动词、终止性动词。瞬间动词可以用于完成时态，但不可以接表示一段时间的状语，若要接表示一段时间的状语，需要做一些相应的变换。瞬间动词的否定式可以接表示一段时间的状语。如：

（×）He has come to Beijing since last year.

（√）He has lived in Beijing since last year.

（×）He has joined the army for 3 years.

（√）He has served in the army for 3 years.

（√）He joined the army 3 years ago.

（√）He has been a soldier for 3 years.

（√）It is 3 years since he joined the army.

（√）He has joined the army.

常见的瞬间动词有：come，go，get to/reach/arrive at/in，leave，buy，sell，open，close，get up，join/take part in，begin/start，return/give，borrow/lend，become/turn，bring/take，die，finish/end，receive/hear from，marry，break，lose，jump 等。

2. 过去完成时

（1）一件事情发生在过去，而另一件事情先于它发生（即表"过去的过去"），那么发生在前的事情的动词须用过去完成时。时间状语可用 before 等介词短语或一个时间状语从句来表示，也可通过上下文来表示。如：

She had learned some English before she came to the institute.

她在来学院前已经学过一些英语。

He said that he had been abroad for 3 years.

他说他在国外待了3年了。

（2）表示从过去某一时间开始，一直延续到过去的另一时间的动作，常用的时间状语有：by then，by that time，until，by the end of，before 2000，by the time+句子等。如：

By then he had learned English for 3 years.

到那时，他已经学了3年英语了。

Until then he had known nothing about it yet.

到那时为止，他对此仍一无所知。

（3）在"hardly/scarcely/rarely... when..."和"no sooner... than..."句型中，when和than从句中用一般过去时，hardly/scarcely/rarely主句中用过去完成时，且位于句首时，主句部分要进行倒装，表示"刚刚……就……"。如：

Hardly/Scarcely/Rarely had I got home when the rain poured down.

我刚到家，大雨就倾盆而下。

No sooner had we started than the car got a flat tyre.

我们才刚刚启动，汽车的轮胎就漏气了。

（4）It was/had been +一段时间+ since从句。since从句的谓语用过去完成时。如：

It was ten years since we had had such a wonderful time.

我们10年没这么高兴了。

（5）That/It/This was the first/second time... + that从句。that从句的谓语要用过去完成时。如：

It was the third time (that) he had made the same mistake.

这是他第三次犯同样的错误了。

That was the first time that I had passed the exam.

那是我第一次考试及格。

（6）表示愿望、打算一类的词，如hope，expect，mean，intend，want，think，suppose等，其过去完成时表示过去未曾实现的愿望或意图。如：

I had hoped to see more of Shanghai.

我本来希望在上海多看看。（但未能如愿）

I had meant to help you, but I was too busy at the moment.

我本来想帮你的，但当时确实太忙了。

I had thought you would come tomorrow.

我原以为你明天才来呢。

3. 将来完成时

将来完成时表示到将来某一时间，某一动作将会完成，常用的时间状语为"by+将来的某个时间"。如：

By this time of next year, all of you will have become college students.

到明年的这个时候，你们大家就都成为大学生了。

1. 一般过去时和现在完成时的用法区别

一般过去时表示过去的一个时间点或一段时间都是可以具体确定的，与其他时间没有牵连，它所表示的事情纯属过去，而现在完成时说的是现在的情况。比较下面几组句子，体会两种时态的不同：

He served in the army from 1952 to 1954.

（这是过去的一件事。）

He has served in the army for 5 years.

（现在他仍在军中服役。）

He wrote many plays when he was at college.

（写剧本是他过去做的事情。）

He has written many plays.

（这意味着他是剧作家。）

I saw *Hero* last year.

（看《英雄》的时间是去年，与现在无关。）

I have seen *Hero* before.

（以前看过，强调现在知道这部电影的内容。before "以前"是表示一个与现在有联系的时间，而不是一个确定的与现在无关的过去时间。）

2. 一般过去时和过去完成时的用法区别

（1）一般过去时是指过去的动作或情况，而过去完成时指过去的一个动作或时间之前发生的事。如：

He had learned 3,000 English words before he came to this school.

他来这个学校之前就已经学了3 000个英语单词了。

（2）过去完成时的时间状语常用by和before引导的短语表示，如by that time，by the end of，before 2000，by the time +句子（一般过去时）等。如：

He had finished writing the book by the end of last month.

到上个月底为止，他已经写完了这本书。

3. 过去完成时与现在完成时的用法区别

两种时态都常与表示一段时间的状语连用，但现在完成时表示的是延续到现在或同现在有关的动作（句中不可有表示过去特定时间的状语），而过去完成时表示的是在过去某时之前已经完成或延续到过去某时的动作（句中有表示过去特定时间的状语）。比较下面的说法：

She had been ill for a week before she came back.

（"回来"发生在过去某一时间，"生病"发生在这一时间之前，即过去的过去。）

She has been ill for a week.

（现在仍然病着。）

▶ 动词的时态 ◀

1. — Have you finished reading *Jane Eyre*?

— No, I _____ my homework all day yesterday.

[A] was doing   [B] would do

[C] had done   [D] do

2. When you are home, give a call to let me know you _____ safely.

[A] are arriving   [B] have arrived

[C] had arrived   [D] will arrive

3. The discovery of gold in Australia led thousands to believe that a fortune _____.

[A] is made   [B] would make

[C] was to be made   [D] had made

4 Excuse me. I _____ I was blocking your way.

[A] didn't realize   [B] don't realize

[C] haven't realized   [D] wasn't realizing

5. — I'm not finished with my dinner yet.

— But our friends _____ for us.

[A] will wait   [B] wait

[C] have waited   [D] are waiting

6. — I'm sorry, but I don't quite follow you. Did you say you wanted to return on September 20?

— Sorry, I _____ myself clear. We want to return on October 20.

[A] hadn't made   [B] wouldn't make

[C] don't make   [D] haven't made

7. It took me a long time before I was able to fully appreciate what they _____ for me.

[A] had done   [B] did

[C] would do   [D] were doing

8. We _____ on this project for four hours. Let's have a rest.

[A] are working   [B] have been working

[C] worked   [D] had worked

9. Every few years, the coal workers _____ their lungs X-rayed to ensure their health.

[A] are having [B] have

[C] have had [D] had had

10. The church tower which _____ will be open to tourists soon. The work is almost finished.

   [A] has restored [B] has been restored

   [C] is restoring [D] is being restored

11. The book has been translated into thirty languages since it _____ on the market in 1973.

   [A] had come [B] has come

   [C] came [D] comes

12. — Why do you want to work for our company?

   — This is the job that I _____ for.

   [A] looked [B] am to look

   [C] had looked [D] have been looking

13. If you plant watermelon seeds in the spring, you _____ fresh watermelon in the fall.

   [A] eat [B] would eat

   [C] have eaten [D] will be eating

14. For many years, people _____ electric cars. However, making them has been more difficult than predicted.

   [A] had dreamed of [B] have dreamed of

   [C] dreamed of [D] dream of

15. — Guess what, we've got our visas for a short-term visit to the UK this summer.

   — How nice! You _____ a different culture then.

   [A] will be experiencing [B] have experienced

   [C] have been experiencing [D] will have experienced

➡ 动词的时态和语态参考答案 ⬅

1. 【答案】A

   【译文】——你读完《简·爱》了吗?

——没有,我昨天一整天都在写作业。

【解析】本题考查动词的时态。从all day yesterday可知,昨天一整天都在写作业,用过去进行时表示过去某段时间一直在进行的动作。一般过去时与过去进行时的区别:一般过去时表示过去完整的、已经结束的动作,而如果表示过去某个时间或某段时间正在做或一直在做某事则用过去进行时。

2. 【答案】B

   【译文】你到家时打个电话给我,让我知道你已经安全抵达。

   【解析】本题考查时态。从语境看,在打电话时对方"已经到达",因此这里的宾语从句要用现在完成时。而不是现在进行时、过去完成时或一般将来时。

3. 【答案】C

   【译文】在澳大利亚发现了黄金,这使数以千计的人认为在那里可以发财。

   【解析】本题考查时态和语态。从语境中动作的先后看可知,"在那里发财"这一动作发生在"发现了金子"这一动作之后且还未发生,因此make a fortune(发财)用过去将来时的被动语态形式。[A]项的一般现在时、[B]项的过去将来时、[D]项的过去完成时都不正确。[C]项was to be made表示过去将来的可能性。故选[C]项。

4. 【答案】A

   【译文】抱歉,我不知道挡了你的路。

   【解析】本题考查时态。动作"没有意识到"应该发生在过去,故答案选[A]项。

5. 【答案】D

   【译文】——我还没有吃完饭呢。

   ——可是朋友们在等我们。

   【解析】本题考查动词的时态。根据语境"正在等我们"可以判断此处为现在进行时,故选择[D]项。

6. 【答案】D

   【译文】——抱歉,我不太明白你的意思。你刚才是说你们要在9月20日返回吗?

   ——对不起,是我没有表述清楚。我们想在10月20日返回。

   【解析】本题考查动词的时态。根据句意可以看出"没有表述清楚"是当前的一种情况，是说话人做过的事情对现在的一种影响，[D]项是现在完成时，表明现在的情况和影响，符合题意。[A]项为过去完成时，[B]项为过去将来时，与语境不符；[C]项为一般现在时，表示通常情况下都如此，也不符合语境。

7. 【答案】A

    【译文】花了很长一段时间我才能完全理解他们为我所做的一切。

    【解析】本题考查动词的时态。根据语境可知整句话的时间是过去，"他们为我做的"这一动作发生在"我可以完全理解"之前，因此用过去完成时更符合题意，故选择[A]项。

8. 【答案】B

    【译文】我们已经连续做这个项目四个小时了，休息一下吧。

    【解析】本题考查动词时态。根据语境中"休息一下吧"可知工作尚未完成，又结合题干中的for four hours，可推知设空处应该用现在完成进行时。

9. 【答案】B

    【译文】每隔几年，煤矿工人们都要对肺部进行X光检查，以确保身体健康。

    【解析】考查动词的时态。根据Every few years（每隔几年）可知动作是经常性的、有规律的，所以用一般现在时。

10. 【答案】D

    【译文】教堂的钟塔正在修复，很快就会对游客开放。修复工作差不多完成了。

    【解析】考查动词的时态和语态。根据语境，主语tower和动词restore之间是被动关系，[A]、[C]两项被排除；又由句意可知修复工作还未完成，而是正在进行中，所以不能使用现在完成时，要用现在进行时。

11. 【答案】C

    【译文】该书自1973年上市以来已被译成三十种语言。

    【解析】考查动词的时态。since从句应该用一般过去时，主句常用现在完成时。

12. 【答案】D

    【译文】——你为什么想为我们公司效力？

    ——这是我一直梦寐以求的工作。

【解析】考查动词时态。由语境得知，这里强调动作开始于过去，并持续到现在且现在还在进行，故用现在完成进行时。

13. 【答案】D

   【译文】如果在春天种下西瓜种子，秋天你就会吃到新鲜的西瓜。

   【解析】本题考查动词时态。[A]项为一般现在时；[B]项为过去将来时；[C]项为现在完成时；[D]项为将来进行时，表示将来某时间点正在进行或某阶段内一直在进行的动作。in the fall为表示将来的时间状语，故答案为[D]项。

14. 【答案】B

   【译文】许多年以来，人们都梦想着电力汽车的出现。但是，制造电力汽车比预想的要更加困难。

   【解析】本题考查动词时态。根据时间状语For many years可知句子时态为完成时态，故排除[C]项和[D]项；句子并没有过去的时间或过去的动作，因此不存在"过去的过去"，排除[A]项。故答案为[B]项。

15. 【答案】A

   【译文】——你猜怎么着，我们获得了今年夏季去英国进行短期访问的签证。

   ——太棒了！到时候，你将会体验到不同的文化。

   【解析】本题考查动词时态。由this summer可知此处应该用将来时，而then表示将来的某个时间点，故用将来进行时。

二、复合句式

英文有三大从句：名词性从句、形容词性从句和副词性从句。从句，顾名思义，就是"从属"于句子的一个组成单位。因为句子的组成单位是单词，所以从句在一个句子中的作用和单词是一样的。由此而言，名词性从句就是在句子中担当名词作用的从句，形容词性从句就是句子中担当形容词作用的从句，而副词性从句就是在句子中担当副词作用的从句。由于名词在一个句子里通常可以作主语、宾语、表语和同位语四种成分，所以名词性从句也就依次分为主语从句、宾语从句、表语从句和同位语从句。形容词一般是对名词进行修饰的，多充当名词的定语，因此，形容词性从句也就是对名词修饰的从句，又称为定语从句。副词在句中主要作状语成分，所以副词性从句又称为状语从句。

1. 名词性从句

名词性从句是都是独立的句子，作用相当于句子中的名词，发挥名词的功能，并且因为它们是句子，所以称为名词性从句。它们在复合句中能担任主语、宾语、表语、同位语等，因此，根据在句中不同的语法功能，名词性从句可分为主语从句、宾语从句、表语从句、同位语从句。下面将逐一讲解。

◆ 主语从句 ◆

若是一个完整的句子充当句子的主语，这种句子就称为主语从句，其谓语动词用第三人称单数。一般而言，主语从句的形式主要表现为以下几种：

（1）由连词that引导，that不作语法成分，无词义，只起引导主语从句的功能，但不可省略。

That they two were bothers was obvious from the facial resemblance between them.

很明显，他们是兄弟俩，因为他们的脸型很相似。

（2）由连词whether引导，whether不作语法成分，只起引导主语从句的功能，但不可省略。

Whether he will secure a job is still uncertain.

他是否能找到一份工作还不好说。

（3）由连接代词who，whom，which，what，whose引导以及缩合连接代词whoever，whomever，whichever，whatever等引导，均不可省略。

Who will be the candidate for the post is still undecided.

谁将成为该职位的候选人尚未决定。

What he prefers is skiing.

他更喜欢滑雪。

Whose proposal will be chosen is still unknown.

谁的提议会被选中仍旧不得而知。

Whoever comes is welcome.

不论谁来都欢迎。

（4）由连接副词when，where，why，how以及缩合连接副词whenever，wherever，however引导，在从句中充当状语，均不可省略。

When we will end this negotiation is quite important.

我们何时结束这场谈判非常重要。

Why he chose to live in the country is still a mystery.

他为何选择住在乡下仍是一个谜。

Wherever you are is my home.

你所在的任何地方就是我的家。

（5）that，whether，why，where，when等引导主语从句时，经常用it作形式主语，而将真正的主语从句置于句末，尤以that从句最为常见。如：

It does not matter whether they turn up or not.

他们来不来没关系。

通常，用it作形式主语替代that从句主要有四种搭配关系：

①It + -ed分词+ that从句

It is said that... 据说……

It is reported that... 据报道……

It is estimated that... 据估计……

It is believed that... 人们认为……

It is known that... 人人皆知……

It must be pointed out that... 必须指出的是……

②It + be +形容词+ that从句

It is possible that... 可能的是……

It is strange that... 奇怪的是……

It is important that... 重要的是……

It is necessary that... 有必要……

It is commonplace that... 司空见惯的是……

It is true that... 诚然……

③It + be +名词+ that从句

It is a pity that... 遗憾的是……

It is a mystery that... 令人迷惑不解的是……

It is no wonder that... 不足为奇的是……

It is no rarity that... ……绝非罕见

It is no accident that... ……绝非偶然

④It +不及物动词+ that从句

It seems that... 似乎……

It happens that... 碰巧……

It turns out that... 结果是……

It occurs to me that... 我突然想起……

It dawns on me that... 我突然明白……

这种句型结构在主语从句中占有相当比例，主要原因是避免头重脚轻，将真正主语放于句末。但是译作汉语时，一般仍将该真正主语放在句首处理，这也符合汉语行文的思维习惯。以下所举的主语从句中，形式主语的例子较多，这正是长难句的一大特点。

宾语从句

用作宾语的从句称为宾语从句。按照不同的引导词，宾语从句可分为三类：

（1）由连词that，whether，if引导

The board meeting decided that this newcomer would get a probationary period.

董事会决定这名新员工将会有一段试用期。

I don't know if you can help me.

我不知你是否能帮我。

We don't know whether or not he comes.

我们不知他是否会来。

注意：在suggest（建议），demand（命令），order（要求）等意义的动词之后的that宾语从句中用虚拟语气should+动词原形，或采用美式英语，直接用动词原形。如：

She suggested that we (should) go shopping after work.

她提议我们下班后去购物。

if与whether用法之区别：

①一般而言，if只用于引导宾语从句，而whether除引导宾语从句之外，还可引导主语从句、表语从句等其他名词性从句。

Whether he supports this proposal or not makes no difference.（whether引导主语从句，不可换用if）

他是否支持这项提议无所谓。

The question is whether he will recover from this illness.（whether引导表语从句，不可换用if）

问题是他能否从这场病中恢复过来。

②if不可用在介词之后，而whether可以。

We are unaware of whether he has finished the work.

我们不知道他完成工作没有。

③if不可用于不定式之前，而whether可以。

She does not know whether to follow him.

她不知道该不该跟他走。

（2）由连接代词who，what，which等引导

We all understand who are our true friends.

我们都知道谁是我们真正的朋友。

I wonder what he is writing to me about.

我不知他要给我写信说什么事。

（3）由连接副词when，where，why，how等引导

I will tell you why I asked you to come.

我会告诉你我为什么要你来。

I should like to see where he lives.

我想去看看他住的地方。

I still remember when this used to be a peaceful village.

我仍记得这曾是一个安静祥和的村庄。

I vaguely remember where I first met her.

我依稀记得第一次见她的地方。

此外，宾语从句的用法还包括：

（1）宾语从句作介词的宾语（介词后不能用that）

We were all unconscious of what had happened that day.

我们都不清楚那天出了什么事。

Your success will largely depend on what you do and how you do it.

你的成功将主要取决于你做什么和怎样做。

I walked over to where he sat.

我朝他坐的地方走去。

（2）宾语从句作形容词的宾语

这类形容词有afraid，anxious，certain，sure，convinced，glad，pleased，satisfied，sorry，worried等。如：

I'm afraid that you will not catch the train.

我恐怕你赶不上那趟火车了。

Now the experts were fully convinced that the animal was a puma.

现在专家们完全相信了那只动物就是美洲狮。

（3）动词+ it + that宾语从句

该结构中的it作形式主语，替代后面由that引导的宾语从句，基本原理类似于主语从句中it作形式主语，主要是避免头重脚轻。这种句型结构在长难句中所占的比重很大，译作汉语时，一般还是省去it，直接翻译that从句。如：

We consider it quite important that parents should place more emphasis on their children's overall development.

我们认为父母应该更加重视孩子的全面发展，这一点很重要。

表语从句

从句放在系动词之后，便构成表语从句。系动词除了be动词，还有以下几类：

（1）表示状态变化的动词，如become，grow，turn，get，fall，go，come等。

He often becomes nervous in the presence of strangers.

在生人面前他经常很紧张。

The little boy grows stronger.

这个小男孩更健壮了。

Food will go bad in hot weather.

天气炎热时，食物容易变质。

（2）表示特征、状态的动词，如look，feel，taste，smell，seem，appear等。

He looked just as he had looked ten years before.

他看起来还与十年前一样。

She felt very uncomfortable at the sight of the snake.

一看到蛇，她就感觉很不舒服。

The strawberries she just picked in the field seemed mouth-watering.

她刚从地里采摘的草莓看起来令人垂涎欲滴。

（3）表示保持某种状态的动词，如remain，stay，keep，hold，prove等。

The situation remains unclear after two rounds of negotiations.

经过两轮谈判，局势依旧不明朗。

The girl kept silent all the time.

女孩一直沉默不语。

The investigation proved not difficult in such a small village.

在这样一个小村子里，调查工作并不难。

引导表语从句的有连接代词that，who，what，which，连接副词when，why，where，how等。在实际应用中，that常省略。

The fact is (that) she has gone to Paris.

事实是她已经去巴黎了。

What we talked about is how to learn English well.

我们所谈论的是如何学好英语。

The problem is who we can get to replace him.

问题是我们能找谁来替换他。

同位语从句

同位语从句就是一个句子中充当同位语的句子。同位语从句放在具有内涵性的名词之后，对前面的名词做进一步的解释说明。常见的同位语引导词或短语有namely，including，that is to say，for example，such as，say，in short，in particular等。

He is fond of pop music, such as Backstreet Boys, Westlife, etc.

他喜欢流行音乐，譬如后街男孩，西城男孩等。

Twenty contestants, including eight women, participated the competition.

二十位选手，其中包括八位女性，参加了这场竞赛。

能接同位语的名词有idea，fact，news，truth，discovery，report，thought，statement，suggestion，conclusion，possibility，opinion等有内涵的名词。从句一般由连词that，whether，连接代词who，which，what和连接副词where，when，why，how等引导。

We have no idea where he has gone.

我们不知他去哪儿了。

Did you hear the news that another hospital was built?

你听说又新建了一所医院这个消息了吗？

There arose the question when we could achieve our purpose.

问题是我们何时能实现目标。

如果句子的谓语较短，同位语从句经常与所修饰的名词分隔，这是长难句中的常见现象，如：

Reports came into London Zoo that a wild puma had been spotted forty-five miles south of

London.

伦敦动物园接到报告，在伦敦以南45英里处发现了一只野生的美洲狮。

这句话的主语是Reports，谓语动词是came，为了避免头重脚轻，故将主语的同位语that从句置于谓语之后。

A saying goes that practice makes perfect.

常言道：熟能生巧。

此外，要注意同位语从句和定语从句的区别。试看下面两个句子：

The news that he passed the exam was encouraging.

他通过考试的消息令人鼓舞。

The news that she told me was encouraging.

她告诉我的消息令人鼓舞。

单从汉语的角度来看，似乎两个that从句都是定语从句，其实不然。第一个是同位语从句，而第二个才是定语从句。依据的标准是：第一句的that从句解释news的内容，两者属于同位关系，而且that只是连接词，不作语法成分，一般不可省略；第二句的that是关系代词，在句中作told的宾语。因此，可以得出这样的结论：定语从句中的that要作语法成分，即主语或宾语，且作宾语时可省略。以下公式可用于判断同位语从句和定语从句：

that +完整的句子→同位语从句

that +不完整的句子→定语从句

2. 定语从句

定语从句即在句中用一个具有主谓结构的完整的句子来充当定语，修饰前面的名词（短语）或代词，这种名词（短语）或代词称为先行词。定语从句一般由关系代词和关系副词引导。定语从句可分为限定性和非限定性，前者就是提供基本信息来限定我们正在谈论的人或事，如果去掉该从句，剩下的主句或意义不成立，或意思表达不清；后者所提供的信息不是必需的，只起补充说明作用，若省去，并不影响原句意义。二者的主要区别是：

（1）形式上而言，限定性定语从句的关系词和先行词之间不用逗号隔开，而非限定性定语从句则用逗号隔开。

（2）意义上而言，一般说来，限定性定语从句与先行词关系密切，对其有限制作用，因此不可缺少，否则会影响全句的意义。如：

Do you know the reason why I came late?

你知道我来晚的原因吗？

非限定性定语从句与先行词关系较为松散，用逗号隔开，从句中的关系代词不能省略，that一般不能引导非限定性定语从句。如：

Water, which is a clear liquid, has many uses.

水是一种清澈的液体，有许多用途。

英译汉时，一般将限定性定语从句直接处理成先行词的前置定语成分，即"……的+先行词"；而非限定性定语从句一般不宜译作先行词的定语成分，常常可处理为状语从句，以表原因、结果、目的、条件、让步等含义。如：

The pedestrians who saw the traffic accident made a detour.

看到那场交通事故的行人绕道而行。（言外之意：没看到交通事故的行人没有绕道，只有部分行人绕道。）

The pedestrians, who saw the traffic accident, made a detour.

行人看到那场交通事故后，就绕道而行。（言外之意：所有的行人都看到了交通事故，都绕道了。）

此外，定语从句与先行词之间常有分割成分，该分割成分中与定语从句紧紧相连的名词，常被误认为是定语从句的先行词，这就要根据上下文和经验认真判断。

3. 状语从句

状语从句是在句子中作状语成分的句子，状语从句可以修饰谓语或整个句子。状语从句的位置灵活，可放在句首、句中或句末。位于句首时，常用逗号隔开，如从句较短且与主句关系密切时，亦可不用逗号，如：

As the house was so small he decided to sell it.

由于房子太小，他决定将它卖掉。（从句和主句关系密切）

状语从句位于句末时，其前一般不用逗号。如从句与其前的主句关系不甚密切，其前则用逗号，如：

She is quite considerate, if I may say so.

恕我直言,她非常体贴人。

按用途来分,状语从句可分为九大类:时间、地点、原因、条件、结果、让步、目的、方式、比较等。

(1)引导时间状语从句的常见关联词有when, whenever, while, after, as, before, no sooner... than..., hardly/scarcely... when..., the minute, the moment, the instant等。

As spring warms the good earth, all flowers begin to bloom.

随着春回大地,百花开始绽放。

I had no sooner arrived home than it began to rain.

我刚到家,就下起了雨。

We will leave the minute you are ready.

你准备好了我们就走。

(2)引导地点状语从句的关联词有where, wherever, anywhere, everywhere等。若地点状语从句位于句首,一般需用逗号将其和主句隔开。

Corn flourishes best where the ground is rich.

谷物在土地肥沃的地方生长得最好。

There were ovations everywhere they went.

他们走到哪里都受到热烈欢迎。

You are able to go wherever you like.

你想去哪儿就去哪儿。

(3)引导原因状语从句的关联词有because, as, for, since, considering, now that, given that等。

You should not get angry just because some people speak ill of you.

你不该仅仅因为有些人说你坏话就生气。

As all the seats were full, he stood up.

所有的座位都满了,他只好站着。

(4)引导条件状语从句的关联词有if, unless, providing/provided, as long as, on condition that，in case等。

If you dream it, you will make it.

如果有梦想，就会获得成功。

Providing there is no objection, we will pass the bill.

如果没有反对意见，我们将通过这项决议。

（5）引导结果状语从句的关联词有so... that...，such... that...，to the degree，to the extent，to such a degree，to such an extent等。

It is so interesting a book that everyone wants to get a copy.

这本书很有趣，人人都想得到一本。

A computer is intelligent only to the extent that it can store information.

计算机的功能只限于它能储存信息。

（6）引导让步状语从句的关联词有though、although、even though、even if，此时，主句前不可用but，但可用yet/still，还有whatever、wherever、however、whenever等。

Even though it was only nine o'clock, there were few people in the street.

尽管才九点钟，街上已没什么人了。

You can't come in, whoever you are.

不管你是谁，都不能进来。

（7）引导目的状语从句的关联词有so that、in order that、so as to、in order to、in the hope that、lest、for fear that、in case等。

In order that the flowers could bloom again, it was necessary that they should be watered regularly.

为了让这些花再度开放，必须要定期浇水。

Take your umbrella with you, lest it should rain.

带上你的伞，以防下雨。

（8）引导方式状语从句的关联词有as、as if、as though、the way等。

You answer as if you did not know this rule.

你回答问题好像不知道这条规则似的。

Do it the way you were taught.

要照教你的那样去做。

（9）引导比较状语从句的关联词有the more... the more...，as... so...，rather than，other than等。

The more rural the community is, the more uniform the customs of child upbringing are.

一个社会越原始，教育孩子的方法就越一致。

As unselfishness is the real test of strong affection, so unselfishness ought to be the real test of the highest kind of art.

正如无私是钟爱的真正考验，无私也是最高艺术的真正考验。

三、特殊结构

1. 并列结构

通常而言，由并列连接词如and，but等连接的两个或多个分句组成的句子就称为并列句。但是并列结构还包括由并列连词连接的词、短语等。在分析该结构的长难句时，首先要确定并列连词，如and，but等，然后再寻找连词之后的关键词语或成分，最后在连词之前定位并列的关键词语或成分。如：

Modesty makes one go forward and pride leaves one far behind.

谦虚使人进步，骄傲使人落后。

Teachers live by selling knowledge, philosophers by selling wisdom and priests by selling spiritual comfort.

教师依靠出售知识生存，哲学家依靠出售智慧生存，而牧师依靠出售精神慰藉生存。

2. 非谓语结构

众所周知，英语中单个的动词（以v.表示）只能充当谓语，那么如果想让v.充当主语、宾语、表语、同位语、状语、补语、独立成分等，则需要改变v.的形式，具体方法有四种：把v.变为不定式（to v.）、现在分词（v.-ing）、动名词（v.-ing）和过去分词（v.-ed），这就是传统意义上的非谓语结构。

不定式

（1）作主语

To see is to believe.

眼见为实。

It is thoughtful of him to tell me the news.（It作形式主语，替代不定式）

他告诉我这个消息，想得真周到。

（2）作宾语

I intend to apply for Tsinghua University.

我打算报考清华大学。

She found it impossible to persuade her husband.（it作形式宾语，替代不定式）

她发现劝说丈夫是不可能的。

（3）作表语

To see is to believe.

眼见为实。

His dream is to be a doctor.

他的梦想是成为一名医生。

（4）作同位语

Her dream, to be a country teacher, surprised her parents.

她梦想成为一名乡村教师，这使父母很吃惊。

（5）作定语

I am impressed by his ability to speak five languages.

他会说五种语言，给我留下很深的印象。

The student has lots of homework to do.

这个学生有许多家庭作业要做。

（6）作状语

He earned much enough to buy himself a big house.（结果状语）

他赚了足够的钱，给自己买了套大房子。

She learned English to find a better job.（目的状语）

她学英语是想找到一份更好的工作。

（7）作补语（主补+宾补）

His boss made him overwork.（作宾补；make是使役动词，后面若有不定式省略to）

老板让他加班。

Really honest people are often made to feel guilty.（作主补；make是使役动词，用于被动语态时后面不定式中的to不能省略）

真正的老实人经常被弄得像犯罪似的。

（8）作独立成分（插入语）

To be honest, she is not the best candidate.

说实话，她并不是最佳候选人。

现在分词

现在分词的形式V-ing与动名词完全一样，但前者在句子中主要起形容词和副词的作用，可以充当表语、定语和状语等；现在分词最主要的作用就是作定语和状语，也可看作是定语从句和状语从句的简化形式。

（1）作定语

The sleeping boy is very cute.

这个睡着的男孩真可爱。

The girl's smiling face impressed me deeply.

那个女孩的笑脸令我印象深刻。

（2）作表语（相当于形容词）

The good news is really encouraging.

这个好消息真令人振奋。

His argument is very convincing.

他的观点很有说服力。

（3）作状语（常常相当于状语从句的省略形式）

Hearing the knock on the door, they stopped talking.（时间状语）

=When they heard the knock on the door, they stopped talking.

听到有人敲门，他们停止了说话。

They stood there waiting for the bus.（伴随状语）

他们站在那儿等车。

（4）作补语

They found the movie boring.（宾补）

他们觉得电影很无聊。

The rabbit was seen rushing into the bush.（主补）

有人看到兔子跑进了灌木丛。

动名词

如果一个动词在句子中想要充当名词成分（如主语、宾语等），就需要把该动词名词化，变成动名词。动名词实际上可以作为名词看待。

（1）作主语

Learning without thinking is the waste of both time and money.

学而不思就是浪费时间和金钱。

Seeing is believing.

眼见为实。

（2）作宾语

I love collecting stamps.

我喜欢集邮。

They avoided speaking to her.

他们不愿和她说话。

（3）作表语

His favorite sport is skiing.

他最爱的运动是滑雪。

My favorite hobby is playing tennis.

我最大的爱好是打网球。

（4）作定语

The baby is sleeping in the sleeping car.

那个小孩正在卧车里睡觉。

Now he is in the dinning room.

他现在正在餐厅里呢。

在这里需要注意现在分词和动名词作定语的区别：

现在分词侧重"动作性"，而动名词强调"用途、功能"，而且前者可以转化为定语从句，后者则不行。如：

a sleeping baby=a baby who/that is sleeping（侧重"睡觉"的动作）

a sleeping car（侧重"用途"）

过去分词

过去分词的形式是V-ed，在句子中主要起形容词和副词的作用，可以充当表语、定语和状语等，与现在分词的区别就是：现在分词表达实施者（多指主语）发出的动作，具有主动性，而过去分词则指实施者接受的动作、状态、性质等；由于过去分词最主要的作用就是作定语和状语，也可看作是定语从句和状语从句的简化形式。

（1）作定语

the broken cup 打破的杯子

the criminals arrested last week 上周被捕的罪犯

（2）作表语

The young girl looked depressed.（过去分词作表语时基本已被视为形容词）

这个年轻女孩看起来情绪低沉。

The little boy seemed excited.

小男孩似乎很兴奋。

（3）作状语

Tired, I soon went to bed after work. （原因状语）

=As I was tired, I soon went to bed after work.

由于身体疲惫，我下班后就上床睡觉了。

（4）作补语（主补/宾补）

I was made disappointed by the bad news. （主补）

我被这个坏消息搞得很失望。

The bad news made me disappointed. （宾补）

这个坏消息让我很失望。

3. 强调结构

"强调"是一种语言表达形式，意在"突出"和"着重"的作用，是英文句子极为常见的表达方法。强调结构最常用的模式是：It is/was... that/who...，即把被强调的部分放在It is/was和that之间，强调人时可用who代替that。按照原理，除了谓语动词之外，一个句子的其他成分都可以用此结构进行强调，但我们在阅读过程中最常见的被强调的成分是主语、宾语、表语和状语四大类型。此外，强调结构翻译成中文时一般可套用"正是……（才）……"模式。如：

It was Frank who/that won the race. （强调主语）

正是弗兰克赢得了比赛。

It was my proposal that the committee finally adopted. （强调宾语）

委员会最终采纳的正是我的提案。

It was because of his diligence and perseverance that he was admitted by Peking University. （强调原因状语）

正是由于他的努力和毅力，他被北大录取了。

4. 倒装结构

英文句子有两种语序：自然语序（又称正装语序）和倒装语序。从形式上看，倒装分为两种：完全倒装和部分倒装。谓语动词全部位于主语前面的称作完全倒装，这里的谓语动词必须是运动性/存在性不及物动词（用vi.表示）；只将谓语的一部分（通常是助动词或情态动词）位于主语前面的称作部分倒装，这里的谓语是及物动词（用vt.表示）。

倒装的主要作用是表示强调或调整句子平衡,具体哪种作用要视情况而定。但是无论是哪种倒装,都必须在最前面加上某些必要成分才能成为完整意义上的倒装,即:

必要成分+ *vi.* +主语+其他成分(完全倒装),

必要成分+助动词/情态动词+主语+ *vt.* +其他成分(部分倒装)。

这些必要成分就是下面讲述的重点内容。

完全倒装

(1)表地点或方位的副词或介词短语置于句首

There came the bus.(come为运动性不及物动词)

公交车来了。

Into the forest ran the small rabbit.(run为运动性不及物动词)

那只小兔子跑进了树林里。

Under the bridge stood a man.(stand为存在性不及物动词)

桥下站着一个人。

(2)时间副词now, then置于句首

Now is the time to tell him the truth.(is为存在性动词)

现在是告诉他真相的时候了。

Then came the order to abandon the ship.(came为运动性不及物动词)

接着传来了弃船的命令。

注意:

①有时为了达到强调或句子平衡的作用,会将作表语的形容词短语置于句首,形成"表语+系动词+主语"的特殊完全倒装结构。如:

More important is your daily performance.

更重要的是你的平时表现。

②主语是代词时不倒装,谓语仍位于主语之后,如:

Here it comes.

它来了。

部分倒装

（1）否定性副词或词组置于句首

常见的否定性副词或词组有：

not, nor, never, seldom, little, hardly, scarcely, nowhere, not until, by no means, not in the least, on no account, in no way, in no case, under no circumstances, under no condition, no sooner... than..., hardly/scarcely... when..., not only... but (also)...

<u>Never</u> have I seen such a strange animal.

我从未见过这么奇怪的动物。

<u>Under no circumstances</u> will China be the first country to use nuclear weapons.

中国在任何情况下都不会首先使用核武器。

（2）only +状语置于句首

<u>Only by working hard</u> can one succeed.

只有勤奋努力才能成功。

<u>Only in this way</u> can we solve this problem.

只有用这种方式我们才能解决这个问题。

此外，在英文阅读过程中还有一些非常规的倒装，严格意义上无法归类到以上两种结构中，下面做一简单介绍。

①对于虚拟语气条件状语从句的倒装，如果虚拟语气条件从句中包含should，were或助动词had，则可将此动词置于句首，同时省略条件状语从句的引导词if。

<u>Should</u> the sun rise in the west, he would lend us money. (=If the sun should rise in the west, he would lend us money.)

如果太阳从西边升起，他才会借给我们钱。

<u>Were</u> he punctual, he would be very likely to get the job. (=If he were punctual, he would be very likely to get the job.)

如果他准时到了，很有可能得到这份工作。

②whether引导的让步状语从句中，谓语如果是系动词be，可省略whether，把be提至句首，句子实行倒装。如：

All substances, be they gaseous, liquid or solid, are made up of atoms. (=All substances, whether they be gaseous, liquid or solid, are made up of atoms.)

所有物质，无论是气态的、液态的或是固态的，都是由原子组成的。

Tears, be they of sorrow, anger, or joy, typically make Americans feel uncomfortable and embarrassed. (=Tears, whether they be of sorrow, anger, or joy, typically make Americans feel uncomfortable and embarrassed.)

无论是悲伤的泪水，愤怒的泪水，还是欢喜的泪水，通常都会使美国人感到不舒服和难为情。

③由so或such引导的结果状语从句，若想表达强调，则可以通过改变语序实现这一目的。如：

So generous is the man that almost all his colleagues turn to him when in trouble. (=The man is so generous that almost all his colleagues turn to him when in trouble.)

这个人非常慷慨，几乎所有同事有难时都求助于他。

Such an extent did she go to that all her friends became indifferent to her. (=She went to such an extent that all her friends became indifferent to her.)

她做得太过分，所有朋友都对她冷漠了。

④对于转述动词的倒装，如果直接引语位于转述动词之前时，转述动词往往放在主语的前面，形成特殊倒装（主语是代词时不能倒装）。如：

"I have been coming here night after night to repair the bell," replied the man. (=the man replied)

"我整夜整夜来这里修钟。"那人答道。

⑤对于让步状语从句的倒装，以as或though引导的让步状语从句，可把从句中作表语的形容词、名词，作状语的副词或者作谓语的动词置于句首，进行特殊倒装。如：

Poor as he is, he is very generous. (=Though he is poor, he is very generous.) （形容词前置）

他虽然很穷，却很慷慨。

Genius as she is, she still studies hard. (=Though she is a genius, she still studies hard.) （名

词前置；注意：前置时须去掉冠词）

她虽然是天才，却仍很用功。

Much as we may pride ourselves on our good taste, we are no longer free to choose the things we want. (=Though we may pride ourselves much on our good taste, we are no longer free to choose the things we want.)（副词前置）

虽然我们对自己的好品味很自豪，却无法自由地选择喜欢的东西了。

5. 分裂结构

分裂结构是英文书面语常用的修辞手段，也是分析理解句子过程中比较复杂的一种现象。顾名思义，分裂结构就是指把英文句子中原本连在一起的两个语言成分进行隔断，一部分留在句子原来的位置，另一部分远离原来的位置。使用分裂结构主要是想达到强调、句子平衡等目的。常见的分裂结构主要有五种：先行词与其修饰成分的分裂，即名词与其修饰语的分裂（简称为"名饰分裂"）；主语与谓语的分裂（简称为"主谓分裂"）；谓语动词与宾语的分裂（简称为"动宾分裂"）；连接词与连接成分的分裂（简称为"连主分裂"）；固定搭配被其他成分隔断造成的分裂（简称为"搭配分裂"）。下面将逐一详细介绍。

▶ 名饰分裂 ◀

一个比较复杂的英文句子中，先行词（名词）后面常有定语、定语从句、同位语、同位语从句等成分修饰。有时为了达到强调或句子平衡的作用，把这些修饰内容与前面的先行词隔断，造成了原本一体的两部分的分裂现象。

（1）名词与定语从句的分裂

He laughs best who laughs last.（名词与定语从句分隔）

谁笑到最后谁笑得最好。

All is well that ends well.（名词与定语从句分隔）

结果好，万事好。

（2）名词与同位语从句的分裂

When reports came into London Zoo that a wild puma had been spotted 45 miles south of

London, they were not taken seriously.（名词与同位语从句分隔）

虽然伦敦动物园接到报告称，伦敦以南45英里的地方发现了一只野生美洲狮，但这些报告并未受到重视。

A saying goes that practice makes perfect.（名词与同位语从句分隔）

常言道：熟能生巧。

◆ 主谓分裂 ◆

一般而言，一个句子的主语和谓语应该紧紧连接在一起，但在大量的阅读材料中情况并非如此。出于强调或句子平衡的作用，主谓之间经常有各种成分将其分隔，这就是主谓分裂。

<u>Verrazano</u>, an Italian about whom little is known, <u>sailed</u> into New York Harbor in 1524.

1524年，一位鲜为人知的意大利人维拉萨诺驾船驶入了纽约港。

<u>Mrs. Ramsay</u>, a very wealthy old lady, <u>has shared</u> a flat with her cat for a great many years.

拉姆齐夫人是一位非常富有的老太太，多年来与她的猫一同住在一所公寓里。

◆ 动宾分裂 ◆

出于强调或句子平衡的作用，一个英文句子的谓语动词和宾语也常常被分隔，这就是动宾分裂。

Wherever it went, the puma <u>left</u> behind it <u>a trail of dead deer and small animals</u>.

美洲狮无论去往何处，都会在身后留下一串死鹿和小动物的痕迹。

The captain <u>realized</u> to his horror <u>that the ship was sinking rapidly</u>.

船长惊恐地意识到船正在迅速下沉。

◆ 连主分裂 ◆

该分裂属于并列句或复合句中出现的现象。一个并列句或复合句正常的顺序是：第一分句+连接词+第二分句。但很多情况下，连接词与第二个分句中间会添加某些成分（多为状语），以上的句型变成了：第一分句+连接词+状语+第二分句，阅读时会有一种突然中断、跳跃之感，这就是连主分裂，即连接词与连接对象的分裂。

The actor decided to play a joke on his colleague to find out if, after so many performances, he had managed to learn the contents of the letter by heart.

这位演员决定与他的搭档开个玩笑，看看他演出那么多场戏后，是否把信件内容记得烂熟。

At first, she decided to go to the police, but fearing that she would never see her son again, she changed her mind.

起初她决定报警，但又怕再也见不到儿子了，于是改变了主意。

➡ 搭配分裂 ⬅

出于强调或句子平衡的作用，或使上下文意义更加紧密，有些固定搭配会被某些成分分隔，这就是搭配分裂。

The big family is dependent to a large extent on this efficient lady.

这个大家庭很大程度上依靠这位能干的女人来支撑。

To love a person is to put up, at least for some time, with his/her inappropriate behaviors.

爱一个人就是至少一定时间内容忍他/她的不良习惯。

6. 否定结构

每一种语言都有一定的形式和方法来表达否定含义，英文的否定方式大致可分为以下五种：全部否定，部分否定，双重否定，否定转移，特殊否定。下面将逐条讲解。

➡ 全部否定 ⬅

通常而言，none/neither/no-和any/either/any-+not表全部否定，如：

Neither of them passed the exam.

他们两人都没通过考试。

Nowhere can you find such a nice guy.

你在哪儿都找不到这么好的人了。

He didn't agree with either side.

两边儿他都不同意。

部分否定

一般而言，both/all/every- + not表部分否定，如：

Both of you are not right.

你们两人中，一个对，一个错。

Everyone can't have such a good luck.

不是每个人都有这种好运气。

双重否定

一个句子里如果出现两个具有否定意义的词，这就是双重否定，其含义往往是强烈的肯定。如：

Cats can never fail to fascinate human beings.

猫总能引起人类的极大兴趣。

Impossible is nothing.

凡事皆有可能。

否定转移

英文句子常有否定移动的现象，即表面上否定A，实则否定B，这就是否定转移。否定转移大致分为两种：

（1）表"看法，感觉"等的动词：think，argue，suppose，believe，imagine，expect，appear，seem，look like等。如果表面上否定词是修饰这些词的，则实际上否定含义应转移到其后的内容上。如：

I don't think he can win the first prize. (= I think he can not win the first prize.)

我认为他得不了一等奖。

She does not appear to reconcile with him. (= She appears not to reconcile with him.)

她似乎不愿和他和好。

（2）否定句中若含有because引导的原因状语从句、as引导的方式状语从句、作目的状语的不定式，如果正常理解出现了偏差歧义，则要把否定词转移到这些状语从句或不定式中。如：

We should not look down on the man because he is lazy. (We should look down on him not because he is lazy.)

我们不能因为他懒就瞧不起他。

She didn't accept the offer to make more money. (She accepted the offer, not to make more money.)

她接受这份工作邀请不是为了多赚钱。

另外，否定词与because引导的原因状语从句连用时，如果产生的含义有两种，则只能根据语境决定哪种是合理的。如：

I didn't go there because I was ill.

我病了，所以没去那儿。（或：我不是因为病了才去那儿的。）

➡ 特殊否定 ⬅

（1）but表示的否定含义

①如果but用于否定句中，且置于名词之后，相当于一个具有否定意义的关联词，可等同于who/that/which... not...，也就是一个具有否定意义的定语从句。如：

There is no rule but has exceptions. (=There is no rule that has no exceptions.)

凡事皆有例外。

②如果but在否定句中不是置于名词之后，也不表示转折含义，则but相当于一个具有否定意义的词，和句中的另一个否定词构成双否结构。如：

It never rains but pours.

不下则已，下则倾盆。（或：祸不单行。）

③nothing but，no one but，none but，nowhere but=only。如：

He cares nothing but his wealth.

他只关心他的财富。

If vacation comes, he wants to go nowhere but his hometown.

如果有假期，他只想回家乡。

（2）the last 和 the least 表示的否定含义

He is the last man I want to see in the world.

他是我最不想见到的人。

Personal safety is the least he thinks about in the face of danger.

个人安危是他面临危险时几乎不考虑的问题。

（3）cannot/can never/can hardly + too/enough/over 表示的肯定含义

The importance of family education cannot be overemphasized.

家庭教育的重要性怎么强调也不为过。

You cannot be too careful to cross the street.

你过马路时可要倍加小心。

A woman can never be too rich or too thin.

一个女人再富有再苗条都不为过。

（4）more than... can... 表示"超出……的限度/能力/范围"等含义

The severity of this disease was more than any doctor could imagine.

这种病的严重性是任何医生无法想象的。

Her rudeness is more than I can bear.

她的粗暴无礼我无法忍受。

7. 比较结构

英文的比较结构是一个相对复杂的语法现象，用来表达人或物的属性或特征的不同程度。广义而言，比较结构有两大类：以than引导的差级比较和以as引导的同级比较。如：

The boy is more diligent than his younger sister.

这个男孩比他的妹妹学习用功。

Every month, I earn as much money as Frank does.

我每月赚的钱和弗兰克一样多。

注意：只有两个同类事物才能比较，不是同类事物是不能比较的。如：

The weather of the South is wetter than the North. (×)

这是典型的错句，因为The weather of the South和the North不是同类事物，故不能比较。所以该句应改写成：The weather of the South is wetter than that of the North.（为避免重复，将前面的the weather 用that替代。）

此外，as引导比较句时前面可加much或just起加强语气的作用。如：

The workstation enables engineers to produce chips right on their desks, much as an editor creates a newsletter on a computer.

工作站可以让工程师们就在他们的桌子上制造芯片，如同一位编辑在电脑上写时事通讯一样。

由于比较结构存在相同性质的比较对象，所以经常出现表达的重复，为了避免累赘，常使用替代和省略手段。如：

Tom likes pop music more than his younger sister likes pop music.

Tom likes pop music more than his younger sister likes it.（it替代pop music）

Tom likes pop music more than his younger sister does.（助动词does替代动词likes）

Tom likes pop music more than his younger sister.（省略谓语）

Tom likes pop music more.（省略从句）

如果than或as引导的比较状语从句中的主语较长（主语必须是名词，代词则不行），则可以将从句中的助动词/情态动词/系动词放到名词主语之前，进行倒装，以避免头重脚轻。如：

He performed much better than did most of his colleagues.

他比大多数同事表现好得多。

然而在实际应用中，有很多复杂的特殊比较结构，下面进行逐一介绍：

（1）not so/as... as...

该结构是as... as...的否定形式，表示"不像……那样……"，强调后者（第二个as后面连接的对象）的程度胜过或重于前者。如：

He is not as stingy as many people assume.

他并不像许多人想象的那么吝啬。

People are not so credulous as they used to be.

人们不像从前那样轻信别人了。

（2）not so much... as... /not... so much as...

该结构有两种形式，但与not as... as...的原理是一样的，只不过多了一个程度副词much，可翻译为"与其……不如……"。如：

Li Yu was not so much a king as a poet.

李煜与其说是个国君，不如说是个词人。

（3）as... so...

该结构是一个固定形式，可翻译为"正如……，同样……"；或"随着……，于是……"，so后面的句子常用倒装形式。如：

As food nourishes the body, so do books enrich the mind.

（正如）食物滋养身体，（同样）书本丰富心灵。

As you sow, so will you reap.

种瓜得瓜，种豆得豆。

（4）A is to B what/as C is to D

该结构是一个固定形式，可理解为"A之于B如同C之于D（同等重要/不可缺少）"。如：

Personality is to man what/as perfume is to a flower.

品格之于人，如同芳香之于花朵（同等重要）。

或：人的品格，犹如花的芳香。

Air is to man what/as water is to fish.

空气对于人，如同水对于鱼不可缺少。

（5）The+比较级+其他成分，the+比较级+其他成分

该结构也是固定形式，可理解为"越……，就越……"。但请注意，这个结构中的两部分意义上并不是并列平行的，而是从句和主句的关系，前面一部分为从句，后面为主句。一般而言，这两部分的逻辑关系是：条件/原因+结果，所以该结构的深层含义是：(If/As) the+比较级+其他成分，the+比较级+其他成分。如：

The greater efforts you make, the more glories you are likely to gain.

付出的努力越多，得到的荣耀就可能越多。

The higher an official is, the greater responsibility he will take.

官员的职位越高，承担的责任就越大。

（6）more than...

①more than+数词，表示"比……多"，同理，less than+数词表示"比……少"。如：

He can earn more than 10,000 yuan per month.

他每月可赚到一万多元。

He stayed in Britain for less than 5 months.

他在英国待了不足5个月。

②more than+形容词/副词/动词，表示程度的强烈，可理解为"非常，远远，极其，加倍"等。如：

You must be more than diligent for the coming terminal test.

你必须为了即将到来的期末考试加倍努力。

His abilities were more than appreciated by the new boss.

新老板对他的能力极其欣赏。

③more than... can...，表示"无法……"或"不能……"。如：

The hot weather is more than I can bear.

这种炎热的天气我简直不能忍受。

His loss is more than money can compensate for.

他的损失是金钱无法补偿的。

④not... any more than... = no more... than...，可理解为"与……一样都不……"，其中than后面的句子表面是肯定形式，实则表达否定含义。如：

Incorporating jazz elements into pop music does not make it jazz, any more than putting chili pepper into a McDonald's hamburger into Sichuan cuisine.

把爵士乐的元素掺进流行乐，并不能将流行乐变成爵士乐，正如同把辣椒放进麦当劳的汉堡包也不能将其变成川菜一样。

⑤常用的、易混淆的几种比较结构，包括：

no more than = only 仅仅，只是

no less than = as much as 多达，高达；简直

no more... than... = neither... nor... 与……都不……

no less... than... = both... and... 与……都……

not more than = less than 至多，比……少

not less than = more than 至少，不少于

not more... than... = less... than... 不如……那么……

not less... than... = more... than... 比……更……

如：

What he did was no less than a miracle.

他所做的简直就是奇迹。

He is no more than 10.

他才10岁。

He is no less than 10.

他都10岁了。

Growing old is no more than a bad habit that a busy man has no time to form.

衰老不过是忙碌之人无暇培养的坏习惯而已。

（7）用times表达的倍数关系

在英文中，除了用than, as来对两个事物进行比较外，还可以用times来说明两个事物之间的倍数关系，可用以下三种句型：

A is twice/three times/four times/etc... + as +形容词+ as + B

A is twice/three times/four times/etc... +形容词比较级+ than + B

A is twice/three times/four times/etc... + the +（形容词对应的名词形式）+ of + B（如：big→size；long→length；wide→width；heavy→weight），如：

The house is three times as big as that one.

这个房子是那个房子的三倍大。

The house is twice bigger than that one.

这个房子比那个房子大两倍。

The house is three times the size of that one.

这个房子是那个房子的三倍大。

8. 独立主格结构

英文中有一种类似于状语从句的结构，称其为结构是因为它不含谓语动词，只包含"名词/名词短语/代词+现在分词/过去分词/不定式/形容词/副词/介词短语"，前面的"名词/名词短语/代词"逻辑上相当于从句的主语，后面的"现在分词/过去分词/不定式/形容词/副词/介词短语"逻辑上相当于从句的谓语或表语。由于该结构逻辑意义上的主语（即"名词/名词短语/代词"）和句子的主语不相同，所以称为独立主格结构。有时，独立主格结构的逻辑主语"名词/名词短语/代词"前面会出现介词with，即：with+名词/名词短语/代词+现在分词/过去分词/不定式/形容词/副词/介词短语。独立主格结构只是一个小短语，而不是主谓完整的句子。另外，该结构作状语时可表伴随、原因、条件等，要依据语境而定，并且在使用时，还要注意分词与逻辑主语的主动（用现在分词）或被动（用过去分词）关系。

（1）(with +) 名词/名词短语/代词+现在分词

(With) weather permitting, the picnic will be held as scheduled.（作条件状语）

天气允许的话，野餐活动将会如期举行。

(With) the strike having been called off, the workers returned to the factory.（作原因状语）

罢工停止了，工人们回到了工厂。

（2）(with +) 名词/名词短语/代词+过去分词

The test finished, we began our holiday.（作原因状语）

考试结束了，我们开始度假。

（3）(with +) 名词/名词短语/代词+不定式

With him to help her, he knew she could succeed.（作原因状语）

他知道有了他的帮助，她会成功的。

（4）(with +) 名词/名词短语/代词+形容词

He slept well with the door open.（作伴随状语）

门开着，他睡得很好。

（5）(with +) 名词/名词短语/代词+副词

He went out with no hat on.（作伴随状语）

他没戴帽子便出去了。

（6）(with +) 名词/名词短语/代词+介词短语

He stood there, with his hat in hand.（作伴随状语）

他站在那，手里拿着帽子。

注意：当独立主格结构的逻辑主语表示"一般人"，如we，you，one时，常可省略。此用法多用于以下表达中：

generally speaking　一般而言

strictly speaking　严格说来

talking of　谈到

speaking of　说到

judging from　从……判断

considering　考虑到

other things being equal　在其他条件等同的情况下

taking all things into consideration/account　把所有事情考虑在内

如：

Speaking of history, Egypt should be one of the oldest countries in the world.

说到历史，埃及应该是世界上最为古老的国家之一。

Judging from his accent, this foreigner should be from Canada.

从口音判断，这个外国人应该来自加拿大。

Other things being equal, a man who expresses himself effectively is sure to succeed more rapidly than the man whose command of language is poor.

在其他条件等同的情况下，语言表达能力强的人肯定比语言能力差的人成功得更快。

Part B 技巧提高篇

- 第三章 英语知识运用
- 第四章 阅读理解（A 部分）
- 第五章 阅读理解（B 部分）
- 第六章 英译汉
- 第七章 英文写作

考点分析 该部分是全书的提高篇，主要讲述考研英语（二）真题中的各个题型。本部分共分为五章，主要讲述了英语知识运用（完形填空）、阅读理解、英译汉，以及英文写作这几个题型的考点及做题技巧。

时间安排 该部分包括真题四大题型，建议考生用 40 天时间精读。在精读过程中，考生重在学习解题思维与技巧。

第三章 英语知识运用

第一节 最新大纲解读与应试策略

（一）大纲要求和命题趋势

1. 大纲要求

（1）英语知识运用（完形填空）

主要考查考生对英语知识的综合运用能力。共20小题，每小题0.5分，共10分。在一篇约350词的文章中留出20个空白，要求考生从每题所给的4个选项中选出最佳答案，使补全后的文章意思通顺、前后连贯、结构完整。

（2）语法知识

考生应能熟练地运用基本的语法知识，其中包括：

①名词、代词的数和格的构成及其用法；

②动词时态、语态的构成及其用法；

③形容词与副词的比较级和最高级的构成及其用法；

④常用连接词的词义及其用法；

⑤非谓语动词（不定式、动名词、分词）的构成及其用法；

⑥虚拟语气的构成及其用法；

⑦各类从句（定语从句、主语从句、表语从句等）及强调句型的结构及其用法；

⑧倒装句、插入语的结构及其用法。

2. 命题趋势

（1）英语知识运用（完形填空）

以下是根据近几年考研英语（二）英语知识运用（完形填空）的文章来源做出的统计：

年份	标题	材料来源	体裁	题材
2018	Curiosity Is Not Intrinsically Good	《科学美国人》	议论文	行为与社会
2017	Would a Work-Free World Be So Bad?	《大西洋月刊》	议论文	社会生活
2016	幸福指数高的城市中的公司更多倾向于长期投资	《哈佛商业评论》	议论文	商业经济
2015	地铁上的沉默，缺少交流	《赫芬顿邮报》	议论文	社会生活
2014	肥胖真的是一种疾病吗？	《大西洋月刊》	说明文	社会生活
2013	对无现金社会的探讨	《万恶之源》	议论文	社会生活

从以上表格中，大概可以总结出几条命题规律：

①文章基本上都来自近几年的英文原版报纸杂志，如：《大西洋月刊》《哈佛商业评论》《赫芬顿邮报》等。因此要多关注这些杂志，将其作为重点阅读对象。

②其次，所选文章绝大多数为议论文和说明文，这就为我们排除掉部分文章，减轻了阅读压力。

③大部分所选文章源于近两年的杂志，甚至来自近一年的文章，可见文章的时效性越来越明显。

（2）语法知识

考研英语（二）没有专项语法知识题，但语法知识贯穿于整个试卷的各个版块，如完形填空、阅读理解、翻译与写作，尤以阅读理解和写作对语法要求最高、最全面。阅读理解中会出现许多长难句，如何快速分清结构、把握文章大意是突破阅读环节的关键；写作部分也对语法提出了相应要求，若想在写作上获得高分，就要使用一些丰富并且复杂的语法结构，如倒装、强调、双重否定等。这就是历年来考研英语（二）在语法层面的命题重点和趋势，希望大家予以足够的重视。

（二）考查重点、命题思路及应对策略

1. 英语知识运用（完形填空）

（1）首段首句不出题

完形填空文章第一段的第一句会是一个完整的句子，因此不会出题。不出题是因为所选的文章基本都是总分结构，文章第一句往往就点明了文章主题。也就是说，第一句是非常重要的做题线索。同时，这一句在词汇和语法层面上难度一般并不大。因此，这一句一定要精读而且要划出关键词。

（2）议论文和说明文为主

考研英语（二）所选的文章多以社会、文化教育类为主，体裁多是议论文和说明文。有关自然科学和科普类的文章只占极少数。之所以这样选材，是为了尽可能做到考试公平。因为，科普类和自然科学类文章对于理工科学生具有优势，但并不是文科类考生擅长的领域。所以在复习时要慎选文章题材。

（3）做题方法和选项规律

有些同学对完形填空没有足够重视，复习时也没投入太多时间，做题时普遍使用代入法：一边看文章，一边把四个选项代入空格，感觉哪个选项合适就选哪个，文章读完题也做完了。这种做法根本没有深入理解文章大意，更谈不上理清上下文之间的逻辑关系。正确的做法是：先快速略读一遍掌握文章大意，然后再开始做题。

2. 语法知识

上面提到，考研英语（二）的语法知识一共涉及八大考点，只要认真将这八点掌握到位，考卷中遇到长难句自然能够快速理解其含义。如果语法混乱，考题中的语句就读不懂，这样会直接导致无法答题，更不要说得分了。所以还是要依托考纲指出的语法重点反查自己是否能够在语法上做到滴水不漏。那么怎样测试自己的语法掌握是否扎实呢？如果在考题中遇到任何长难句能够迅速抓住其主干，分清从句类型，理解句子大意，那就说明语法掌握到位；否则必须按照考纲规定将语法从头梳理一遍，理解语法基本知识点。八大考点的后四点是复习和考查重

点，即：非谓语动词（不定式、动名词、分词）的构成及其用法；虚拟语气的构成及其用法；各类从句（定语从句、主语从句、表语从句等）及强调句型的结构及其用法；倒装句、插入语的结构及其用法。

（三）复习备考指南

1. 英语知识运用（完形填空）

有些同学因为从心理上不重视完形填空，也就不会花太多时间研究完形填空及做题方法和技巧。因此，很多考生并不真正了解完形填空，而且形成了两种误区。

首先，他们认为完形填空阅读量小，一般每篇文章只有350个单词左右，看上去并不难，因此从一开始就没准备下大力气复习，也就是在主观上轻视。其次，很多同学认为完形填空所填的空都是单词，而且很简单，所以只需每天花时间记单词就可以，不用刻意再去做练习。

事实上，完形填空并不是大家所认为的那样，而是有更多价值尚未挖掘。首先，完形填空题本身就是检验考生掌握单词是否牢固的一个大好机会。因为对于准备考研的考生们来说，记单词是从开始复习到考试前一天每天的必备工作。所以在做阅读和完形填空时，遇到不熟悉的、尚未记牢的单词一定多下功夫，尤其是同义词、近义词、形近词等，应该随时整理出来，每天花时间复习。

其次，做完形填空也有助于提高阅读能力，特别是根据上下文判断推理的能力。因为完形填空的做题规则就是用已知信息确定未知信息。另外，完形填空真题都是经过精挑细选和深加工完成的，并不仅仅是一道题，同时也是一篇高质量的文章。积累背诵其中优美的句子，尝试着用高级词汇替换简单词汇，也会对提升写作能力大有帮助。

完形填空想取得不错的成绩，语法和词汇是基础。对于语法，一般只要有中学水平即可，复习重点在于词汇辨析和逻辑关系。主要考查的是常规词汇，还有形近词、近义词等。一般不考偏词、难词，更不会考查超纲词汇。

另外，完形填空的正确答案中，A、B、C、D四个选项的出现概率一般是一样的，不会出现正确答案中某个选项被选次数多、某个选项被选次数少的问题，这是为了最大公平原则而设置的。所以，做完题后如有时间要把答案粗略浏览检查，20个选项要合理分配。

总之，要重新理解和认识完形填空这种题型的巨大价值，同时深入了解其考查重点和命题规律，自然也就知道了复习重点。

2. 语法知识

上面提到，虽然语法在考研英语（二）中不再单独考查，但是语法知识贯穿在整个英语试卷中。完形填空题会直接考查语法知识；阅读理解题和英译汉中有大量长难句，这些句子只有具备一定的语法知识才能正确分析；作文中要写出正确无误的句子，也需要语法知识，所以语法知识是英语学习的基础。

在大纲列出的八大考点中，非谓语动词、虚拟语气、倒装等都是复习重点。比如非谓语动词，要了解它包括几个形式：不定式、现在分词/动名词和过去分词，以及具体的作用和功能。

从句也是考查重点。学习从句前首先要了解英语的基本句子构成。按结构划分有：简单句、并列句和复合句。简单句：句子里只有一个主谓结构，且各个成分都只由单词或短语构成。共有五种结构，即主谓、主谓宾、主系表、主谓双宾和主谓宾宾补。并列句是用并列连词把两个或两个以上的简单句连接起来的句子。并列连词有and，but，or等。复合句是指一个句子里又包含一个或多个句子充当成分的句子。大句子叫主句；充当成分、附属于大句子的句子叫从句。英语有三大从句，分别是名词性从句、定语从句和状语从句。

看语法书的同时，既要对基本的语法知识进行整理，形成一个体系，也要对一些特殊的语法现象进行归纳，要手眼并用，不能只看不动手。另外，语法复习重在语法现象本身，而不是记住那些枯燥无味的术语。

建议大家通过做题巩固所学的语法知识。复习过程中单纯看语法书很枯燥，复习效果也不好，跟题目结合起来复习效果会好一些，并且可以通过做题检查对语法知识的掌握情况。

复习语法的目的是读懂文章、做对题目。英语成绩好的同学，语法基础肯定也不差，并且能熟练地将语法知识应用到阅读、写作等环节中。英语成绩不好的同学，可能是语法基础不扎实，也可能是囫囵吞枣，对语法知识一知半解。如果在阅读中面对一个长难句，你能快速准确地理解这个句子的成分、各个成分之间的关系、涉及什么样的语法知识，并能正确翻译，那就说明对这部分语法知识掌握得不错；如果达不到这个要求，就需要强化复习。

第二节 英语知识运用精讲

（一）考点分布及解题技巧

完形填空一般是总分的结构，而且体裁一般是议论文和说明文。要高效做题，就要最短时间内准确抓住全文主旨。而议论文的主旨很明显，往往在全文首段，尤其是首段首句。只要读懂了首段，考生便能了解作者描述的对象、发生了什么事，以及作者的态度。因此，从完形填空的题型特点看，要养成读首段尤其是首段首句的习惯。

其次，有必要了解一下完形填空的考点。总体而言，考点基本分为两点：逻辑关系以及词义辨析。这两部分所占的比例却不相同：前者只占 30%，而后者占 70%。就逻辑关系而言，考生可主要记忆关联词，如表示因果、递进、转折、让步等关系的常用词汇或短语。对于 70% 的词义辨析，其实就是词汇的积累。所以，加强单词记忆，尤其是在背一词多义、熟词僻义等方面要多加重视。

（二）历年真题精讲

Section I Use of English (2017)

Directions: Read the following text. Choose the best word (s) for each numbered blank and mark A, B, C or D on the ANSWER SHEET. (10 points)

People have speculated for centuries about a future without work. Today is no different, with academics, writers, and activists once again __1__ that technology is replacing human workers.

Some imagine that the coming work-free world will be defined by __2__: A few wealthy people will own all the capital, and the masses will struggle in an impoverished wasteland.

A different and not mutually exclusive __3__ holds that the future will be a wasteland of a different sort, one __4__ by purposelessness: Without jobs to give their lives __5__, people will simply become lazy and depressed. __6__, today's unemployed don't seem to be having a great time. One Gallup poll found that 20 percent of Americans who have been unemployed for at least a year report having depression, double the rate for __7__ Americans. Also, some research suggests that the __8__ for rising rates of mortality, mental-health problems, and addiction __9__ poorly-educated middle-aged people is a shortage of well-paid jobs. Perhaps this is why many __10__ the agonizing dullness of a jobless future.

But it doesn't __11__ follow from findings like these that a world without work would be filled with unease. Such visions are based on the __12__ of being unemployed in a society built on the concept of employment. In the __13__ of work, a society designed with other ends in mind could __14__ strikingly different circumstances for the future of labor and leisure. Today, the __15__ of work may be a bit overblown. "Many jobs are boring, degrading, unhealthy, and a waste of human potential," says John Danaher, a lecturer at the National University of Ireland in Galway.

These days, because leisure time is relatively __16__ for most workers, people use their free time to counterbalance the intellectual and emotional __17__ of their jobs. "When I come home from a hard day's work, I often feel __18__," Danaher says, adding, "In a world in which I don't have to work, I might feel rather different" —perhaps different enough to throw himself __19__ a hobby or a passion project with the intensity usually reserved for __20__ matters.

1. [A] boasting   [B] denying   [C] warning   [D] ensuring
2. [A] inequality   [B] instability   [C] unreliability   [D] uncertainty
3. [A] policy   [B] guideline   [C] resolution   [D] prediction
4. [A] characterized   [B] divided   [C] balanced   [D] measured

5. [A] wisdom [B] meaning [C] glory [D] freedom
6. [A] Instead [B] Indeed [C] Thus [D] Nevertheless
7. [A] rich [B] urban [C] working [D] educated
8. [A] explanation [B] requirement [C] compensation [D] substitute
9. [A] under [B] beyond [C] alongside [D] among
10. [A] leave behind [B] make up [C] worry about [D] set aside
11. [A] statistically [B] occasionally [C] necessarily [D] economically
12. [A] chances [B] downsides [C] benefits [D] principles
13. [A] absence [B] height [C] face [D] course
14. [A] disturb [B] restore [C] exclude [D] yield
15. [A] model [B] practice [C] virtue [D] hardship
16. [A] tricky [B] lengthy [C] mysterious [D] scarce
17. [A] demands [B] standards [C] qualities [D] threats
18. [A] ignored [B] tired [C] confused [D] starved
19. [A] off [B] against [C] behind [D] into
20. [A] technological [B] professional [C] educational [D] interpersonal

◆ 试题详解 ◆

1. 【答案】C

【解析】词义辨析。根据前文语境，本句题干意为"现在也没什么不同，学者、作家还有活动家都又一次毫无例外地____，技术将会代替人类工作"。[A]夸耀；[B]拒绝；[C]警告；[D]保证。依次代入原文，结合本段最后一句"少数富豪将会占据全部资本，而广大群众只能在贫困的荒芜之地挣扎度日"这一后果，显然是在发出"警告"，可确定[C]为正确答案。

2. 【答案】A

【解析】词义辨析语义衔接。结合本段最后一句"少数富豪将会占据全部资本，而广大群众只能在贫困的荒芜之地挣扎度日"，再看四个选项，[A]不平等；[B]不稳定性；[C]不可靠；[D]不确定。因此这个即将到来的世界是不平等的。可确定[A]为正确答案。

3. 【答案】D

【解析】词义辨析语义衔接。分析句子，that从句后面接will是将来时态，"未来将是一个完全不同的荒芜之地"。[A]政策；[B]指导；[C]决心；[D]预测。浏览四个选项，只有[D]符合句意。

4. 【答案】A

【解析】词义辨析语义衔接。one ____ by purposelessness是前面wasteland的补充成分，起修饰作用。[A]以……为特点的；[B]分开的；[C]平衡的；[D]基于……标准的。依次代入原句，[A]符合句意，这个荒芜之地以毫无意义为特点，因此[A]为正确答案。

5. 【答案】B

【解析】词义辨析。本句题干意为"当工作不能给人们的生活带来____，人们就会变得懒惰，心情低落。"[A]智慧；[B]意义；[C]荣耀；[D]自由。依次代入题目，[B]最符合题意，因此[B]为正确答案。

6. 【答案】B

【解析】语义衔接。空格后面句意为"失业者的日子并不好过"，因此该句与前一句"当工作不能给人们的生活带来____，人们就会变得懒惰，心情低落。"之间是一种递进关系。[A]反而，表示转折；[B]甚至，表示递进；[C]因此，表示因果；[D]然而，表示转折。因此[B]为正确答案。

7. 【答案】C

【解析】语义衔接。本句题干意为"盖勒普的一次民意调查显示，失业至少一年以上的美国人中，大约20%的人会患上抑郁症，比____美国人比例高出一倍"。[A]富有的；[B]城市的；[C]工作的；[D]受教育的。根据题意可知，空格处应与前半句中失业的美国人形成对比，因此[C]为正确答案。

8. 【答案】A

【解析】语义衔接。分析句子结构可知，空格处为主语，for后面为主语的修饰成分，简化该句意为"呈上升趋势的____是高薪工作匮乏"。[A]解释，原因；[B]需求；[C]补偿；[D]代替品。依次代入原文，[A]最符合题意，因此[A]为正确答案。

9. 【答案】D

【解析】结构衔接。分析句子可知，空格处连接前后的关系词，...mortality, mental-health problems, and addiction ____ poorly-educated middle-aged people...。[A]在……之下；[B]超出……之处；[C]在……旁边；[D]在……之中。依次代入，[D]最符合题意，因此[D]为正确答案。

10. 【答案】C

【解析】语义衔接。本句题干意为"或许这就是很多人对未来失业前景令人痛苦的沉闷____的原因"。[A]留下，遗留；[B]组成；[C]担心；[D]留出，撤回。分析上下文可知应为"担心"，因此[C]为正确答案。

11. 【答案】C

【解析】语义衔接。本句题干意为"但是这些发现也未必____得出结论：没有工作的世界会充满不安"。[A]统计上地；[B]偶尔，间或；[C]必要地；[D]经济地。依次代入可知，[C]最符合题意，因此[C]为正确答案。

12. 【答案】B

【解析】语义衔接。本句题干意为"类似的看法基于人们在一个以就业为本的社会失业后的____"。[A]机会；[B]不利方面；[C]福利；[D]原则。依次代入，[B]最符合题意，因此[B]为正确答案。

13. 【答案】A

【解析】惯用搭配语义衔接。[A]缺乏（in the absence of表示缺乏，缺少）；[B]顶点（in the height of表示在……的顶峰）；[C]面容（in the face of表示面对）；[D]行动方向（in the course of表示在……的过程中）。依次代入，只有[A]最符合题意，因此[A]为正确答案。

14. 【答案】 D

    【解析】语义衔接。该空格所选词汇的主语是a society，宾语是different circumstances。[A]打扰；[B]修复；[C]排斥；[D]产生。根据主谓一致的原则，只有[D]最符合题意，因此[D]为正确答案。

15. 【答案】 C

    【解析】语义衔接。overblow意为"吹散，吹倒"，表贬义。后面的内容"Many jobs are boring, degrading, unhealthy, and a waste of human potential," says John Danaher, a lecturer at the National University of Ireland in Galway.是对本句题干的进一步解释，结合上下文语义理解，应选择virtue，其他选项均排除。因此[C]为正确答案。

16. 【答案】 D

    【解析】语义衔接。本句题干意为"最近，由于休闲时间对大多数员工来说是____，所以人们就利用工作之余的时间来弥补他们工作中带来的理智与情感____"。[A]狡猾的；[B]漫长的；[C]秘密的；[D]匮乏的。依次代入，只有[D]最符合题意，因此[D]为正确答案。

17. 【答案】 A

    【解析】语义衔接。本句题干意为"最近，由于休闲时间对大多数员工来说是____，所以人们就利用工作之余的时间来弥补他们工作中带来的理智与情感____"。[A]需求；[B]标准；[C]质量；[D]威胁。依次代入，只有[A]最符合题意，因此[A]为正确答案。

18. 【答案】 B

    【解析】语义衔接。本句题干意为"我累了一天回到家，经常觉得____"。[A]被忽视的；[B]疲惫的；[C]疑惑的；[D]饥饿的。根据语义，正确答案应为[B]。

19. 【答案】 D

    【解析】惯用搭配。throw oneself off意为"摆脱，抛弃，关闭"；throw against意为"向……投掷"；throw behind意为"把……抛在身后"；throw oneself into意为"一头

扎进；投身于，积极从事"。分析句意可知，[D]为正确答案。

20. 【答案】 B

【解析】词义辨析。[A]技术的；[B]职业的，专业的；[C]教育的；[D]人际的。因为第19题谈到，"他才会投入到某种爱好，或者一个热爱的激情项目"，由此可见，[B]与爱好或喜欢之事逻辑顺畅，因此[B]为正确答案。

参考译文

几百年以来人们一直在思考，未来不用工作会是什么景象。现在也没什么不同，学者、作家、活动家都又一次警告说，技术将会替代人类工作。有些人设想，未来人们不用工作，世界将会充满不平等：少数富豪将会占据全部资本，而广大群众只能在贫困的荒芜之地挣扎度日。

一个虽然不同但是并不矛盾的预言认为，未来将是一个不同的荒芜之地，特征就是漫无目的。当工作不能给人们的生活带来意义，人们就会变得懒惰，心情低落。的确，现在失业者的日子并不好过。盖勒普的一次民意调查显示，失业至少一年以上的美国人中，有20%的人会患上抑郁症，比工作的美国人比例高出一倍。同时，一些研究表明，没有受过良好教育的中年人中，死亡、患精神病、染上毒瘾的比例节节攀升，其中一个原因就是缺乏高薪工作。或许这就是很多人对未来失业前景令人痛苦的沉闷产生焦虑的原因。

但是这些发现也未必一定能得出结论：没有工作的世界会充满不安。类似的看法基于人们在一个以就业为本的社会失业后的消极面。在没有工作的情况下，社会还要完成其他目标，要产生截然不同的未来就业与休闲环境。如今，关于就业的积极面有点言过其实。爱尔兰国立高威大学的讲师John Danaher指出："不少工作枯燥乏味，缺乏体面，有损健康，浪费人力。"

最近，由于休闲时间对大多数员工来说是不够的，所以人们就利用工作之余的时间来弥补他们工作中带来的理智与情感需求。Danaher补充说："我累了一天回到家，经常觉得疲惫，假如身处一个不需要干活的世界，我的心境可能完全不同。"也许因为心境大大不同，他才会投入到某种爱好，或者一个热爱的激情项目，人们一般会保留这份热情应对工作上的事务。

Section I   Use of English (2016)

Directions: Read the following text. Choose the best word(s) for each numbered blank and mark A, B, C or D on the ANSWER SHEET. (10 points)

Happy people work differently. They're more productive, more creative, and willing to take greater risks. And new research suggests that happiness might influence __1__ firms work, too.

Companies located in places with happier people invest more, according to a recent research paper. __2__, firms in happy places spend more on R&D (research and development). That's because happiness is linked to the kind of longer-term thinking __3__ for making investments for the future.

The researchers wanted to know if the __4__ and inclination for risk-taking that come with happiness would __5__ the way companies invested. So they compared U.S. cities' average happiness __6__ by Gallup polling with the investment activity of publicly traded firms in those areas.

__7__ enough, firms' investment and R&D intensity were correlated with the happiness of the area in which they were __8__. But is it really happiness that's linked to investment, or could something else about happier cities __9__ why firms there spend more on R&D? To find out, the researchers controlled for various __10__ that might make firms more likely to invest—like size, industry, and sales—and for indicators that a place was __11__ to live in, like growth in wages or population. The link between happiness and investment generally __12__ even after accounting for these things.

The correlation between happiness and investment was particularly strong for younger firms, which the authors __13__ to "less codified decision making process" and the possible presence of "younger and less   14   managers who are more likely to be influenced by sentiment." The relationship was   15   stronger in places where happiness was spread more   16 . Firms seem to invest more in places where most people are relatively happy, rather than in places with happiness inequality.

  17   this doesn't prove that happiness causes firms to invest more or to take a longer-term view, the authors believe it at least   18   at that possibility. It's not hard to imagine that local culture and sentiment would help   19   how executives think about the future. "It surely seems plausible that happy people would be more forward-thinking and creative and   20   R&D more than the average," said one researcher.

1. [A] why   [B] where   [C] how   [D] when
2. [A] In return   [B] In particular   [C] In contrast   [D] In conclusion
3. [A] sufficient   [B] famous   [C] perfect   [D] necessary
4. [A] individualism   [B] modernism   [C] optimism   [D] realism
5. [A] echo   [B] miss   [C] spoil   [D] change
6. [A] imagined   [B] measured   [C] invented   [D] assumed
7. [A] Sure   [B] Odd   [C] Unfortunate   [D] Often
8. [A] advertised   [B] divided   [C] overtaxed   [D] headquartered
9. [A] explain   [B] overstate   [C] summarize   [D] emphasize
10. [A] stages   [B] factors   [C] levels   [D] methods
11. [A] desirable   [B] sociable   [C] reputable   [D] reliable
12. [A] resumed   [B] held   [C] emerged   [D] broke
13. [A] attribute   [B] assign   [C] transfer   [D] compare
14. [A] serious   [B] civilized   [C] ambitious   [D] experienced
15. [A] thus   [B] instead   [C] also   [D] never
16. [A] rapidly   [B] regularly   [C] directly   [D] equally

17. [A] After   [B] Until   [C] While   [D] Since

18. [A] arrives   [B] jumps   [C] hints   [D] strikes

19. [A] shape   [B] rediscover   [C] simplify   [D] share

20. [A] pray for   [B] lean towards [C] give away   [D] send out

◆ 试题详解 ◆

1. 【答案】 C

   【解析】连词辨析。"近期的一项研究表明：快乐也可能会影响公司____运作。"[A]为什么；[B]哪里；[C]怎样，多么；[D]当……时候。根据语义分析，[C]填入原文，意为"快乐也可能会影响公司如何运作"，因此[C]为正确答案。

2. 【答案】 B

   【解析】上下文语义以及短语辨析。[A]反过来；[B]尤其是；[C]相反；[D]总的来说。根据前文语境，第二段第一句意为"根据近期的研究报告，拥有更多快乐员工的公司会投资更多"。而第二句"____那些在快乐氛围中的公司会做更多的研发以及发展。"第二句是在第一句的基础上进一步强调说明，[B]更符合语境要求，因此[B]为正确答案。

3. 【答案】 D

   【解析】上下文语义及形容词词义辨析。[A]充足的；[B]著名的；[C]完美的；[D]必要的。首先，本句题干That's because happiness is linked to the kind of longer-term thinking ____ for making investments for the future.意为"这是因为对未来进行投资____做出长远决策，而这种决策与快乐相关。"要求填写形容词，我们要考虑其搭配与其修饰成分。空格处搭配介词for，并且修饰"长远决策"，[D]最符合语境要求，因此[D]为正确答案。

4. 【答案】 C

   【解析】上下文语义及名词词义辨析。[A]个人主义；[B] 现代主义；[C]乐观主义；[D]现实主义。本题考查同后缀的名词辨析。根据原文主旨，探讨happy people与公司的关系。衡量四个选项，只有[C]符合主旨要求，因此[C]为正确答案。

5. 【答案】 D

   【解析】 上下文语义及动词词义辨析。[A]发出回声；[B]想念，错过；[C]破坏；[D]改变。根据原文语境，...would ____ the way companies invested...，本题考查动宾搭配，宾语为"公司投资的方式"，只有[D]搭配最为合理，因此[D]为正确答案。

6. 【答案】 B

   【解析】上下文语义及动词词义辨析。[A]想象；[B]衡量，测量；[C]发明；[D]假定，设想。So they compared U.S. cities' average happiness ____ by Gallup polling with the investment activity of publicly traded firms in those areas.意为"他们把盖洛普咨询公司所____的美国城市平均幸福指数与该地区的上市公司投资活跃度进行对比。"根据原文语境，盖洛普咨询公司所做的应该是一个既定事实，所以排除[A]、[C]、[D]。因此[B]为正确答案。

7. 【答案】 A

   【解析】上下文语义及固定搭配。[A]确信地；[B]奇怪的；[C]不幸运的；[D]经常的。本题考查固定搭配sure enough，意为"足以肯定的是"，因此[A]为正确答案。

8. 【答案】 D

   【解析】上下文语义及形容词词义辨析。[A]广告的；[B]划分的；[C]课税过重的；[D]位于总部的。根据原文...firms' investment and R&D intensity were correlated with the happiness of the area in which they were ____. "……公司投资与研发力度与公司____的幸福指数密切相关。"in which引导表示地点的定语从句，先行词为area。对比四个选项，[A]、[B]、[C]均不足以说明此地点的真实含义。[D]和area构成"总部所在地"最为合理，因此[D]为正确答案。

9. 【答案】 A

   【解析】上下文语义及动词词义辨析。[A]解释；[B]夸大；[C]概述；[D]重点强调。根据原文"...or could something else about happier cities ____ why firms there spend more on

R&D?" explain常和后文why搭配使用，因此[A]为正确答案。

10. 【答案】 B

    【解析】上下文语义及名词词义辨析。[A]阶段；[B]因素；[C]等级；[D]方法。根据原文语境"To find out, the researchers controlled for various ____ that might make firms more likely to invest—like size, industry, and sales..."，本题中，破折号后面"大小，产业，销售"这些都是"促使公司投资"的因素。[B]最符合原文语境，因此[B]为正确答案。

11. 【答案】 A

    【解析】上下文语义和形容词词义辨析。该空填的是形容词，用来修饰前面的名词place，并且在意义上也是对后面like growth in wages or population的解释，可以看出应该是填褒义词，并且能修饰place。[A] desirable合适的；[B] sociable社交的；[C] reputable受尊敬的；[D] reliable可靠的。只有[A]符合题意，因此[A]为正确答案。

12. 【答案】 B

    【解析】上下文语义及动词词义辨析。该句是这一段的总结句，该段整体在描述幸福与投资之间的关系。[A] resumed重新开始；[B] held得出；[C] emerged浮现；[D] broke破坏。只有[B]符合语境，因此[B]为正确答案。

13. 【答案】 A

    【解析】上下文逻辑关系以及动词词组辨析。该空是一个which引导的定语从句的谓语动词所在地，动词的宾语就是前面的主句，强调"幸福与投资之间的关系尤其适用于新公司"这一结论与后面"决策时更容易受情绪影响"之间的关系，能看出是一个因果关系。[A] attribute to归因于……；[B] assign to指派；[C] transfer to转移到；[D] compare to与……比较。[A]含有因果关系，其他均不符合题意，因此[A]为正确答案。

14. 【答案】 D

    【解析】上下文语义及形容词词义辨析。此处很简单，前面有一个并列连词and，与前面的young一致修饰managers，强调新公司的领导年轻并缺乏经验，只有[D] experienced最合适，因此[D]为正确答案。

15. 【答案】C

【解析】上下文逻辑关系以及副词词义辨析。前面说到了"年轻的新经理决策时更容易受情绪影响"，与后面的"这种关系在幸福度分布更加____的地方尤为明显。公司似乎乐于投资那些相对快乐的员工所在的部门，而不是那些不快乐的部门。"之间很明显是一种递进关系，只有[C] also最合适，因此[C]为正确答案。

16. 【答案】D

【解析】上下文语义及副词词义辨析。这道题考查副词修饰spread。"这种关系在幸福度分布更加____的地方尤为明显。公司似乎乐于在大多数人都相对幸福的地方投资，而不是那些幸福感分布不公平的地方。"该空与后面的inequality形成复现关系，所以很容易判断出答案选择equally，因此[D]为正确答案。

17. 【答案】C

【解析】上下文逻辑关系。该题考查上下文逻辑关系，因此着力点应该放在上一段和这一段之间的关系。这一段第一句明确说出"____这并不能证明幸福导致公司大量投资……"，所以两句话之间是一个转折关系，因此[C]为正确答案。

18. 【答案】C

【解析】上下文语义及动词词义辨析。该题考查动词与at的固定搭配，[A] arrive at到达，抵达；[B] jump at扑向，欣然接受；[C] hint at暗示；[D] strike at袭击，攻击。文章中的at least和that possibility论证了这是一种可能，只有hint at有这层含义，因此[C]为正确答案。

19. 【答案】A

【解析】上下文语义及动词词义辨析。根据上下文应该选一个"影响"未来看法含义的动词，[A]塑造，形成，影响；[B]再发现；[C]使简化，使单纯；[D]分享。[A]带有"影响"含义，因此[A]为正确答案。

20.【答案】 B

【解析】 上下文语义及动词词组词义辨析。本空考查动词词组，且该词组词义应与and前面意思保持一致，且作用对象为研发。[A] pray for祈祷；[B] lean towards倾向；[C] give away放弃，泄露；[D] send out放出，给予。只有[B]选项能表达一种递进含义，因此[B]为正确答案。

◆ 参考译文 ◆

快乐的人工作起来会有不同。他们更有效率，更有创造力，也更愿意去冒险。近期的一项研究表明快乐也可能会影响公司如何运作。

根据近期的研究报告，拥有更多快乐员工的公司会投资更多。尤其是那些在快乐氛围中的公司会投入更多的钱在研发上。这是因为对未来进行投资需要做出长远决策，而这种决策与快乐相关。

研究人员希望了解乐观精神和随快乐而来的冒险倾向是否会改变公司投资的方式。因此，他们把盖洛普咨询公司所评估出的美国城市平均幸福指数与该地区的上市公司投资活跃度进行对比。

果然，公司投资与研发力度与公司总部所在地的幸福指数密切相关。但是幸福真的与投资相关吗？或者说，幸福指数更高的城市的其他方面能不能够说明公司为何加大研发投入？为了弄清这一点，研究人员掌握了多种可能促使公司投资的因素，例如规模、产业、销售，也要掌握各种指标，如适宜居住地，工资涨幅及人口变化。了解这些问题后，幸福与投资的关系就能够轻松得出了。

幸福与投资之间的关系尤其适用于新公司，这是因为新公司的决策过程不太规范，而且年轻的新经理决策时更容易受情绪影响。同样，这种关系在幸福度分布更加公平的地方尤为明显。公司似乎乐于在大多数人都相对幸福的地方投资，而不是那些幸福感分布不公平的地方。

尽管这并不能证明幸福导致公司大量投资或把目标放得更远，研究人员认为至少它预示着这种可能性。不难想象，当地文化以及情绪有助于影响高管对于未来的看法。一位研究者说："快乐的人比普通人更有远见、更有创造力，更善于研发，这种说法似乎很可信。"

（三）实战操练

Passage 1

Directions: Read the following text. Choose the best word(s) for each numbered blank and mark A, B, C or D on the ANSWER SHEET. (10 points)

Jose Rommel Umano, who is __1__ from the Philippines, moved to New York last autumn. He came __2__ a family-reunification visa and joined his wife, who had been living in America for some time. This is a __3__ tale: America gives more __4__ to close family members when considering immigration applications than some other rich countries do. More __5__ is that Mr Rommel Umano arrived with a master's degree from the University of Tokyo and 20 years of experience as an architect in Japan. Yet this, it __6__, is typical too. Nearly half of all immigrants who arrived between 2011 and 2015 were college-educated. This is a level "__7__" in America, says Jeanne Batalova, co-author of the paper __8__ the finding published by the Migration Policy Institute (MPI), a think-tank.

One of Donald Trump's many executive orders __9__ the Departments of Labour, Justice and Homeland Security to __10__ immigration rules. The president, whose hostility __11__ illegal migrants is well-known, has also said that he would like to change the criteria for choosing legal ones, pointing to Canada or Australia as models for America to copy. In 1967 Canada became the first country to introduce a points system for immigration; Canada and Australia now both give __12__ to would-be migrants with degrees, work experience and fluent English (and, in Canada,

81

French). Some of the president's advisers think this more hard-headed system is better than America's family-centred __13__ . The __14__ immigration bill from 2013 that died in the House of Representatives also reflected widespread enthusiasm for a points-based system.

Two things ought to __15__ this enthusiasm. First, Canada and Australia have concluded that pure points systems do not work well. A surprisingly high share of the people admitted this way __16__ unemployed. Both countries have since changed their immigration __17__ so that applicants who have job offers in their pockets may __18__ the queue. Second, migrants who move to America to join family members have become much better educated. Of the more than 1m new green-card holders (or permanent residents) in 2015, the most recent year with numbers __19__ , almost half were __20__ relatives of citizens.

1. [A] currently   [B] previously   [C] originally   [D] lately
2. [A] on   [B] with   [C] by   [D] for
3. [A] standard   [B] stereotypical   [C] extraordinary   [D] typical
4. [A] quantity   [B] weight   [C] quality   [D] amount
5. [A] excellent   [B] spectacular   [C] surprising   [D] strange
6. [A] turns out   [B] turns up   [C] turns down   [D] turns to
7. [A] heard of   [B] unheard of   [C] heard   [D] unheard
8. [A] connecting   [B] improving   [C] correcting   [D] containing
9. [A] inspired   [B] instructed   [C] expected   [D] hoped
10. [A] examine   [B] boost   [C] change   [D] control
11. [A] with   [B] on   [C] to   [D] against
12. [A] superiority   [B] nobility   [C] popularity   [D] priority
13. [A] tactic   [B] approach   [C] plan   [D] goal
14. [A] predicted   [B] hoped   [C] doomed   [D] calculated

15.	[A] temper	[B] control	[C] suppress	[D] regulate
16.	[A] finished up	[B] split up	[C] tore up	[D] ended up
17.	[A] processes	[B] criteria	[C] strategies	[D] methods
18.	[A] cross	[B] stand	[C] jump	[D] walk
19.	[A] available	[B] predictable	[C] controllable	[D] imaginable
20.	[A] instant	[B] near	[C] intimate	[D] immediate

试题详解

1.【答案】C

【解析】语义衔接+词汇辨析。[A] currently现在；[B] previously先前；[C] originally最初；[D] lately最近。该空格所处的句子大意是：何塞·隆美尔·乌马诺来自菲律宾，于去年秋天搬到了纽约。根据句意，选项C为正确答案，originally from the Philippines表示原籍是菲律宾。

2.【答案】A

【解析】词汇辨析。[A] on依靠，在……上面；[B] with用；[C] by按照，依据；[D] for为了。该空格所处的句子大意是：他是以家庭团聚签证移民的，与妻子实现了团聚。根据句意，选项A为正确答案。构成干扰的是选项B和选项C。with常与具体可见的物质类名词搭配，如with a stick（用棍子）；by则常与某种方式构成搭配，如by sea（乘船），by bike（骑车）。

3.【答案】D

【解析】语义衔接+词汇辨析。[A] standard标准的；[B] stereotypical带有成见的；[C] extraordinary非凡的；[D] typical典型的。该空格所处的句子大意是：这是一个＿＿＿故事。冒号后面的内容是对这个故事做出解释说明：当考虑移民申请时，美国比其他发达国家更加重视家庭成员。通过逻辑判断以及与tale的搭配关系，选项D为正确答案。此外，从第6个空格后面的论述也可推出选项D是正确的。

4. 【答案】B

   【解析】固定搭配。[A] quantity数量；[B] weight 重量；[C] quality 质量；[D] amount 数量。give weight to sth.表示"重视某事"，根据句意，选项B为正确答案。

5. 【答案】C

   【解析】逻辑衔接+词汇辨析。[A] excellent优秀的；[B] spectacular壮观的；[C]surprising令人吃惊的；[D] strange奇怪的。该空格所处的句子大意是：更_____的是，隆美尔·乌马诺拥有东京大学的硕士学位和作为建筑师在日本从业20年的经验。从空格后面的内容判断，只有选项C符合逻辑。选项A有所干扰，但excellent一般修饰人，不修饰某个事件。

6. 【答案】A

   【解析】语义衔接。[A] turns out结果是，生产；[B] turns up出现；[C] turns down拒绝；[D] turns to求助。该空格所处的句子大意是：然而，_____，这也很典型。由此看出，只有选项A符合句意。

7. 【答案】B

   【解析】语义衔接。[A] heard of听说；[B] unheard of未听说；[C] heard听见；[D] unheard未听见。该空格所处的句子大意是：这种程度在美国"_____"。根据句意，只有选项B符合逻辑。

8. 【答案】D

   【解析】语义衔接+词汇辨析。[A] connecting连接，联系；[B] improving改进，提高；[C] correcting改正，纠正；[D] containing包含，容纳。该空格所处的句子大意是：一家名为"移民政策研究所（MPI）"的智库出版的_____该结论的论文的作者之一。从该句前后的语义和逻辑判断，只有选项D符合题意。

9. 【答案】B

   【解析】词汇辨析。[A] inspired激励，鼓舞；[B] instructed指示，指派；[C]expected期待；[D] hoped希望。该空格所处的句子大意是：在唐纳德·特朗普众多行政命令中，有一条命令_____劳动部、司法部及国土安全部对移民规定进行审查。因为空格前出现了orders，且是总统发出的，所以选项B正确，表示上级对下级发号施令。

10. 【答案】A

【解析】词汇辨析。[A] examine检查，审查；[B] boost促进，提升；[C] change改变；[D] control控制。该空格所处的句子大意是：指示劳动部、司法部及国土安全部对移民规定_____。空格里所填动词的宾语是rules，首先排除选项B和选项D，因为没有这类搭配；如果发现规章制度可能有漏洞，首先要进行审查，一旦有问题才会修改，所以选项A正确，选项C应排在选项A之后。

11. 【答案】C

【解析】语义衔接+固定搭配。[A] with和……一起，用；[B] on在……上面，依靠；[C] to朝向；[D] against反对。该空格所处的句子大意是：总统先生对非法移民的敌对态度是世人皆知的。从语义和与hostility的搭配角度来看，只有选项C符合要求。

12. 【答案】D

【解析】词汇辨析。[A] superiority优越性；[B] nobility高贵；[C] popularity流行；[D] priority优先选项。该空格所处的句子大意是：如今加拿大与澳大利亚都把学历、工作经验与英语流利程度（在加拿大还包括法语）作为预备移民的_____。从句意看，只有选项D符合要求。

13. 【答案】B

【解析】词汇辨析。[A] tactic策略；[B] approach方法；[C] plan计划；[D] goal目标。该空格所处的句子大意是：总统先生的一些顾问认为这套更加讲究实际的系统要优于美国以家庭为中心的_____。空格里所填的词应和前面的system（系统）形成对照和呼应，所以选项D不符要求；选项C（计划）表示尚未实施的内容，而美国以家庭为中心的这个内容早已实施，所以选项C排除；选项A和B比较容易混淆，但tactic一般指战争或竞赛中采用的策略，所以应排除；因此选项B为正确答案。

14. 【答案】C

【解析】语义衔接+词汇辨析。[A] predicted预测的；[B] hoped希望的；[C] doomed难逃死劫的；[D] calculated计算的。该空格所处的句子大意是：2013年以来_____移民法案在众议院被否决，这也反映出人们对积分系统的普遍热情。该句中出现了from 2013和died等表述，说明这是过去的事件，所以选项A和B可以排除，选项D与句意不符，因此选项C正确。

15. 【答案】A

【解析】词汇辨析。[A] temper缓和；[B] control控制；[C] suppress镇压，压制；[D] regulate调节。该空格所处的句子大意是：有两件事会_____这种热情。空格里所填的词要与enthusiasm构成动宾搭配，根据句意，选项B和选项D均不符合要求，只有选项A符合要求，与选项C搭配的宾语一般是emotion，desire等。

16. 【答案】D

【解析】语义衔接。[A] finished up完成；[B] split up分开；[C] tore up撕开；[D] ended up最终，结果。该空格所处的句子大意是：很大比例获得准许的人_____失业状态。A surprisingly high share of the people admitted this way _____ unemployed，该句中的admitted是过去分词修饰people，表示"获得准许的人"，this way的意思是"以这种方式"。从语义看，只有选项D符合要求。

17. 【答案】B

【解析】词汇辨析。[A] processes过程；[B] criteria尺度，标准；[C] strategies策略；[D] methods方法。该空格所处的句子大意是：这两个国家都已改变了各自的移民_____，使得那些已经得到工作录用机会的申请人拥有优先权。选项A、C、D一般是对应申请者的，只有选项B是对应移民国的，所以该选项是正确答案。

18. 【答案】C

【解析】固定搭配。[A] cross穿过；[B] stand站立；[C] jump跳跃；[D] walk行走。该空格所处的句子大意是：使得那些已经得到工作录用机会的申请人_____。jump the queue是固定搭配，本意是"插队"，这里引申为"优先得到某物"，所以选项C为正确答案。

19.【答案】**A**

【解析】词汇辨析。[A] available可利用的，可提供的；[B] predictable可预见的；[C] controllable可控的；[D] imaginable可以想象的。该空格所处的句子大意是：在2015年，也就是_____数据的最近的年份。选项B、D都表示数据是尚未得出的，可排除；选项C不合句意；选项A搭配numbers符合句意，所以该选项是正确答案。

20.【答案】**D**

【解析】词汇辨析。[A] instant立即的；[B] near近的；[C] intimate亲密的；[D] immediate直接的。该空格所处的句子大意是：有近一半是美国公民的_____亲属。选项A、B不能修饰relatives，所以首先排除；选项C虽然可以修饰relatives，但逻辑不符；选项D除了有"立刻的"之意，还有"直接的、直系的"之意，属于熟词僻义的现象，所以该选项是正确答案。

◆ 参考译文 ◆

何塞·隆美尔·乌马诺自菲律宾，于去年秋天搬到了纽约。他是以家庭团聚签证移民的，与妻子实现了团聚，他的妻子已经在美国生活了一段时间。这是一个典型的故事：当考虑移民申请时，美国比其他发达国家更加重视家庭成员。令人更惊讶的是，隆美尔·乌马诺拥有东京大学的硕士学位和作为建筑师在日本从业20年的经验。然而，事实证明，这也很典型。在2011年至2015年来到美国的移民中，有将近一半的人拥有大学学历。珍妮·贝塔罗娃，一家名为"移民政策研究所（MPI）"的智库出版的包含该结论的论文的作者之一，说到这种程度在美国"前所未闻"。

在唐纳德·特朗普众多行政命令中，有一条命令指示劳动部、司法部及国土安全部对移民规定进行审查。总统先生对非法移民的敌对态度是世人皆知的，他也说过他希望改变遴选合法移民的标准，指明要把加拿大与澳大利亚作为美国效仿的典范。1967年，加拿大成为第一个把积分系统引入移民政策的国家；如今加拿大与澳大利亚都把学历、工作经验与英语流利程度（在加拿大还包括法语）作为预备移民的优先选项。总统先生的一些顾问认为这套更加讲究实际的系统要优于美国以家庭为中心的方法。2013年以来难逃死劫的移民法案在众议院被否决，这也反映出人们对积分系统的普遍热情。

有两件事会缓和这种热情。第一，加拿大与澳大利亚已经得出结论，单一的积分系统并不能有效地运行。很大比例获得准许的人最后会处于失业状态。这两个国家都已改变了各自的移民标准，使得那些已经得到工作录用机会的申请人拥有优先权。第二，搬到美国与家庭成员团聚的移民已经拥有更好的教育背景。在2015年，也就是可提供数据的最近的年份，在超过100万的新绿卡持有者（或永久居民）中，有近一半是美国公民的直系亲属。

Passage 2

Directions: Read the following text. Choose the best word(s) for each numbered blank and mark A, B, C or D on the ANSWER SHEET. (10 points)

The homeless make up a growing percentage of America's population. __1__ homelessness has reached such proportions that local government can't possibly __2__. To help homeless people __3__ independence, the federal government must support job training programs, __4__ the minimum wage, and fund more low-cost housing.

__5__ everyone agrees on the numbers of Americans who are homeless. Estimates __6__ anywhere from 600,000 to 3 million. __7__ the figure may vary, analysts do agree on another matter: that the number of the homeless is __8__, one of the federal government's studies __9__ that the number of the homeless will reach nearly 19 million by the end of this decade.

Finding ways to __10__ this growing homeless population has become increasingly difficult. __11__ when homeless individuals manage to find a __12__ that will give them three meals a day and a place to sleep at night, a good number still spend the bulk of each day __13__ the street. Part of the problem is that many homeless adults are addicted to alcohol or drugs. And a significant number of the homeless have serious mental disorders. Many others, __14__ not addicted or mentally ill, simply lack the everyday __15__ skills needed to turn their lives __16__. *Boston Globe* reporter Chris Reidy notes that the situation will improve only when there are __17__ programs that address the many needs of the homeless. __18__ Edward Zlotkowski, director of community service at Bentley College in Massachusetts, __19__ it, "There has to be __20__ of programs. What we need is a package deal."

1. [A] Indeed [B] Likewise [C] Therefore [D] Furthermore
2. [A] stand [B] cope [C] approve [D] retain
3. [A] in [B] for [C] with [D] toward
4. [A] raise [B] add [C] take [D] keep
5. [A] Generally [B] Almost [C] Hardly [D] Not
6. [A] cover [B] change [C] range [D] differ
7. [A] Now that [B] Although [C] Provided [D] Except that
8. [A] inflating [B] expanding [C] increasing [D] extending
9. [A] predicts [B] displays [C] proves [D] discovers
10. [A] assist [B] track [C] sustain [D] dismiss
11. [A] Hence [B] But [C] Even [D] Only
12. [A] lodging [B] shelter [C] dwelling [D] house
13. [A] searching [B] strolling [C] crowding [D] wandering
14. [A] when [B] once [C] while [D] whereas
15. [A] life [B] existence [C] survival [D] maintenance
16. [A] around [B] over [C] on [D] up
17. [A] complex [B] comprehensive [C] complementary [D] compensating
18. [A] So [B] Since [C] As [D] Thus
19. [A] puts [B] interprets [C] assumes [D] makes
20. [A] supervision [B] manipulation [C] regulation [D] coordination

试题详解

1. 【答案】 A

   【解析】语义衔接+逻辑衔接。The homeless make up a growing percentage of America's population. ____ homelessness has reached such proportions that... "流浪者在美国人口中所占的比例越来越高。____流浪者所占的比例已经达到如此地步，以至于……"[A] Indeed表示强调；[B] Likewise与……相似；[C] Therefore因此；[D] Furthermore进一步说（表递进）。根据前一句"make up a growing percentage"与后一句"has reached such proportions that"确定后者是对前者的例证强调，因此正确答案为[A]。

2. 【答案】 B

   【解析】语义衔接。本题选择动词在定语从句中充当谓语。Indeed homelessness has reached such proportions that local government can't possibly____. "事实上流浪者所占的比例已经达到地方政府都无法____的地步。"[A] stand忍受；[B] cope对付，应对；[C] approve赞成，批准；[D] retain保留。[A] stand作为及物动词在句子中要直接连接宾语，但是句子中没有宾语，因此该词不符合句子结构；[B] cope作为不及物动词，可以在句子中表达完整的含义；[C]、[D]与句意不符。因此正确答案为[B]。

3. 【答案】 D

   【解析】语义衔接。本题选择介词，选择介词与句子中的动词有直接关系。原文意为：帮助流浪者达到独立。[D] toward达到。[C] with可与help构成搭配to help sb. with sth. "帮助某人做某事"，与题意不符。因此正确答案为[D]。

4. 【答案】 A

   【解析】语义衔接。The federal government must support job training programs, ____ the minimum wage, and fund more low-cost housing. "联邦政府必须支持职业培训计划，____最低工资，资助更多低价住房。"句子中"the minimum wage"与前面的短语"support job training programs"（支持职业培训计划）和后面的短语"fund more low-cost housing"（资助更多低价住房）是并列关系。由提供信息确定选择"提高"之意。[A] raise增

90

加，提高，"提高最低工资"，符合句子含义；[B] add也意为"增加"，但它的宾语一般是具体数字。因此正确答案为[A]。

5. 【答案】 D

【解析】语义衔接+词汇辨析。本题选择副词，在句子中限定范围。____ every one agrees on the numbers of Americans who are homeless. "____每个人同意美国人中流浪者的数量。"由于本题包含反义选项，而上文又没有提示，因此应看下面句中的信息。第6题所在的语境句意为"人们对此的估计数字从60万到300万不等"。因此本题意思应该为"关于美国流浪者的数量，众说不一"。[A]、[B]表示肯定含义，所以排除。[C]、[D]同样表示否定含义，但hardly一般与anyone，anything搭配；not与all，every搭配表示部分否定。

6. 【答案】 C

【解析】语义衔接+惯用衔接。句子中的主语、宾语以及介词决定所选择的动词。Estimates ____ anywhere from 600,000 to 3 million. "估计数字____60万到300万之间。" [A] cover覆盖，包括；[B] change改变，变化；[C] range在某范围中变化；[D] differ不同。句子中选择的动词要与"from 600,000 to 3 million"构成搭配，句子提供信息确定选择"在……范围波动"之意。[A] cover覆盖，包括，与要表达的句意不符；[B] change from...to...意为"由……变为……"，此处不表示变化的意思，故排除。[D] differ可与from搭配，表示"不同于……"。因此[C]为正确答案。

7. 【答案】 B

【解析】逻辑衔接。____ the figure may vary, analysts do agree on another matter... "（估计的）____数字不同，分析专家们对另一个问题却有共识。" [A] Now that既然；[B] Although虽然……；[C] Provided假设……；[D] Except that除去……。根据本题所在的语境，前文中的may vary与后文中的do agree互为反义，确定二者为转折让步关系。因此正确答案为[B]，句子译为"尽管（估计的）数字各有不同，但是分析专家们对另一个问题却有共识。"

8. 【答案】 C

【解析】语义衔接+词汇辨析。Although the figure may vary, analysts do agree on another matter: that the number of the homeless is ____ "尽管（估计的）数字各有不同，但是分析专家们对另一个问题却有共识：流浪者的人数正在____" [A] inflating 膨胀；[B] expanding 发展，扩张；[C] increasing 增加；[D] extending 延伸。文章首句便提到 "流浪者在美国人口中所占的比例越来越高（growing percentage）。" 本空格要与growing构成呼应，应该填入increasing。因此正确答案为[C]。

9. 【答案】 A

【解析】语义衔接。One of the federal government's studies ____ that the number of the homeless will reach nearly 19 million by the end of this decade. "联邦政府的调查之一____流浪者的数量在近十年内将会达到大约1 900万。" [A] predicts 预测，预计；[B] displays 展示；[C] proves 证明；[D] discovers 发现。that the number of the homeless will reach nearly 19 million by the end of this decade. "流浪者的数量将在十年内逼近1 900万。" "十年内达到1 900万" 表达未来的状况，确定选择 "预测" 之意。因此正确答案为[A]。

10. 【答案】 A

【解析】语义衔接。Finding ways to ____ this growing homeless population has become increasingly difficult. "寻找办法____越来越多的流浪者将变得逐渐困难起来。" [A] assist 帮助；[B] track 追踪；[C] sustain 承受，支持，供养；[D] dismiss 解散。本文前两段提出流浪者的问题并略加分析，本段开始解决方法的探讨。句子提供信息确定选择 "帮助" 之意。assist 帮助，符合句子含义。因此正确答案为[A]。

11. 【答案】 C

【解析】逻辑衔接。本题选择逻辑关系词，体现前后两句的逻辑关系。____ when homeless individuals manage to find a ____ that will give them three meals a day and a place to sleep at night, a good number still spend the bulk of each day ____ the street. "____当流浪

者找到____能提供一日三餐，晚上能睡觉，很多人仍然会把大部分时间花费在____街头。"[A] Hence 因此；[B] But 但是；[C] Even 即使；[D] Only 仅仅。不难发现，前后句子之间体现出让步关系。[A] Hence表示因果关系，与本句逻辑关系不符；[B] But表示转折关系，与本句逻辑关系不符；[C] Even表示让步关系，与本句逻辑关系相符，句子译为"当流浪者找到地方能提供一日三餐，晚上能睡觉，很多人仍然会把大部分时间花费在流浪街头"；[D] Only仅仅，表示递进关系，与本句逻辑关系不符。因此正确答案为[C]。

12. 【答案】 B

【解析】词汇辨析。本题目选择名词，同时这个名词由定语从句来修饰。Even when homeless individuals manage to find a ____ that will give them three meals a day and a place to sleep at night，"即使流浪者能够找到一个____，可以给他们提供一日三餐和夜里睡觉的地方"。[A] lodging借宿地，寄宿处；[B] shelter庇护所，避难所；[C] dwelling住处；[D] house房屋。从定语从句"that will give them three meals a day and a place to sleep at night"（能够提供一日三餐和夜里睡觉的地方）确定选择"庇护所或避难所"之意。因此正确答案为[B]。

13. 【答案】 D

【解析】语义衔接。...a good number still spend the bulk of each day ____ the street."很多人仍然会把大部分时间花费在____街头。"[A] searching搜寻；[B] strolling漫步，闲逛；[C] crowding拥挤；[D] wandering游荡，徘徊，流浪。流浪者是流浪街头的，wandering符合句子含义。因此正确答案为[D]。

14. 【答案】 C

【解析】逻辑衔接。本题选择连词，体现句子之间的逻辑关系。Many others, ____ not addicted or mentally ill, simply lack the everyday ____ skills needed to turn their lives ____."其他许多人，____既不吸毒，也没有精神障碍，____缺乏起码的可以自食其力的生存技能____。"句子中"既不吸毒，也没有精神障碍"与"缺乏生存技能"构成转折关系。因此空格处的词应该表示让步，所以首先排除[A] when和[B] once，而[C] while和[D] whereas都能表示让步，但whereas不能用于省略句，而while常可用于省略句。故[C]为正确答案。

15.【答案】C

【解析】语义衔接+词汇辨析。...simply lack the everyday ____ skills needed to turn their lives."但是缺乏起码的让自己生活____的技巧。"[A] life生活，生命；[B] existence存在；[C] survival生存，存活；[D] maintenance维护，维持。英语中"生活/生存技能"的固定搭配是survival skills，因此正确答案为[C]。maintenance skills意思是"维修技术，保养技术"。

16.【答案】A

【解析】语义衔接+惯用衔接。本题选择与turn构成的短语。...to turn their lives ____."使生活变____"这里表达出"出现转机"之意。[A] around, turn around"（使）逆转，（使）出现转机"；[B] over, turn over"仔细考虑，移交"；[C] on, turn on"打开开关"；[D] up, turn up"调大，开大；出现"。因此正确答案为[A]。

17.【答案】B

【解析】词汇辨析。Boston Globe reporter Chris Reidy notes that the situation will improve only when there are ____ programs that address the many needs of the homeless."《波士顿环球邮报》记者克莉斯·雷蒂认为，只有通过____规划才能解决这些流浪者的大多需求，局面才能够有所改善。"[A] complex复杂的；[B] comprehensive综合的，全面的；[C] complementary补充的，互补的；[D] compensating补偿的。由于要满足流浪者的大多需求（many needs of the homeless），所以这份计划应该是考虑周全、无所不包的。[B] comprehensive"综合的、全面的"，"全面的计划"与"解决这些流浪者的大多需求"直接关联，符合句子含义。因此正确答案为[B]。

18.【答案】C

【解析】逻辑衔接+惯用衔接。...director of community service at Bentley College in Massachusetts，是Edward Zlotkowski这个人物的同位语成分，这样就更容易看出句子结构了：as sb. puts it "正如某人说的那样……"，put此处意为"表达"。因此正确答案为[C]。

19. 【答案】 A

【解析】语义衔接+惯用衔接。解析见上题。

20. 【答案】 D

【解析】语义衔接。本题选择名词，句子中的所有格关系决定所选名词。There has to be ____ of programs. What we need is a package deal. "各项计划必须____运行，所需的是一整套的措施。"[A] supervision监督，管理；[B] manipulation操作，处理；[C] regulation管理，调节，规定；[D] coordination协调。综合前文中的comprehensive programs that address the many needs of the homeless（……的综合性计划）和后文中的a package deal（一整套的措施），所以需要对它们进行协调，即coordination。因此正确答案为[D]。

◆ 参考译文 ◆

流浪者在美国人口中所占的比例越来越高。事实上，流浪者问题已经严重到了地方政府不能应付的程度。为了帮助流浪者独立生存，联邦政府必须支持职业培训计划，提高最低工资，资助更多低价住房。

并不是所有人都同意美国人中流浪者的数量。估计数字会有从60万到300万的差异。尽管估计的数字各有不同，但是分析专家们对另一个问题却有共识：流浪者的数目在不断增加。联邦政府的调查之一预言流浪者的数量将在十年内逼近1 900万。

寻找方法去帮助越来越多的流浪者将变得逐渐困难起来。即使流浪者能够找到一个提供一日三餐和夜里睡觉的地方，很多人仍然会把大部分时间花费在流浪街头。部分原因是因为许多流浪者都会酗酒或是吸毒。相当一部分的流浪者都患有严重精神病。其他许多人既不吸毒，也没有精神障碍，但是缺乏起码的可以自食其力的生存技能。《波士顿环球邮报》记者克莉斯·雷蒂认为，只有当实施了能解决流浪者大多需求的综合计划后，局面才能够有所改善。正如马萨诸塞州本特立学院社区服务部的主任爱德华·资罗特可夫所说：

"各项计划必须要相互协调合作，所需的是一整套的措施。"

Passage 3

Directions: Read the following text. Choose the best word(s) for each numbered blank and mark A, B, C or D on the ANSWER SHEET. (10 points)

By 1830 the former Spanish and Portuguese colonies had become independent nations. The roughly 20 million __1__ of these nations looked __2__ to the future. Born in the crisis of the old regime and Iberian Colonialism, many of the leaders of independence __3__ the ideals of representative government, careers __4__ to talent, freedom of commerce and trade, the __5__ to private property, and a belief in the individual as the basis of society. __6__ there was a belief that the new nations should be sovereign and independent states, large enough to be economically viable and integrated by a __7__ set of laws.

On the issue of __8__ of religion and the position of the Church, __9__, there was less agreement __10__ the leadership. Roman Catholicism had been the state religion and the only one __11__ by the Spanish crown. __12__ most leaders sought to maintain Catholicism __13__ the official religion of the new states, some sought to end the __14__ of other faiths. The defense of the Church became a rallying __15__ for the conservative forces.

The ideals of the early leaders of independence were often egalitarian, valuing equality of everything. Bolivar had received aid from Haiti and had __16__ in return to abolish slavery in the areas he liberated. By 1854 slavery had been abolished everywhere except Spain's __17__ colonies. Early promises to end Indian tribute and taxes on people of mixed origin came much __18__ because the new nations still needed the revenue such policies __19__. Egalitarian sentiments were often tempered by fears that the mass of the population was __20__ self-rule and democracy.

1. [A] natives   [B] inhabitants   [C] peoples   [D] individuals

2. [A] confusedly   [B] cheerfully   [C] worriedly   [D] hopefully

3. [A] shared   [B] forgot   [C] attained   [D] rejected

4. [A] related   [B] close   [C] open   [D] devoted

5. [A] access   [B] succession   [C] right   [D] return

6. [A] Presumably   [B] Incidentally   [C] Obviously   [D] Generally

7. [A] unique   [B] common   [C] particular   [D] typical

8. [A] freedom   [B] origin   [C] impact   [D] reform

9. [A] therefore   [B] however   [C] indeed   [D] moreover

10. [A] with   [B] about   [C] among   [D] by

11. [A] allowed   [B] preached   [C] granted   [D] funded

12. [A] Since   [B] If   [C] Unless   [D] While

13. [A] as   [B] for   [C] under   [D] against

14. [A] spread   [B] interference   [C] exclusion   [D] influence

15. [A] support   [B] cry   [C] plea   [D] wish

16. [A] urged   [B] intended   [C] expected   [D] promised

17. [A] controlling   [B] former   [C] remaining   [D] original

18. [A] slower   [B] faster   [C] easier   [D] tougher

19. [A] created   [B] produced   [C] contributed   [D] preferred

20. [A] puzzled by   [B] hostile to   [C] pessimistic about   [D] unprepared for

试题详解

1. 【答案】B

【解析】词汇辨析。[A] natives 当地人；[B] inhabitants 居民；[C] peoples 民族；[D] individuals 个人。独立后的国家居民由原住民和移民共同构成，因此强干扰项[A]可排除。而居民既包括原住民也包括移民，故选[B]。

2. 【答案】 D

   【解析】语义衔接。[A] confusedly混淆地；[B] cheerfully欢乐地；[C] worriedly担心地；[D] hopefully有希望地。前一句指出各殖民地已经独立，所以人们对未来的态度应该是积极的，而"充满希望地"与"对未来的展望"应该是最恰当的，所以选[D]。

3. 【答案】 A

   【解析】语义衔接。[A] shared分享；[B] forgot忘记；[C] attained达到；[D] rejected拒绝。从…the ideals of representative government, careers ____ to talent, freedom of commerce and trade, the ____ to private property, and a belief in the individual as the basis of society…的字里行间看出这些ideals是现代制度和法律所支持的观念，虽然这些领导人出身于旧政体和伊比利亚殖民主义的危难之刻，他们（都认同）这些观念。可先排除否定意义的[B]、[D]。[C]attained这个词一般指的是通过不断的努力获得某种知识或达到某个目标。因此正确答案为[A]，许多独立国家领导人都认同代议制政府。

4. 【答案】 C

   【解析】语义衔接+固定搭配。[A] related相关的；[B] close近的；[C] open开放的；[D] devoted投入的。本题选择形容词，在句子中体现前后名词之间的关系。many of the leaders of independence shared the ideals of representative government, careers ____ to talent…"许多独立国家领导人都认同代议制政府，职业向有才能的人____"，符合语境的只有[C] careers open to talent "职位向有才能的人开放"。

5. 【答案】 C

   【解析】语义衔接。本题选择名词，在句子中体现句子内容的连贯性。many of the leaders of independence shared the ideals of representative government, careers open to talent, freedom of commerce and trade, the ____ to private property, and a belief in the individual as the basis of society. "许多独立国家的领导人都认同代议制政府，认为职业应该向人才开放，认可商业和贸易自由，认可人们对私有财产的____，认可个人是社会的基础。"代入[A] access to接近；有权使用；代入[B] succession to 继承；代入[C] right to…的权利；代入[D] return to

返回。从前面的"代议制政府","向人才开放的职业","商业和贸易自由"可以看出这里提到的是推动国家进步和发展,充分调动人们积极性的另一个理念"人们对私有财产的所有权",故此处选择right。因此正确答案为[C]。

6. 【答案】 D

   【解析】语义衔接。本题选择副词,体现前后两个句子之间的逻辑关系。____ there was a belief that the new nations should be sovereign and independent states,"有一种____的信念,新国家应该是自主、独立的国家"。[A] Presumably大概;[B] Incidentally偶然地;[C] Obviously 显然地;[D] Generally 普遍地。在上文中:...many of the leaders of independence shared the ideals of representative government, careers open to talent, freedom of commerce and trade, the right to private property, and a belief in the individual as the basis of society."许多独立国家的领导人都认同代议制政府,认为职业应该向人才开放,认可商业和贸易自由,认可人们对私有财产的……,认为个人是社会的基础。" 该句与后面的句子没有任何内容相反或转折的信号词,可以判断两个句子是顺接关系,后面承接上一句内容,继续介绍新的独立国家领导人都认同的理念。因此正确答案为[D]。

7. 【答案】 B

   【解析】语义衔接+词义辨析。本题选择形容词,在句子中充当定语。Generally there was a belief that the new nations should be sovereign and independent states, large enough to be economically viable and integrated by a ____ set of laws."普遍存在这样的信念,新国家应该是自主、独立的国家,足以在经济上运行良好,通过一套____的法律使国家完整。" [A] unique唯一的;[B] common普通的;[C] particular特别的,独有的;[D] typical 典型的。想要"使国家完整"只有通过普遍适用的法律才能够实现。因此正确答案为[B]。

8. 【答案】 A

   【解析】语义衔接。本题选择名词,在句子中做宾语。On the issue of ____ of religion and the position of the Church..."针对宗教的____和教会的地位问题。"[A] freedom自

由；[B] origin 起源；[C] impact 影响；[D] reform 改革。四个选项在句子中似乎都合理，确定该题目为语义衔接题。由于前文叙述内容未涉及宗教，所以信息在后文。浏览下面语句发现，罗马天主教是西班牙国教，是西班牙王室唯一认可的宗教。多数领导人致力于保留天主教为新国家的官方宗教；而另一些领导人致力于终结排斥其他宗教的状况。显然是关于宗教信仰的自由问题产生分歧。因此正确答案为[A]。

9. 【答案】 B

 【解析】逻辑衔接。本题选择逻辑关系词，体现前后句子之间的逻辑关系。On the issue of freedom of religion and the position of the Church, ____, there was less agreement... "针对宗教信仰自由和教会的地位问题，____，领导阶层之间的意见就不那么一致了。"[A] therefore 因此；[B] however 然而；[C] indeed 的确；[D] moreover 而且。第一段中叙述到 Generally there was a belief that the new nations should be sovereign and independent states, large enough to be economically viable and integrated by a common set of laws. "普遍存在这样的信念，新国家应该是自主、独立的国家，足以在经济上运行良好，通过一套普遍适用的法律使国家完整"，介绍了新成立的独立国家领导人之间在治国理念方面的共识。而随后的语句 there was less agreement the ____ leadership，提到的是他们之间存在的分歧，显然两部分之间为转折关系。因此正确答案为[B]。

10. 【答案】 C

 【解析】惯用衔接。本题选择介词，体现叙述内容的范围。On the issue of freedom of religion and the position of the Church, however, there was less agreement ____ the leadership. "针对宗教信仰自由和教会的地位问题，领导阶层在主导地位____方面存在分歧。"本句表明各国领导人之间在宗教问题方面不那么有默契了，[C] among 表示"在……之间"，这里 among the leadership 表范围。其他几个介词与后面内容搭配作状语时，都不表示范围。因此正确答案为[C]。

11. 【答案】 A

 【解析】语义衔接。本句说：罗马天主教一直是国教，是西班牙王室准许的唯一宗教。

与前一句"宗教自由"相对。由句中的only可推断，西班牙王室只承认罗马天主教。各个选项中只有[A] allowed有"允许"之意，故为答案。[C] granted准予，给予，为强干扰项。[C] granted所接的间接宾语应当是该动作发出者能力范围或自身特点所拥有的东西。此句中，"天主教"并非源自皇室，皇室无法赋予他人某种宗教，故[C]不合适。[B] preached布道，宣扬；[D] funded提供资金，赞助。两个选项都不符合题意。

12.【答案】 D

【解析】逻辑衔接。本题选择连词，体现句子之间的逻辑关系。____ most leaders sought to maintain Catholicism... some sought to end the..."____大多数领导人致力于保留天主教……一些领导人却试图结束……"关于宗教信仰问题，领导人分成两个派别，即多数领导人致力于保留天主教为新国家的官方宗教，而一些领导人致力于终结不能有其他宗教信仰的状况。显然，二者观点相异。因此，正确答案为[D]。

13.【答案】 A

【解析】语义衔接。本题选择介词，衔接后面的名词和前面句子的逻辑关系。While most leaders sought to maintain Catholicism ____ the official religion of the new states,"大多数领导人致力于保留天主教____新国家的官方宗教"。[A] as 作为；[B] for 为了；[C] under 在……之下；[D] against 反对。显然这里as the official religion of the new states是方式状语，与maintain搭配使用，符合语义关系。因此正确答案为[A]。

14.【答案】 C

【解析】语义衔接。本题选择名词，在句子中做宾语。句子叙述到：...some sought to end the ____ of other faiths."一些领导人却试图结束将其他宗教信仰的____"。[A] spread 传播；[B] interference干涉；[C] exclusion 排除；[D] influence 影响。"天主教已经成为国家信仰，并且是西班牙国王承认的唯一信仰；虽然大多数领导人致力于保留天主教作为新国家的官方宗教"，此处与之对立的观点是：结束对其他宗教的排斥，即允许人们信奉其他宗教。exclusion用在此处符合语境，表示"结束对于其他宗教的排挤"。因此正确答案为[C]。

15. 【答案】 B

【解析】语义衔接+固定搭配。选择名词，构成rallying...的固定搭配。在句子中充当表语。The defense of the Church became a rallying ____ for the conservative forces.这里rallying cry为固定搭配，意为"（起号召作用的）战斗口号"。因此正确答案为[B]。

16. 【答案】 D

【解析】语义衔接。本题选择动词，与to构成搭配，在句子中充当谓语动词。Bolivar had received aid from Haiti and had ____ in return to abolish slavery in the areas he liberated."玻利瓦尔得到海地的援助，作为回报，他____废除他所解放地区的奴隶制。"[A] urged 敦促；[B] intended 打算；[C] expected 期望；[D] promised 承诺。从句中的in return可以看出，海地对玻利瓦尔的帮助并非无条件的，其条件就是后者承诺废除奴隶制度。因此正确答案为[D]。

17. 【答案】 C

【解析】词汇辨析。本题选择形容词，修饰名词colonies。By 1854 slavery had been abolished everywhere except Spain's ____ colonies."到1854年，除了西班牙____殖民地外，其他地区都已经废除奴隶制。"[A] controlling 正在统治的；[B] former 原来的；[C] remaining 遗留的；[D] original 原始的。因此应选[C]。

18. 【答案】 A

【解析】语义辨析。Early promises to end Indian tribute and taxes on people of mixed origin came much ____ because..."实现停止征收印第安人贡物以及各民族人民赋税的早期承诺____因为……"[A] slower 较慢地；[B] faster 较快地；[C] easier 较容易地；[D] tougher 较强硬地。上文提到玻利瓦尔承诺废除奴隶制，到1854年除了西班牙剩余的殖民地外，其他地区都已废除奴隶制，因此根据上下文可知，此处是说这个承诺实现得缓慢。正确答案为[A]。

19. 【答案】 B

【解析】语义衔接。本题选择动词，在定语从句中充当谓语动词。...the new nations still needed the revenue such policies ____."新国家仍然需要这些政策所____的税收收入。"[A] created 创建；[B] produced 产生，生产；[C] contributed 有助于；[D] preferred 更喜欢。本题所在部分意为"新国家仍然需要这些政策所带来的税收收入"，这些税收收入是这些policies带来的，这里使用produce意思相近。created 不能与revenue "收入"构成合理的主谓关系；contributed 有助于，一般要构成"contribute to"短语才能够接宾语，在此不符合句子含义；[D] preferred 更喜欢，一般要构成"prefer to"短语。句子中没有提供比较的参照，所以不涉及"更喜欢"，不符合句子含义。因此正确答案为[B]。

20. **【答案】** D

【解析】语义衔接+固定搭配。Egalitarian sentiments were often tempered by fears that the mass of the population was ____ self-rule and democracy. "平等主义的情绪往往被民众对自治和民主____恐惧所减缓。" [A] puzzled by 感到困惑；[B] hostile to 敌对；[C] pessimistic to 悲观；[D] unprepared to 未准备好。由于新的独立国家的人们刚刚摆脱了殖民统治，因此人们还没有充分了解和熟悉自治和民主，这里使用unprepared for符合语境。因此正确答案为[D]。

◆ 参考译文 ◆

到1830年，西班牙和葡萄牙的前殖民地已经成为独立国家。这些国家的大约两千万居民满怀希望地展望着未来。出生于旧体制以及伊比利亚殖民主义的危难之刻，许多独立国家的领导人都认同代议制政府，认为职业应该向人才开放，认可商业和贸易自由，认可人们对私有财产的所有权，认为个人是社会的基础。当时，普遍存在这样的信念——新国家应该是自主、独立的国家，足以在经济上运行良好，并且通过一套普遍适用的法律使国家完整。

不过，针对宗教信仰自由以及教会的地位问题，领导阶层之间的意见就不那么一致了。天主教已经成为国家信仰，并且是西班牙国王承认的唯一信仰。虽然大多数领导人致力于保留天主教作为新国家的官方宗教，但是一些领导人却试图终止对其他信仰的排斥。保护教会成为保守力量的战斗号角。

独立国家的早期领导人的理想通常是实行平等主义，重视一切事物的平等。玻利瓦尔得到海地的援助，作为回报，他承诺废除他所解放地区的奴隶制。到1854年，除了西班牙遗留的殖民地外，其他地区都已经废除奴隶制。实现停止征收印第安人贡物以及各民族人民赋税的早期承诺晚了许久才得以实现，因为新国家仍然需要这些政策所带来的税收收入。平等主义的情绪往往被民众对自治和民主尚未做好准备的恐惧所减缓。

Passage 4

Directions: Read the following text. Choose the best word(s) for each numbered blank and mark A, B, C or D on the ANSWER SHEET. (10 points)

In 1924 America's National Research Council sent two engineers to supervise a series of industrial experiments at a large telephone-parts factory called the Hawthorne Plant near Chicago. It hoped they would learn how shop-floor lighting __1__ workers' productivity. Instead, the studies ended __2__ giving their name to the "Hawthorne effect", the extremely influential idea that the very __3__ of being experimented upon changed subjects' behavior.

The idea arose because of the __4__ behavior of the women in the plant. According to __5__ of the experiments, their hourly output rose when lighting was increased, but also when it was dimmed. It did not __6__ what was done in the experiment; __7__ something was changed, productivity rose. A(n) __8__ that they were being experimented upon seemed to be __9__ to alter workers' behavior __10__ itself.

After several decades, the same data were __11__ to econometric the analysis. The Hawthorne experiments had another surprise in store. __12__ the descriptions on record, no systematic __13__ was found that levels of productivity were related to changes in lighting.

It turns out that the peculiar way of conducting the experiments may have led to __14__ interpretations of what happened. __15__, lighting was always changed on a Sunday. When work started again on Monday, output __16__ rose compared with the previous Saturday and

__17__ to rise for the next couple of days. __18__, a comparison with data for weeks when there was no experimentation showed that output always went up on Mondays. Workers __19__ to be diligent for the first few days of the week in any case, before __20__ a plateau and then slackening off. This suggests that the alleged "Hawthorne effect" is hard to pin down.

1. [A] affected   [B] achieved   [C] extracted   [D] restored
2. [A] at   [B] up   [C] with   [D] off
3. [A] truth   [B] sight   [C] act   [D] proof
4. [A] controversial [B] perplexing   [C] mischievous   [D] ambiguous
5. [A] requirements [B] explanations   [C] accounts   [D] assessments
6. [A] conclude   [B] matter   [C] indicate   [D] work
7. [A] as far as   [B] for fear that [C] in case that   [D] so long as
8. [A] awareness   [B] expectation   [C] sentiment   [D] illusion
9. [A] suitable   [B] excessive   [C] enough   [D] abundant
10. [A] about   [B] for   [C] on   [D] by
11. [A] compared   [B] shown   [C] subjected   [D] conveyed
12. [A] Contrary to [B] Consistent with [C] Parallel with [D] Peculiar to
13. [A] evidence   [B] guidance   [C] implication   [D] source
14. [A] disputable [B] enlightening   [C] reliable   [D] misleading
15. [A] In contrast [B] For example   [C] In consequence [D] As usual
16. [A] duly   [B] accidentally   [C] unpredictably [D] suddenly
17. [A] failed   [B] ceased   [C] started   [D] continued
18. [A] Therefore   [B] Furthermore   [C] However   [D] Meanwhile
19. [A] attempted   [B] tended   [C] chose   [D] intended
20. [A] breaking   [B] climbing   [C] surpassing   [D] hitting

试题详解

1. 【答案】A

   【解析】词汇辨析。[A] affected影响，感动；[B] achieved达成，完成；[C] extracted提取，榨出；[D] restored恢复，重建。本句意为：该委员会希望他们弄清楚车间照明是如何影响工人的生产效率的，所以答案选[A]。

2. 【答案】B

   【解析】语义衔接。本题考查了固定短语end up 的用法，end up 意思是"最终成为……"，end 和其他三个介词的搭配都无此意，故选[B]。

3. 【答案】C

   【解析】词汇辨析。本句意为：研究最终总结为一个极具影响力的概念"霍桑效应"，也正是成为研究对象这个行为改变了工人们的表现。[A] truth真相；[B] sight视力，视野；[C] act行为；[D] proof证明。所以应选择[C]。

4. 【答案】B

   【解析】词汇辨析。本句意为：这个问题之所以引起大家的注意是因为工厂女工的行为令人费解。四个选项中[A] controversial争议的；[B] perplexing令人费解的；[C] mischievous恶作剧的，有害的；[D] ambiguous模棱两可的。所以正确答案为[B]。

5. 【答案】C

   【解析】语义衔接。本句意为：根据实验的描述，照明强度增加时，女工每小时的产出增加，照明强度减小时，亦是如此。四个选项中[A] requirements要求；[B] explanations解释；[C] accounts描述，叙述；[D] assessments评价。有描述含义的是[C] accounts，所以答案为[C]。

6. 【答案】B

   【解析】固定搭配。本句意为：实验中做什么无关紧要。[A] conclude总结；[B] matter重要，有关系；[C] indicate表明；[D] work工作。it doesn't matter是固定表达，意为"没关系，不要紧"，故选[B]。

7. 【答案】D

【解析】语义衔接。考查so long as短语，意思是"只有"，本句意为：只要发生了某种变化，生产率就会上升。[A] as far as与……一样远；[B] for fear that唯恐，以防；[C] in case that万一，以防。

8. 【答案】A

【解析】语义衔接+词汇辨析。[A] awareness意识；[B] expectation期望；[C] sentiment观点，意见；[D] illusion幻觉。本句意为：似乎仅仅是意识到自己被当作实验对象就足以促使工人改变行为。所以选[A]。

9. 【答案】C

【解析】词汇辨析。见第8题解析。[A] suitable适合的；[B] excessive过量的，过多的；[C] enough足够的；[D] abundant充足的。

10. 【答案】D

【解析】固定搭配。见第8题解析，by itself是固定表达，意为"本身而言"。

11. 【答案】C

【解析】语义衔接。be subjected to表示"服从于，与……一致"，为固定短语。[A] compared比较；[B] shown展示；[D] conveyed传递。

12. 【答案】A

【解析】逻辑衔接。contrary to表示"与……相反"。根据语境提示，空白处需要填写一个能表示转折意味的连接词，所以选[A]。[B] Consistent with与……一致；[C] Parallel with与……平行/相似；[D] Peculiar to ……所独有的，……所特有的。

13. 【答案】A

【解析】语义衔接+词汇辨析。[A] evidence证据；[B] guidance指导；[C] implication含义；[D] source来源。只有evidence一词可与found呼应，表示"发现或找到证据"。

14. 【答案】D

【解析】词汇辨析。[D] misleading欺骗性，误导性的，意思上来看，符合语境所表达的

107

意思，所以答案为[D]。[A] disputable有争议的；[B] enlightening启发的，启迪的；[C] reliable可靠的。

15. 【答案】 B

【解析】逻辑衔接。[B] For example与上句呼应，举例说明问题，所以答案为[B]。[A] In contrast相反，相比而言；[C] In consequence结果；[D] As usual按照往常。

16. 【答案】 A

【解析】词汇辨析。[A] duly准时地，在同一个时间地，填入句中后意思表达更精确。[B] accidentally意外地，偶然地；[C] unpredictably不可预测地；[D] suddenly突然地。

17. 【答案】 D

【解析】语义衔接。与前句duly rose呼应，递进说明问题，故应选continued。[A] failed失败，无法……；[B] ceased停止；[C] started开始；[D] continued继续。

18. 【答案】 C

【解析】逻辑衔接。此句意思与上句相反，说明另一种情况，故应使用转折词however，答案为[C]。[A] Therefore因此；[B] Furthermore而且；[D] Meanwhile同时。

19. 【答案】 B

【解析】词汇辨析。[A] attempted尝试；[B] tended倾向于；[C] chose选择；[D] intended打算。tend to do "倾向于做某事"，说明一种常规的事实。所以答案选[B]。

20. 【答案】 D

【解析】固定搭配。[A] breaking打破；[B] climbing攀爬；[C] surpassing超越；[D] hitting打击，触及。hit能与a plateau搭配，意为"到达高地，触及顶点"，句意符合语境。所以答案为[D]。

参考译文

1924年，美国国家研究委员会派出两名工程师到芝加哥附近的一家电话配件厂（霍桑工厂）指导一系列实验研究。该委员会希望他们弄清楚车间照明是如何影响工人的生产效率的。然而，研究最终总结为一个极具影响力的概念"霍桑效应"，也正是成为研究对象本身这个行为改变了工人们的表现。

这个问题之所以引起大家的注意是因为工厂女工的行为令人费解。根据实验的描述，照明强度增加时，女工每小时的产出增加，照明强度减小时，亦是如此。实验中做什么无关紧要，只要发生了某种变化，生产效率就会上升。似乎仅仅是意识到自己被当作实验对象就足以促使工人改变行为。

几十年后，同一实验数据被用于计量经济分析。得到的却是霍桑试验中另一个令人吃惊的结果。与所记载的描述相反，没有系统的证据证明生产效率与照明的变化之间存在关联。

结果发现可能是进行试验的特殊方式导致实验者对所发生事实的误导性解释。比如，照明条件总是在周日被改变。当周一重新开工时，工人的产出与上周六相比如期上升了，并在接下来的几天内持续增长。然而，与没有进行试验的几周的数据对比显示，周一工人的产出总是会增加。无论什么情况，工人在每周前几天往往都会勤奋工作，随后达到一个停滞期，继而懒散下来。这表明，所谓的"霍桑效应"是很难解释清楚的。

Passage 5

Directions: Read the following text. Choose the best word(s) for each numbered blank and mark A, B, C or D on the ANSWER SHEET. (10 points)

Research on animal intelligence always makes us wonder just how smart humans are. __1__ the fruit-fly experiments described by Carl Zimmer's piece in *the Science Times* on Tuesday. Fruit flies who were taught to be smarter than the average fruit fly __2__ to live shorter lives. This suggests that __3__ bulbs burn longer, that there is a(n) __4__ in not being too bright.

Intelligence, it __5__, is a high-priced option. It takes more upkeep, burns more fuel and is slow __6__ the starting line because it depends on learning—a(n) __7__ process—instead of instinct. Plenty of other species are able to learn, and one of the things they've apparently learned is when to __8__.

Is there an adaptive value to __9__ intelligence? That's the question behind this new research. Instead of casting a wistful glance __10__ at all the species we've left in the dust I.Q.-wise, it implicitly asks what the real __11__ of our own intelligence might be. This is __12__ the mind of every animal we've ever met.

Research on animal intelligence also makes us wonder what experiments animals would __13__ on humans if they had the chance. Every cat with an owner, __14__, is running a small-scale study in operant conditioning. We believe that __15__ animals ran the labs, they would test us to __16__ the limits of our patience, our faithfulness, our memory for locations. They would try to decide what intelligence in humans is really __17__, not merely how much of it there is. __18__, they would hope to study a(n) __19__ question: Are humans actually aware of the world they live in? __20__ the results are inconclusive.

1. [A] Suppose   [B] Consider   [C] Observe   [D] Imagine
2. [A] tended   [B] feared   [C] happened   [D] threatened
3. [A] thinner   [B] stabler   [C] lighter   [D] dimmer
4. [A] tendency   [B] advantage   [C] inclination [D] priority
5. [A] insists on   [B] sums up   [C] turns out   [D] puts forward
6. [A] off   [B] behind   [C] over   [D] along
7. [A] incredible   [B] spontaneous   [C] inevitable   [D] gradual
8. [A] fight   [B] doubt   [C] stop   [D] think
9. [A] invisible   [B] limited   [C] indefinite   [D] different
10. [A] upward   [B] forward   [C] afterward   [D] backward
11. [A] features   [B] influences   [C] results   [D] costs
12. [A] outside   [B] on   [C] by   [D] across
13. [A] deliver   [B] carry   [C] perform   [D] apply

14. [A] by chance   [B] in contrast   [C] as usual   [D] for instance

15. [A] if   [B] unless   [C] as   [D] lest

16. [A] moderate   [B] overcome   [C] determine   [D] reach

17. [A] at   [B] for   [C] after   [D] with

18. [A] Above all   [B] After all   [C] However   [D] Otherwise

19. [A] fundamental   [B] comprehensive   [C] equivalent   [D] hostile

20. [A] By accident   [B] In time   [C] So far   [D] Better still

◆ 试题详解 ◆

1. 【答案】B

   【解析】语义衔接+词汇辨析。本题选择动词，放在祈使句句首。[A] Suppose认为，假定；[B] Consider考虑；[C] Observe观察；[D] Imagine想象。文章开篇指出：Research on animal intelligence always makes us wonder just how smart humans are."对动物智慧的研究总是让我们对人类到底有多聪明感到好奇"，接着举了果蝇的例子，该句要选择的动词应与上句在语义上衔接。用consider意为"让读者考虑一下（果蝇实验）"，从而引出下文，其他选项均不符合题意。

2. 【答案】A

   【解析】语义衔接+固定搭配。本题目选择动词，与介词to构成动词短语，在句子中充当谓语。[A] tended to易于，往往会……；[B] feared to害怕做某事；[C] happened to碰巧做某事；[D] threatened to威胁要做某事。Fruit flies who were taught to be smarter than the average fruit fly ____ to live shorter lives.原文讲述的是在实验中经常发生的一种情况，即"通过训练变得更聪明的果蝇，其寿命往往比普通果蝇短"。故选[A]。

3. 【答案】D

   【解析】语义衔接+词汇辨析。本题选择形容词比较级，在句中作定语修饰bulbs。This suggests that ____ bulbs burn longer, "这表明____的灯泡照明时间比较长"。上句讲到

111

聪明的果蝇寿命往往较短，这句接着用灯泡作类比，承接上句语义，应该是越不亮的灯泡用的时间越长，所以选[D] dimmer较暗的。[C] lighter更亮的，与前文意思相悖；[A] thinner更薄的，更瘦的；[B] stabler更稳定的。这三项均不符合题意。

4. 【答案】B

   【解析】词汇辨析+固定搭配。本题选择名词，并与in搭配。[A] tendency 趋势，倾向，后面常接介词for或动词不定式；[B] advantage 优势，后常接介词in，即an advantage in sth.在某方面具有优势；[C] inclination倾向，意愿，倾斜度，后常接介词for或动词不定式；[D] priority优先权，后常接over。从上下文语义来看，前面说聪明的果蝇寿命短，越不亮的灯泡用的时间越长，所以这里语义大意为"不太聪明（灯泡不太亮）是有优势的"，故[B]为正确选项。注意，bright在此处是一语双关，既可表示"灯泡不那么亮"，也可表示"人不那么聪明"。

5. 【答案】C

   【解析】语义衔接+词汇辨析。本题目要选择动词短语，使插入语完整。从上文可知，"通过训练变得更聪明的果蝇，其寿命往往比普通果蝇短"，以及"暗淡是灯泡的一个优势"，由此推出的结果是：聪明也是要付出代价的。[C] turns out意为"结果是……"，把it turns out用作插入语，使该句与上段内容紧紧联系起来，因此选[C]。[A] insists on坚持；[B] sums up总计，总结；[D] puts forward提出。这三项均不符合题意。

6. 【答案】A

   【解析】语义衔接。本题选择介词，体现与the starting line（起跑线）之间的逻辑关系。[B] behind和[C] over可以首先排除，因为这里没有涉及空间位置关系；若选[D] along则是"沿着起跑线徘徊"之意，这与后面的process意思不符；[A] off 有"离开"之意，slow off the starting line表示"离开起跑线慢了"，即"起步慢了"，但仍在进步，与后文逻辑一致，故选[A]。

7. 【答案】D

   【解析】语义衔接+词汇辨析。本题目选择形容词，作process的定语。破折号表示对前面内容即learning的解释。这里把learning（学习）与instinct（本能）做对比，结合前文的slow，以及学习自身的特点可知，只有gradual"渐进的"符合题意。其他三项[A] incredible难以置信的；[B] spontaneous自发的；[C] inevitable不可避免的；均不符合题意，故本题答案为[D]。

8. 【答案】C

【解析】语义衔接+词汇辨析。Plenty of other species are able to learn, and one of the things they've apparently learned is when to ____."许多其他物种都能够学习，很显然他们学到的东西之一就是知道何时____（学习）。"由上文可知，聪明需要学习，很多物种都能够学习，但都没有变聪明，这是因为它们还学会了适时停止学习。因此选[C]，其他三项在语义上均不通。

9. 【答案】B

【解析】语义衔接+词汇辨析。本题选择形容词，作定语修饰intelligence。由上文可知，智慧越多，付出的代价越多，因此智慧肯定是有限的，而且根据value也可以推断这里是关于intelligence多少的问题。[A] invisible看不见的；[C] indefinite不确定的；[D] different不同的；均与数量多少无关，只有limited"有限的，不多的"符合题意，故选[B]。

10. 【答案】D

【解析】语义衔接+词汇辨析。本题选择副词以表明逻辑关系。"we've left in the dust I.Q.-wise"是定语从句，修饰the species。cast a glance at...意为"对……投以目光"；"leave sb. in the dust"是固定搭配，"将某人远远抛在后面"的意思；I.Q.-wise是派生词，后缀wise表示方式，意为"在I.Q.方面"。本句意为"该研究不是要我们对那些在智力方面已被人类远远抛在后面的物种投以悲怜的眼光。"人类看这些被抛在后面的物种，自然是往后看了，所以[D] backward为正确选项，[A] upward向上；[B] forward向前；[C] afterward之后，后来（表时间）；该三项均不符合题意。

11. 【答案】D

【解析】语义衔接+词汇辨析。本题选择名词，做宾语从句的主语。...it implicitly asks

what the real ____ of our own intelligence might be."这项实验含蓄地提出一个问题：人类智慧的真正____可能是什么？"前文已经提到Intelligence... is a high-priced option，因此应选[D] costs。[A] features 特征；[B] influences 影响；[C] results 结果，均不符合题意。

12. 【答案】 B

【解析】固定搭配。本题选择介词，与mind搭配。on one's mind或on the mind of sb.是固定短语，意为"有心事，总是想着"，其他三项均不能与mind构成固定搭配。

13. 【答案】 C

【解析】固定搭配。本题选择动词，作为wonder后面宾语从句的谓语。选择的动词应与experiments搭配。[A] deliver 递送；[D] apply 应用；两者均不能与experiments搭配。若用carry，则为carry out experiments，故只能选[C] perform 执行，perform experiments意为"做实验"。

14. 【答案】 D

【解析】词汇辨析。本题选择介词短语在句中做插入语，表明逻辑关系。前文已经讲到作者很好奇，如果动物有机会的话，会对人类进行何种实验。本句接着说：Every cat with an owner, ____, is running a small-scale study in operant conditioning."每一只有主人的猫都在进行一项有关操作性条件反射的小规模研究"。这是以cat为例进一步论述动物对人进行实验，因此应选择表示举例的介词短语，故选[D] for instance 例如。[A] by chance 偶然；[B] in contrast 与……相比；[C] as usual 像往常一样；均不符合题意。

15. 【答案】 A

【解析】逻辑衔接。本题选择连词，体现句子之间的逻辑关系。由ran, would可知，本句使用了虚拟语气，是对动物可能对人类进行实验进行了假设，故选[A]。[B] unless 除非；[C] as 因为；[D] lest 唯恐，均不符合题意。

16. 【答案】 C

【解析】语义衔接+词汇辨析。本题选择动词，与limits搭配，作为test的目的。[A]

moderate 缓和；[B] overcome 克服；[D] reach 达到。既然作为测试的目的，应为确定某些内容，故选[C] determine，这里是"查明，测定"的意思。

17. 【答案】 B

【解析】语义衔接+词汇辨析。本题选择介词，体现逻辑关系。该句承接上一句，继续论述假设动物对人类进行实验的内容。[A] at表示方位；[C] after表示时间；[D] with表示伴随，均不符合语义，只有[B] for表示目的，构成what...for符合语境，表明动物们想了解人类智慧是用来干什么的。

18. 【答案】 A

【解析】逻辑衔接。本题选择逻辑关系词，体现前后句子之间的逻辑关系。前面两句解释了假设动物对人类进行实验会进行的的内容：它们想了解人类的某些极限，想知道人类智慧的用途。本句与前两句构成并列排比，they would hope to study a(n) ____ question "它们希望研究一个____问题"，与前两句应为顺承关系，表示强调或递进，所以选[A] Above all尤其是。[B] After all 毕竟；[C] However但是；[D] Otherwise 否则；三者均不符合题意。

19. 【答案】 A

【解析】语义衔接+词汇辨析。本题选择形容词作定语修饰question。[A] fundamental基本的；[B] comprehensive 综合的；[C] equivalent 相等的；[D] hostile 敌对的。由下文可知，这个question是Are humans actually aware of the world they live in？"人类是否真正了解他们生活的这个世界？"这应该是个最基本的问题，故选[A]。

20. 【答案】 C

【解析】逻辑衔接+词汇辨析。本题选择短语，体现与前面句子的逻辑关系。前面句子提出一个问题，本句讲the results are inconclusive（对比……仍无定论）。因此[C] so far "迄今为止"最符合题意，[A] By accident偶然；[B] In time 及时；[D] Better still更好；三者都不符合语义。

参考译文

　　对动物智慧的研究总是让我们对人类到底有多聪明感到好奇。让我们看一下卡尔·齐默周二发表在《科学时代》上的文章所描述的果蝇试验。通过训练变得更聪明的果蝇，其寿命往往比普通果蝇短。这表明暗淡的灯泡照明时间比较长，暗淡是灯泡的一个优势。

　　事实证明，智力是要付出昂贵的代价。它需要更多的保养、消耗更多的燃料，因为智力依靠的是学习，这是一个循序渐进的过程，而不是一种本能，所以离开起点时进展缓慢。许多其他物种都能够学习，很显然他们学到的东西之一就是知道何时停止。

　　有限的智力是否有适应值呢？这也是此项研究的课题。该研究不是要我们对那些在智力方面已被人类远远抛在后面的物种投以悲怜的眼光，这项实验含蓄地提出一个问题：人类智慧的真正代价可能是什么。我们所遇到的每种动物也都在思考着这个问题。

　　对动物智力的研究也让我们思考，如果动物有机会的话，他们会对人类做什么样的实验。比如说，每一只有主人的猫都在进行一项有关操作性条件反射的小规模研究。我们认为如果动物也能进行实验的话，他们会测定我们的忍耐度，忠诚度，以及对地形的记忆力。他们会试图判定人类智力的实际用处，而不仅仅是判定人类智力的高低。最重要的是他们希望研究一个最基本的问题：人类是否真正了解他们生活的这个世界？对此目前仍无定论。

第四章 阅读理解（A 部分）

第一节 最新大纲解读与命题趋势

（一）大纲要求

考研英语（二）阅读理解 Part A 通常由 4 篇文章组成，总长度约 1 500 词，每篇短文设有 5 道题，共计 20 个问题，要求考生从每题给出的四个选项中选出最佳答案。大纲要求"考生应能读懂不同题材和体裁的文字材料，题材包括经济、管理、社会、文化、科普等，体裁包括说明文、议论文和记叙文等"。根据阅读材料，考生应能：(1) 理解主旨要义；(2) 理解文中的具体信息；(3) 理解语篇的结构和上下文的逻辑关系；(4) 根据上下文推断重要生词或词组的含义；(5) 进行一定的判断和推理；(6) 理解作者的意图、观点或态度。

（二）命题趋势

大纲明确指出"题材包括经济、管理、社会、文化、科普等，体裁包括说明文、议论文和记叙文等"。注意它是把经济和管理放在最前边的，也就是说经济类文章、管理类文章可能是比较重要的，考生复习时可以有所侧重。

为了测试考生的上述能力，每年考试中心的命题者们要从国外的核心期刊中选取相应的阅读材料，然后对所选材料进行题目设计。通过对近十年考研阅读理解的分析不难发现：考试所选材料的体裁多是议论文和说明文，记叙文较少。词汇通常不超出考纲规定的范围，生词量不会超过所选材料的 3%；生词不会影响对短文内容的理解，而且这些生词很可能就是命题点，需要通过上下文推测其含义。所选短文材料内容宽广，题材多样；超纲词汇偶尔出现；有的文章句子结构十分复杂，出现大量长难句，例如常常采用多重并列句、省略句、倒装句和双重否定句等；而文章的逻辑结构也是重点中的重点。

因此，在备考阶段的前期考生要多背单词，对长难句进行分析、积累和整理，多读国外核心期刊中的文章，训练英语思维，把握文章方向，在后期做真题时，理解能力和阅读速度才会大幅度提升。

考研英语（二）中阅读理解所占的分值比重最大，因而有这样一个说法：得阅读者，得天下。对于同学们而言，无论你是什么专业，想让自己的分数在考试的大军当中能够脱颖而出，阅读理解部分的得分都会直接影响到考试的总成绩。因此，考生需要具备相应的阅读基本功以及应试技巧。与写作不同，阅读理解都是客观题型，只要理解和选择正确，得满分完全有可能。

英语（二）的阅读理解题，无非是从宏观和微观两个角度进行考查，体现在题型上，从广义的角度可分为两类：主旨态度和细节事实。主旨态度是全文的论点，细节事实是全文的论据。两者相结合，才是一篇逻辑严谨的文章。主旨态度对应的题型就是常见的主旨大意题、文章标题题和作者态度题。文章中的细节，即论据，通常是作者论证文章主题或是论证段落大意而使用的具体信息。因为就议论文而言，作者阐明所要阐述的问题和观点之后，通常会使用大量的具体细节去支持这些问题和观点并加以说明。这些细节可能是原因、事例、数字等。从对历年的试题分析中不难发现，细节事实题的比例占据了阅读理解试题的一半以上，尤其对于英语（二）的考生来说，细节题决定了阅读理解的成败，因此，重视细节题，考研阅读就有了很大希望。细节题首先考查的便是考生迅速回到原文进行定位的能力。定位准确，快速得出答案是非常容易的。之后考生再重点分析这个句子，充分理解、分析之后，再仔细排除错误选项。细节题的精髓就在于精确查找信息，这一考法一直沿用至今。

（三）备考指南

阅读是考研英语中最为重要的部分，这一点已经得到一致认同。但是怎样才能提高阅读能力并在考试中获得好的成绩呢？

大量的实践练习是提升阅读能力的前提。但同时也必须指出，大量的实践未必就能积累起我们所期望的高超"技巧"。考生在进行阅读训练的同时，更要善于总结，找出其中规律，提炼科学的做题方法和技巧，提高效率，以最短的复习时间达到最佳的学习效果。

1.阅读本质：速度+理解

阅读过程就是一个"读懂"别人思想的过程，阅读的质量主要取决于阅读者的理解能力，而考研英语阅读的应试要求是考生要在规定时间内完成阅读任务，因此还必须考虑阅读"速度"的问题。因此，从一定意义上讲，如何提高阅读理解能力和阅读速度就是在阅读中要解决的两大根本问题。

2. 阅读速度：略读+查读

大多数考生学习英语学了十几年，阅读文章时依然是一字一句地抠，动不动就翻字典，少看几个词心里就不踏实，总觉得考试时间不够，题目经常做不完，最后胡乱勾选几个草草了事。结果可想而知。针对这种现象，考生必须提高阅读效率，学会应用阅读策略。我们在这里提供两种阅读策略。

一是略读（Skimming）策略：略读时，不需要详尽地理解文章的每一句话，要求考生只是了解文章基本内容、主要观点以及文章的篇章结构，可以跳过具体细节和例子。略读能帮助考生把精力集中到文章的重点信息上，还能避免因"只见树木，不见森林"而浪费时间，以及避免因关注细节而忘了文章主题而造成困惑。它还能帮助你发现重点难点，以达到高效解题的效果。

二是查读（Scanning）策略：解题时，需要寻找特定信息，如主题句、相关细节、难句等。应用这种方法的关键是记住所需信息中最独特的词和词组（如专有名词、年代、数字等）。找到这些词之后，考生立即放慢速度，精读所需要的信息直至弄懂为止。

考试过程中，考生要想缩短时间，就应根据需要适当调整阅读速度，快慢结合。浏览文章时，要求考生尽快掌握文章主旨和大意，检索信息、寻找答案时，速度也要快一些。但是找到有关句子或段落时，考生则需放慢速度，仔细研读，理解其含义。

3. 提升理解：全面+定位

阅读过程是一个重新整合思维的过程，在这个过程中，考生利用已有知识同新信息进行比较、分析、总结、归纳，从而构建自己对文章的理解。阅读理解绝不是一个简单地把英语词汇和句子翻译成相应的汉语的过程，它需要考生思维敏捷，将输入的信息融会贯通，全面理解，在答题时才能做出正确的判断。

总而言之，若想提高考研英语阅读理解的解题能力，首先，在思维能力上，考生要从微观和宏观的角度出发，从思维的角度去战胜考试，才能够真正做到透过现象挖掘试题的本质，方能以不变应万变，破解任何一种题型，掌控任何一年的考题；其次，内化到题型角度，便是从细节事实题和主旨态度题这广义角度上的两大分类分别入手，对于不同的题型，采用不同的解题方法。知其法，方可解其意。最终才能百战不殆。

第二节 题型分类与解题技巧

（一）题型分类

一般而论，英语（二）Part A阅读文章的试题可大致分为5类，即：细节题（事实、原因、排除、正误判断、词汇等）、推理判断题、主旨大意题、观点态度题、例子题。首先要在题干中圈定几个关键词，这些关键词通常可以被设定为：首字母大写的名词如人名、地名、机构名，引号里的内容等。然后将这些关键词做一个简单的叠加，得出的大致意思一般就是文章的主要内容。最后，利用这些关键词回文定位，再对照每个问题的四个选项，就可得出正确答案。

干扰项的典型特点：（1）所述和原文相反；（2）无中生有；（3）和常识一致，却和文中科学论述相悖；（4）是原文不严谨的改写或推理；（5）违背常理；（6）语气极端，过于绝对。

（二）解题技巧

1. 细节题

细节题正确选项的特点：一般照抄原文的选项不是正确答案，而同义替换的选项往往才是正确选项。最常见的改写原文的方法是词性变换，同义词、同义词组的替换等，这些变化往往体现了选项与原文之间精确的对应；还有一种很普遍的方式就是句式和表达法的转换。一般来说，含有一些概括性太强的词（如：only, everything, all, none, must, never, always, too, so, alone, everyone, entirely, absolutely, mainly, any, have to, no, very, completely, hardly, the most, no longer等）的选项往往是错误的。而含有一些不肯定词（如some, sometimes, certain, someone, more... than, (not) as... as, less等）的选项往往是正确的。这类题的答案往往在两个意义相近或相反的选项之中。

细节题干扰项的典型特点：（1）照抄部分原文信息；（2）含有原文中没有的内容；（3）与原文相矛盾；（4）张冠李戴（把A的特征加在B上）；（5）偷梁换柱（与原文内容一半相同一半不同，即选项仍使用文章中的句法结构和大部分词汇，但换掉关键词，造成意思上的改变）；（6）与原句内容相似但过于绝对化；（7）虽是原文信息，但与问题答案无关。

（1）事实类细节题

这是最为常见的细节题之一。通常是对事件的参与人物、人物的行为、发生时间、发生地点等提问。通过题干关键信息词找到原文对应的句子，正确答案一般是对原文句子的适度改写，如词汇替换、句式改写（双重否定句改为肯定句、反问句改为肯定句）等。

例1：In delivering lessons for high-schoolers, Flatiron has considered their_____.

[A] experience

[B] academic backgrounds

[C] career prospects

[D] interest

【对应原文】The high-schoolers get the same curriculum, but "we try to gear lessons toward things they're interested in," said Victoria Friedman, an instructor. For instance, one of the apps the students are developing suggests movies based on your mood.

【要点解析】题干关键词lessons对应原文的curriculum，原文but之后"we try to gear lessons toward things they're interested in（我们试图让课程满足学生的兴趣）"就是该题的答案，故interest为正确答案。

例2：According to the last paragraph, Flatiron students are expected to_____.

[A] compete with a future army of programmers

[B] stay longer in the information technology industry

[C] become better prepared for the digitalized world

[D] bring forth innovative computer technologies

【对应原文】Indeed, the Flatiron students might not go into IT at all. But creating a future army of coders is not the sole purpose of the classes. These kids are going to be surrounded by computers—in their pockets, in their offices, in their homes—for the rest of their lives. The younger they learn how computers think, how to coax the machine into producing what they want—the earlier they learn that they have the power to do that—the better.

【要点解析】题干问：根据最后一段，Flatiron的学生被期望_____。据此句定位到原文中These kids are going to be处，该处内容是题干的同义复现。定位句"These kids are... be surrounded by computers... for the rest of their lives. The younger they learn how computers think... the better."的大意是学生们越早学越好。选项C "为数字化世界做更好的准备"是对该句的同义概述。

（2）原因类细节题

一般有表原因的标志性的词如because、in that等出现在题干中时，答案应在原文描述原因的句子里寻找。

例：Parkrun is different from Olympic games in that it _____.

[A] aims at discovering talents

[B] focuses on mass competition

[C] does not emphasize elitism

[D] does not attract first-timers

【对应原文】Parkrun is not a race but a time trial: Your only competitor is the clock. The ethos welcomes anybody. There is as much joy over a puffed-out first-timer being clapped over the line as there is about top talent shining. The Olympic bidders, by contrast, wanted to get more people doing sport and to produce more elite athletes. The dual aim was mixed up: The stress on success over taking part was intimidating for newcomers.

【要点解析】题干大意是：公园跑步不同于奥运会是因为它_____。选项C中的does not emphasize elitism是to produce more elite athletes的反面说法，即公园跑步与运动会不同在于公园跑步并不是以培养体育精英为目的，所以该选项是正确答案；选项A对应原文第四句中的to produce more elite athletes，这是奥运会的宗旨，而不是公园跑步的目标；选项B与首句Parkrun is not a race 相悖；选项D对应的是末句was intimidating for newcomers（使新来者恐惧），这也是在谈奥运会的特点。

（3）排除类细节题

常见的题干形式是：All the following statements are mentioned in the passage EXCEPT_____. 这种题型相对而言不好处理，因为题干提供的关键信息太少，难以在原文中确定对应的出处。这时就得分别找到四个选项的关键词，再在原文寻找对应的内容。一种可能是，四个选项所描述的内容分布在同一段落中，对于这种设计套路，锁定答案相对容易；另一种可能是，四个选项所描述的内容分布在不同段落中，这就需要阅读大量内容才能锁定答案，使得解题难度增大很多。

例：All of the following are true EXCEPT _____.

[A] men tend to talk more in public than women

[B] nearly 50 percent of recent divorces are caused by failed conversation

[C] women attach much importance to communication between couples

[D] a female tends to be more talkative at home than her spouse

【对应原文】This episode crystallizes the irony that although American men tend to talk more than women in public situations, they often talk less at home. And this pattern is wreaking havoc with marriage.

The pattern was observed by political scientist Andrew Hacker in the late 1970s. Sociologist Catherine Kohler Riessman reports in her new book *Divorce Talk* that most of the women she interviewed—but only a few of the men—gave lack of communication as the reason for their divorces. Given the current divorce rate of nearly 50 percent, that amounts to millions of cases in the United States every year—a virtual epidemic of failed conversation.

【要点解析】题干中没有明显的关键词，但根据出题顺序原则和选项中的关键词可以大致进行定位。选项A论述的内容在第一段首句复现；根据选项B中的关键词nearly 50 percent可定位到第二段第三句，但原文中的Given表示"假如"，是一种假设条件，而选项B中的是事实陈述，所以选项B为答案；根据选项C中的关键词communication可定位到第二段第二句gave lack of communication... divorces，由此可以推断，女性比较重视沟通，选项C中所论述的内容正确；综合上下文，选项D中所论述的内容在文章多处均有体现。

（4）正误判断类细节题

常见的题干形式是：Which of the following statements is TRUE/FALSE? 这种题型与排除类细节题解题套路基本相同，可以说是后者的姐妹版题型。这里不再详述。

（5）词汇类细节题

常见的题干形式是：The word "xxx" in Paragraph x is closest in meaning to＿＿＿＿＿. 解题方法是先找到该词所处的句子，然后通过该句与上下文的逻辑关系（因果、递进、让步等）来确定所考查词汇的含义。要得出该词的精准含义并非易事，但有时只要能判断其属性如褒义、贬义，也可锁定正确选项。

猜词技巧是阅读中一项非常重要和常用的技巧，是一种应对生词时用来确定词汇在具体语言环境中的确切含义的手段。阅读中的生词不是孤立的，而是与其上下文中的词、句乃至整个篇章在意义上、结构上和逻辑上存在联系的，这些联系便是我们推测词义的依据，通常被称为词的上下文线索（context clues）。

常用的上下文线索有以下几种：①举例线索；②上下文推理线索；③比较与对照性线索（包括同义词、反义词线索及重复线索）。

词汇类细节题正确选项的特点：①与所考查词汇词形相近的往往是错误的；②如果考查的是熟词，要考虑其在特定上下文中的意义，尤其注意含有该词常规含义的选项一般是错误选项。

词汇类细节题干扰项的特点：①与所考查的词汇形似；②含有该词常规含义；③与该词意义无关或相反；④对句子的释义太宽或太窄。

例：The word "coax" (Line 4, Para.6) is closest in meaning to＿＿＿＿＿.

[A] challenge

[B] persuade

[C] frighten

[D] misguide

【对应原文】Indeed, the Flatiron students might not go into IT at all. But creating a future army of coders is not the sole purpose of the classes. These kids are going to be surrounded by computers—in their pockets, in their offices, in their homes—for the rest of their lives. The younger they learn how computers think, how to <u>coax</u> the machine into producing what they want—the earlier they learn that they have the power to do that—the better.

【要点解析】根据题干中的coax可定位到最后一句"how to coax the machine into producing what they want"。选项A"挑战"，选项B"劝服"，选项C"使恐慌"，选项D"误导"。将四个选项代入原句，再结合上下文的逻辑，可断定选项B正确。

123

2. 推理判断题

推理判断题的常用标志词：imply，infer，suggest，would probably agree等。

推理判断题的解题方法：注意那些话中有话的间接表达句，含义深刻或结构复杂的句子，以及文章或段落的开头或结尾处。

推理判断题干扰项的特点：①以假乱真，编造信息（不是在文章事实或上下文逻辑基础上进行推理而得出的观点）；②混淆本末，主次不分（虽然是以文章提供的事实或内在逻辑为基础进行的推理，但推理过头，概括过度）；③直接间接不分（把文章中明确表明的事实当成是推理出来的）；④因果颠倒（原文中的原因变成了选项中的结果，或反之）；⑤手段与目的颠倒（原文中的手段变成了选项中的目的，或反之）。

例：Jay Lininger would most likely support _____.

[A] industry groups

[B] the win-win rhetoric

[C] environmental groups

[D] the plan under challenge

【对应原文】Not everyone buys the win-win rhetoric. Some Congress members are trying to block the plan, and at least a dozen industry groups, four states, and three environmental groups are challenging it in federal court. Not surprisingly, industry groups and states generally argue it goes too far; environmentalists say it doesn't go far enough. "The federal government is giving responsibility for managing the bird to the same industries that are pushing it to extinction," says biologist Jay Lininger.

【要点解析】题干问的是杰伊·林恩格最可能支持_____。题干中出现了most likely，可以断定这是一道推理判断题。根据人名可定位到最后一句。该句提到，生物学家杰伊·林恩格说联邦政府要把管理鸟类的责任交给导致鸟类灭绝的企业，显然杰伊·林恩格对政府和企业持反对意见。再往前看一句，该句指出：企业团体和政府部门观点一致，而环境保护主义者与政府和企业的观点相反。因此杰伊·林恩格最可能支持环保组织的观点，选项C正确。选项A指的是企业团体，杰伊·林恩格对企业是持反对意见的，故排除；选项B、D实际上指的是同一事物，即政府提出的保护计划，该题只能有一个正确答案，所以选项B、D均应排除。

3. 主旨大意题

主旨大意题常见的题干形式有：

a. The passage is mainly about _____.

b. What is the major point the author makes in the passage?

c. What is the main idea of the passage?

d. What is the main topic of this passage?

e. The proper subject of this text is _____.

f. The best title for this article is _____.

g. The passage was written to explain _____.

主旨大意题的解题方法：①重点关注首末段信息，尤其是首末段的首末句；②重点关注综合性例证的前后，及以事例开头的后面的部分；③将各段落首句相加或各段落主题句相加；④重点关注首末段的转折连接词后；⑤关注各题干复现率最高的信息表达；⑥正确选项往往具有概括总结性；⑦过于具体、仅涉及文章单方面内容的选项常为干扰项。

主旨大意题正确选项的特点是：有概括性强的词汇，但通常不含过分肯定或绝对意义的词，如all，no one，only，absolutely，entirely等。

例：The most suitable title for this text would be _____.

[A] In Favor of the Gap Year

[B] The ABCs of the Gap Year

[C] The Gap Year Comes Back

[D] The Gap Year: A Dilemma

【对应原文】Today, widespread social pressure to immediately go to college in conjunction with increasingly high expectations in a fast-moving world often causes students to completely overlook the possibility of taking a gap year. After all, if everyone you know is going to college in the fall, it seems silly to stay back a year, doesn't it? And after going to school for 12 years, it doesn't feel natural to spend a year doing something that isn't academic.

But while this may be true, it's not a good enough reason to condemn gap years. There's always a constant fear of falling behind everyone else on the socially perpetuated "race to the finish line," whether that be toward graduate school, medical school or a lucrative career. But despite common misconceptions, a gap year does not hinder the success of academic pursuits—in fact, it probably enhances it.

Studies from the United States and Australia show that students who take a gap year are generally better prepared for and perform better in college than those who do not. Rather than pulling students back, a gap year pushes them ahead by preparing them for independence, new responsibilities and environmental changes—all things that first-year students often struggle with the most. Gap year experiences can lessen the blow when it comes to adjusting to college and being thrown into a brand new environment, making it easier to focus on academics and activities rather than acclimation blunders.

If you're not convinced of the inherent value in taking a year off to explore interests, then consider its financial impact on future academic choices. According to the National Center for

Education Statistics, nearly 80 percent of college students end up changing their majors at least once. This isn't surprising, considering the basic mandatory high school curriculum leaves students with a poor understanding of the vast academic possibilities that await them in college. Many students find themselves listing one major on their college applications, but switching to another after taking college classes. It's not necessarily a bad thing, but depending on the school, it can be costly to make up credits after switching too late in the game. At Boston College, for example, you would have to complete an extra year were you to switch to the nursing school from another department. Taking a gap year to figure things out initially can help prevent stress and save money later on.

【要点解析】第二至四段的首句分别是："But while this may be true, it's not a good enough reason to condemn gap years"，"Studies from the United States and Australia show that students who take a gap year are generally better prepared for and perform better in college than those who do not."，以及"If you're not convinced of the inherent value in taking a year off to explore interests, then consider its financial impact on future academic choices."。根据这些句子可以得知，作者对gap year持赞同态度，选项A正确。

4. 观点态度题

观点态度题的解题方法：①在强烈肯定之后的转折关系是观点态度题命题的重点；②首段、第二段和末段最容易出现作者的态度倾向；③在两方观点的文章中，要看有无作者的观点，判断是主观还是客观；④回归到态度句，注意混合型的观点：I like, but... （关注作者在相关出处所用形容词的褒贬性质；关注作者所引用对象的身份或立场对比）。

观点态度题的正确选项通常是比较有限度、有保留的词语，如partially correct，critical，skeptical，approve，disapprove等。而包含有具有过于中性、攻击、热情等特点的词语的选项一般可排除，如indifferent，neutral，condemn，absolutely，fervent等。

例：The author's attitude to what UK governments have done for sports is _____.

    [A] tolerant

    [B] critical

    [C] uncertain

    [D] sympathetic

【对应原文】But successive governments have presided over selling green spaces, squeezing money from local authorities and declining attention on sport in education. Instead of wordy, worthy strategies, future governments need to do more to provide the conditions for sport to thrive. Or at least not make them worse.

【要点解析】题干大意是：作者对于英国政府在体育方面的作为的态度是_____。根据原文中but一词就可知此处是作者真正要表达的意图，英国政府本该为民众提供更多的体育基础设施,却做出大规模出售绿地及压缩地方政府资金等不人道的行为,由此可见作者的批评态度,选项B的critical也可体现作者的批评态度。该题也可从应试技巧入手,首先排除选项C这个中性词,同时选项A和D都属于观点态度题的常规排除对象。

5. 例子题

例子题题干的常见形式是:The example in Paragraph 2 is used to show _____.

例子题的解题方法是:通过题干中的定位词如人名、地名或某些首字母大写的名词在文中找到例子所在位置。关于例子本身的叙述可迅速扫过,不需细读。考题答案往往在例子前后具有哲理性或总结性的话里,一般来说,答案在例子前的概率更大。

例:Radesky cites the "still face experiment" to show that _____.

  [A] it is easy for children to get used to blank expressions

  [B] verbal expressions are unnecessary for emotional exchange

  [C] children are insensitive to changes in their parents' mood

  [D] parents need to respond to children's emotional needs

【对应原文】Radesky cites the "still face experiment" devised by developmental psychologist Ed Tronick in the 1970s. In it, a mother is asked to interact with her child in a normal way before putting on a blank expression and not giving them any visual social feedback: The child becomes increasingly distressed as she tries to capture her mother's attention. "Parents don't have to be exquisitely present at all times, but there needs to be a balance and parents need to be responsive and sensitive to a child's verbal or nonverbal expressions of an emotional need," says Radesky.

【要点解析】题干大意是:拉德斯基引用"静止面部实验"表明_____。例子题的答案往往在例子前后具有归纳总结性的话语里,该题的答案在例子后,即"but there needs to be a balance and parents need to be responsive and sensitive to a child's verbal or nonverbal expressions of an emotional need",选项D中的parents need to respond to children's emotional needs是本句的同义替换,因此该选项是正确答案。

第三节　真题同源实战

Text 1

1　With two and a half years left in office, Barack Obama wants to shed his image as a president who is hostile to business. In an interview with *The Economist* last week aboard Air Force One, which was supposed to focus on foreign policy, Mr. Obama introduced the subject of business and launched a strident defence of his record. Bosses, he argued, have not given him due credit for running the economy well. And rather than grumbling about the burden of regulation and casting him as a class warrior, chief executives should think harder about society as a whole.

2　The full interview is here. But Mr. Obama's impatience with Main Street is interesting, because the feeling is mutual. His administration provokes quiet fury from many corporate leaders: even Democrat-voting bosses moan about a White House that "doesn't get it." Some cite a president bent on redistribution and red tape as a reason not to invest in America.

3　But who is correct? The president's strongest card is macroeconomic policy. Mr. Obama points to such measures as high stockmarket values, record corporate profits and job growth. How much of this he can claim credit for is a question debated by economists. But, given the mess that he inherited, it is hard to claim that he has done badly. Indeed, CEOs tend to give fairly high marks to his economic team: they may not have enjoyed being lectured about Keynesian stimulus by Larry Summers and Tim Geithner, both now departed, but they sensed the economists knew their subject.

4 The main complaints from business are threefold. First, Mr. Obama rarely misses a chance to cast them as the bad guys. In a speech in Kansas City just before the interview, he raised whoops by lambasting "unpatriotic" companies which (perfectly legally) register their headquarters overseas for tax purposes—or, as he puts it, "stash their money offshore." A fairer stance would be that America's corporate-tax system is a mess, which the president deserves part of the blame for failing to fix.

5 The second element is more personal. In face-to-face meetings, the White House's starting point is contempt. Bosses exchange horror stories about being herded in for photo-opportunities or being invited to the White House to suggest policy ideas—only to find themselves accused of special pleading. Sooner or later the CEOs mention Valerie Jarrett, who many depict as the commissar of the West Wing.

6 The third complaint is over-regulation. Businesses moan that the White House has become a red-tape machine. Mr. Obama responds that businesses will always find some regulations inconvenient, which is fair. Asked about the crushing

complexity of flagship laws passed on his watch, such as the Dodd-Frank financial reforms or the Affordable Care Act ("Obamacare"), he is defensive. Given a blank canvas and a calmer political environment, they could have been "far more elegant." But democracy is "messy," he explains.

极其烦琐复杂的重大法律时，如多德-弗兰克金融改革法案或平价医疗法案（即"奥巴马医改"），奥巴马总会自圆其说。若处于像一块空白画布一样的社会和一个更温和的政治环境中，这些规定会"更完善"。但是民主却是"一团糟"，他这样解释道。

1. What does Obama decide to do within his not-very-long rule in office?

   [A] Business leaders are to blame for poor economy.

   [B] Obama tries to be humane to business leaders.

   [C] Obama wants to be tougher to business leaders.

   [D] Bosses can rely on the president for their troubles.

2. Obama administration provokes quiet fury mainly because of _____.

   [A] his impatience

   [B] his economic team

   [C] his inefficiency

   [D] his macroeconomic policy

3. In Kansa City, Obama criticized some companies for _____.

   [A] their poor tax management

   [B] calling him a bad guy

   [C] laying off American employees

   [D] promoting prosperity of other countries

4. We can learn from Paragraph 5 that _____.

   [A] business leaders are uneasy with the White House's accusation

   [B] business leaders are often invited for photo-opportunities

   [C] Valerie Jarrett is admired by business leaders

   [D] business leaders are free to suggest public ideas

5. The appropriate title for this text may be _____.

   [A] Harmony: Mutual Pursuit

   [B] Hostility: Like a Volcano

[C] Settlement: on the Horizon

[D] Obligation: Fair Deal

◆ 解题之路 ◆

1. 【答案】B 【题型】事实细节题。
   【思路】根据出题段落顺序和题干关键词within his not-very-long rule in office可定位到原文首段，within his not-very-long rule in office是对with two and a half years left in office的改写；再根据题干关键词decide可知答案就在首句：Obama wants to shed his image as a president who is hostile to business, decide是want的替换词，所以答案为选项[B]，使用了正话反说的方法。选项[A]属于无中生有；选项[C]与原文相悖；选项[D]与原文首段第四句中的And rather than grumbling about the burden of regulation意思相反。

2. 【答案】C 【题型】原因细节题。
   【思路】根据题干关键词administration provokes quiet fury可定位到第二段的第三句，答案就在其中的doesn't get it和第四句的red tape上，稍加推导就可知选项[C]是正确选项。选项[A]在第二段第二句，选项[B]在第三段第六句，选项[D]在第三段第二句，均属于张冠李戴。

3. 【答案】D 【题型】事实细节题。
   【思路】根据题干关键词Kansas City, criticized, companies可定位到第四段的第三句，答案就是stash their money offshore，选项[D]是对该句的改写，故为正确选项。选项[A]在该段末句可找到，但属于故意曲解原文；选项[B]是对该段第二句的曲解，原文说Obama认为商界领袖是bad guys；选项[C]属于无中生有。

4. 【答案】A 【题型】事实细节题。
   【思路】选项[A]可从第五段的contempt, horror stories以及only to find themselves accused of...推导而出。选项[B]可在第三句找到信息，但often一词未提及；选项[C]错在admire一词，因为该段末句关于Valerie Jarrett的描述中commissar（政委）具有贬义含义；选项[D]在该段的第三句可找到信息，但are free to suggest却未提及。

5. 【答案】B 【题型】主旨大意题。
   【思路】纵观全文，Obama和商界领袖的矛盾摩擦是文章主题，只有选项[B]符合题意。

◆ 词汇精解 ◆

1. shed [ʃed] v. 摆脱；解雇	3. interview [ˈɪntəvju:] n. 面试；采访
2. hostile [ˈhɒstaɪl] a. 敌对的；敌视的	4. launch [lɔ:ntʃ] v. 启动；发射

5. strident ['straɪdnt] a. 刺耳的；尖锐的
6. defence [dɪ'fens] n. 捍卫；辩护
7. due [dju:] a. 适当的；合适的
8. credit ['kredɪt] n. 信誉；荣誉
9. grumble ['grʌmbl] v. 抱怨；埋怨
10. cast [kɑ:st] v. 刻画；描绘
11. warrior ['wɒrɪə(r)] n. 卫士；捍卫者
12. chief [tʃi:f] a. 主要的；重要的
13. executive [ɪɡ'zekjʊtɪv] n. 管理者；执行官
14. mutual ['mju:tʃʊəl] a. 相互的；彼此的
15. administration [ədˌmɪnɪ'streʃn] n. 管理；政府；当局
16. provoke [prə'vəʊk] v. 激发；引起
17. fury ['fjʊərɪ] n. 愤怒；生气
18. corporate ['kɔ:pərət] a. 企业的；公司的
19. moan [məʊn] v. 抱怨；埋怨
20. redistribution [ˌri:dɪstrɪ'bju:ʃn] n. 重新分配
21. macroeconomic [ˌmækrəʊˌi:kə'nɒmɪk] a. 宏观经济的
22. debate [dɪ'beɪt] v. 争论；辩论
23. given ['ɡɪvn] prep. 鉴于；由于；假设
24. inherit [ɪn'herɪt] v. 继承
25. stimulus ['stɪmjələs] n. 刺激；激励

26. depart [dɪ'pɑ:t] v. 离去；离开
27. complaint [kəm'pleɪnt] n. 抱怨；投诉
28. threefold ['θri:fəʊld] a. 三重的；三倍的
29. unpatriotic [ˌʌnˌpætrɪ'ɒtɪk] a. 不爱国的
30. headquarters [ˌhed'kwɔ:təz] n. 总部
31. stash [stæʃ] v. 储藏；藏匿
32. offshore [ˌɒf'ʃɔ:(r)] ad. 在岸边；海外
33. stance [stæns] n. 立场；观点
34. deserve [dɪ'zɜ:v] v. 值得；配得上
35. fix [fɪks] v. 处理；解决
36. contempt [kən'tempt] n. 蔑视；轻视
37. horror ['hɒrə(r)] n. 惊恐；恐惧
38. herd [hɜ:d] v. 召集；召唤
39. accuse [ə'kju:z] v. 指责；指控
40. pleading ['pli:dɪŋ] n. 请求；呼吁
41. depict [dɪ'pɪkt] v. 描绘；描述
42. commissar [ˌkɒmɪ'sɑ:(r)] n. 政委
43. respond [rɪ'spɒnd] v. 回应；回答
44. blank [blæŋk] a. 空白的
45. canvas ['kænvəs] n. 画布
46. environment [ɪn'vaɪrənmənt] n. 环境；情形
47. elegant ['elɪɡənt] a. 优雅的；得体的
48. democracy [dɪ'mɒkrəsɪ] n. 民主；民主制度

→ 难句解析 ←

1. With two and a half years left in office, Barack Obama wants to shed his image as a president who is hostile to business.

在离任期还有两年半之际，贝拉克·奥巴马希望摆脱他对商界有敌意的总统形象。

结构分析：这个句子可以划分为：With two and a half years left in office, Barack Obama wants to shed his image *as a president (who is hostile to business)*. 下划线部分是独立主格结构，即 with+n.+过去分词，作时间状语；斜体部分是一个介词短语，作 image 的后置定语，括号里 who 引导的是修饰 president 的定语从句。

2. In an interview with *The Economist* last week aboard Air Force One, which was supposed to focus on foreign policy, Mr. Obama introduced the subject of business and launched a strident defence of his record.	上周在空军一号上《经济学人》杂志的一场采访中，奥巴马本应该关注外交政策，但他却谈论起了经济话题，并对自己过去的言论进行了强硬的辩护。

结构分析：这个句子可以划分为：In an interview with *The Economist* last week aboard Air Force One, (which was supposed to focus on foreign policy), Mr. Obama *introduced* the subject of business and launched a strident defence of his record. 下划线部分是一个介词短语，作时间状语，括号里 which 引导的从句作 an interview 的定语；introduced 和 launched 是并列的谓语动词。

3. And rather than grumbling about the burden of regulation and casting him as a class warrior, chief executives should think harder about society as a whole.	而且企业的首席执行官们应该多为社会这一整体考虑问题，不要总是抱怨政策使他们不堪重负，还将他视作阶级捍卫者。

结构分析：这个句子可以划分为：And rather than grumbling about the burden of regulation and casting him as a class warrior, chief executives should think harder about society (as a whole). 下划线部分作状语；括号里的介词短语作 society 的后置定语。

4. Some cite a president bent on redistribution and red tape as a reason not to invest in America.	一些人甚至说总统热衷于再分配和官僚作风，这是他们不愿在本国投资的原因。

结构分析：这个句子可以划分为：Some cite (a president *bent on redistribution and red tape*) as a reason (not to invest in America). cite... as... 可视作一个固定搭配，意思相当于 regard... as...；第一个括号里的名词短语作 cite 的宾语，斜体部分的过去分词短语作 president 的后置定语，be bent on sth. 表示"专注于某事"；第二个括号里不定式的否定形式作 reason 的后置定语。

> 5. Mr. Obama points to such measures as high stockmarket values, record corporate profits and job growth.
>
> 奥巴马指出了一些措施，例如提高股票市值、使企业利润创历史新高和提高就业率等。

结构分析：这个句子可以划分为：Mr Obama points to (such measures as high stockmarket values, record corporate profits and job growth). 括号里的并列名词短语作 point to 的宾语；point to 表"指出，谈到"之意，such... as... 是固定搭配；as 后面的内容是实施 such measures 后希望实现的结果。

> 6. How much of this he can claim credit for is a question debated by economists.
>
> 这些有多少可以归功于他也是经济学家们争论的问题。

结构分析：这个句子可以划分为：<u>How much of this he can claim credit for</u> is a question (debated by economists). 下划线部分为 How 引导的从句作主语，括号里的过去分词短语作 question 的后置定语。

> 7. But, given the mess that he inherited, it is hard to claim that he has done badly.
>
> 但是考虑到他接手时的混乱局面，很难说他表现糟糕。

结构分析：这个句子可以划分为：But, <u>given the mess (that he inherited)</u>, it is hard to claim (that he has done badly). 下划线部分是一个介词短语，given 的意思是"鉴于，考虑到"，其中括号里 that 引导的从句作 mess 的后置定语；it 作形式主语，指代后面的不定式，最后括号里 that 引导的从句是 claim 的宾语。

> 8. In a speech in Kansas City just before the interview, he raised whoops by lambasting "unpatriotic" companies which (perfectly legally) register their headquarters overseas for tax purposes—or, as he puts it, "stash their money offshore."
>
> 就在此次采访之前，奥巴马在堪萨斯城的一次演讲中怒斥"不爱国的"公司，这些公司出于避税的目的将公司总部注册在海外（而这是完全合法的），或者正如他所说，"把钱藏到海外"。

结构分析：这个句子可以划分为：In a speech in Kansas City just before the interview, he raised whoops <u>by lambasting "unpatriotic" companies</u> *which (perfectly legally) register their headquarters overseas for tax purposes—or, (as he puts it), "stash their money offshore."* 下划线部分作方式状语，

修饰 raised whoops；该状语中斜体部分 which 引导的从句作 "unpatriotic" companies 的定语，其中括号里的 as he puts it 作方式状语从句，it 指代后面的 stash their money offshore，put 是 "表述，说明" 的意思。

> 9. Bosses exchange horror stories about being herded in for photo-opportunities or being invited to the White House to suggest policy ideas—only to find themselves accused of special pleading.
>
> 企业家们经常互相交流一些令其恐惧的情形：他们被召集到白宫与总统合影留念，或受白宫之邀去建言献策，结果却被指责是在诡辩诉苦。

结构分析：这个句子可以划分为：Bosses exchange horror stories (about being herded in for photo-opportunities or being invited to the White House to suggest policy ideas)—*only to find themselves accused of special pleading*. 括号里的介词短语作 horror stories 的后置定语，破折号之后的不定式结构作结果状语，过去分词短语 accused of... 作宾语 themselves 的补语。

> 10. Given a blank canvas and a calmer political environment, they could have been "far more elegant."
>
> 若处于像一块空白画布一样的社会和一个更温和的政治环境中，这些规定会"更完善"。

结构分析：这个句子可以划分为：<u>Given a blank canvas and a calmer political environment</u>, they could have been "far more elegant." 下划线部分是一个介词短语，given 表 "假如" 之意，参看第 7 句中 given 的不同含义（鉴于，考虑到），多加留意一词多义的现象。

Text 2

> 1 Early in the age of affluence that followed World War II, an American retailing analyst named Victor Lebow proclaimed, "Our enormously productive economy demands that we make consumption our way of life, that we convert the buying and use of goods into rituals, that we seek our spiritual satisfaction, our ego satisfaction, in consumption. We need things consumed, burned up, worn out, replaced and discarded at an ever increasing rate."
>
> 1 "二战"之后经济繁荣之初，美国零售业分析家维克托·勒博宣称："我们巨大的生产力经济要求我们把消费作为自己的生活方式，把购买和使用商品变成一种生活习惯，在消费中寻求精神满足和自我满足，我们以不断增长的比例消耗、烧尽、用完、更换和丢弃东西"。

135

2   Americans have responded to Lebow's call, and much of the world has followed.

3   Consumption has become a central pillar of life in industrial lands and is even embedded in social values. Opinion surveys in the world's two largest economies—Japan and the United Sates—show consumerist definitions of success becoming ever more prevalent.

4   Overconsumption by the world's fortunate is an environmental problem unmatched in severity by anything but perhaps population growth. Their surging exploitation of resources threatens to exhaust or unalterably spoil forests, soils, water, air and climate.

5   Ironically, high consumption may be a mixed blessing in human terms, too. The time-honored values of integrity of character, good work, friendship, family and community have often been sacrificed in the rush to riches.

6   Thus many in the industrial lands have a sense that their world of plenty is somehow hollow—that, misled by a consumerist culture, they have been fruitlessly attempting to satisfy what are essentially social, psychological and spiritual needs with material things.

7   Of course, the opposite of overconsumption poverty is no solution to either environmental or human problems. It is infinitely worse for people and bad for the natural world too. Dispossessed peasants

2   美国人已在响应勒博的号召，世界其他地方也纷纷效仿。

3   在工业社会，消费已成为生活的中心支柱，甚至已嵌入社会价值中。在世界两大经济强国——日本和美国所进行的民意调查显示，消费主义所界定的成功论正在日益盛行。

4   对世界财富的过度消费是一种环境问题，其严重性或许除了人口增长的危害外没有其他问题能与之相比。人类对资源的肆意开发很可能将资源耗尽或对森林、土壤、水、空气以及气候造成不可挽回的破坏。

5   具有讽刺意味的是，高度消费对人类而言也是祸福相依。长期以来受人推崇的价值观念，如诚实的品质、良好的工作、友谊、家庭和社团等往往在追逐财富的过程中被牺牲掉了。

6   因此，工业国家里许多人都感觉他们富足的世界实际上空空如也——那是因为被消费主义的文化误导了，他们试图用物质来满足社会的、心理的和精神的必要需求，却一无所获。

7   当然，过度消费的对立面——贫穷——绝不是环境问题或人类问题的解决之道。贫穷对人类来说更加糟糕，对自然界也没什么好处。被剥夺

slash-and-burn their way into the rain forests of Latin America, and hungry nomads turn their herds out onto fragile African grassland, reducing it to desert.

8 If environmental destruction results when people have either too little or too much, we are left to wonder how much is enough. What level of consumption can the earth support? When does having more cease to add noticeably to human satisfaction?

得一无所有的农民为了生存，一路朝着拉丁美洲的雨林刀耕火种，饥饿的游牧民族把他们的牧群赶进贫瘠的非洲草地，使草地退化成沙漠。

8 如果过于贫穷或过于富裕都会导致环境破坏，那么，我们想知道，多么富裕才恰到好处。地球能支撑什么样的消费水平？什么时候拥有更多财富无法再明显增加人们的满足感呢？

1. The emergence of the affluent society after World War II _____.

    [A] gave birth to a new generation of upper class consumers

    [B] gave rise to the dominance of the new egoism

    [C] led to the reform of the retailing system

    [D] resulted in the worship of consumerism

2. Apart from enormous productivity, another important impetus to high consumption is _____.

    [A] the conversion of the sale of goods into rituals

    [B] the people's desire for a rise in their living standards

    [C] the imbalance that has existed between production and consumption

    [D] the concept that one's success is measured by how much they consume

3. Why does the author say high consumption is a mixed blessing?

    [A] Because poverty still exists in an affluent society.

    [B] Because moral values are sacrificed in pursuit of material satisfaction.

    [C] Because overconsumption won't last long due to unrestricted population growth.

    [D] Because traditional rituals are often neglected in the process of modernization.

4. According to the passage, consumerist culture _____.

    [A] cannot thrive on a fragile economy

    [B] will not aggravate environmental problems

    [C] cannot satisfy human spiritual needs

    [D] will not alleviate poverty in wealthy countries

5. It can be inferred from the passage that _____.

   [A] human spiritual needs should match material affluence

   [B] there is never an end to satisfying people's material needs

   [C] whether high consumption should be encouraged is still an issue

   [D] how to keep consumption at a reasonable level remains a problem

◆ 解题之路 ◆

1. 【答案】D 【题型】事实细节题。

   【思路】根据题干关键词affluent society和after World War II，可从第一段找到信息："……我们巨大的生产力经济……要求我们把消费作为自己的生活方式，把购买和使用商品变成一种生活习惯，在消费中寻求精神满足和自我满足……我们以不断增长的比例消耗、烧尽、用完、更换和丢弃东西。"这几句引用的话其实表达的是一个主题："二战"后的富裕时代，人们崇拜消费主义，故选项[D]正确。

2. 【答案】D 【题型】事实细节题。

   【思路】根据题干关键词high consumption可定位到第三段，答案在第二句；本题也用排除法。选项[A]的说法与第一段不符；选项[B]、[C]文中并未提及，只有选项[D]正确。第三段首句说："消费已成为工业社会上生活的中心支柱，甚至已嵌入社会价值中。"有关"社会价值"，本段末句说"……消费主义所界定的成功论正在日益盛行"。综合这两处，可知选项[D]正确。

3. 【答案】B 【题型】原因细节题。

   【思路】根据题干关键词a mixed blessing可定位到第五段："具有讽刺意味的是，高度消费对人类而言也是祸福相依的。长期以来受人推崇的价值观念，如诚实的品质、良好的工作、友谊、家庭和社团等往往在追求财富的过程中被牺牲掉了。"前一句是果，后一句是因，故选项[B]正确。

4. 【答案】C 【题型】事实细节题。

   【思路】根据题干关键词consumerist culture可定位到第六段："因此，工业国家里许多人都感觉：他们富足的世界实际上空空如也——那是因为被消费主义的文化误导了，他们试图用物质的东西来满足社会的、心理的和精神的必要需求，却一无所获"，综合全段，只有选项[C]的说法符合原文。

5. 【答案】D 【题型】推理判断题。

   【思路】最后一段有两个问句：地球能承受什么水平的消费？什么时候拥有更多财富无

138

法再明显增加人们的满足感呢？这两个问题其实都是在针对"如何保持合理的消费水平"而提出的。故只有选项[D]正确。

词汇精解

1. affluence [ˈæfluəns] n. 富足，富裕
2. retailing [ˈriːteɪlɪŋ] a. 零售的，零售业的
3. analyst [ˈænəlɪst] n. 分解者，分析家
4. proclaim [prəˈkleɪm] v. 宣布；显示；声称
5. enormously [ɪˈnɔːməsli] ad. 巨大地；非常
6. productive [prəˈdʌktɪv] a. 生产性的；能产的；富有成效的
7. consumption [kənˈsʌmpʃn] n. 消费；消费量
8. convert [kənˈvɜːt] v. 使改变；使转换
9. ritual [ˈrɪtʃuəl] n. 典礼；仪式；惯例
10. spiritual [ˈspɪrɪtʃuəl] a. 精神的；灵魂的
11. satisfaction [ˌsætɪsˈfækʃn] n. 满意，满足；令人满足的事物
12. prevalent [ˈprevələnt] a. 普遍的，盛行的，流行的
13. overconsumption [ˌəʊvəkənˈsʌmpʃn] n. 过度消费
14. environmental [ɪnˌvaɪrənˈmentl] a. 周围的；环境的
15. severity [sɪˈverɪti] n. 严肃；严格；严重性
16. but [bʌt] prep. 除了
17. plenty [ˈplenti] n. 大量；丰富；富足
18. somehow [ˈsʌmhaʊ] ad. 不知何故
19. hollow [ˈhɒləʊ] a. 空的；虚伪的；空腹的
20. mislead [mɪsˈliːd] v. 误导
21. fruitlessly [ˈfruːtləsli] ad. 徒劳地；无益地；毫无效果地
22. essentially [ɪˈsenʃəli] ad. 本质上，实质上
23. psychological [ˌsaɪkəˈlɒdʒɪkl] a. 心理的
24. nomad [ˈnəʊmæd] n. 游牧民族，流浪者
25. herd [hɜːd] n. 兽群，牧群
26. fragile [ˈfrædʒaɪl] a. 易碎的；脆弱的（活译为"贫瘠的"）
27. grassland [ˈɡrɑːslænd] n. 牧草地；草原
28. destruction [dɪˈstrʌkʃn] n. 毁灭，破坏
29. result [rɪˈzʌlt] v. 导致；出现
30. wonder [ˈwʌndə(r)] v. 对……感到惊奇；想知道
31. noticeably [ˈnəʊtɪsəbli] ad. 显著地，明显地

难句解析

1. Early in the age of affluence that followed World War Ⅱ, an American retailing analyst named Victor Lebow proclaimed, "Our enormously productive economy demands that we make consumption our way of life, that we convert the buying and use of goods into rituals, that we seek our spiritual satisfaction, our ego satisfaction, in consumption."

"二战"之后经济繁盛之初,美国零售业分析家维克托·勒博宣称:"我们巨大的生产力经济要求我们把消费作为自己的生活方式,把购买和使用商品变成一种生活习惯,在消费中寻求精神满足和自我满足。"

结构分析:这个句子可以切分为:(Early in the age of affluence//that followed World War Ⅱ//), (an American retailing analyst//named Victor Lebow//proclaimed), ("Our enormously productive economy... demands//that we make consumption our way of life,//that we convert the buying and use of goods into rituals,//that we seek our spiritual satisfaction, our ego satisfaction, in consumption."//) 第一部分是时间状语,分隔号内是 that 引导的从句作 age 的定语;第二部分是主干的主谓结构,即:an American retailing analyst... proclaimed,过去分词短语 named Victor Lebow 是 retailing analyst 的后置定语;第三部分是 proclaimed 的宾语从句,该从句的主干是 Our enormously productive economy demands that... that... that...,第一个 that 引导的宾语从句中,our way of life 是宾语 consumption 的补足语,第二个 that 引导的宾语从句中,into rituals 也是宾语 the buying and use of goods 的补足语。

2. Opinion surveys in the world's two largest economies—Japan and the United States—show consumerist definitions of success becoming ever more prevalent.

在世界两大经济强国——日本和美国所进行的民意调查显示,消费主义所界定的成功论正在日益盛行。

结构分析:这个句子的主干是 Opinion surveys... show... definitions,in... economies 是主语的后置定语,Japan and the United Sates 是 two largest economies 的同位语,现在分词短语 becoming... prevalent 是宾语 definitions 的补足语。

3. Overconsumption by the world's fortunate is an environmental problem unmatched in severity by anything but perhaps population growth.

对世界财富的过度消费是一种环境问题，其严重性或许除了人口增长的危害外没有其他问题能与之相比。

结构分析：这个句子的主干是 Overconsumption... is an environmental problem，by the world's fortunate 是主语 Overconsumption 的后置定语，过去分词 unmatched 是表语 environmental problem 的后置定语，in severity 是范围状语，by... growth 是状语，其中的 but 是介词，相当于 except。

4. Thus many in the industrial lands have a sense that their world of plenty is somehow hollow—that, misled by a consumerist culture, they have been fruitlessly attempting to satisfy what are essentially social, psychological and spiritual needs with material things.

因此，工业国家里许多人都感觉他们富足的世界实际上空空如也——那是因为被消费主义的文化误导了，他们试图用物质来满足社会的、心理的和精神的必要需求，却一无所获。

结构分析：这是一个主从复合句，可以切分为：(Thus many in the industrial lands have a sense) (that their world of plenty is somehow hollow)—(that,//misled by a consumerist culture,//they have been fruitlessly attempting to satisfy//what are essentially social, psychological and spiritual needs//with material things)。第一部分是主句，in... lands 是主语 many 的后置定语；第二、三部分均是前面 sense 的同位语从句；第三部分中的过去分词短语 misled... culture 是原因状语，what...needs 是 satisfy 的宾语从句，with material things 是方式状语。

5. And hungry nomads turn their herds out onto fragile African grassland, reducing it to desert.

饥饿的游牧民族把他们的牧群赶进贫瘠的非洲草地，使草地退化成沙漠。

结构分析：这个句子的主语是 hungry nomads，宾语是 their herds，out... grassland 是方位状语，现在分词结构 reducing... desert 是结果状语，it 指代前面的 grassland，介词短语 to desert 是宾语 it 的补足语。

6. If environmental destruction results when people have either too little or too much, we are left to wonder how much is enough.

如果过于贫穷或过于富裕都会导致环境破坏，那么，我们想知道多么富余才恰到好处。

结构分析：If 引导的条件状语从句中，主语是 environmental destruction，谓语是 results， when 引导的时间状语从句中，主语是 people，谓语是 have，宾语是 either too little or too much；主句的主语是 we，谓语是 are left to wonder，宾语是 how much 引导的从句。

| 7. When does having more cease to add noticeably to human satisfaction? | 什么时候拥有更多财富无法再明显增加人们的满足感呢？ |

结构分析：这个问句的主语是动名词结构 having more，谓语是 cease to add... to，宾语是 human satisfaction。

Text 3

1 Technological revolutions are best appreciated from a distance. The great inventions of the 19th century, from electric power to the internal-combustion engine, transformed the human condition. Yet for workers who lived through the upheaval, the experience of industrialisation was harsh: full of hard toil in crowded, disease-ridden cities.

2 The modern digital revolution—with its hallmarks of computer power, connectivity and data ubiquity—has brought iPhones and the internet, not crowded tenements and cholera. But it is disrupting and dividing the world of work on a scale not seen for more than a century. Vast wealth is being created without many workers; and for all but an elite few, work no longer guarantees a rising income.

3 So far, the upheaval has been felt most by low- and mid-skilled workers in rich countries. The incomes of the highly educated—those with the skills to complement computers—have soared, while pay for others lower down the skill ladder has been squeezed. In half of all OECD countries real median

1 要认识科技革命，最好是与它保持些距离。19世纪的伟大发明，从电力到内燃机，改变了人类境况。但是对于经历了这场剧变的工人来说，工业化是一段艰苦之旅：在人潮汹涌、疾病肆虐的城市里，他们做的都是苦工。

2 现代数字革命，以计算机能力、计算机连接性能、无处不在的数据为标志，为人类带来的是苹果手机和因特网，而不是人满为患的公寓和霍乱。但数字革命正在以百余年来未有之规模打乱和分割职业领域。巨额财富的创造靠的不再是工人；除少数精英外，努力工作不再是收入提高的保障。

3 目前，对于这场剧变感触最深的是富裕国家的中低级技术工人。受过高等教育又能熟练操作电脑的工作者，收入高速增长；技术水平低的工作者，收入却在缩减。在经济合作与发展组织成员国中，半数国家的实

wages have stagnated since 2000. Countries where employment is growing at a decent clip, such as Germany or Britain, are among those where wages have been squeezed most.

4   In the coming years the disruption will be felt by more people in more places, for three reasons. First, the rise of machine intelligence means more workers will see their jobs threatened. The effects will be felt further up the skill ladder, as auditors, radiologists and researchers of all sorts begin competing with machines. Technology will enable some doctors or professors to be much more productive, leaving others redundant.

5   Second, wealth creation in the digital era has so far generated little employment. Entrepreneurs can turn their ideas into firms with huge valuations and hardly any staff. Oculus VR, a maker of virtual-reality headsets with 75 employees, was bought by Facebook earlier this year for $2 billion. With fewer than 50,000 workers each, the giants of the modern tech economy such as Google and Facebook are a small fraction of the size of the 20th century's industrial behemoths.

6   Third, these shifts are now evident in emerging economies. Foxconn, long the symbol of China's manufacturing economy, at one point employed 1.5m workers to assemble electronics for Western markets. Now, as the costs of labour rise

and those of automated manufacturing fall, Foxconn is swapping workers for robots. China's future is more Alibaba than assembly line: the e-commerce company that recently made a spectacular debut on the New York Stock Exchange employs only 20,000 people.

7   The digital transformation seems to be undermining poor countries' traditional route to catch-up growth. Moving the barely literate masses from fields to factories has become harder. If India, for instance, were to follow China's development path, it would need skilled engineers and managers to build factories to employ millions of manufacturing workers. But, thanks to technological change, its educated elite is now earning high salaries selling IT services to foreigners. The digital revolution has made an industrial one uneconomic.

加和自动化制造成本的下降，富士康已开始使用机器人来取代工人。中国未来主要依靠的将不再是生产线，而是阿里巴巴那样的企业：这家仅拥有2万名员工的电商最近在纽约证券交易所华丽上市。

7   数字时代的转变似乎破坏了贫穷国家追赶式增长的传统路线，鼓励受教育程度低的农村人口去工厂打工变得更加困难。比如印度要想效仿中国的发展路线，就需要娴熟的工程师和管理人才去建造工厂，并且雇用数百万制造业工人。但是由于发生了技术变革，印度受到良好教育的精英开始通过向外国人提供IT服务来获得高收入。数字革命使工业革命显得效益低下。

1. Technological revolutions are best appreciated from a distance mainly because _____.

   [A] the great inventions transformed human lives

   [B] humans suffered a lot while enjoying benefits

   [C] vast wealth has been accumulated automatically

   [D] a rising income can't be guaranteed

2. Germany and Britain are mentioned to illustrate that _____.

   [A] skills are necessary for a higher pay

   [B] their economy has stopped growing

   [C] employment is growing at a decent pace

   [D] real median wages have stagnated

3. It can be inferred from Paragraph 4 that _____.

   [A] competing with machines is nonsense

   [B] redundancy is becoming a trend

[C] machine intelligence offers more jobs

[D] many workers feel threatened

4. In order to follow the digital transformation, poor countries need to _____.

[A] move illiterate masses to factories

[B] expand employment scale

[C] renovate outdated factories

[D] produce more highly-skilled people

5. The proper title for this text may be _____.

[A] Technological Revolutions: a Disaster

[B] Digital Transformation: a Hopeless Story

[C] Technological Revolutions: a Disguised Blessing

[D] Digital Transformation: Struggling for Survival

◆ 解题之路 ◆

1. 【答案】B 【题型】主旨大意题。

【思路】根据题干关键词可定位到首段。出题点在第三句，即Yet之后，符合转折词后是答案的解题原则。该句意思是：但是对于经历了这场剧变的工人来说，工业化是一段艰苦之旅；在人潮汹涌、疾病肆虐的城市里，他们做的都是苦工。而该段第二句主要说明了技术革命给人类带来的好处。由此可知，技术革命优劣明显。综合对比四个选项，选项[B]正确。选项[A]中的transformed属于积极意义的词汇，只涉及了技术革命之影响的好的一方面，故排除；选项[C]、[D]均是对第二段第三句的改写，与该题干所问的问题无关。

2. 【答案】A 【题型】例子题。

【思路】根据题干关键词Germany和Britain可定位到第三段末句。但例子题的解题方法是：找到例子出处后，要在例子前面寻找答案信息，即答案不在例子中，例子是为所处段落的主旨服务的。按照这种逻辑，该段首句就是这段文字的主旨：目前，对于这场剧变感触最深的是富裕国家的中低级技术工人。对比四个选项，选项[A]最符合题意，属于正话反说的出题套路。选项[B]的信息在该段没有描述，属于无中生有；选项[C]属于例子里面的内容，故排除；选项[D]的信息在该段第三句，属于张冠李戴。

3. 【答案】B 【题型】推理判断题。

【思路】推理判断题的特点是：答案相对比较深刻，需要适度推导，即文中直接可找到的信息一般不是答案。选项[A]的competing with machines在该段第三句，但nonsense属于无中生有，故排除；选项[C]与该段内容相悖；选项[D]在第二句可直接找到，直白肤浅无须推理判断，故排除；选项[B]在该段末句有所提及，但需要适度推理，因此符合题意。

4. 【答案】D 【题型】事实细节题。

   【思路】根据题干关键词the digital transformation，poor countries可定位到末段。选项[A]与该段论述相悖；选项[B]、[C]均属于无中生有；选项[D]在第三句体现出来：If India, for instance, were to follow China's development path, it would need skilled engineers and managers...，故为正确选项。

5. 【答案】C 【题型】主旨大意题。

   【思路】纵观全文，主要谈及技术革命给人类社会带来的有利与不利两方面。选项[A]的disaster过于负面，应排除；选项[B]的hopeless也是过于消极的负面之词；选项[D]的struggling for survival没有信息支持；故正确答案为选项[C]。一般而言，主旨大意题不要选择过于消极负面的选项作为答案，这是出题人一贯的题目设置思路，也是常用的应试技巧。

词汇精解

1. technological [ˌteknəˈlɒdʒɪkl] a. 技术的；科技的
2. revolution [ˌrevəˈluːʃn] n. 革命
3. appreciate [əˈpriːʃɪeɪt] v. 欣赏；体会；理解
4. transform [trænsˈfɔːm] v. 改变；改造
5. upheaval [ʌpˈhiːvl] n. 剧变；动乱
6. industrialisation [ɪnˌdʌstrɪəlaɪˈzeɪʃn] n. 工业化
7. harsh [hɑːʃ] a. 艰苦的；艰难的
8. toil [tɔɪl] n. 劳作；劳动
9. disease-ridden a. 疾病肆虐的
10. digital [ˈdɪdʒɪtl] a. 数字的；数码的
11. hallmark [ˈhɔːlmɑːk] n. 标志；特点
12. connectivity [kɒnekˈtɪvɪtɪ] n. 连接性；连贯性
13. ubiquity [juːˈbɪkwətɪ] n. 无处不在
14. tenement [ˈtenəmənt] n. 地产；公寓
15. cholera [ˈkɒlərə] n. 霍乱
16. vast [vɑːst] a. 巨大的
17. elite [eɪˈliːt] n. 精英；精英阶层
18. guarantee [ˌɡærənˈtiː] v. 保证；保障
19. complement [ˈkɒmplɪmənt] v. 补充
20. soar [sɔː(r)] v. 翱翔；飙升
21. ladder [ˈlædə(r)] n. 梯子；阶梯
22. stagnate [stæɡˈneɪt] v. 停滞
23. decent [ˈdiːsnt] a. 体面的；得体的
24. intelligence [ɪnˈtelɪdʒəns] n. 智力；智能
25. threaten [ˈθretn] v. 威胁
26. auditor [ˈɔːdɪtə(r)] n. 审计员
27. radiologist [reɪdɪˈɒlədʒɪst] n. 放射科医生

28. redundant [rɪˈdʌndənt] a. 富余的；被解雇的	38. assemble [əˈsembl] v. 组装；装配
29. generate [ˈdʒenəreɪt] v. 生产；产生	39. electronics [ɪlekˈtrɒnɪks] n. 电子；电子学
30. entrepreneur [ˌɒntrəprəˈnɜː(r)] n. 企业家；实业家	40. automated [ˈɔːtəˌmeɪtɪd] a. 自动的；自动化的
31. staff [stɑːf] n. 员工；工人	41. swap [swɒp] v. 交换
32. virtual-reality a. 虚拟现实的	42. spectacular [spekˈtækjəl(r)] a. 壮观的；辉煌的
33. headset [ˈhedset] n. 耳麦；头戴式视图器	43. debut [deɪbjuː] n. 首秀；首次演出
34. fraction [ˈfrækʃn] n. 小部分	44. undermine [ˌʌndəˈmaɪn] v. 危害；迫害
35. behemoth [bɪˈhiːmɒθ] n. 巨兽；巨头	45. barely [ˈbeəlɪ] ad. 几乎没有
36. emerging [ɪˈmɜːdʒɪŋ] a. 出现的；新兴的	46. literate [ˈlɪtərət] a. 有知识的；有文化的
37. symbol [ˈsɪmbl] n. 标志；象征	47. mass [mæs] n. 人群；大块

难句解析

1. The great inventions of the 19th century, from electric power to the internal-combustion engine, transformed the human condition.

19世纪的伟大发明，从电力到内燃机，改变了人类境况。

结构分析：这个句子可以划分为：The great inventions of the 19th century, (from electric power to the internal-combustion engine), transformed the human condition. 句子主语是 The great inventions of the 19th century，谓语是 transformed，宾语是 the human condition；括号里的介词短语作主语的后置定语。

2. The modern digital revolution—with its hallmarks of computer power, connectivity and data ubiquity—has brought iPhones and the internet, not crowded tenements and cholera.

现代数字革命，以计算机能力、计算机连接性能、无处不在的数据为标志，为人类带来的是苹果手机和因特网，而不是人满为患的公寓和霍乱。

结构分析：这个句子可以划分为：The modern digital revolution—with its hallmarks of computer power, connectivity and data ubiquity—has brought *iPhones and the internet, not crowded tenements and cholera*. 句子主语是 The modern digital revolution，谓语是 has brought，宾语是斜体部分的名

词短语；破折号之间下划线部分的介词短语作主语的后置定语。

> 3. But it is disrupting and dividing the world of work on a scale not seen for more than a century.
>
> 但数字革命正在以百余年来未有之规模打乱和分割职业领域。

结构分析：这个句子可以划分为：But it is disrupting and dividing the world of work *on a scale (not seen for more than a century)*. 斜体部分的介词短语作状语；括号里的过去分词短语作 scale 的后置定语。

> 4. The incomes of the highly educated—those with the skills to complement computers—have soared, while pay for others lower down the skill ladder has been squeezed.
>
> 受过高等教育又能熟练操作电脑的工作者，收入高速增长；技术水平低的工作者，收入却在缩减。

结构分析：这个句子可以划分为：The incomes of the highly educated—those (with the skills to complement computers)—have soared, //while pay for others (lower down the skill ladder) has been squeezed. 以 "//" 为界，while 连接了两个并列分句；前一个分句的主语是 The incomes of the highly educated，谓语是 have soared，破折号之间的名词短语作前面 the highly educated 的同位语，括号里的介词短语作 those 的后置定语；后一个分句的主语是 pay for others，谓语是 has been squeezed，括号里的介词短语作 others 的后置定语。

> 5. Countries where employment is growing at a decent clip, such as Germany or Britain, are among those where wages have been squeezed most.
>
> 在就业增长有所放缓的国家，比如德国或英国，工资水平下滑最快。

结构分析：这个句子可以划分为：Countries (where employment is growing at a decent clip), (such as Germany or Britain), are among those (where wages have been squeezed most). 括号外的内容是主干；前两个括号里的内容均是修饰 Countries 的；第三个括号里的内容是修饰 those 的。

> 6. Technology will enable some doctors or professors to be much more productive, leaving others redundant.
>
> 对于一部分医生或教授来说，科技能大大提高他们的工作效率，但是其他行业的工作者将丢掉饭碗。

结构分析：这个句子可以划分为：Technology will enable some doctors or professors to be much more productive, *leaving others redundant*. 句子使用了 enable sb. to do sth. 结构；斜体部分的

现在分词短语作结果状语，leave 这里相当于 make，形容词 redundant 作宾语 others 的补语。

> **7.** Foxconn, long the symbol of China's manufacturing economy, at one point employed 1.5m workers to assemble electronics for Western markets.
>
> 富士康公司长期以来都是中国制造业经济的代表，过去曾雇用过 150 万名员工为西方市场组装电子设备。

结构分析：这个句子可以划分为：Foxconn, (long the symbol of China's manufacturing economy), *at one point* employed 1.5m workers <u>to assemble electronics for Western markets</u>. 句子主干是 Foxconn employed 1.5m workers；括号里的名词短语作主语 Foxconn 的同位语，其中的 long 是副词，相当于 for long；斜体部分的介词短语作时间状语；下划线部分的不定式作目的状语。

> **8.** The digital revolution has made an industrial one uneconomic.
>
> 数字革命使工业革命显得效益低下。

结构分析：这个句子的主语是 The digital revolution，谓语是 has made，宾语是 an industrial one，其中的 one 指代 revolution；形容词 uneconomic 作宾语补足语。

Text 4

1 Central bankers once used to inveigh against wage inflation. Guarding against a return to the ruinous price-wage spirals of the 1970s was a constant preoccupation. Since the financial crisis, however, they have started to fret about the opposite concern: stagnant wages and the growing risk of deflation.

2 There has been a squeeze on pay in the rich world for several years now. Between 2010 and 2013 real (inflation-adjusted) wages were flat across the OECD, according to its annual "Employment Outlook," published on September 3rd. Real wages have barely grown at all in America over that period and have fallen in the euro area and Japan. Declines have been particularly sharp in the

1 央行行长们过去常常猛烈抨击工资的通胀，防止再次发生20世纪70年代工资毁灭性的螺旋式快速上涨的局面是他们一贯的关注焦点。但自金融危机发生以后，他们开始担忧起恰好相反的问题：停滞不前的工资以及不断增长的通货紧缩的风险。

2 工资停滞增长的现象在富裕国家已经持续好几年了。根据经济合作与发展组织9月3日发布的年度"就业展望"报告，从2010年到2013年其成员国的实际（扣除物价上涨因素）工资几乎没有变化。在这一段时期，美国的实际工资几乎没有增长，而欧元区和日本则出现了工资下降。下降的幅度在欧元

troubled peripheral economies of the euro zone, such as Portugal and Spain, but real wages have also tumbled in Britain.

3   These sharp adjustments have hurt but were in large part unavoidable. Real wages can grow in the long run only at the pace of productivity. If productivity has deteriorated, as for example in Britain since 2007, real wages must fall. The crisis-hit countries of the euro area, meanwhile, needed to lower labour costs to reverse their loss of competitiveness relative to their northern neighbours (the currency union makes the more common form of adjustment, a devaluation, impossible).

4   In most advanced countries—though not in Britain or Italy—labour productivity is picking up again. Moreover, the downward pressure on wages from high unemployment is easing in some countries, including America and Britain (in the euro area, alas, the jobless rate is still 11.5%). Yet even though unemployment in America has dropped from a peak of 10% in late 2009 to 6.2%, growth in even nominal wages (i.e., not adjusted for inflation) is tame. In the private sector, they had been rising by around 3.5% a year before the crisis, but are currently increasing by less than 2% a year. In Britain, where unemployment has fallen from a peak of 8.4% to 6.4%, nominal pay is growing by 0.6% a year, far below the pre-crisis average of 4%.

5   Divergent trends in the supply of labour

区那些陷入困境的经济边缘化的国家尤为严重，比如葡萄牙和西班牙，但在英国实际工资也出现了大幅度下降。

3   这些大幅的调整其过程是痛苦的，但在很大程度上也是不可避免的。从长远看，实际工资只能按照劳动生产率变化的速度来增长。如果生产率下降了，比如像2007年后的英国，实际工资也一定会下降。与此同时，欧元区受金融危机冲击严重的国家，需要通过降低劳工成本来提升相较北方邻国下降的竞争力（欧元区货币联盟的形式使得更常见的经济调整政策，如货币贬值变得不可能）。

4   在大多数发达国家（不包括英国和意大利），劳动生产率正在提高。并且在美国、英国等一些国家，高失业率带来的工资下行压力也正在减小（在欧元区，失业率仍高达11.5%）。但是，虽然美国的失业率已经从2009年末峰值的10%降到了6.2%，名义工资（未经过通胀调整）的上涨仍然十分缓慢。在私有部门，发生危机前工资的年均增速还达到了大约3.5%，而现在每年的增速还不到2%。在英国，失业率已经从高峰时的8.4%回落到了6.4%，名义工资每年的增速还是只有0.6%，远低于危机前每年4%的平均水平。

5   劳动力供给的趋势差异有助

help to explain why the pay squeeze has been more intense in Britain than in America. The British labour participation rate—the proportion of adults who are either in work or looking for jobs—has returned to its previous peak of almost 64% and looks set to rise further. By contrast, America's participation rate has declined by three percentage points since the financial crisis and is now bumping along at around 63%.

6 Working out to what extent the low participation rate is structural, meaning that it will persist, rather than cyclical, caused by a weaker-than-usual recovery, will be crucial in determining when the Federal Reserve raises interest rates. The Fed has seen quiescent nominal wages as evidence the labour market has more slack than falling unemployment suggests. But Janet Yellen, its chairman, recently said that the weakness in wages might be deceptive. New research by the San Francisco Fed suggests that many employers froze pay during the recession because workers resist cuts in nominal pay more fiercely than the erosion of their purchasing power by inflation. Employers, unable to reduce wages when times were bad, have not been raising them now that times are better. But once this "pent-up wage deflation" has run its course, pay growth might take off.

1. Between 2010 and 2013, real wages in many regions and countries go down EXCEPT _____.
   [A] Japan

[B] Britain

[C] Spain

[D] America

2. Real wages see a downward trend mainly because of _____.

   [A] low productivity

   [B] redundancy of employees

   [C] frugality of bosses

   [D] expansion of industry

3. In most advanced countries, with productivity gaining speed, wages _____.

   [A] will see a sharp increase in near future

   [B] still remain stagnant or grow slowly

   [C] have no hope to rise at all

   [D] differ little from country to country

4. The pay squeeze is more serious in Britain than in America because _____.

   [A] more British adults lose their jobs

   [B] more American adults lose their jobs

   [C] more British adults participate in work

   [D] more American adults participate in work

5. According to the Federal Reserve, quiescent nominal wages _____.

   [A] result in failing unemployment

   [B] result from failing unemployment

   [C] lead to weaker purchasing power

   [D] result from unsatisfactory labor market

➡ 解题之路 ⬅

1. 【答案】D 【题型】事实细节题。

   【思路】根据题干关键词Between 2010 and 2013，real wages，go down可定位到原文第二段第二句及之后的内容，重点关注提到的几个国名或地名。可以看出，欧元区、日本、葡萄牙、西班牙和英国都是属于工资下降的国家，提到美国时说工资没有增长，但没有说下降，因此正确答案就是美国，选项[D]正确。

2. 【答案】A 【题型】原因细节题。

【思路】根据题干关键词Real wages see a downward trend以及出题段落顺序原则可定位到第三段。答案存在于第二句和第三句：从长远看，实际工资只能按照劳动生产率变化的速度来增长。如果生产率下降了，比如像2007年后的英国，实际工资也一定会下降。选项[A]是对这两句的浓缩提炼，故为正确选项。其余三个选项的信息在该段及其他各段均未提及，属于无中生有。

3. 【答案】B 【题型】事实细节题。

   【思路】根据题干关键词In most advanced countries, productivity可定位到第四段。该段大意是：大多数发达国家的劳动生产率正在提高，但工资未见明显增长。选项[A]与原文论述相悖；选项[B]符合文意，为正确答案；选项[C]过于绝对，一般要排除；选项[D]在文中没有信息支持，属于无中生有。

4. 【答案】C 【题型】原因细节题。

   【思路】根据题干关键词The pay squeeze, Britain, America以及出题段落顺序原则可定位到第五段。答案就在第二句：英国的劳动人口参与率——成年人中在职或求职人口的占比，已经恢复到早先约64%的峰值，而且看起来还将继续上升。选项[C]体现了该句的含义，故为正确答案。选项[A]、[B]均属于无中生有；选项[D]与该段论述相反，故排除。

5. 【答案】D 【题型】事实细节题。

   【思路】根据题干关键词the Federal Reserve, quiescent nominal wages可定位到原文末段，答案在第二句：美联储将静止的名义工资看作是劳动力市场比失业率下降所表现得更加疲软的依据。选项[D]符合该句的描述，unsatisfactory替换了原文的slack。其余三个选项属于张冠李戴。

词汇精解

1. inflation [ɪnˈfleɪʃn] n. 通货膨胀
2. ruinous [ˈruːɪnəs] a. 灾难性的；毁灭性的
3. spiral [ˈspaɪrəl] n. 螺旋
4. constant [ˈkɒnstənt] a. 持续的
5. preoccupation [prɪˌɒkjʊˈpeɪʃn] n. 全神贯注；关注
6. concern [kənˈsɜːn] n. 关注；忧虑
7. stagnant [ˈstæɡnənt] a. 停滞的；不变的
8. deflation [dɪˈfleɪʃn] n. 通货紧缩
9. annual [ˈænjʊəl] a. 年度的；每年的
10. peripheral [pəˈrɪfərəl] a. 边缘的
11. tumble [ˈtʌmbl] v. 跌倒；翻腾
12. adjustment [əˈdʒʌstmənt] n. 调整；调节
13. deteriorate [dɪˈtɪərɪəreɪt] v. 恶化；变坏
14. meanwhile [ˈmiːnwaɪl] ad. 同时
15. reverse [rɪˈvɜːs] v. 逆转；改变
16. currency [ˈkʌrənsɪ] n. 货币
17. union [ˈjuːnɪən] n. 同盟；联盟

18. devaluation [ˌdiːvæljʊ'eɪʃn] n. 贬值
19. downward ['daʊnwəd] a. 向下的；下行的
20. ease [iːz] v. 缓解；减轻
21. peak [piːk] n. 巅峰；峰值
22. nominal ['nɒmɪnl] a. 名义的；名字的
23. divergent [daɪ'vɜːdʒənt] a. 不同的；差异的
24. intense [ɪn'tens] a. 强烈的；剧烈的
25. proportion [prə'pɔːʃn] n. 比例
26. persist [pə'sɪst] v. 坚持；持续
27. cyclical ['sɪklɪkəl] a. 循环的；周期的
28. recovery [rɪ'kʌvərɪ] n. 恢复；康复
29. crucial ['kruːʃl] a. 关键的；重要的
30. quiescent [kwɪ'esnt] a. 静止的；沉寂的
31. deceptive [dɪ'septɪv] a. 欺骗性的
32. froze [frəʊz] v.（使）结冰（freeze 的过去式）；冻结；（使）冻住
33. recession [rɪ'seʃn] n. 衰退；后退
34. fiercely ['fɪəslɪ] ad. 猛烈地；剧烈地
35. erosion [ɪ'rəʊʒn] n. 腐蚀；侵蚀

难句解析

1. Guarding against a return to the ruinous price-wage spirals of the 1970s was a constant preoccupation.

防止再次发生 20 世纪 70 年代工资毁灭性的螺旋式快速上涨的局面是他们一贯的关注焦点。

结构分析：这是一个特殊倒装句，正常语序是 A constant preoccupation was guarding against a return to the ruinous price-wage spirals of the 1970s，倒装的目的是强调 guarding against a return...；介词短语 to the ruinous price-wage spirals of the 1970s 作 return 的后置定语。

2. The crisis-hit countries of the euro area, meanwhile, needed to lower labour costs to reverse their loss of competitiveness relative to their northern neighbours.

与此同时，欧元区受金融危机冲击严重的国家，需要通过降低劳工成本来提升相较北方邻国下降的竞争力。

结构分析：这个句子可以划分为：The crisis-hit countries of the euro area, meanwhile, needed to lower labour costs to reverse their loss of competitiveness (relative to their northern neighbours). 下划线部分的不定式作目的状语，括号里的形容词短语作 their loss of competitiveness 的后置定语。

3. The currency union makes the more common form of adjustment, a devaluation, impossible.

欧元区货币联盟的形式使得更常见的经济调整政策，如货币贬值变得不可能。

结构分析：这个句子可以划分为：The currency union makes the more common form of adjustment, a devaluation, *impossible.* 句子主语是 The currency union，谓语是 makes，宾语是 the more common form of adjustment，下划线部分是一个名词，作宾语的同位语；斜体的 impossible 作宾语补足语。

4. The British labour participation rate—the proportion of adults who are either in work or looking for jobs—has returned to its previous peak of almost 64% and looks set to rise further.

英国的劳动人口参与率——成年人中在职或求职人口的占比，已经恢复到早先约64%的峰值，而且看起来还将继续上升。

结构分析：这个句子可以划分为：The British labour participation rate—*the proportion of adults (who are either in work or looking for jobs)*—has returned to its previous peak of almost 64% and looks set to rise further. 句子主语是 The British labour participation rate，谓语是 has returned 和 looks set to rise；破折号之间斜体部分是一个名词短语，作主语的同位语，其中括号里 who 引导的是 adults 的定语从句。

5. Working out to what extent the low participation rate is structural, meaning that it will persist, rather than cyclical, caused by a weaker-than-usual recovery, will be crucial in determining when the Federal Reserve raises interest rates.

弄清由比往常更为缓慢的经济复苏造成的低劳动人口参与率在多大程度上是结构性的，也就是说它是持续性的而不是周期性的，对于美联储确定什么时候升息至关重要。

结构分析：这个句子可以划分为：Working out to what extent (that) the low participation rate is structural, (meaning that it will persist), rather than cyclical, (caused by a weaker-than-usual recovery), will be crucial in determining when the Federal Reserve raises interest rates. 下划线部分是主干，主语是动名词短语 Working out... rather than cyclical，其中 structural 和 cyclical 属于并列关系，谓语是系动词 will be，表语是 crucial；to what extent 作 work out 的宾语，之后的句子是 extent 的同位语，省略了引导词 that；现在分词 meaning 作伴随状语；过去分词短语 caused... recovery 作定语修饰 the low participation rate；介词短语 in determining 属于 in doing 结构，作状语，when 引导的从句作 determine 的宾语。

6. The Fed has seen quiescent nominal wages as evidence the labour market has more slack than falling unemployment suggests.

美联储将静止的名义工资看作是劳动力市场比失业率下降所表现得更加疲软的依据。

结构分析：这个句子可以划分为：The Fed has seen quiescent nominal wages as evidence (that the labour market has more slack <u>than falling unemployment suggests</u>)。see... as... 属于固定搭配，意思是：把……视作……；括号里的从句作 evidence 的同位语，省略了引导词 that；下划线部分是比较状语从句。

> 7. New research by the San Francisco Fed suggests that many employers froze pay during the recession because workers resist cuts in nominal pay more fiercely than the erosion of their purchasing power by inflation.
>
> 美联储旧金山分行的一份新的研究指出，相比通胀对工资购买力造成的侵蚀，工人们更为强烈地抗议名义工资的下降问题，所以即使在经济衰退期许多雇主仍维持工资水平不变。

结构分析：这个句子可以划分为：New research (by the San Francisco Fed) suggests <u>that many employers froze pay during the recession//because workers resist cuts in nominal pay more fiercely than the erosion of their purchasing power (by inflation)</u>。主语是 New research，之后的括号里的介词短语作其后置定语；谓语是 suggests，宾语是下划线部分 that 引导的从句。在该从句中，"//" 前面是主句，froze 是谓语动词；because 引导的原因状语从句中的比较级结构 more... than... 是修饰 resists 的，最后的括号里的介词短语 by inflation 作 the erosion of their purchasing power 的后置定语。

> 8. Employers, unable to reduce wages when times were bad, have not been raising them now that times are better.
>
> 雇主们不能在境遇糟糕的时候降低工资，也不愿意在经济状况好转时调高工资。

结构分析：这个句子可以划分为：Employers, (unable to reduce wages when times were bad), have not been raising them *now that times are better*. 括号里的形容词短语作原因状语；斜体部分是 now that 引导的原因状语从句，修饰前面的 have not been raising them，但理解时要将否定词 not 转移至 now that 之前，即 not 是否定该状语从句的，所以正常含义是：have been raising them not now that times are better，这叫作否定转移现象。

Text 5

1 For more than a decade, Japan has been perceived as the rich world's exception; it has been mired in deflation, with slow growth and ultra-low bond yields. Economists have debated whether its problems

1 十多年来，日本一直被认为是发达国家的例外；它已深陷通货紧缩的泥潭，经济增长缓慢并且国债利息超低。经济学家们曾辩论日本的问

are down to its ageing population, conservative monetary policy or outdated business models.

2　But these days western Europe looks quite Japan-like. Inflation in the euro zone has been heading remorselessly downwards and was just 0.3% in the year to August. The trend rate of economic growth is perceived to be 1% or below. Ten-year bond yields in Germany and Switzerland are well under 1%. Albert Edwards, a strategist at Société Générale, has dubbed these conditions an "ice age" which he predicts will extend across the rich world.

3　If there is an exception in the rich world, it looks like America. The gap between yields on its bonds and on Germany's is now almost as wide as it has been at any point since the euro was created. Despite a rally since the depths of the euro crisis, European equities trade at much lower valuations than those on Wall Street: the cyclically-adjusted price-earnings ratio (or CAPE) for the euro zone is 14.7, according to Absolute Strategy Research, a consulting firm. That for America is 25.7, according to Robert Shiller of Yale University.

4　But is this American exceptionalism based on sound fundamentals, such as a faster-growing economy and better demography? Or will the world's largest economy eventually succumb to the same pressures as Europe and Japan?

5　Part of the explanation for the divergence in sentiment must be America's growth in the second quarter, which was 4.2% at an annual rate.

Unemployment has also fallen much faster than most economists would have predicted a year ago. However, it is a little early to declare that America has returned to the glory days of the 1990s. The healthy numbers for the second quarter followed a surprise drop in GDP in the first. Falling unemployment has in part been caused by people dropping out of the workforce: participation in the labour market is close to its lowest level since the 1970s.

6   As baby boomers retire, it will be hard for America's workforce to grow significantly without a jump in participation. Robert Gordon of Northwestern University predicts that, even if productivity growth is maintained at the 1.3% annual rate seen for much of the past 40 years, future growth in real (adjusted for inflation) GDP per person will be just 0.9%. The IMF believes America's long-term growth rate has fallen to 2%—better than in Europe, but below the 3~3.5% once thought possible.

7   Some forecasters are cheerier. Morgan Stanley, an investment bank, argues that the American recovery could last another five years (leading its strategists to hope that the S&P 500, which recently passed 2,000 for the first time, could reach 3,000). "Debt dynamics paint the picture of a more prudent household sector and well-managed corporate sector, both of which remain far from the heights of leverage typically associated with risks to business-cycle expansions," the bank's economists write. Bulls also

比一年前多数经济学家预测的下降很多。然而，现在宣布美国已重返20世纪90年代的繁荣还为时过早。因为在第二季度看似健康的数据之前是第一季度GDP惊人的下降。失业率的降低部分是由脱离劳动力大军的人们引起的：劳动力市场的参与度接近于20世纪70年代以来的最低水平。

6   随着婴儿潮时代出生的人开始退休，没有劳动力市场参与者的大幅增加，美国的劳动力队伍很难大规模扩大。西北大学的罗伯特·戈登预测，即使生产率增长能保持在过去40年来的高水平，即年增长率为1.3%，未来人均实际GDP增长（调整通货膨胀以后）也仅为0.9%。国际货币基金组织相信美国的长期增长率已经降至2%，比欧洲稍好一些，但是比预想的3%～3.5%低。

7   一些预言者们对此更为高兴。投资银行摩根士丹利称，美国经济复苏还会持续五年（导致其战略家们希望近来首次超过2 000点的标准普尔500指数能够达到3 000点）。"债务的运转情况描绘了一幅更为审慎的房地产和管理良好的公司的画面，二者远远达不到与商业周期扩张有关的风险的杠杆高度。"摩根的经济学家这样写道。多头投资者也指出，美国在

point to America's success in exploiting shale oil and gas, which has lowered energy costs.

8 It is easy to explain how America's distinctive qualities affect the bond markets. Inflation is 1.6 percentage points higher than the euro-zone equivalent (so investors need compensation in the form of a higher yield). Meanwhile, the Federal Reserve is winding down its bond purchases whereas many expect the European Central Bank to be pushed into adopting quantitative easing (and thus buying bonds) later this year.

8 美国独特的品质是如何影响到债券市场的，这很容易解释。通货膨胀率较欧元区经济实力相当的国家高出1.6个百分点（因此投资者需要以更高的债券收益得以补偿）。同时，美联储缩减了债券购买量，而许多人期望欧洲中央银行今年晚些时候被推动采取量化宽松政策（因此而购买债券）。

1. According to the text, western Europe looks similar to Japan in that _____.

   [A] both are advanced regions

   [B] both enjoy high-speed development

   [C] both face ageing population

   [D] both suffer an economic dilemma

2. According to Paragraph 3, which statement is true?

   [A] America's bonds perform worse than those of Germany.

   [B] Wall Street is No.1 financial center in the world.

   [C] America's economy is generally better than Europe.

   [D] Yale University conducted a research for the euro zone.

3. Falling unemployment in America is mainly the result of _____.

   [A] economic growth in the second quarter

   [B] lower participation in the labour market

   [C] a surprise drop in GDP in the first quarter

   [D] economic recession in the second quarter

4. About America's future growth, Robert Gordon's prediction seems _____.

   [A] a little pessimistic

   [B] rather bold

   [C] very optimistic

[D] very accurate

5. Morgan Stanley is optimistic about America's economy because _____.

   [A] America has successfully shed all its debts

   [B] risks about business-cycle expansions are under control

   [C] America has distinctive qualities

   [D] America begins to exploit shale oil and gas

➡ 解题之路 ⬅

1. 【答案】D 【题型】原因细节题。

   【思路】根据题干关键词western Europe和Japan定位到首段和第二段。首段主要讲述了日本所面临的社会问题，如通缩、经济增长缓慢、老龄化等；第二段则主要论述了西欧的问题：通胀水平无休止地下滑、经济增长缓慢等。可以看出，两段文字均是围绕经济问题的。对比四个选项，选项[A]、[B]首先排除；选项[C]涉及的是日本面临的问题，而西欧则没有提及，所以也应排除；选项[D]符合文意，故为正确答案。

2. 【答案】C 【题型】事实细节题。

   【思路】第三段通过债券收益率、股票交易、市盈率等数据比较了美国和欧洲的经济现状，可以看出前者总体比后者表现要好。选项[C]符合这一论述，所以为正确答案。选项[A]与该段所述内容相悖；选项[B]在该段没有提及，属于无中生有；选项[D]属于张冠李戴，因为Yale University所做的研究是针对美国的，而非欧元区。

3. 【答案】B 【题型】事实细节题。

   【思路】根据题干关键词Falling unemployment和America可定位到第五段的第二句和第五句。研读后发现答案应在第五句的冒号之后，即选项[B]的内容。选项[A]在该段首句可找到信息支持，但和题干的问题无关；选项[C]在第四句也有信息支持，但错误属性和选项[A]相同；选项[D]则属于无中生有。

4. 【答案】A 【题型】推理判断题。

   【思路】根据题干关键词Robert Gordon可定位到第六段的第二句。根据该句论述和两个数据1.3%、0.9%的前后对比，可推导出Robert Gordon的预测不甚乐观，所以选项[A]符合文意。

5. 【答案】B 【题型】原因细节题。

   【思路】根据题干关键词Morgan Stanley可定位到倒数第二段的第二句，但该句主要是说"美国经济复苏还会持续"，这只是一种现象，不是题干所问的原因，所以答案应在下面的内容里。第三句说"债务的运转情况基本良好"，似乎和选项[A]有关联，但选项[A]是说"美国成功地摆脱了债务"，表述毫无关系，故排除；接着后半句说到"风险还没到杠杆高度",这与选项[B]的描述一致,故选项[B]为正确答案;选项[C]的信息可在末段的首句找到,但与题干所问无关,属于张冠李戴;选项[D]在第七段的末句,也属于张冠李戴。

词汇精解

1. decade ['dekeɪd] n. 十年
2. perceive [pə'siːv] v. 感知;感觉;认为
3. mire ['maɪə(r)] v. 受困于;陷入泥潭
4. deflation [dɪ'fleɪʃn] n. 通货紧缩
5. bond [bɒnd] n. 债券
6. yield [jiːld] n. 收益;产出
7. conservative [kən'sɜːvətɪv] a. 保守的
8. monetary ['mʌnɪtri] a. 货币的;金钱的
9. outdated [ˌaʊt'deɪtɪd] a. 过时的;淘汰的
10. remorselessly [rɪ'mɔːsləsli] ad. 不懊悔地;无情地
11. downwards ['daʊnwədz] ad. 向下
12. strategist ['strætədʒɪst] n. 战略家
13. dub [dʌb] v. 起绰号;称呼
14. gap [gæp] n. 差距;鸿沟
15. rally ['ræli] n. 恢复;振作
16. cyclically-adjusted a. 周期性调整的
17. exceptionalism [ɪk'sepʃənəˌlɪzəm] n. 例外性
18. demography [dɪ'mɒɡrəfi] n. 人口学;人口状况
19. eventually [ɪ'ventʃuəli] ad. 最终
20. sentiment ['sentɪmənt] n. 感情;观点
21. quarter ['kwɔːtə(r)] n. 四分之一;季度
22. workforce ['wɜːkfɔːs] n. 劳动力
23. maintain [meɪn'teɪn] v. 维持;保持
24. forecaster ['fɔːkɑːstə(r)] n. 预测者
25. last [lɑːst] v. 持续
26. dynamics [daɪ'næmɪks] n. 动力学;活力;活跃
27. prudent ['pruːdnt] a. 谨慎的;审慎的
28. corporate ['kɔːpərət] a. 企业的;公司的
29. leverage ['liːvərɪdʒ] n. 杠杆作用
30. exploit [ɪk'splɔɪt] v. 开发;利用
31. distinctive [dɪ'stɪŋktɪv] a. 有特色的
32. equivalent [ɪ'kwɪvələnt] n. 对等物;等同物
33. compensation [kɒmpen'seɪʃn] n. 补偿;弥补
34. whereas [weər'æz] conj. 而;却
35. adopt [ə'dɒpt] v. 采纳;采用

难句解析

1. Economists have debated whether its problems are down to its ageing population, conservative monetary policy or outdated business models.

经济学家们曾辩论日本的问题是否可归因于人口老龄化、保守的货币政策或者落伍的商业模式。

结构分析：这个句子可以划分为：Economists have debated <u>whether its problems are down to its ageing population, conservative monetary policy or outdated business models.</u> 下划线部分是 whether 引导的从句，作 have debated 的宾语；be down to sth. 表示"归因于某事"。

2. Albert Edwards, a strategist at Société Générale, has dubbed these conditions an "ice age" which he predicts will extend across the rich world.	法国兴业银行的战略家阿尔伯特·爱德华兹称这些境况为"冰川世纪"，他预测这种状况的影响将扩大至所有发达国家。

结构分析：这个句子可以划分为：Albert Edwards, *a strategist at Société Générale,* has dubbed these conditions <u>an "ice age"</u> (which he predicts will extend across the rich world). 斜体部分是一个名词短语，作主语 Albert Edwards 的同位语；下划线部分也是一个名词短语，作宾语 these conditions 的补足语；括号里 which 引导的是从句作 an "ice age" 的定语，其中的 he predicts 可看作插入语。

3. The gap between yields on its bonds and on Germany's is now almost as wide as it has been at any point since the euro was created.	美国与德国的债券收益率差距自欧元出现以来差不多已达到最大。

结构分析：这个句子可以划分为：The gap (between yields on its bonds and on Germany's) is now almost as wide as it has been <u>at any point</u> *since the euro was created.* 括号里的介词短语作主语 The gap 的后置定语；as wide as it has been 作表语，使用了同级比较结构，it 指代前面的 The gap；下划线部分的介词短语作时间状语，最后的斜体部分是 since 引导的时间状语从句。

4. As baby boomers retire, it will be hard for America's workforce to grow significantly without a jump in participation.	随着婴儿潮时代出生的人开始退休，没有劳动力市场参与者的大幅增加，美国的劳动力队伍很难大规模扩大。

结构分析：这个句子可以划分为：*As baby boomers retire,* it will be hard for America's workforce to grow significantly (without a jump in participation). 斜体部分是 as 引导的时间状语从句；it 作形式主语，指代后面的不定式，括号里的介词短语作方式状语，修饰 grow。

5. Robert Gordon of Northwestern University predicts that, even if productivity growth is maintained at the 1.3% annual rate seen for much of the past 40 years, future growth in real (adjusted for inflation) GDP per person will be just 0.9%.

西北大学的罗伯特·戈登预测，即使生产率增长能保持在过去40年来的高水平，即年增长率为1.3%，未来人均实际GDP增长（调整通货膨胀以后）也仅为0.9%。

结构分析：这个句子可以划分为：Robert Gordon of Northwestern University predicts that, *even if productivity growth is maintained at the 1.3% annual rate (seen for much of the past 40 years),* <u>future growth in real (adjusted for inflation) GDP per person will be just 0.9%</u>. 句子主语是 Robert Gordon，谓语是 predicts，宾语是 that 引导的从句，即下划线部分，该从句被斜体部分 even if 引导的让步状语从句所分裂，该状语从句中括号里的过去分词短语作 the 1.3% annual rate 的后置定语。

6. "Debt dynamics paint the picture of a more prudent household sector and well-managed corporate sector, both of which remain far from the heights of leverage typically associated with risks to business-cycle expansions," the bank's economists write.

"债务的运转情况描绘了一幅更为审慎的房地产和管理良好的公司的画面，二者远远达不到与商业周期扩张有关的风险的杠杆高度。"摩根的经济学家这样写道。

结构分析：这个句子可以划分为："Debt dynamics paint the picture *of a more prudent household sector and well-managed corporate sector,* <u>both of which remain far from the heights of leverage (typically associated with risks to business-cycle expansions),</u>" the bank's economists write. 斜体部分的介词短语作 the picture 的后置定语；下划线部分 both of which 引导的定语从句修饰前面的 a more prudent household sector and well-managed corporate sector，括号里的过去分词短语作 the heights of leverage 的后置定语。

7. Meanwhile, the Federal Reserve is winding down its bond purchases whereas many expect the European Central Bank to be pushed into adopting quantitative easing (and thus buying bonds) later this year.

同时，美联储缩减了债券购买量，而许多人期望欧洲中央银行今年晚些时候被推动采取量化宽松政策（因此而购买债券）。

结构分析：这个句子可以划分为：Meanwhile, the Federal Reserve is winding down its bond purchases//whereas many expect the European Central Bank to be pushed into adopting quantitative easing (and thus buying bonds) later this year. 以 "//" 为界，whereas 连接了两个并列分句；后一个分句使用了 expect sb. to do sth. 的结构。

Text 6

1 Since the dawn of human ingenuity, people have devised ever more cunning tools to cope with work that is dangerous, boring, burdensome, or just plain nasty. That compulsion has resulted in robotics—the science of conferring various human capabilities on machines. And if scientists have yet to create the mechanical version of science fiction, they have begun to come close.

2 As a result, the modern world is increasingly populated by intelligent gizmos whose presence we barely notice but whose universal existence has removed much human labor. Our factories hum to the rhythm of robot assembly arms. Our banking is done at automated teller terminals that thank us with mechanical politeness for the transaction. Our subway trains are controlled by tireless robo-drivers. And thanks to the continual miniaturization of electronics and micro-mechanics, there are already robot systems that can perform some kinds of brain and bone surgery with submillimeter accuracy—far greater precision than highly skilled physicians can achieve with their hands alone.

3 But if robots are to reach the next stage of laborsaving utility, they will have to operate with less human supervision and be able to make at least a few decisions for themselves—goals that pose a real

1　自从人类的创造智慧诞生以来，人类设计了越来越多的巧妙工具去应付危险、枯燥、繁重或是实在不堪忍受的工作。这使得机器人科学诞生了——这门科学研究如何将人的各种能力赋予机器。如果说科学家还没有创造出科幻小说中的现实版机器人，他们也离实现目标不远了。

2　因此，现代世界中智能化的新玩意越来越多，尽管这些东西不引人注意，但它们的普遍存在已经取代了很多人类劳动。工厂生产随着机械装配手臂的节奏嗡嗡作响。银行业务在自动化的柜员终端设备中进行，自动化的柜员终端还能用机器特有的礼貌对我们的交易表示感谢。我们的地铁列车由无线机器人司机操纵。由于电子技术和小型机械的不断微型化，已经有机器人系统能够进行某些大脑和骨骼手术，精确度达到了亚毫米——远比技术精湛的内科医生徒手所能达到的精确度要高。

3　但如果要机器人进入下一阶段，使其成为节约劳动的工具，机器人运作时就必须减少人类的监控，而且机器人至少应该能够独立做出一些

challenge. "While we know how to tell a robot to handle a specific error," says Dave Lavery, manager of a robotics program at NASA, "we can't yet give a robot enough 'common sense' to reliably interact with a dynamic world."

4   Indeed the quest for true artificial intelligence has produced very mixed results. Despite a spell of initial optimism in the 1960s and 1970s when it appeared that transistor circuits and microprocessors might be able to copy the action of the human brain by the year 2010, researchers lately have begun to extend that forecast by decades if not centuries.

5   What they found, in attempting to model thought, is that the human brain's roughly one hundred billion nerve cells are much more talented—and human perception far more complicated—than previously imagined. They have built robots that can recognize the error of a machine panel by a fraction of a millimeter in a controlled factory environment. But the human mind can glimpse a rapidly changing scene and immediately disregard the 98 percent that is irrelevant, instantaneously focusing on the monkey at the side of a winding forest road or the single suspicious face in a big crowd. The most advanced computer systems on Earth can't approach that kind of ability, and neuroscientists still don't know quite how we do it.

1. Human ingenuity was initially demonstrated in _____.

   [A] the use of machines to produce science fiction

   [B] the wide use of machines in manufacturing industry

   [C] the invention of tools for difficult and dangerous work

   [D] the elite's cunning tackling of dangerous and boring work

2. The word "gizmos" (Line 2, Paragraph 2) most probably means _____.

   [A] programs

   [B] experts

   [C] devices

   [D] creatures

3. According to the text, what is beyond man's ability now is to design a robot that can _____.

   [A] fulfill delicate tasks like performing brain surgery

   [B] interact with human beings verbally

   [C] have a little common sense

   [D] respond independently to a changing world

4. Besides reducing human labor, robots can also _____.

   [A] make a few decisions for themselves

   [B] deal with some errors with human intervention

   [C] improve factory environments

   [D] cultivate human creativity

5. The author uses the example of a monkey to argue that robots are _____.

   [A] expected to copy human brain in internal structure

   [B] able to perceive abnormalities immediately

   [C] far less able than human brain in focusing on relevant information

   [D] best used in a controlled environment

◆ 解题之路 ◆

1. 【答案】C 【题型】事实细节题。

   【思路】根据题干关键词human ingenuity可定位到首段。本题主要考查考生是否看懂了该段，尤其是"That compulsion has resulted in robotics—the science of conferring various human capabilities on machines"这句话。这句话的意思是：（设计了越来越多的巧妙工

具去应付危险、枯燥、繁重或是实在不堪忍受的工作。）这使得机器人科学诞生了——这门科学研究如何将人的各种能力赋予机器。所以答案是选项[C]，属于同义转述。

2. 【答案】C 【题型】词义猜测题。

　　【思路】本题考查考生从上下文猜测词义的能力。根据第二段中出现的"robot assembly arms"，"automated teller terminals"，"tireless robo-drivers"等信息，考生可以猜出"gizmos"是"设备，装置"的意思。所以答案是选项[C]。

3. 【答案】D 【题型】事实细节题。

　　【思路】根据题干关键词beyond man's ability和design a robot可定位到第三段，Dave Lavery的后半句话，即"we can't yet give a robot enough 'common sense' to reliably interact with a dynamic world"，该句中的"dynamic"意思是"动态的，变化的"，对应选项[D]中的changing，该选项即是对原文的同义改写。

4. 【答案】B 【题型】事实细节题。

　　【思路】根据题干关键reducing human labor可定位到第三段，reducing human labor对应首句的laborsaving utility，但答案在下面Dave Lavery说的前半句话里：While we know how to tell a robot to handle a specific error，即"尽管我们知道如何指示机器人去纠正一个具体的错误"。看懂了这句话，这道题就很容易了。所以答案为选项[B]。

5. 【答案】C 【题型】例子题。

　　【思路】根据题干关键词the example of a monkey可定位到末段的第三句。例子题的一般做法是：找到例子出处后，在例子前寻找比较深刻的句子，这个句子往往就是答案。该例子之前的内容大意是：机器人能够在很短的时间内发现机器的问题，而人脑能很快忽略不相关的信息，而将注意力集中到相关的信息上来，这是先进的机器人都做不到的。对比四个选项，选项[C]是正确选项。

☞ 词汇精解 ☜

1. ingenuity [ˌɪndʒəˈnjuːətɪ] n. 聪明，智慧	9. capability [ˌkeɪpəˈbɪlətɪ] n. 能力
2. devise [dɪˈvaɪz] v. 设计，策划	10. mechanical [məˈkænɪkl] a. 机械的
3. cunning [ˈkʌnɪŋ] a. 聪明的；狡猾的	11. version [ˈvɜːʃn] n. 版本
4. burdensome [ˈbɜːdnsəm] a. 麻烦的，令人劳累的	12. gizmo [ˈɡɪzməʊ] n. 装置，设备
5. nasty [ˈnɑːstɪ] a. 恶心的，讨厌的	13. hum [hʌm] v. 嗡嗡作响
6. compulsion [kəmˈpʌlʃn] n. 迫使，推动	14. rhythm [ˈrɪðəm] n. 节奏，韵律
7. robotics [rəʊˈbɒtɪks] n. 机器人学	15. assembly [əˈsemblɪ] n. 组装线，流水线
8. confer [kənˈfɜː(r)] v. 授予，给予	16. teller [ˈtelə(r)] n. 银行出纳员
	17. terminal [ˈtɜːmɪnl] n. 终端机；终点

18. transaction [træn'zækʃn] n. 交易，贸易
19. miniaturization [ˌmɪnətʃəraɪ'zeɪʃn] n. 微型化
20. accuracy ['ækjərəsɪ] n. 精确，精度
21. precision [prɪ'sɪʒn] n. 精确，精度
22. utility [juː'tɪlətɪ] n. 应用，实用性
23. supervision [ˌsuːpə'vɪʒn] n. 监督，监控
24. dynamic [daɪ'næmɪk] a. 有活力的；动态的
25. quest [kwest] n. 追求，渴望
26. initial [ɪ'nɪʃl] a. 最初的
27. optimism ['ɒptɪmɪzəm] n. 乐观；乐观主义
28. perception [pə'sepʃn] n. 感知，感觉
29. instantaneously [ˌɪnstən'teɪnɪəslɪ] ad. 立刻，立即
30. suspicious [sə'spɪʃəs] a. 令人怀疑的；疑心的
31. neuroscientist ['njʊərəʊ'saɪəntɪst] n. 神经系统科学家

难句解析

1. Since the dawn of human ingenuity, people have devised ever more cunning tools to cope with work that is dangerous, boring, burdensome, or just plain nasty.

自从人类的创造智慧诞生以来，人类设计了越来越多的巧妙工具去应付危险、枯燥、繁重或实在不堪忍受的工作。

结构分析：该句是一个复合句，前面是 since 引导的一个时间状语，这个地方的 dawn 取其比喻义，表示"早期"，句中有一个定语从句 that is dangerous, boring, burdensome, or just plain nasty 用来修饰 work。

2. As a result, the modern world is increasingly populated by intelligent gizmos whose presence we barely notice but whose universal existence has removed much human labor.

因此，现代世界中智能化的新玩意越来越多，尽管这些东西不引人注意，但它们的普遍存在已经取代了很多人类劳动。

结构分析：本句的主句是 the modern world is increasingly populated by intelligent gizmos，后面是两个定语从句，中间用 but 来连接。as a result 相当于一个连词，表示"因此"。

3. And thanks to the continual miniaturization of electronics and micro-mechanics, there are already robot systems that can perform some kinds of brain and bone surgery with submillimeter accuracy—far greater precision than highly skilled physicians can achieve with their hands alone.

由于电子技术和小型机械的不断微型化，已经有机器人系统能够进行某些大脑和骨骼手术，精确度达到了亚毫米——远比技术精湛的内科医生徒手所能达到的精确度要高。

结构分析：该句是一个there be句型结构，注意robot systems后面有一个修饰它的定语从句。而后面的破折号引出一个名词短语 far greater precision，起补充说明作用，作前面 submillimeter accuracy 的同位语。句首的 thanks to 引导的是原因状语。

4. But if robots are to reach the next stage of laborsaving utility, they will have to operate with less human supervision and be able to make at least a few decisions for themselves—goals that pose a real challenge.

但如果要机器人进入下一个阶段，使其成为节约劳动的工具，机器人运作时就必须减少人类的监控，而且机器人至少应该能够独立做出一些决定——这些目标才是真正富有挑战性的。

结构分析：这是一个主从复合句。起首的是一个条件句，主句是两个并列结构，一个是 they will have to operate with less human supervision，一个是 (they will have to) be able to make at least a few decisions for themselves。破折号之后是一个名词短语，修饰整个主句，作主句的同位语。

5. Despite a spell of initial optimism in the 1960s and 1970s when it appeared that transistor circuits and microprocessors might be able to copy the action of the human brain by the year 2010, researchers lately have begun to extend that forecast by decades if not centuries.

尽管20世纪六七十年代人们起初着实乐观了一阵——当时看起来晶体管电路和微处理器到2010年应该将能够模仿人类大脑活动了，研究人员最近将这个预测时间延后，即使不用几百年，也是几十年。

结构分析：句子的主干是 researchers lately have begun to extend that forecast by decades if not centuries。句首的 Despite a spell of initial optimism in the 1960s and 1970s 是让步状语，其后的 when 引导的是一个定语从句，比较冗长，因而整个句子显得比较令人费解。

Text 7

1　Cybercrime affected more than half those surveyed, yet fewer than a third said they had reported it. Many Britons have been the victim of a cybercrime such as identity theft, hacking or abuse on social media, new research has found. UK losses from online fraud are now running at more

1　网络犯罪影响了超过一半的受访者，然而只有不到三分之一的受害者进行了举报。最新研究显示，许多英国民众有过被盗号、遭受黑客袭击以及网络欺凌的经历。每年英国的网络诈骗案件涉案金额超过6.7亿英

169

than £670m a year, though with many cases going unreported, the true economic cost is likely to be significantly higher.

2 The data—which follows the outcry over private photos of celebrities published by hackers—was produced to coincide with Get Safe Online Week, which runs until 26 October and is aimed at raising awareness of internet security issues. Just over half (51%) of the 2,075 people surveyed said they had been a victim of online crime, a category which includes internet-based fraud, ID theft, hacking and online abuse. Of those, 50% said they felt either very or extremely violated by their ordeal, according to Get Safe Online, an internet security awareness initiative that is a joint partnership between the government, the National Crime Agency, the telecoms regulator Ofcom, law enforcement bodies and a number of major companies including Barclays and PayPal.

3 However, fewer than a third (32%) of the cybercrime victims said they had reported the incident. Around half (47%) of those affected did not know who to report an online crime to, though a spokesman for the initiative said this figure was expected to fall as a result of the ongoing work of Action Fraud, the UK's national fraud reporting centre, and the "considerable government resources" now dedicated to fighting cybercrime.

4 On a more positive note, those who

had suffered some form of cybercrime said the experience had shocked them into changing their behaviour for the better, with almost half (45%) opting for stronger passwords and 42% saying they were now more vigilant when shopping online.

5   Tony Neate, chief executive of Get Safe Online, said: "Our research shows just how serious a toll cybercrime can take, both on the wallet and on wellbeing, and this has been no more apparent than in the last few weeks, with various large-scale personal photo hacks of celebrities and the general public. Unfortunately, this is becoming more common now that we live more of our lives online."

6   He added: "Get Safe Online Week this year is all about 'Don't be a victim', and we can all take simple steps to protect ourselves, including putting a password on your computer or mobile device, never clicking on a link sent by a stranger, using strong passwords and always logging off from an account or website when you are finished. The more the public do this, and together with better conviction rates, the more criminals won't be able to hide behind a cloak of anonymity."

7   If you think you have been a victim of cyber-enabled economic fraud (where you have lost money), report it to Action Fraud by calling 0300 123 20 40 or visiting actionfraud.police.uk. If you are a victim of online abuse or harassment, report it to your local police force. For general advice on how to stay safe online go to getsafeonline.org.

称在经历过网络犯罪之后，这种经历使他们警醒，促使他们养成了良好的上网行为习惯，其中将近一半的人（45%）使用了强度更高的密码，42%的人表示在网络购物时提高了警觉。

5   "安全上网"的首席执行官托尼·尼特说："我们的调查表明，网络犯罪无论是对于人们的钱财或是心理健康都造成了巨大伤害，这在过去几周再明显不过——大量名人以及公众的私人照片被侵入。不幸的是，这种事情变得愈加普遍，因为我们的生活越来越依赖网络。"

6   他又说道："'安全上网周'今年的主题围绕着'不做受害者'展开，我们只需要通过简单几步就可以保护自己：设置电脑或手机密码、不点击陌生人发送的链接、设置更高强度的密码以及在完成上网之后退出登录账号。越多的民众这么做，再加上定罪越为严厉，越多的罪犯将无处可藏。"

7   如果你觉得自己遭受了网络经济诈骗（遭受了经济损失），请拨打0300 123 20 40 或登录actionfraud.police.uk 进行举报。如果你在网络上受到侮辱或侵犯，请向当地警察部门举报。如有安全上网方面的疑问，请浏览 getsafeonline.org。

1. About cybercrime in Britain, which statement is TRUE?

   [A] More than one third of victims reported crimes.

   [B] Hacking is the most serious kind of crime.

   [C] Losses of online fraud may be more serious than expected.

   [D] Cybercrimes have hit a record high.

2. Get Safe Online Week was launched in order to _____.

   [A] meet the demand of some victims

   [B] strengthen cyber security awareness

   [C] protect private photos of celebrities

   [D] facilitate mutual joint partnership

3. A spokesman for Get Safe Online Week predicted that _____.

   [A] more victims will know the channel to report

   [B] fewer victims will report

   [C] fighting cybercrime will be harder

   [D] government resources will be less

4. According to Tony Neate, cybercrime in Britain now _____.

   [A] is less serious than before

   [B] gets out of control

   [C] is not serious at all

   [D] can be controlled

5. The text centres mainly on _____.

   [A] cybercrime and counteractions

   [B] seriousness of cybercrime

   [C] ordeal of cybercrime victims

   [D] varieties of cybercrime

◆ 解题之路 ◆

1. 【答案】C 【题型】事实细节题。

   【思路】根据题干关键词cybercrime in Britain和出题段落顺序原则可定位到首段，根据首句yet fewer than a third said they had reported it 可知选项[A]错误；选项[B]中的hacking可从第二句找到信息：Many Britons have been the victim of a cybercrime such as identity theft, hacking or abuse on social media，但most serious无法推断，所以该选项排除，一般而言，选项中若出现绝对意义的词汇，如most、extremely等，该选项就是错误的；选项[C]可从末句找到信息：the true economic cost is likely to be significantly higher，是对该句的同义改写，所以选项[C]为正确选项；选项[D]无法从原文推断出来，而且a record high属于绝对意义的短语，应该排除。

2. 【答案】B 【题型】事实细节题。

   【思路】根据题干关键词Get Safe Online Week可定位到第二段首句，考点就在该句which引导的从句中：which... is aimed at raising awareness of internet security issues，题干中的in order to与is aimed at对应，选项[B]正是对该句raising awareness of internet security issues的正确改写。

3. 【答案】A 【题型】事实细节题。

   【思路】根据题干关键词A spokesman可定位到第三段第二句though a spokesman for the initiative said this figure was expected to fall as a result of the ongoing work of Action Fraud，题干中predicted所需的答案就是原文said之后的内容，this figure指的是前面的47%，由此得出选项[A]正确，使用了正话反说的方法。

4. 【答案】D 【题型】事实细节题。

   【思路】根据题干关键词Tony Neate定位到第五段和第六段。第五段主要说网络犯罪的严重性及其危害；第六段主要说通过一些方法，安全上网是可以做到的。综合这些内容，选项[D]为正确选项。选项[A]只说明了第五段的内容，而未涉及第六段，显得片面、不完整；选项[B]、[C]都属于包含过于绝对含义的表述，均应排除。

5. 【答案】A 【题型】主旨大意题。

   【思路】纵观全文，文章首先谈论了英国网络犯罪的危害及其严重性，接着重点转到如何防范的措施方法上，因此可断定选项[A]为正确选项，它包含了以上所说的两个方面。

◆ 词汇精解 ◆

1. cybercrime [ˈsaɪbəkraɪm] n. 网络犯罪	8. case [keɪs] n. 案例；情形
2. victim [ˈvɪktɪm] n. 受害人；牺牲者	9. outcry [ˈaʊtkraɪ] n. 大声呼喊；强烈抗议
3. identity [aɪˈdentəti] n. 身份	10. celebrity [səˈlebrəti] n. 名人；名流
4. theft [θeft] n. 盗窃；盗窃行为	11. coincide [ˌkəʊɪnˈsaɪd] v. 符合；同时发生
5. hacking [ˈhækɪŋ] n. 黑客行为	12. awareness [əˈweənəs] n. 意识；意识程度
6. abuse [əˈbjuːs] n. 辱骂；滥用；虐待	13. extremely [ɪkˈstriːmli] ad. 极其；非常地
7. fraud [frɔːd] n. 诈骗；欺骗	14. violate [ˈvaɪəleɪt] v. 侵犯；违背

15. ordeal [ɔːˈdiːl] *n.* 巨大痛苦	24. positive [ˈpɒzətɪv] *a.* 积极的；肯定的
16. initiative [ɪˈnɪʃətɪv] *n.* 倡议；举动；主动性	25. vigilant [ˈvɪdʒɪlənt] *a.* 警觉的；警惕的
17. joint [dʒɔɪnt] *a.* 联合的；共同的	26. toll [təʊl] *n.* 代价；损失
18. regulator [ˈreɡjuleɪtə(r)] *n.* 管理者；调整者	27. wellbeing [ˌwelˈbiːɪŋ] *n.* 健康；幸福
19. enforcement [ɪnˈfɔːsmənt] *n.* 执行，强迫	28. apparent [əˈpærənt] *a.* 明显的；显然的
20. major [ˈmeɪdʒə(r)] *a.* 主要的；重要的	29. account [əˈkaʊnt] *n.* 账户
21. incident [ˈɪnsɪdənt] *n.* 事件；事变	30. conviction [kənˈvɪkʃn] *n.* 定罪
22. spokesman [ˈspəʊksmən] *n.* 发言人	31. criminal [ˈkrɪmɪnl] *n.* 罪犯
23. considerable [kənˈsɪdərəbl] *a.* 相当大的；重要的，值得考虑的	32. cloak [kləʊk] *n.* 斗篷；遮盖物
	33. anonymity [ˌænəˈnɪməti] *n.* 匿名；匿名状态
	34. harassment [ˈhærəsmənt] *n.* 骚扰；打扰

难句解析

1. Cybercrime affected more than half those surveyed, yet fewer than a third said they had reported it.	网络犯罪影响了超过一半的受访者，然而只有不到三分之一的受害者进行了举报。

结构分析：这个句子可以划分为：Cybercrime affected more than half those (surveyed),//yet fewer than a third said (that) they had reported it. 以"//"为界，yet 连接了两个并列分句；第一个分句括号里的过去分词作 those 的后置定语；第二个分句 said 之后是其宾语从句，省略了引导词 that。

2. UK losses from online fraud are now running at more than £670m a year, though with many cases going unreported, the true economic cost is likely to be significantly higher.	每年英国的网络诈骗案件涉案金额超过 6.7 亿英镑，然而若将那些未被举报的案件计算在内，实际的犯罪金额无法估量。

结构分析：这个句子可以划分为：UK losses from online fraud are now running at more than £670m a year, *though with many cases going unreported*, the true economic cost is likely to be significantly higher. 斜体部分 though 引导的让步状语从句中下划线部分是独立主格结构，即 with+*n.*+现在分词。

3. The data—which follows the outcry over private photos of celebrities published by hackers—was produced to coincide with Get Safe Online Week, which runs until 26 October and is aimed at raising awareness of internet security issues.

以上数据是在公众对黑客泄露明星隐私照进行强烈抗议之后发布的，发布该数据是为了配合"安全上网周"活动，该活动将持续到10月26日，旨在提高公众的网络安全意识。

结构分析：这个句子可以划分为：The data—(which follows the outcry over private photos of celebrities published by hackers)—was produced to coincide with Get Safe Online Week, (which runs until 26 October and is aimed at raising awareness of internet security issues). 句子主干是 The data was produced；第一个括号里 which 引导的从句作 The data 的定语；下划线部分的不定式作目的状语，其中括号里 which 引导的从句作 Get Safe Online Week 的定语。

4. Just over half (51%) of the 2,075 people surveyed said they had been a victim of online crime, a category which includes internet-based fraud, ID theft, hacking and online abuse.

在2 075名受采访者中，只有一半的人（51%）表明曾经遭受过网络犯罪，包括网络诈骗、盗号、黑客袭击以及网络欺凌。

结构分析：这个句子可以划分为：Just over half (51%) of the 2,075 people (surveyed) said they had been a victim of online crime, a category (which includes internet-based fraud, ID theft, hacking and online abuse). 第一个括号里的过去分词 surveyed 作 the 2,075 people 的后置定语；下划线部分是一个名词短语，作 online crime 的同位语，其中括号里 which 引导的从句作 a category 的定语。

5. Of those, 50% said they felt either very or extremely violated by their ordeal, according to Get Safe Online, an internet security awareness initiative that is a joint partnership between the government, the National Crime Agency, the telecoms regulator Ofcom, law enforcement bodies and a number of major companies including Barclays and PayPal.

这其中又有50%的人表示这些痛苦的经历让他们觉得受到了重度或强烈侵犯。这是"安全上网"的调查结果，"安全上网"是一项旨在提高网络安全意识的倡议，是由多个单位共同发起的，其中包括政府、国家打击犯罪局、电信监管机构 Ofcom、执法部门以及巴克莱银行和贝宝支付等大型企业。

结构分析：这个句子可以划分为：Of those, 50% said they felt either very or extremely violated by their ordeal, according to Get Safe Online, an internet security awareness initiative (that is a joint partnership *between the government, the National Crime Agency, the telecoms regulator Ofcom, law enforcement bodies and a number of major companies including Barclays and PayPal*). 下划线部分是一个名词短语，作 Get Safe Online 的同位语，起解释说明的作用；该同位语中括号里 that 引导的从句作 an internet security awareness initiative 的定语，斜体部分的介词短语作 a joint partnership 的后置定语。

> 6. Around half (47%) of those affected did not know who to report an online crime to, though a spokesman for the initiative said this figure was expected to fall as a result of the ongoing work of Action Fraud, the UK's national fraud reporting centre, and the "considerable government resources" now dedicated to fighting cybercrime.
>
> 近一半（47%）的受访者仍不知向谁举报，不过该倡议的一位发言人表示，随着英国国家诈骗举报中心"防欺诈局"推行相关举措，以及"相当可观的政府资源"已投入到打击网络犯罪方面，该数据将会降低。

结构分析：这个句子可以划分为：Around half (47%) of those (affected) did not know (who to report an online crime to), though a spokesman for the initiative said this figure was expected to fall <u>as a result of the ongoing work of Action Fraud, *the UK's national fraud reporting centre*, and the "considerable government resources"</u> (now dedicated to fighting cybercrime). 第一个括号里的过去分词 affected 作 those 的后置定语；第二个括号里 who 引导的从句作 did not know 的宾语；下划线部分的介词短语作原因状语，the ongoing work 和 and the "considerable government resources" 是并列关系；该状语中斜体部分是一个名词短语，作 Action Fraud 的同位语，起解释说明作用；最后括号里的过去分词短语作 the "considerable government resources" 的后置定语。

> 7. On a more positive note, those who had suffered some form of cybercrime said the experience had shocked them into changing their behaviour for the better, with almost half (45%) opting for stronger passwords and 42% saying they were now more vigilant when shopping online.
>
> 从积极层面看，这些受访者称在经历过网络犯罪之后，这种经历使他们警醒，促使他们养成了良好的上网行为习惯，其中将近一半的人（45%）使用了强度更高的密码，42% 的人表示在网络购物时提高了警觉。

结构分析：这个句子可以划分为：On a more positive note, those (who had suffered some form of cybercrime) said <u>the experience had shocked them into changing their behaviour for the better</u>, *with almost half (45%) opting for stronger passwords and 42% saying they were now more vigilant when (they were) shopping online.* 括号里 who 引导的从句作 those 的定语；下划线部分作 said 的宾语从句；斜体部分是独立主格结构，即 with+*n.*+doing，作伴随状语；最后的括号里是 when 引导的时间状语从句省略的内容。

8. Tony Neate, chief executive of Get Safe Online, said: "Our research shows just how serious a toll cybercrime can take, both on the wallet and on wellbeing, and this has been no more apparent than in the last few weeks, with various large-scale personal photo hacks of celebrities and the general public."

"安全上网"的首席执行官托尼·尼特说："我们的调查表明，网络犯罪无论是对于人们的钱财或是心理健康都造成了巨大伤害，这在过去几周再明显不过——大量名人以及公众的私人照片被侵入。"

结构分析：这个句子可以划分为：Tony Neate, <u>chief executive of Get Safe Online</u>, said: "Our research shows (just how serious a toll cybercrime can take, *both on the wallet and on wellbeing*, //and this has been no more apparent than in the last few weeks, *with various large-scale personal photo hacks of celebrities and the general public*). 下划线部分的名词短语作 Tony Neate 的同位语。括号里的内容作 shows 的宾语，以 "//" 为界，and 连接了两个并列分句；两个斜体部分均为介词短语作状语。

9. Unfortunately, this is becoming more common now that we live more of our lives online.

不幸的是，这种事情变得愈加普遍，因为我们的生活越来越依赖网络。

结构分析：这个句子可以划分为：Unfortunately, this is becoming more common <u>now that we live more of our lives online</u>. 下划线部分是 now that 引导的原因状语从句。

10. The more the public do this, and together with better conviction rates, the more criminals won't be able to hide behind a cloak of anonymity.

越多的民众这么做，再加上定罪越为严厉，越多的罪犯将无处可藏。

结构分析：这个句子可以划分为：*The more* the public do this, and <u>together with better conviction rates</u>, *the more* criminals won't be able to hide behind a cloak of anonymity. 句子使用了 "The+比较级，the+比较级"结构，其中前半部分表条件，后半部分表结果；下划线部分是一个介词短语，逻辑上和前面的 do this 构成并列关系，together with sth. 表示"连同……；以及……"。

Text 8

1 Not long ago, Barack Obama was hoping that high-speed trains would provide America with the desired "twofer." First, building the special tracks and locomotives would put a division or two of America's army of unemployed back to work. Then, once built, the trains would get people out of cars and planes and to their destinations in a way that would be cleaner and use less foreign oil. But those dreams have mostly died. Republicans have decided that government spending, not outdated infrastructure, is the real bogeyman, and Republican governors in Florida, Wisconsin and Ohio have rejected federal money to begin building.

2 Only in California does the dream live on. As Governor Jerry Brown, aged 73 and a Democrat, likes to remember, another big railway project in the 19th century connected the young state to the rest of America. In the 1970s Mr. Brown became governor for the first time, and had visions of his grand projects.

3 Today Mr. Brown still sparkles as he mocks the "dystopian journalists" and "declinists" who obstinately fail to see that California's population will grow from just under 38m now to about 50m in 2030; and that, unless the state has something like Japan's bullet trains, Californians will choke in traffic jams or go mad waiting for delayed flights in inadequate airports.

1 不久前，贝拉克·奥巴马还期望高铁能给美国人民带来双重效益。首先，建造特殊铁轨和火车头将会使美国的一两股失业大军重回岗位。其次，一旦修建成功，高铁可以使人们出行不再选择使用汽车、飞机等交通工具，从而以更加清洁且减少使用进口油的方式到达目的地。但是这些梦想基本已经破灭了。共和党人认为问题不在于基础设施陈旧，政府开支才是真正可怕的问题。佛罗里达州、威斯康星州和俄亥俄州的州长们都已拒绝了联邦政府对高铁的投资。

2 只有在加利福尼亚州（加州），高铁梦仍在延续。73岁的州长杰里·布朗是一位民主党人，他总喜欢回忆19世纪的一个大型铁路项目将加州这个年轻的州与美国其他地方连接了起来的往事。20世纪70年代，布朗首次出任州长，当时脑海里就产生了一个宏大的铁路工程构想。

3 如今，布朗先生讽刺起那些"反乌托邦主义的记者"和"唱衰主义者"时依然两眼放光，他认为这些人没有认识到加州人口将会从目前的不足3 800万增长到2030年的5 000万左右，他们更没有认识到，除非加州有像日本一样的高速子弹头列车，

4   California's voters used to agree. In a 2008 ballot measure, they approved $9 billion in bonds to fund just such a train. As advertised, it was to connect the two big population centres, Los Angeles and the San Francisco Bay area. Speeds were to reach 220mph, giving a travel time of less than three hours; the project was to cost $33 billion and be completed as early as 2020.

5   Then the iron law of infrastructure projects asserted itself. According to current estimates, the train would in fact cost three times as much or more, and take 13 years longer to build. Mr. Obama still wants to help; he has asked Congress for $35 billion in railway funding over five years, of which $3.5 billion may go to California. But even with the bond funds, those dollops would cover less than 13% of the estimated cost. Republicans are in no mood to allocate more.

6   It gets worse. After the ballot measure, it was decided that construction should begin not in the two population centres but in the vast and flat farmlands of the Central Valley, where building is much easier. This means that funds could run dry before the big cities are even connected to the network. A high-speed train would then run through sparsely populated countryside, with hardly anybody riding it. Some call this a "train to nowhere," others

a white elephant. Using a rather more original metaphor Richard White, a professor of history at Stanford, calls it "a Vietnam of transportation: easy to begin and difficult and expensive to stop."

> 德·怀特更具独创性的比喻：越南式的交通方式——起步容易停下则又贵又难（上车容易下车又贵又难）。

1. High-speed trains are expected to benefit people by _____.

   [A] creating job opportunities for people in military service

   [B] helping the Republicans to save government spending

   [C] making a better and cleaner transportation system

   [D] stopping the usage of foreign oil

2. The word "bogeyman" (Paragraph 1) is closest in meaning to _____.

   [A] nightmare

   [B] support

   [C] goal

   [D] approval

3. We can learn from Paragraphs 2 and 3 that _____.

   [A] a high-speed train is under construction in California

   [B] Jerry Brown strongly supports the high-speed train project

   [C] California has a severe public transportation problem

   [D] most of the journalists are against the high-speed train project

4. High-speed trains are difficult to achieve mainly because of _____.

   [A] the advanced technology

   [B] the vast area

   [C] the iron law

   [D] the high expenses

5. Which of the following best summarizes the text?

   [A] High-speed train in the U.S. is still an untouchable dream.

   [B] California is advanced in high-speed train construction.

   [C] Outdated infrastructure of U.S. needs to be renewed.

   [D] U.S. government should save their budget expenditure.

第四章 阅读理解（A部分）

> 解题之路

1. 【答案】**C** 【题型】事实细节题。

   【思路】本题意在考查高铁能给人们带来哪些好处。根据题干关键词High-speed trains和benefit people定位到首段。该段首句开门见山地指出，不久前，贝拉克·奥巴马还期望高铁能给美国人民带来双重效益（provide America with the desired "twofer"）。接着第二至第三句具体介绍了这两大好处，其中第三句指出，高铁可以使人们不选择使用汽车、飞机等交通工具，从而以更加清洁且减少使用进口油的方式到达目的地（to their destination in a way that would be cleaner and use less foreign oil），由此可推知，便捷、低污染以及低油耗是高铁能够造福于人们的一个方面，故选项[C]为答案。首段第二句指出了高铁可能带来的好处之一：修建高铁轨道与高铁火车头可以使一两股的美国失业人员重新回到工作岗位（would put a division or two of America's army of unemployed back to work），原文的army不是"军队"之意，而是用作量词，an army of=a group of，选项[A]与原文不符，故可排除；首段第四句指出高铁梦基本已经破灭了，紧接着第五句指出真正可怕的问题在于政府开支，而且由常识可知，修建高铁肯定会耗费政府开支，不可能节省政府开支，故选项[B]也可排除；该段第三句指出，高铁可以减少进口原油的消耗，但并非说明高铁可以使人们停止使用进口原油，选项[D]与原文不符，故应排除。

2. 【答案】**A** 【题型】词汇题。

   【思路】本题就第一段第五句中的bogeyman一词的含义进行提问，故应结合其所在句上下文，推出该词在文中的具体意思。本段第一句至第三句首先介绍了高铁可以给人们带来的两大好处，接着第四句笔锋一转，指出关于高铁的美梦基本已经破灭（those dreams have mostly died）。紧接着第五句指出，共和党人已经断定，政府的开支才是真正的bogeyman，而不是过时的基础设施，而且佛罗里达州、威斯康星州以及俄亥俄州的共和党州长都已经拒绝了联邦政府修建高铁的资金援助（have rejected federal money to begin building），既然梦想已经破灭，且州长们都拒绝修建高铁，可推知bogeyman是一个负面意义的词，表明政府的开支同过时的基础设施一样，带给人们的是不利的影响，将四个选项分别代入文中，只有选项[A]最符合文意，故为答案。bogeyman一词所在的第五句处于第一段的后半部分，根据上文分析可知，该部分主要说明了高铁建设不容乐观的现状，故bogeyman一词的意思应该能说明这种不容乐观的现状，分别将"支持""目标"以及"许可"代入文中，均无法与上下文构成通顺的文意，故选项[B]、[C]、[D]可排除。

3. 【答案】**B** 【题型】事实细节题。

【思路】根据题干关键词Paragraphs 2 and 3可定位至文章第二段至第三段。第二段第一句指出，只有在加州，高铁梦仍在延续（Only in California does the dream live on）。紧接着该段最后一句提到加州州长杰里·布朗于20世纪70年代任职，并产生了其宏大的铁路工程构想。第三段首句指出，布朗先生讽刺起那些"反乌托邦主义的记者"和"唱衰主义者"时依然两眼放光，他认为这些人没有认识到加州人口将会从目前的不足3800万增长到2030年的5000万左右，他们更没有认识到，除非加州有像日本一样的高速子弹头列车，否则加州人民将会在交通堵塞中窒息，或因机场资源不足而在等待延误的航班中发疯。由此可知，加州州长布朗先生认为高铁的修建是很有必要的，即他非常支持修建高速铁路，选项[B]与原文相符，故为答案。第二段至第三段主要说明了加州州长对修建高速铁路的态度，并没有说明加州已经有正在建设中的高速铁路了，故选项[A]可以排除；第三段中作者指出，布朗州长经常会嘲讽那些"反乌托邦主义记者"以及"唱衰主义者"，因为这些人看不到加州人口的迅速增长，更没有意识到人口的增长将会给加州交通带来巨大的压力，文中并没有说明加州目前面临着严重的交通问题，故选项[C]也可以排除；文中并未指出大多数记者都反对修建高铁，故选项[D]可排除。

4. 【答案】D 【题型】原因细节题。

【思路】本题就高铁很难实现的原因提问，按照出题段落顺序原则可定位至第四段至第五段。第四段首先说明了计划中的高铁蓝图。而第五段第二句则开始指出，根据目前的估计，修建高铁的花费将会是预计的三倍甚至更多，奥巴马总统也尝试资助，但只有35亿美元资金会分配给加州，且即使加上之前的债券，那些钱也不足预计资金的13%，而共和党也不想继续拨款了，由此可知，资金不足是高铁建设困难重重的最主要原因，而这从根本上也是由高铁建设花费高昂所造成的，故选项[D]最符合原文。文章中并没有提到高铁先进技术对高铁建设形成障碍的信息，故选项[A]属无中生有，可排除；文章第六段提到了加州广阔的地域，该段第二句指出，加州的铁路建设最终决定在广袤平坦的农田间进行，这会更容易，但这意味着在大城市和铁路网相连之前，资金就已经耗尽了，由此可知，这一规划会耗费更多的资金，并不能说明地域广阔就能阻止高铁的建设，故选项[B]可以排除；选项[C]中的iron law出现在第五段第一句，该句指出，基础设施建设的铁规则显示了其威力，即基础设施建设总会使人们投入许多资金，但这并非是建设高铁的主要障碍，故选项[C]也可排除。

5. 【答案】A 【题型】主旨大意题。

【思路】该题需要梳理全文各段的段落大意。文章首段首先说明了高速铁路将会给美国带来的双重好处：为失业的人创造就业机会，以及建设更加清洁便捷的交通系统。但首段后半部分笔锋一转，指出高铁的美好愿望几乎已经破灭了，而最大的问题则是政府开支。接着第二段至第三段则说明了加州的高铁建设情况，加州州长认为高铁的建设十分必要并大力支持高铁的工程建设。第四段则具体说明加州高铁建设的规划，第五段至第六段回归现实，说明了加州高铁建设的实际状况：资金严重不足，修建时间长，跨越地区广等。文章最后引用不同人的话对美国高铁的建设做出了评价。由以上对各段内容的分析可知，本文核心内容是美国高铁，而讨论的重点是高铁建设的种种困境，纵观四个选项，只有选项[A]比较准确地概括了文章内容，故为正确选项。文章第五段至第六段中对加州高铁建设所遇到的种种困难的说明可知，加州并没有在高铁建设方面遥遥领先，故选项[B]可排除；选项[C]中的outdated infrastructure出现在第一段倒数第一句中，但文中意为"过时的基础设施建设并不是真正的问题"，选项[C]是对此细节的错误解读，且不能全面地概括全文的内容，故可排除；选项[D]仅是高铁建设面临困难的一方面原因，没有体现原文的核心内容——高铁建设，故也不够全面，应排除。

➡ 词汇精解 ⬅

1. desired [dɪˈzaɪə(r)d] a. 渴望的；称心的
2. twofer [ˈtuːfə] n. 两份；两方面（常用复数形式）；可半价优待的两张戏票
3. track [træk] n. 轨道；路径
4. locomotive [ˌləʊkəˈməʊtɪv] n. 火车头
5. division [dɪˈvɪʒn] n. 分支；部门
6. republican [rɪˈpʌblɪkən] n. 共和党人
7. infrastructure [ˈɪnfrəstrʌktʃə(r)] n. 基础设施；基础建设
8. bogeyman [ˈbəʊɡɪmæn] n. 怪物；令人害怕的人
9. governor [ˈɡʌvənə(r)] n. 州长；省长
10. federal [ˈfedərəl] a. 联邦的；n. 联邦主义者
11. democrat [ˈdeməkræt] n. 民主党人
12. rest [rest] n. 其余；剩余部分
13. vision [ˈvɪʒn] n. 视野；愿景
14. grand [ɡrænd] a. 盛大的；宏伟的
15. sparkle [ˈspɑːkl] v. 闪耀；发光
16. mock [mɒk] v. 取笑；戏弄
17. dystopian [dɪsˈtəʊpɪən] a. 反面乌托邦的
18. journalist [ˈdʒɜːnəlɪst] n. 记者
19. declinist [dɪˈklaɪmɪst] n. 唱衰主义者
20. obstinately [ˈɒbstɪnətli] ad. 固执地；执拗地
21. choke [tʃəʊk] v. 阻塞；塞满
22. delayed [dɪˈleɪd] a. 延迟的；推延的
23. flight [flaɪt] n. 航班；飞行
24. inadequate [ɪnˈædɪkwət] a. 不足的；不够的
25. voter [ˈvəʊtə(r)] n. 投票人
26. ballot [ˈbælət] n. 选票；投票
27. approve [əˈpruːv] v. 赞同；同意
28. fund [fʌnd] v. 投资

29. advertise [ˈædvətaɪz] v. 做广告；宣传	33. allocate [ˈæləkeɪt] v. 分配
30. assert [əˈsɜːt] v. 声明；表明	34. sparsely [ˈspɑːslɪ] ad. 稀疏地；稀少地
31. estimate [ˈestɪmət] n. 估算；估计	35. metaphor [ˈmetəfə(r)] n. 比喻
32. dollop [ˈdɒləp] n. 少量；一点儿	36. Vietnam [ˌvjetˈnæm] n. 越南

难句解析

1. First, building the special tracks and locomotives would put a division or two of America's army of unemployed back to work.	首先，建造特殊铁轨和火车头将会使美国的一两股失业大军重回岗位。

结构分析：这个句子可以划分为：First, <u>building the special tracks and locomotives</u> would put a division or two of America's army of unemployed back to work. 主语是下划线部分的动名词短语；谓语是 put，宾语是 a division or two of America's army of unemployed，最后的 back to work 作宾语补足语；也可将 put sb. back to work 视作固定短语，意思是：让某人重新就业。

2. Then, once built, the trains would get people out of cars and planes and to their destinations in a way that would be cleaner and use less foreign oil.	其次，一旦修建成功，高铁可以使人们出行不再选择使用汽车、飞机等交通工具，从而以更加清洁且减少使用进口油的方式到达目的地。

结构分析：这个句子可以划分为：Then, <u>once (the trains were) built</u>, the trains would get people out of cars and planes and to their destinations in a way (that would be cleaner and use less foreign oil). 下划线部分是时间状语从句，其中括号里是省略的内容；第二个括号里 that 引导的从句作 way 的定语。

3. Republicans have decided that government spending, not outdated infrastructure, is the real bogeyman, and Republican governors in Florida, Wisconsin and Ohio have rejected federal money to begin building.	共和党人认为问题不在于基础设施陈旧，政府开支才是真正可怕的问题。佛罗里达州、威斯康星州和俄亥俄州的州长们都已拒绝了联邦政府对高铁的投资。

结构分析：这个句子可以划分为：Republicans have decided <u>that government spending, not</u>

outdated infrastructure, is the real bogeyman,//and Republican governors in Florida, Wisconsin and Ohio have rejected federal money to begin building. 以 "//" 为界，and 连接了两个并列分句；第一个分句中下划线部分 that 引导的是 have decided 的宾语从句；第二个分句中下划线部分的不定式作 federal money 的后置定语。

> 4. As Governor Jerry Brown, aged 73 and a Democrat, likes to remember another big railway project in the 19th century connected the young state to the rest of America.
>
> 73 岁的州长杰里·布朗是一位民主党人，他总喜欢回忆 19 世纪的一个大型铁路项目将加州这个年轻的州与美国其他地方连接了起来的往事。

结构分析：这个句子可以划分为：As Governor Jerry Brown, aged 73 and a Democrat, likes to remember *(that) another big railway project in the 19th century connected the young state to the rest of America*. 下划线部分 and 连接的过去分词短语和名词短语分别作 Governor Jerry Brown 的后置定语；斜体部分的从句作 remember 的宾语，省略了引导词 that。

> 5. Today Mr. Brown still sparkles as he mocks the "dystopian journalists" and "declinists" who obstinately fail to see that California's population will grow from just under 38m now to about 50m in 2030; and that, unless the state has something like Japan's bullet trains, Californians will choke in traffic jams or go mad waiting for delayed flights in inadequate airports.
>
> 如今，布朗先生讽刺起那些"反乌托邦主义的记者"和"唱衰主义者"时依然两眼放光，他认为这些人没有认识到加州人口将会从目前的不足 3 800 万增长到 2030 年的 5 000 万左右，他们更没有认识到，除非加州有像日本一样的高速子弹头列车，否则加州人民将会在交通堵塞中窒息，或因机场资源不足而在等待延误的航班中发疯。

结构分析：这个句子可以划分为：Today Mr. Brown still sparkles//as he mocks the "dystopian journalists" and "declinists" *who obstinately fail to see that California's population will grow from just under 38m now to about 50m in 2030; and that, (unless the state has something like Japan's bullet trains), Californians will choke in traffic jams or go mad waiting for delayed flights in inadequate airports*. 以 "//" 为界，前面是主句，后面是 as 引导的时间状语从句；该从句中斜体部分 who 引导的从句作 the "dystopian journalists" and "declinists" 的定语；其中下划线部分 that...and that... 是并列的从句，作 fail to see 的宾语；括号里 unless 引导的条件状语从句将引导词 that 和

其主干分裂，起强调作用。

> 6. After the ballot measure, it was decided that construction should begin not in the two population centres but in the vast and flat farmlands of the Central Valley, where building is much easier.
>
> 投票过后，加州的铁路建设最终决定在中央峡谷广袤平坦的农田间进行，而不是两大人口聚集区，这会使施工更容易。

结构分析：这个句子可以划分为：After the ballot measure, it was decided <u>that construction should begin not in the two population centres but in the vast and flat farmlands of the Central Valley,</u> (where building is much easier). it 作形式主语，指代后面下划线部分 that 引导的从句；该从句中使用了 not... but...（不是……而是……）的并列结构；括号里 where 引导的从句作 farmlands of the Central Valley 的定语。

> 7. A high-speed train would then run through sparsely populated countryside, with hardly anybody riding it.
>
> 高铁将穿越人迹罕至的地域，几乎没人乘坐。

结构分析：这个句子可以划分为：A high-speed train would then run through sparsely populated countryside, <u>with hardly anybody riding it.</u> 下划线部分是独立主格结构，即 with+n.+doing，作结果状语。

> 8. Some call this a "train to nowhere," others a white elephant.
>
> 有人称其为"迷失了方向的列车"，另有人称之为"废物"。

结构分析：这个句子可以划分为：Some call this a "train to nowhere," others (call this) a white elephant. 括号内的内容是承前省略的内容。

> 9. Using a rather more original metaphor Richard White, a professor of history at Stanford, calls it "a Vietnam of transportation: easy to begin and difficult and expensive to stop."
>
> 或借用斯坦福大学教授理查德·怀特更具独创性的比喻：越南式的交通方式——起步容易停下则又贵又难（上车容易下车又贵又难）。

结构分析：这个句子可以划分为：<u>Using a rather more original metaphor</u> Richard White, (a professor of history at Stanford), calls it *"a Vietnam of transportation: easy to begin and difficult and expensive to stop."* 下划线部分的现在分词短语作方式状语；括号里的名词短语作主语 Richard

White 的同位语；斜体部分的名词短语作宾语 it 的补足语；冒号后面的形容词短语作 a Vietnam of transportation 的后置定语。

Text 9

1   Not too many decades ago it seemed "obvious" both to the general public and to sociologists that modern society has changed people's natural relations, loosened their responsibilities to kin and neighbors, and substituted in their place superficial relationships with passing acquaintances. However, in recent years a growing body of research has revealed that the "obvious" is not true. It seems that if you are a city resident, you typically know a smaller proportion of your neighbors than you do if you are a resident of a smaller community. But, for the most part, this fact has few significant consequences. It does not necessarily follow that if you know few of your neighbors you will know no one else.

2   Even in very large cities, people maintain close social ties within small, private social worlds. Indeed, the number and quality of meaningful relationships do not differ between more and less urban people. Small-town residents are more involved with kin than are big-city residents. Yet city dwellers compensate by developing friendships with people who share similar interests and activities. Urbanism may produce a different style of life, but the quality of life does not differ between town and city. Nor are residents of large communities any likelier to display psychological symptoms of stress

1 现代社会改变了人们的自然关系，淡化了他们对亲戚和邻居的责任感，取而代之的是表面上结交一些泛泛之交，这是多年来普通大众和社会学家都了解的一个"明显的"事实。但是，近年来越来越多的研究表明，这个"明显的"事实并不是真的。如果你是城市居民，那么通常你认识的邻居会比你住在小型社区认识的邻居要少。但是在极大程度上，这个事实没什么大不了。这并不一定意味着如果你认识的邻居少，就等于你不认识其他人。

2 即使在大城市，人们也在小的私人社交圈子里保持着紧密的联系。确实，有意义的关系的数量和质量在大城市居民和小城镇居民之间并无差别。同大城市居民相比，小城镇居民亲戚之间的关系更加亲密，而大城市的居民则与拥有相同兴趣及喜欢相同活动的人发展彼此的友谊。都市生活形成了不同的生活风格，但城市和小城镇的生活质量并无差别。同小城镇居民相比，大城市居民也没有更易于表现出压力、疏远或者没有归属

or alienation, a feeling of not belonging, than are residents of smaller communities. However, city dwellers do worry more about crime, and this leads them to a distrust of strangers.

 3 These findings do not imply that urbanism makes little or no difference. If neighbors are strangers to one another, they are less likely to sweep the sidewalk of an elderly couple living next door or keep an eye out for young trouble makers. Moreover, as Wirth suggested, there may be a link between a community's population size and its social heterogeneity (多样性). For instance, sociologists have found much evidence that the size of a community is associated with bad behavior including gambling, drugs, etc. Large-city urbanites are also more likely than their small-town counterparts to have a cosmopolitan outlook, to display less responsibility to traditional kinship roles, to vote for leftist political candidates, and to be tolerant of nontraditional religious groups, unpopular political groups, and so-called undesirables. Everything considered, heterogeneity and unusual behavior seem to be outcomes of large population size.

感的心理症状。但城市居民的确更为担心犯罪，这使他们不信任陌生人。

 3 这些发现并不意味着都市生活乏善可陈。如果邻居互不认识，就不大可能有人帮助清扫隔壁老夫妇门前的人行道，也不会时刻警惕捣乱的青年人。而且，正如沃思所认为的，社区人口的多少与其社会群体的多样性之间可能有关联。例如，社会学家发现，许多证据表明，社区规模同赌博、吸毒等恶习有关。同小镇居民相比，大城市的居民可能见识更广，对传统意义的亲属关系责任感更少，更可能投票给左翼政治候选人，对非传统宗教团体、不受欢迎的政治集团和所谓的不良分子也很宽容。从对各方面的因素考虑来看，多样混杂性和反常行为似乎是人口众多的结果。

1. Which of the following statements best describes the organization of the first paragraph?

 [A] Two contrasting views are presented.

 [B] An argument is examined and possible solutions are given.

 [C] Research results concerning the quality of urban life are presented in order of time.

 [D] A detailed description of the difference between urban and small-town life is given.

2. According to the passage, it was once a common belief that urban residents _____.

 [A] did not have the same interests as their neighbors

[B] could not develop long-standing relationships

[C] tended to be associated with bad behavior

[D] usually had more friends

3. One of the consequences of urban life is that impersonal relationships among neighbors _____.

[A] disrupt people's natural relations

[B] make them worry about crime

[C] cause them not to show concern for one another

[D] cause them to be suspicious of each other

4. It can be inferred from the passage that the bigger a community is, _____.

[A] the better its quality of life

[B] the more similar its interests

[C] the more tolerant and open-minded it is

[D] the likelier it is to display psychological symptoms of stress

5. What is the passage mainly about?

[A] Similarities in the interpersonal relationships between urbanites and small-town dwellers.

[B] Advantages of living in big cities as compared with living in small town.

[C] The positive role that urbanism plays in modern life.

[D] The strong feeling of alienation of city inhabitants.

解题之路

1. 【答案】A 【题型】段落大意题。

   【思路】该题考查的是段落的主旨大意。要解决这类考题，应注意表示各种关系的连词、副词、句与句之间的关系，在本题中只要注意到however就可以推出选项[A]是正确答案。

2. 【答案】B 【题型】事实细节题。

   【思路】文章第一段所展示的第一种观点substituted in their place superficial relationships with passing acquaintances说明人们以往是认为城市居民不可能发展长久的友谊的，所以对应的正确答案是选项[B]。

3. 【答案】C 【题型】事实细节题。

   【思路】文章第三段提到：If neighbors are strangers to one another, they are less likely to

189

sweep the sidewalk of an elderly couple living next door or keep an eye out for young trouble makers，说明邻里之间很可能出现彼此都不关心的状况，即选项[C]所述内容。

4. 【答案】C 【题型】推理判断题。

   【思路】文章最后提到，大城市的居民比小城镇居民更见多识广，to be tolerant of nontraditional religious groups，说明社区越大，人们越容易变得包容，思想也越开明，所以答案为选项[C]。

5. 【答案】A 【题型】主旨大意题。

   【思路】本篇文章对比了大城市与小城镇的人际关系，但并没有强调在大城市中居住的优越之处，所以选项[B]不对；文中提到了很多在城市居住的负面影响，显然选项[C]也不对；文章第二段中提到Nor are residents of large communities any likelier to display psychological symptoms of stress or alienation，说明选项[D]是错误的。由此可以判断答案为选项[A]。

词汇精解

1. decade [ˈdekeɪd] n. 十年
2. obvious [ˈɒbvɪəs] a. 明显的，显而易见的
3. sociologist [ˌsəʊsɪˈɒlədʒɪst] n. 社会学家
4. loosen [ˈluːsn] v. 解开，松开；放松
5. kin [kɪn] n. 家属（总称）；家族；血缘关系
6. substitute [ˈsʌbstɪtjuːt] v. 代替，替换
7. superficial [ˌsuːpəˈfɪʃl] a. 表面的，肤浅的，浅薄的
8. typically [ˈtɪpɪklɪ] ad. 代表性地；有特色地；一般地
9. proportion [prəˈpɔːʃn] n. 比例；均衡；部分
10. necessarily [ˈnesəs(ə)rəlɪ] ad. 必要地，一定
11. compensate [ˈkɒmpenseɪt] v. 偿还；补偿；付报酬
12. activity [ækˈtɪvətɪ] n. 活动；行动
13. display [dɪˈspleɪ] v. 陈列，展览；展示
14. psychological [ˌsaɪkəˈlɒdʒɪkl] a. 心理学的，心理的
15. symptom [ˈsɪmptəm] n. 症状，征兆
16. alienation [ˌeɪlɪəˈneɪʃn] n. 疏远，离间
17. sweep [swiːp] v. 打扫，扫过；席卷；掠过
18. couple [ˈkʌpl] n. 一对，一双；夫妇
19. urbanite [ˈɜːbənaɪt] n. 都市人，城市居民
20. counterpart [ˈkaʊntəpɑːt] n. 副本；对应的人或物
21. cosmopolitan [ˌkɒzməˈpɒlɪtən] a. 世界性的；见多识广的
22. outlook [ˈaʊtlʊk] n. 景色，风光；展望；眼界
23. leftist [ˈleftɪst] a. 左翼的，左派的
24. candidate [ˈkændɪdət] n. 候选人；投考者

25. nontraditional [ˌnɒntrəˈdɪʃənəl] *a.* 不符合传统的；非传统的	受欢迎的人
26. undesirable [ˌʌndɪˈzaɪərəbl] *n.* 不良分子；不	27. heterogeneity [ˌhetərədʒəˈniːəti] *n.* 异种；异质
	28. outcome [ˈaʊtkʌm] *n.* 成果；结果

难句解析

> 1. Not too many decades ago it seemed "obvious" both to the general public and to sociologists that modern society has changed people's natural relations, loosened their responsibilities to kin and neighbors, and substituted in their place superficial relationships with passing acquaintances.
>
> 现代社会改变了人们的自然关系，淡化了他们对亲戚和邻居的责任感，取而代之的是表面上结交一些泛泛之交，这是多年来普通大众和社会学家都了解的一个"明显的"事实。

结构分析：这是一个形式主语句，可以切分为：(Not too many decades ago) (it seemed "obvious") (both to the general public and to sociologists) (that modern society has changed people's natural relations, loosened their responsibilities//to kin and neighbors//, and substituted//in their place//superficial relationships with passing acquaintances). 第一部分是时间状语；第二部分是主干，是一个形式主语句，主语 it 指代第四部分 that 引导的从句；第三部分是 both... and 连接的并列介词短语，作范围状语；第四部分 that 从句由三个句子组成，即 modern society has changed... loosened... and substituted...，介词短语 to kin and neighbors 是 responsibilities 的后置定语，in their place 是地点状语，substitute 与后面的 with 形成固定搭配。

> 2. It seems that if you are a city resident, you typically know a smaller proportion of your neighbors than you do if you are a resident of a smaller community.
>
> 如果你是城市居民，那么通常你认识的邻居会比你住在小型社区认识的邻居要少。

结构分析：这个句子可以切分为：(It seems that//if you are a city resident//, you typically know a smaller proportion of your neighbors) (than you do//if you are a resident of a smaller community//). 第一部分是一个形式主语句，it 指代之后的 that 引导的从句，即：that... you typically know... neighbors，分隔号内是 if 引导的条件状语从句；第二部分的 than 引导比较状语从句，与前面的 smaller 相呼应，谓语 do 指代前面的 know。

3. It does not necessarily follow that if you know few of your neighbors you will know no one else.

这并不一定意味着如果你认识的邻居少，就等于你不认识其他人。

结构分析：这是一个主从复合句，可以切分为：(It does not necessarily follow) (that//if you know few of your neighbors//you will know no one else). 第一部分是主句，是形式主语句，it 指代第二部分 that 从句的内容；第二部分中的主干是 you will know no one else，分隔号内是 if 引导的条件状语从句，即：if you...neighbors。

4. Yet city dwellers compensate by developing friendships with people who share similar interests and activities.

而大城市的居民则与拥有相同兴趣及喜欢相同活动的人发展彼此的友谊。

结构分析：这个句子可以切分为：(Yet city dwellers compensate) (by developing friendships with people) (who share similar interests and activities). 第一部分是主干；第二部分是 by 引导的方式状语；第三部分是 who 引导的定语从句，修饰 people。

5. Nor are residents of large communities any likelier to display psychological symptoms of stress or alienation, a feeling of not belonging, than are residents of smaller communities.

同小城镇居民相比，大城市居民也没有更易于表现出压力、疏远或者没有归属感的心理症状。

结构分析：这是一个倒装句，否定词 Nor 移至句首，形成部分倒装；句子可以切分为：(Nor are residents of large communities any likelier to display psychological symptoms of stress or alienation), (a feeling of not belonging), (than are residents of smaller communities). 第一部分是主干，主语是 residents，谓语是 are not any likelier to display，宾语是 psychological... alienation；第二部分 a feeling... belonging 是一个名词短语，作前面 alienation 的同位语；第三部分是 than 引导的比较状语从句，与前面的 likelier 相呼应，也使用了倒装结构，且有省略现象，正常语序是 than residents of smaller communities are (not any likely to display...)。

6. If neighbors are strangers to one another, they are less likely to sweep the sidewalk of an elderly couple living next door or keep an eye out for young trouble makers.

如果邻居互不认识，就不大可能有人帮助清扫隔壁老夫妇门前的人行道，也不会时刻警惕捣乱的青年人。

结构分析：这是一个主从复合句，逗号之前是 if 引导的条件状语从句，其中的介词短语 to one another 作状语；主句的主干是 they are less likely to sweep the sidewalk... or keep an eye out for young trouble makers，现在分词 living 是 elderly couple 的后置定语，名词短语 next door 是方位状语，keep an eye out for 是固定短语。

> 7. Large-city urbanites are also more likely than their small-town counterparts to have a cosmopolitan outlook, to display less responsibility to traditional kinship roles, to vote for leftist political candidates, and to be tolerant of nontraditional religious groups, unpopular political groups, and so-called undesirables.

同小镇居民相比，大城市的居民可能见识更广，对传统意义的亲属关系责任感更少，更可能投票给左翼政治候选人，对非传统宗教团体、不受欢迎的政治集团和所谓的不良分子也很宽容。

结构分析：这个句子的主干是 Large-city urbanites are also more likely...to have...to display...to vote for...and to be tolerant of...，四个 to 引导的是并列不定式，与 likely 构成固定搭配；第二个不定式中的介词短语 to...roles 是 responsibility 的后置定语。

> 8. Everything considered, heterogeneity and unusual behavior seem to be outcomes of large population size.

从对各方面的因素考虑来看，多样混杂性和反常行为似乎是人口众多的结果。

结构分析：这个句子的主语是 heterogeneity and unusual behavior，谓语是 seem to be，表语是 outcomes；Everything considered 是独立主格结构，considered 是过去分词，与 Everything 构成动宾关系。

Text 10

1 Everybody loves a fat pay rise. Yet pleasure at your own can vanish if you learn that a colleague has been given a bigger one. Indeed, if he has a reputation for slacking, you might even be outraged. Such behaviour is regarded as "all too human," with the underlying assumption that other animals would not be capable of this finely developed sense of

1　人人都喜欢大幅加薪，但是当你知道一个同事薪水加得比你还要多的时候，那么加薪带给你的喜悦感就消失得无影无踪了。事实上，如果他还以懒散出名的话，你甚至会变得怒不可遏。这种行为被看作是"人之常情"，其潜在的假定是：其他动物

grievance. But a study by Sarah Brosnan and Frans de Waal of Emory University in Atlanta, Georgia, which has just been published in *Nature*, suggests that it is all too monkey, as well.

2 The researchers studied the behaviour of female brown capuchin monkeys. They look cute. They are good-natured, co-operative creatures, and they share their food readily. Above all, like their female human counterparts, they tend to pay much closer attention to the value of "goods and services" than males.

3 Such characteristics make them perfect candidates for Dr. Brosnan's and Dr. de Waal's study. The researchers spent two years teaching their monkeys to exchange tokens for food. Normally, the monkeys were happy enough to exchange pieces of rock for slices of cucumber. However, when two monkeys were placed in separate but adjoining chambers, so that each could observe what the other was getting in return for its rock, their behaviour became markedly different.

4 In the world of capuchins, grapes are luxury goods (and much preferable to cucumbers). So when one monkey was handed a grape in exchange for her token, the second was reluctant to hand hers over for a mere piece of cucumber. And if one received a grape without having to provide her token in exchange at all, the other either tossed her own token

at the researcher or out of the chamber, or refused to accept the slice of cucumber. Indeed, the mere presence of a grape in the other chamber (without an actual monkey to eat it) was enough to induce resentment in a female capuchin.

5   The researchers suggest that capuchin monkeys, like humans, are guided by social emotions. In the wild, they are a co-operative, group-living species. Such co-operation is likely to be stable only when each animal feels it is not being cheated. Feelings of righteous indignation, it seems, are not the preserve of people alone. Refusing a lesser reward completely makes these feelings abundantly clear to other members of the group. However, whether such a sense of fairness evolved independently in capuchins and humans, or whether it stems from the common ancestor that the species had 35 million years ago, is, as yet, an unanswered question.

1. In the opening paragraph, the author introduces his topic by _____.

    [A] posing a contrast

    [B] justifying an assumption

    [C] making a comparison

    [D] explaining a phenomenon

2. The statement "it is all too monkey" (Last line, Paragraph 1) implies that _____.

    [A] monkeys are also outraged by slack rivals

    [B] resenting unfairness is also monkeys' nature

    [C] monkeys, like humans, tend to be jealous of each other

    [D] no animals other than monkeys can develop such emotions

3. Female capuchin monkeys were chosen for the research most probably because they are _____.

[A] more inclined to weigh what they get

[B] attentive to researchers' instructions

[C] nice in both appearance and temperament

[D] more generous than their male companions

4. Dr. Brosnan and Dr. de Waal have eventually found in their study that the monkeys _____.

[A] prefer grapes to cucumbers

[B] can be taught to exchange things

[C] will not be co-operative if feeling cheated

[D] are unhappy when separated from others

5. What can we infer from the last paragraph?

[A] Monkeys can be trained to develop social emotions.

[B] Human indignation evolved from an uncertain source.

[C] Animals usually show their feelings openly as humans do.

[D] Cooperation among monkeys remains stable only in the wild.

◆ 解题之路 ◆

1. 【答案】C 【题型】段落结构题。

    【思路】这种题型一般不多见。本题涉及首段与文章主题之间的逻辑联系。题干问："在文章首段，作者引入主题的手段是……"首段说，人会对不公正待遇感到愤懑，并自以为这是人类才有的一种感觉；段末说，研究表明猴也有这种感觉；下文接着探讨猴对不公正的详细感受。可见，作者通过把猴与人做比较（comparison），来引出文章的主题，所以答案为选项[C]。选项[A]则认为，猴与人在进行对照，两者不一样，这显然与首段的意思不吻合。误选选项[A]的原因是，一方面被"But"误导，将首段理解反了，另一方面没能区分comparison（强调相同性）和contrast（强调不同）之间的差异，两词的含义不同。

2. 【答案】B 【题型】句意理解题。

    【思路】题干问："首段末行'it is all too monkey'暗示了……"本题可以定位在首段，分析该段的逻辑关系，不难发现作者指出了两者的相似之处，就是选项[B]"对不公平的怨恨也是猴子的本性"的含义。选项[D]"除了猴子之外其他动物都不会有这种感情"与篇章的思想相矛盾；选项[A]"懒散的对手也会使猴子大发雷霆"是对原文片语信息的断章取义；选项[C]"像人类一样，猴子往往会互相嫉妒"不是作者谈论的重点，作者谈论的是义愤的情感。

3. 【答案】**A** 【题型】原因细节题。

   【思路】该题涉及句意的因果逻辑。题干问："研究选用了雌性卷尾猴，最可能的原因是它们……"第二段末句 pay much closer attention to the value of...（更关注……的价值）换词后就是 are more inclined to weigh（更会掂量），可见答案为选项[A]"更倾向于权衡它们所获得的东西"。选项[B]"专心聆听研究者们的指导"，选项[C]"漂亮且性情温和"，以及选项[D]"比雄性伙伴更大方"，都是对原文片语信息的断章取义，或者是原文未提及的信息。

4. 【答案】**C** 【题型】事实细节题。

   【思路】题干问："布罗斯南博士和德瓦尔博士在他们的研究中最后发现猴子……"如果注意到题干中"eventually"一词，就可以定位在第五段而选择选项[C]："如果感到被欺骗就不再合作"，该选项是对第五段第三句的正确改写：Such co-operation is likely to be stable only when each animal feels it is not being cheated。其实，关于群居动物在公平条件下合作的思想在上文第二段第三句就有提及：They are good-natured, co-operative creatures。选项[A]"更喜欢葡萄，而不是黄瓜"与选项[B]"可以被教会交换东西"不是研究者的发现，而选项[D]"当与其他卷尾猴分开时感到不高兴"是对原文片语信息的断章取义。

5. 【答案】**B** 【题型】推理判断题。

   【思路】题干问："从最后一段我们可以得出什么推论？"本题直接定位在第五段的末句，即 However 之后：whether such a sense of fairness evolved independently in capuchins and humans, or whether it stems from the common ancestor that the species had 35 million years ago, is, as yet, an unanswered question，由此可知选项[B]"人类义愤填膺情感的进化来源不确定"正确。选项[A]不对，因为 social emotions 是猴子天生具有的（末段首句），谈不上 develop（培养）；选项[C]"动物常常像人类那样公开显示出它们的感情"不正确，篇章中没有明显提出这一信息；选项[D]"猴子间的合作只有在野外时才保持稳定"错误，这是对第五段第二句、第三句的曲解，原文强调的是在受到公平对待时关系才会保持稳定。

词汇精解

1. pleasure [ˈpleʒə(r)] n. 乐趣，快乐	5. underlying [ˌʌndəˈlaɪɪŋ] a. 潜在的，内含的
2. reputation [ˌrepjuˈteɪʃn] n. 声望，名声	6. assumption [əˈsʌmpʃn] n. 假定，假说
3. slacking [ˈslækɪŋ] n. 懒散，懒惰	7. capable [ˈkeɪpəbl] a. 有能力的，有技能的
4. outraged [ˈaʊtreɪdʒd] a. 义愤的，愤怒的	8. grievance [ˈgriːvəns] n. 委屈，抱怨

9. good-natured [gʊd'neɪtʃəd] a. 脾气好的，温厚的
10. counterpart ['kaʊntəpɑːt] n. 与对方地位作用相当的人（或物）
11. characteristic [ˌkærəktə'rɪstɪk] n. 特色，特点
12. candidate ['kændɪdət] n. 候选人；投考者
13. exchange [ɪks'tʃeɪndʒ] v. 交换；交流
14. token ['təʊkən] n. 代币；信物，纪念品
15. slice [slaɪs] n. 薄片；一份，部分
16. cucumber ['kjuːkʌmbə(r)] n. 黄瓜
17. adjoining [ə'dʒɔɪnɪŋ] a. 相邻的，紧挨的
18. chamber ['tʃeɪmbə(r)] n.（特殊用途的）房间；会所
19. markedly ['mɑːkɪdli] ad. 明显地，显著地
20. luxury ['lʌkʃəri] n. 奢侈品；奢华
21. preferable ['prefrəbl] a. 更可取的，更好的，更合意的
22. reluctant [rɪ'lʌktənt] a. 不乐意的，不情愿的
23. toss [tɒs] v. 扔，抛
24. resentment [rɪ'zentmənt] n. 憎恨，痛恨
25. stable ['steɪbl] a. 稳定的；沉稳的
26. righteous ['raɪtʃəs] a. 正当的，合理的
27. indignation [ˌɪndɪg'neɪʃn] n. 愤怒，愤慨
28. preserve [prɪ'zɜːv] n. 专门领域
29. abundantly [ə'bʌndəntli] ad. 十分清楚；非常明白
30. evolve [ɪ'vɒlv] v. 进化，发展
31. ancestor ['ænsestə(r)] n. 祖先；先驱

◆ 难句解析 ◆

1. Such behaviour is regarded as "all too human," with the underlying assumption that other animals would not be capable of this finely developed sense of grievance.	这种行为被看作是"人之常情"，其潜在的假定是：其他动物不可能具有如此高度发达的不公平意识。

结构分析：逗号之前的内容是句子的主干，逗号之后的介词短语 with the underlying assumption... 作伴随状语，assumption 之后的 that 引导一个同位语从句，解释前面的名词 assumption。

2. But a study by Sarah Brosnan and Frans de Waal of Emory University in Atlanta, Georgia, which has just been published in *Nature*, suggests that it is all too monkey, as well.	但是由佐治亚州亚特兰大市埃默里大学的萨拉·布罗斯南和弗朗斯·德瓦尔进行的一项研究表明，它也是"猴之常情"。这项研究成果刚刚发表在《自然》杂志上。

结构分析：本句的主干是 a study... suggests that...，其中主语 study 有两个定语：一个是介词结构 by Sarah Brosnan and Frans de Waal...，另一个是 which 引导的非限定性定语从句。谓语动词 suggests 后面的 that 引导一个宾语从句，其中的 it 指代前文提到的 sense of grievance。

| 3. However, when two monkeys were placed in separate but adjoining chambers, so that each could observe what the other was getting in return for its rock, their behaviour became markedly different. | 但是，当两只猴子被安置在隔开但相邻的两个房间里，能够互相看见对方用石头换回来什么东西时，猴子的行为就会变得明显不同。 |

结构分析：本句是一个复合句。主句在最后：their behaviour became markedly different；起头的是 when 引导的时间状语从句，其中包含 so that 引导的目的状语从句，而 observe 之后是 what 引导的宾语从句。

| 4. And if one received a grape without having to provide her token in exchange at all, the other either tossed her own token at the researcher or out of the chamber, or refused to accept the slice of cucumber. | 如果一只猴子根本无须用代币就能够得到一颗葡萄的话，那么另外一只就会将代币掷向研究人员或者扔出房间外，又或者拒绝接受那片黄瓜。 |

结构分析：本句是一个复合句。起头的是 if 引导的条件状语从句，第一个逗号之后的部分是主句：the other either tossed her own token... or refused to...，其中包含两个并列的谓语：tossed 和 refused。本句的难点是找到主句的三个并列谓语，并判断出第二个谓语 tossed 被省略，补全后是：either tossed her own token at the researcher or (tossed her own token) out of the chamber。

| 5. However, whether such a sense of fairness evolved independently in capuchins and humans, or whether it stems from the common ancestor that the species had 35 million years ago, is, as yet, an unanswered question. | 但是，这种公平感是在卷尾猴和人类身上各自独立演化而成，还是源自 3 500 万年前他们共同的祖先，依然是一个悬而未决的问题。 |

结构分析：本句的主语很复杂，由 whether... or...（是……还是……）结构充当，其中 whether... 引导一个主语从句，or... 后面也是一个主语从句，而且这一从句的宾语 ancestor 后面的 that 又引导了一个定语从句，修饰 ancestor；主句的谓语是系动词 is，an unanswered question 是表语；as yet 是一个时间状语，意思是"迄今为止"。注意：本句的主语由两个从句充当。这

种"头重脚轻"的句子在学术文章中很常见，阅读时应该迅速把握主干，进而再理解复杂的主语成分。

Text 11

1 **Prior** to the 20th century, many languages with small numbers of speakers **survived** for centuries. The increasingly interconnected modern world makes it much more difficult for small language **communities** to live in **relative isolation**, a key factor in language **maintenance** and **preservation**.

2 It remains to be seen whether the world can maintain its **linguistic** and cultural **diversity** in the centuries ahead. Many powerful forces appear to work against it: population growth, which pushes **migrant** populations into the world's last isolated locations; mass **tourism**; global telecommunications and mass media; and the spread of **gigantic** global corporations. All of these forces appear to **signify** a future in which the language of advertising, popular culture, and consumer products becomes similar. Already English and a few other major **tongues** have emerged as global languages of **commerce** and communication. For many of the world's peoples, learning one of these languages is viewed as the key to education, economic opportunity, and a better way of life.

3 Only about 3,000 languages now in use are expected to survive the coming century. Are most of the rest **doomed** in the century after that?

4 Whether most of these languages survive will probably depend on how strongly cultural

1 20世纪以前，很多种只有少数人使用的语言都留存了若干个世纪。联系日益密切的现代世界使小语种团体更难存在于相对隔绝的环境中，而这种相对隔绝的环境对于语言的维系来说是至关重要的因素。

2 在未来的几个世纪，语言和文化的多样性能否保持下来还有待证实。许多强大的影响力似乎不利于这种多样性的保持：人口增长促使移民人口涌入世界最后一些僻静之地；大规模的观光旅游；全球电信和大众媒体；以及巨型跨国公司的扩张。所有的这些影响力似乎预示着一个广告语言、流行文化、消费品逐渐趋同的未来。英语和其他几种主要的语言早已成为全球性的商务交流语言。全球众多人将学习一种这样的语言视为是通往教育、谋生机会和更好生活方式的关键。

3 只有大约3 000种现存语言有望在下个世纪中存续下去。21世纪内剩余的大多数语言接下来就要消失了吗？

4 这些剩余的大多数语言是否能够留存下来，可能要取决于文化群

groups wish to keep their identity alive through a native language. To do so will require an emphasis on bilingualism (mastery of two languages). Bilingual speakers could use their own language in smaller spheres—at home, among friends, in community settings—and a global language at work, in dealings with government, and in commercial spheres. In this way, many small languages could sustain their cultural and linguistic integrity alongside global languages rather than yield to the homogenizing forces of globalization.

5 Ironically, the trend of technological innovation that has threatened minority languages could also help save them. For example, some experts predict that computer software translation tools will one day permit minority language speakers to browse the Internet using their native tongues. Linguists are currently using computer-aided learning tools to teach a variety of threatened languages.

6 For many endangered languages, the line between revival and death is extremely thin. Language is remarkably resilient, however. It is not just a tool for communicating, but also a powerful way of separating different groups, or of demonstrating group identity. Many indigenous communities have shown that it is possible to live in the modern world while reclaiming their unique identities through language.

体通过母语来维持自身特性的意愿是否强烈。要做到这一点，就要强调对双语的掌握。掌握双语的人能够在较小范围内（在家，和朋友一起，在社团中）使用他们自己的语言，而在工作中、与政府打交道时或者在商务领域使用全球通用语言。这样很多小语种就能够跟全球通用语言并存，可以维系它们的文化和语言的完整，而不受制于全球化的同化影响。

5 具有讽刺意味的是，使小语种受到威胁的技术革新趋势却也有助于挽救小语种。比如，一些专家预测，计算机翻译软件终有一天能够让使用小语种的人用他们的母语上网浏览。语言学家目前正在使用计算机辅助教学工具教授多种濒临失传的语言。

6 对于许多濒临灭亡的语言来说，复兴还是消失只是一线之隔。然而，语言具有强大的适应性。它不仅是交流的工具，也是划分不同族群或展现族群特性的有力方法。许多土著居民区已经证明，在现代社会生活的同时通过语言恢复其独特的（族群）特性是可能的。

1. Minority languages can be best preserved in _____.

   [A] an increasingly interconnected world

   [B] maintaining small numbers of speakers

   [C] relatively isolated language communities

   [D] following the tradition of the 20th century

2. According to Paragraph 2, that the world can maintain its linguistic diversity in the future is _____.

   [A] uncertain

   [B] unrealistic

   [C] foreseeable

   [D] definite

3. According to the author, bilingualism can help _____.

   [A] small languages become acceptable in work places

   [B] homogenize the world's languages and cultures

   [C] global languages reach home and community settings

   [D] speakers maintain their linguistic and cultural identity

4. Computer technology is helpful for preserving minority languages in that it _____.

   [A] makes learning a global language unnecessary

   [B] facilitates the learning and using of those languages

   [C] raises public awareness of saving those languages

   [D] makes it easier for linguists to study those languages

5. In the author's view, many endangered languages are _____.

   [A] remarkably well-kept in this modern world

   [B] exceptionally powerful tools of communication

   [C] quite possible to be revived instead of dying out

   [D] a unique way of bringing different groups together

➡ 解题之路 ⬅

1. 【答案】C 【题型】细节题。

   【思路】根据题干中的关键词Minority languages和preserved可定位到首段第二句，Minority languages对应原文的small language, be preserved in对应in language preservation,

选项[C]中的relatively isolated对应原文的relative isolation，属于同义替换。选项[A]与原文说法矛盾；选项[B]为小语种的特征，与其能否得到保存无关；选项[D]属于无中生有。

2. 【答案】A 【题型】细节题。

   【思路】根据题干的关键词the world can maintain its linguistic diversity可定位到第二段的首句，题干中的in the future对应原文的in the centuries ahead，uncertain与It remains to be seen对应。选项[B]、[C]、[D]过于绝对，且与原文意思相悖。

3. 【答案】D 【题型】细节题。

   【思路】根据题干的关键词bilingualism可定位到原文的第四段第三句话：Bilingual speakers...，以及最后一句话：In this way... globalization，选项[D]中的maintain对应原文的sustain，identity对应integrity。选项[A]、[B]、[C]均与原文相悖。

4. 【答案】B 【题型】细节题。

   【思路】根据题干的关键词Computer technology定位到第五段首句。题干是对原文的同义改写：Computer technology对应technological innovation，is helpful对应could also help，preserving对应save。选项[A]、[C]属于无中生有，而[D]中的study与原文的teach矛盾。

5. 【答案】C 【题型】推理判断题。

   【思路】根据题干的关键词endangered languages定位到末段首行。第二句的转折词however意义重大，表明可能是作者观点的隐藏处。选项[A]中的remarkably well-kept与文章主旨矛盾；[B]中的exceptionally过于绝对；[D]中的bringing... together与原文的separating意思相反。

▶ 词汇精解 ◀

1. prior ['praɪə(r)] a. 在……之前的；优先的	9. diversity [daɪ'vɜːsətɪ] n. 多样性，种类
2. survive [sə'vaɪv] v. 幸存；活下来	10. migrant ['maɪɡrənt] a. 移动的，流动的
3. community [kə'mjuːnətɪ] n. 社区；领域	11. tourism ['tʊərɪzəm] n. 旅游，旅游业
4. relative ['relətɪv] a. 相对的	12. gigantic [dʒaɪ'ɡæntɪk] a. 巨大的
5. isolation [ˌaɪsə'leɪʃn] n. 隔离；孤立	13. signify ['sɪɡnɪfaɪ] v. 预示，标志着
6. maintenance ['meɪntənəns] n. 维持，维护	14. tongue [tʌŋ] n. 舌头；语言
7. preservation [ˌprezə'veɪʃ(ə)n] n. 保护，保存	15. commerce ['kɒmɜːs] n. 商业
8. linguistic [lɪŋ'ɡwɪstɪk] a. 语言的，语言学的	16. doomed [duːmd] a. 注定的，气数已尽的
	17. identity [aɪ'dentətɪ] n. 身份

18. bilingualism [baɪ'lɪŋgwəlɪzəm] n. 双语性，双语现象
19. sphere [sfɪə(r)] n. 范围；领域；球体
20. sustain [sə'steɪn] v. 维持，维系
21. yield [ji:ld] v. 屈从，屈服
22. homogenizing [hə'mɒdʒənaɪzɪŋ] a. 同化的，有同化作用的
23. globalization [ˌgləʊbəlaɪ'zeɪʃn] n. 全球化，全球一体化
24. ironically [aɪ'rɒnɪklɪ] ad. 讽刺地
25. innovation [ˌɪnə'veɪʃn] n. 革新，创新
26. threaten ['θretn] v. 威胁
27. minority [maɪ'nɒrətɪ] n. 少数（人），少数民族
28. browse [braʊz] v. 浏览
29. a variety of... 大量的，许多
30. revival [rɪ'vaɪvl] n. 复兴，复活
31. resilient [rɪ'zɪlɪənt] a. 适应性强的；有弹性的
32. indigenous [ɪn'dɪdʒənəs] a. 原生的，土著的
33. reclaim [rɪ'kleɪm] v. 要求，索回
34. unique [ju:'ni:k] a. 独特的，唯一的

难句解析

1. The increasingly interconnected modern world makes it much more difficult for small language communities to live in relative isolation, a key factor in language maintenance and preservation.

联系日益密切的现代世界使小语种团体更难存在于相对隔绝的环境中，而这种相对隔绝的环境对于语言的维系来说是至关重要的因素。

结构分析：这个句子的主语是 The increasingly interconnected modern world，谓语是 makes，宾语是 it，指代后面的不定式 to live in relative isolation；名词短语 a key factor 是前面 small language communities to live in relative isolation 的同位语，in language maintenance and preservation 是 a key factor 的后置定语。

2. It remains to be seen whether the world can maintain its linguistic and cultural diversity in the centuries ahead.

在未来的几个世纪，语言和文化的多样性能否保持下来还有待证实。

结构分析：这是一个主从复合句。主句是：It remains to be seen，其中的 it 指代后面 whether 引导的从句。

3. Many powerful forces appear to work against it: population growth, which pushes migrant populations into the world's last isolated locations; mass tourism; global telecommunications and mass media; and the spread of gigantic global corporations.

许多强大的影响力似乎不利于这种多样性的保持：人口增长促使移民人口涌入世界最后一些僻静之地；大规模的观光旅游；全球电信和大众媒体；以及巨型跨国公司的扩张。

结构分析：冒号之前的内容是主干，主语是 Many powerful forces，谓语是 appear to work against，宾语是 it，指代上文的 whether the world can maintain its linguistic and cultural diversity in the centuries ahead；冒号之后是并列的几个名词短语：population growth; mass tourism; global telecommunications and mass media; and the spread of gigantic global corporations，均是前面 Many powerful forces 的同位语，第一个名词短语 population growth 之后还有一个 which 引导的定语从句。

4. All of these forces appear to signify a future in which the language of advertising, popular culture, and consumer products becomes similar.

所有的这些影响力似乎预示着一个广告语言、流行文化、消费品逐渐趋同的未来。

结构分析：这是一个主从复合句。主句的主语是 All of these forces，谓语是 appear to signify，宾语是 a future；in which 引导的是 a future 的定语从句，属于"介词+关系代词"的模式。

5. Whether most of these languages survive will probably depend on how strongly cultural groups wish to keep their identity alive through a native language.

这些剩余的大多数语言是否能够留存下来，可能要取决于文化群体通过母语来维持自身特性的意愿是否强烈。

结构分析：这个句子的主语是 Whether... will depend on...，即 Whether 引导主语从句，谓语是 will depend on，宾语是 how 引导的从句；该从句中的主语是 cultural groups，谓语是 wish to keep，宾语是 their identity，形容词 alive 是宾语补足语，介词短语 through a native language 是谓语的方式状语。

6. For example, some experts predict that computer software translation tools will one day permit minority language speakers to browse the Internet using their native tongues.

比如，一些专家预测，计算机翻译软件终有一天能够让使用小语种的人用他们的母语上网浏览。

结构分析：这是一个主从复合句。主句的主语是 some experts，谓语是 predict，宾语是 that 引导的从句；该从句中使用了固定搭配 permit sb. to do sth.，现在分词 using 是方式状语，修饰前面的 browse。

> 7. Many indigenous communities have shown that it is possible to live in the modern world while reclaiming their unique identities through language.
>
> 许多土著居民区已经证明，在现代社会生活的同时并通过语言恢复其独特的（族群）特性是可能的。

结构分析：这是一个主从复合句。主句的主语是 Many indigenous communities，谓语是 have shown，宾语是 that 引导的从句；该从句的主语是 it，指代后面的不定式 to live in the modern world，句末的 while 引导的是时间状语从句，其中使用了省略手段，复原后是：while (they are) reclaiming their unique identities through language。

Text 12

1 Everyone, it seems, has a health problem. After pouring billions into the National Health Service, British people moan about dirty hospitals, long waits and wasted money. In Germany, the new chancellor, Angela Merkel, is under fire for suggesting changing the financing of its health system. Canada's new Conservative Prime Minister, Stephen Harper, made a big fuss during the election about reducing the country's lengthy medical queues. Across the rich world, affluence, ageing and advancing technology are driving up health spending faster than income.

2 But nowhere has a bigger health problem than America. Soaring medical bills are squeezing wages, swelling the ranks of the uninsured and pushing huge firms and perhaps even the government towards bankruptcy. Ford's announcement this week

1 似乎每个人都存在医疗问题。在向国民医疗保健系统投入了数十亿的资金后，英国人民开始抱怨医院的脏乱、候诊的漫长以及金钱的浪费。在德国，新当选的总理安吉拉·默克尔因为建议改变医疗系统的融资方案而受到抨击。加拿大保守党新任总理史蒂芬·哈珀在竞选期间对减少本国就医排队的问题大做文章。在发达国家，富裕、老龄化以及技术进步正在使医疗花费的涨速快于收入的涨速。

2 然而，任何国家的医疗问题都不如美国严重。激增的医疗费挤占了工资，增加了无保险人数，致使一些大公司甚至可能连政府都濒临破产。本周，福特宣布到 2012 年缩减

that it would cut up to 30,000 jobs by 2012 was as much a sign of its "legacy" health-care costs as of the ills of the car industry. Pushed by polls that show health-care is one of his main domestic problems and by forecasts showing that the retiring baby-boomers will crush the government's finances, George Bush is expected to unveil a reform plan in next week's state-of-the-union address.

3   America's heath system is unlike any other. The United States spends 16% of its GDP on health, around twice the rich country average, equivalent to $6,280 for every American each year. Yet it is the only rich country that does not guarantee universal health coverage. Thanks to an accident of history, most Americans receive health insurance through their employers, with the government picking up the bill for the poor and the elderly.

4   This curious hybrid (混合物) certainly has its strengths. Americans have more choices than anybody else, and their health-care system is much more innovative. Europeans' bills could be much higher if American medicine were not doing much of their Research and Development (R&D) for them. But there are also huge weaknesses. The one most often cited—especially by foreigners—is the army of uninsured. Some 46 million Americans do not have cover. In many cases that is out of choice and, if they fall seriously ill, hospitals have to treat them. But it is still deeply unequal. And there are also shocking inefficiencies: by some measures, 30% of American

health spending is wasted.

5   Then there is the question of state support. Many Americans disapprove of the "Socialized Medicine" of Canada and Europe. In fact, even if much of the administration is done privately, around 60% of America's health-care bill ends up being met by the government. Proportionately, the American state already spends as much on health as the OECD (Organization of Economic Cooperation and Development) average, and that share is set to grow as the baby-boomers run up their Medicare bills and ever more employers avoid providing health-care coverage. America is, in effect, heading towards a version of socialized medicine by default.

30%的医疗费用浪费掉了。

5   紧接着就是政府支持问题。许多美国人不赞成加拿大和欧洲实施的"全民公费医疗制度"。实际上，即使大部分医保由私人负责，美国仍有约60%的医保费最终由政府支出。从比例上看，美国政府在医疗上的开销已经相当于经合组织（经济合作与发展组织）的平均水平，而随着生育高峰期出生的人们医疗账单越积越多，以及越来越多的雇主逃避提供医疗保险，这一比例还会进一步增长。事实上，美国正默认走上一种全民公费医疗的模式。

1. Health problems mentioned in the passage include all the following EXCEPT _____.

    [A] poor hospital conditions in UK

    [B] Angela Merkel under attack

    [C] health financing in Germany

    [D] long waiting lines in Canada

2. Ford's announcement of cutting up to 30,000 jobs by 2012 indicates that Ford _____.

    [A] has the biggest health problem of the car industry

    [B] has made profits from its health-care legacy

    [C] has accumulated too heavy a health-care burden

    [D] owes a great deal of debt to its employees

3. In the author's opinion, America's health system is _____.

    [A] inefficient

    [B] feasible

    [C] unpopular

    [D] successful

4. It is implied in the passage that _____.

   [A] America's health system has its strengths and weaknesses

   [B] the US government pays medical bills for the poor and the elderly

   [C] some 46 million Americans do not have medical insurance

   [D] Europeans benefit a lot from America's medical research

5. From the last paragraph we may learn that the "Socialized Medicine" is _____.

   [A] a practice of Canada and Europe

   [B] a policy adopted by the US government

   [C] intended for the retiring baby-boomers

   [D] administered by private enterprises

解题之路

1. 【答案】**B** 【题型】反选题。

   【思路】反选题的标志一般是在题干中出现大写的NOT、EXCEPT等字眼，正确答案是原文未出现的内容。根据题干的关键词Health problems定位到首段。选项[A]、[C]和[D]都是对原文首段内容的改写：poor hospital conditions对应dirty hospitals，health financing对应the financing of its health system，long waiting lines对应lengthy queues，所以均是原文提到的内容。选项[B]虽然在首段中有所提及，但不是具体的医疗问题，而是选项[C]提到的问题的后果。

2. 【答案】**C** 【题型】推理判断题。

   【思路】根据题干的关键词Ford's定位到第二段第三句，[C]是对原文的推理的结果，其中的accumulated对应原文的legacy。选项[A]中的biggest属于无中生有；选项[B]中的profits和原文第二段的bankruptcy相矛盾；选项[D]也属于无中生有。

3. 【答案】**A** 【题型】作者态度题。

   【思路】根据题干中的关键词America's health system定位到第三段、第四段。选项[A]中的inefficient是对第四段末句中shocking inefficiencies的同义改写。选项[B] feasible（可行的）、选项[C] unpopular（不受欢迎的）、选项[D] successful（成功的）均与原文矛盾。

4. 【答案】**D** 【题型】作者态度题。

   【思路】本题没有关键词可以定位，但根据出题顺序以及第三题和第五题分别定在第三段、第四段和末段，该题也应在第三段、第四段。选项[A]直接对应第四段首句和第四句，选项[B]对应第三段末句，选项[C]对应第四段第六句，无须推理；而选项[D]中的

benefits a lot是原文Europeans' bills could be much higher…的正话反说，需要推理得出，所以是正确选项。

5. 【答案】A 【题型】细节题。

【思路】根据题干的关键词Socialized Medicine定位到末段第二句，选项[A]是对原文的同义改写。选项[B]的adopted与原文的disapprove矛盾，[C]和[D]均属无中生有。

词汇精解

1. moan [məʊn] v. 呻吟；抱怨
2. chancellor [ˈtʃɑːnsələ(r)] n.（英国）大臣，（德国）总理
3. fuss [fʌs] n. 小题大做
4. lengthy [ˈleŋθɪ; ˈleŋkθɪ] a. 冗长的，累赘的
5. queue [kjuː] n. 长队
6. affluence [ˈæfluəns] n. 富裕，富足
7. soaring [ˈsɔːrɪŋ] a. 高飞的；（情绪、价格等）飞涨的
8. swell [swel] v. 增加，增多；膨胀
9. uninsured [ˌʌnɪnˈʃʊəd] a. 未入保险的
10. bankruptcy [ˈbæŋkrʌptsɪ] n. 破产
11. legacy [ˈlegəsɪ] n. 遗产；遗留问题
12. baby-boomer [ˈbeɪbɪˌbuːmə] n. 生育高峰期出生的人
13. crush [krʌʃ] v. 压碎，压垮
14. unveil [ˌʌnˈveɪl] v. 揭开面纱；将……公布于众
15. equivalent [ɪˈkwɪvələnt] a. 相等的，相当的
16. hybrid [ˈhaɪbrɪd] n. 混合物
17. strength [streŋθ] n. 力量；优点
18. innovative [ˈməʊətɪv] a. 创新的，革新的
19. cite [saɪt] v. 引用；引证
20. administration [ədˌmɪnɪˈstreɪʃn] n. 管理
21. proportionately [prəˈpɔːʃənətlɪ] ad. 成比例地
22. default [dɪˈfɔːlt] n. 违约；拖欠；默认状态

难句解析

1. Pushed by polls that show health-care is one of his main domestic problems and by forecasts showing that the retiring baby-boomers will crush the government's finances, George Bush is expected to unveil a reform plan in next week's state-of-the-union address.

民意调查显示，医保问题是其国内主要问题之一；预测表明，那些在生育高峰期出生并面临退休的人员将会拖垮政府的财政。在这双重压力之下，乔治·布什将在下周的国情咨文中宣布一项改革计划。

结构分析：这个句子的主干在最后：George Bush is expected to unveil a reform plan in next week's state-of-the-union address, 这里的 is expected to... 表示"预计"；句首的过去分词结构 Pushed by... and by... 是原因状语，polls 之后的 that 从句是其定语从句，forecasts 之后的现在分词 showing 是其后置定语，that 引导的从句是 showing 的宾语，该从句的主语是名词短语 the retiring baby-boomers。

> 2. The United States spends 16% of its GDP on health, around twice the rich country average, equivalent to $6,280 for every American each year.
>
> 美国要花费其国内生产总值的 16% 用于医疗方面，这大约是发达国家平均水平的两倍，相当于每年人均 6 280 美元。

结构分析：这个句子的主语是 The United States，谓语是 spends，宾语是 16% of its GDP，spend sth. on sth. 是固定搭配；后面的 around twice... 和形容词短语 equivalent to... 都是 16% of its GDP 的后置定语。

> 3. Thanks to an accident of history, most Americans receive health insurance through their employers, with the government picking up the bill for the poor and the elderly.
>
> 由于历史的偶然，绝大多数美国人通过他们的雇主获得医疗保险，而政府则为那些穷人和上了年纪的人支付医疗费用。

结构分析：这个句子的主谓宾结构是 most Americans receive health insurance，介词短语 through their employers 是 receive 的方式状语；句末的 with... elderly 是独立主格，即 with+*n.*+现在分词，在句中作伴随状语；句首的 Thanks to... 是原因状语，修饰整个句子。

> 4. Proportionately, the American state already spends as much on health as the OECD (Organization of Economic Cooperation and Development) average, and that share is set to grow as the baby-boomers run up their Medicare bills and ever more employers avoid providing health-care coverage.
>
> 从比例上看，美国政府在医疗上的开销已经相当于经合组织（经济合作与发展组织）的平均水平，而随着生育高峰期出生的人们医疗账单越积越多，以及越来越多的雇主逃避提供医疗保险，这一比例还会进一步增长。

结构分析：第二个逗号之前是一个简单句，其中使用了两个固定短语：spend... on... 和 as much as...；第二个逗号之后是由 and 连接的一个主从复合句，与前一个简单句构成并列结构；该复合句的主句是 that share is set to grow，as 引导的是时间状语从句，由 and 连接的两个句子组成。

Text 13

1   When Thomas Keller, one of America's foremost chefs, announced that on Sept. 1 he would abolish the practice of tipping at Per Se, his luxury restaurant in New York City, and replace it with a European-style service charge, I knew three groups would be opposed: customers, servers and restaurant owners. These three groups are all committed tipping—as they quickly made clear on Web sites. To oppose tipping, it seems, is to be anti-capitalist, and maybe even a little French.

2   But Mr. Keller is right to move away from tipping—and it's worth exploring why just about everyone else in the restaurant world is wrong to stick with the practice.

3   Customers believe in tipping because they think it makes economic sense. "Waiters know that they won't get paid if they don't do a good job" is how most advocates of the system would put it. To be sure, this is a tempting, apparently rational statement about economic theory, but it appears to have little applicability to the real world of restaurants.

4   Michael Lynn, an associate professor of consumer behavior and marketing at Cornell's School of Hotel Administration, has conducted dozens of studies of tipping and has concluded that consumers' assessments of the quality of service correlate weakly to the amount they tip.

5   Rather, customers are likely to tip more in

1   当作为美国顶级厨师之一的托马斯·凯勒宣布从9月1日起将在其位于纽约名为Per Se的豪华饭店取消小费制度，并将实行欧式服务费制度时，我就知道会有三个群体表示反对：顾客、服务员和饭店老板。正如这三个群体迅速在网上声明的那样，他们都坚定拥护小费制度。反对小费制度似乎是反对资本主义，甚至可能有些草率。

2   但是，凯勒先生取消小费制度的做法是正确的，并且也有必要弄清楚：为什么餐饮界几乎所有人都坚守小费制度这一点是错误的。

3   顾客之所以拥护小费制度，是因为他们觉得这样做在经济层面是有意义的。大多数小费制度的支持者都会这样说："服务员知道，如果服务不周就不会得到小费。"诚然，这种说法在经济学理论上十分诱人且明显在理，但是它似乎不适合现实中的餐饮界。

4   康奈尔大学酒店管理学院消费者行为与营销学的副教授马歇尔·林恩对付小费行为进行了大量研究后得出结论：消费者对服务质量的评价与他们所付小费的数额之间关系不大。

5   更准确地说，相较于频频为

response to servers touching them lightly and leaning forward next to the table to make conversation than to how often their water glass is refilled—in other words, customers tip more when they like the server, not when the service is good. Mr. Lynn's studies also indicate that male customers increase their tips for female servers while female customers increase their tips for male servers.

6 What's more, consumers seem to forget that the tip increases as the bill increases. Thus, the tipping system is an open invitation to what restaurant professionals call "up selling": every bottle of imported water, every espresso and every cocktail is extra money in the server's pocket. Aggressive up selling for tips is often rewarded while low-key, quality service often goes unrecognized.

7 In addition, the practice of tip pooling, which is the norm in fine-dining restaurants and is becoming more common in every kind of restaurant above the level of a greasy spoon, has ruined whatever effect voting with your tip might have had on an individual waiter. In an unreasonable outcome, you are punishing the good waiters in the restaurant by not tipping the bad one. Indeed, there appears to be little connection between tipping and good service.

客人斟满水杯的那些侍者，顾客更愿意给那些与他们轻微接触并在餐桌旁俯身和他们聊上几句的侍者多付一些小费。换句话说，顾客多给小费是因为喜欢这个侍者，而不是因为其服务周到。林恩的研究还表明，男性顾客会多给女侍者小费，而女性顾客也会多给男性侍者小费。

6 而且，消费者似乎忘记了，消费越高，小费也越多。因此，这样的小费制度就是公开要求餐饮业进行内行所说的"向上销售"：每一瓶进口水、每一瓶浓咖啡和每一杯鸡尾酒都意味着要额外付给侍者小费。极力地向上销售以赚取小费常常得到奖励，而低调的优质服务却往往被人们忽略。

7 此外，作为高档饭店惯用并正被各类饭店（只要不是脏兮兮的小餐馆）所接受的集中支付小费的做法破坏了顾客通过支付小费对个体侍者本可能产生的任何影响。一个不合理的结果就是，在饭店里，你通过不给服务差的侍者小费会惩罚到服务好的侍者。实际上，支付小费与优质服务之间看来并不存在什么联系。

1. It may be inferred that a European-style service _____.

    [A] is tipping-free

    [B] charges little tip

    [C] is the author's initiative

    [D] is offered at Per Se

2. Which of the following is NOT true according to the author?

    [A] Tipping is a common practice in the restaurant world.

    [B] Waiters don't care about tipping.

    [C] Customers generally believe in tipping.

    [D] Tipping has little connection with the quality of service.

3. According to Michael Lynn's studies, waiters will likely get more tips if they _____.

    [A] have performed good service

    [B] frequently refill customers' water glass

    [C] win customers' favor

    [D] serve customers of the same sex

4. We may infer from the context that "up selling" (Para. 6) probably means _____.

    [A] selling something up

    [B] selling something fancy

    [C] selling something unnecessary

    [D] selling something more expensive

5. This passage is mainly about _____.

    [A] reasons to abolish the practice of tipping

    [B] economic sense of tipping

    [C] consumers' attitudes towards tipping

    [D] tipping for good service

➡ 解题之路 ⬅

1. 【答案】A 【题型】推理判断题。

    【思路】根据题干的关键词European-style service定位到原文第一段首句。在abolish和replace... with a European-style service charge中，abolish和replace含义相近，replace it中的it指代tipping，因此tipping与European-style service charge是不同的服务费制度，[A]为正

确答案。[B]中的little与原文的abolish矛盾；[C]明显错误，要取消小费的是托马斯·凯勒；[D]中的is offered与原文的would... replace...相比，前者的时态错误。

2. 【答案】**B** 【题型】反选题。

   【思路】该题没有关键词可以定位，但根据出题顺序原则和第一题、第三题，应该位于原文的前四段。[B]中的waiters是原文servers的近义词，而don't care与首段的be opposed相矛盾，所以为正确选项。[C]是原文第三段首句的重现，[D]是第四段末句的同义改写。

3. 【答案】**C** 【题型】细节题。

   【思路】根据题干中的关键词Michael Lynn's定位到原文第四段和第五段。选项[C]是对原文...they like the server...的同义转述。选项[A]中的good、选项[B]、选项[C]中的same分别与原文第四段末句、第五段首句及末句相矛盾。

4. 【答案】**D** 【题型】词汇题。

   【思路】其实本题答案就在原文这个词后面的那句话中：every bottle of imported water, every espresso and every cocktail is extra money in the server's pocket，这句话就解释了up selling一词的含义。很显然，这些东西就是饭馆经营者搭卖给消费者的，另外，该段第一句也提到消费越高，小费也越多。

5. 【答案】**A** 【题型】主旨大意题。

   【思路】该题比较简单。文章的结构很清晰，作者首先引出一个话题，第二段表明立场，并引用其他众人的观点，分析了问题的原因，因此[A]选项正确。[B]、[C]、[D]均是废除小费制度的细节，属于以偏概全。

◆ 词汇精解 ◆

1. foremost ['fɔːməʊst] a. 最前面的，顶尖的	10. anti-capitalist [ˌæntɪˈkæpɪtəlɪst] a. 反资本主义的
2. chef [ʃef] n. 厨师	11. explore [ɪkˈsplɔː] v. 探索，研究
3. abolish [əˈbɒlɪʃ] v. 废除，终止	12. advocate [ˈædvəkeɪt] n. 提倡者；支持者
4. tip [tɪp] v. 给小费	13. tempting [ˈtemptɪŋ] a. 诱惑的，诱人的
5. luxury [ˈlʌkʃərɪ] a. 奢华的，豪华的	14. rational [ˈræʃnəl] a. 合理的
6. replace... with... 以……替代……	15. applicability [ˌæplɪkəˈbɪlətɪ] n. 实用性
7. charge [tʃɑːdʒ] n. 收费	16. conduct [kənˈdʌkt] v. 做，从事
8. oppose [əˈpəʊz] v. 反对	17. assessment [əˈsesmənt] n. 评估，评价
9. committed [kəˈmɪtɪd] a. 坚定的，坚信的	

18. correlate to... 与……有关系
19. lean [li:n] v. 倚靠
20. refill [ˌriːˈfɪl] v. 再充满
21. indicate [ˈɪndɪkeɪt] v. 表明
22. aggressive [əˈgresɪv] a. 气势汹汹的；志在必得的
23. greasy [ˈgriːsɪ] a. 油腻的
24. ruin [ˈruːɪn] v. 毁坏，破坏

难句解析

1. When Thomas Keller, one of America's foremost chefs, announced that on Sept. 1 he would abolish the practice of tipping at Per Se, his luxury restaurant in New York City, and replace it with a European-style service charge, I knew three groups would be opposed: customers, servers and restaurant owners.

当作为美国顶级厨师之一的托马斯·凯勒宣布从9月1日起将在其位于纽约名为Per Se的豪华饭店取消小费制度，并将实行欧式服务费制度时，我就知道会有三个群体表示反对：顾客、服务员和饭店老板。

结构分析：这是一个主从复合句。主句是 I knew three groups would be opposed，冒号之后的三个并列的名词性成分 customers, servers 和 restaurant owners 是 three groups 的同位语，起解释说明的作用；句首的 When 引导的时间状语从句中，主语是 Thomas Keller，谓语是 announced，宾语是 that 引导的从句，该从句包括两部分：he would abolish... 与 replace it...；名词短语 one of America's foremost chefs 和 his luxury restaurant 分别是 Thomas Keller 和 Per Se 的同位语。

2. Michael Lynn, an associate professor of consumer behavior and marketing at Cornell's School of Hotel Administration, has conducted dozens of studies of tipping and has concluded that consumers' assessments of the quality of service correlate weakly to the amount they tip.

康奈尔大学酒店管理学院消费者行为与营销学的副教授马歇尔·林恩对付小费行为进行了大量研究后得出结论：消费者对服务质量的评价与他们所付小费的数额之间关系不大。

结构分析：这是一个主从复合句。句子主干的主语是 Michael Lynn，谓语由并列的两部分组成：has conducted 和 has concluded，第二部分的 that 引导的是 concluded 的宾语从句，其中的谓语 correlate to... 是固定搭配，中间的副词 weakly 造成了搭配分裂，起强调作用；句末的 they tip 是省略引导词 that 的定语从句，修饰 amount；句子主干主谓之间的名词短语 an associate professor... Administration 是主语的同位语，这种现象就是我们熟知的主谓分裂。

3. Rather, customers are likely to tip more in response to servers touching them lightly and leaning forward next to the table to make conversation than to how often their water glass is refilled.

更准确地说，相较于频频为客人斟满水杯的那些侍者，顾客更愿意给那些与他们轻微接触并在餐桌旁俯身和他们聊上几句的侍者多付一些小费。

结构分析：这个句子的主语是 customers，谓语是 are likely to tip，后面出现了一个固定比较结构 more in response to... than to...，其中 than 之后使用了省略形式，复原后是：more in response to... than (in response) to...；现在分词 touching... and leaning 均是 servers 的后置定语，不定式 to make conversation 是目的状语；句末的 how 引导的从句是介词 to 的宾语。

4. In addition, the practice of tip pooling, which is the norm in fine-dining restaurants and is becoming more common in every kind of restaurant above the level of a greasy spoon, has ruined whatever effect voting with your tip might have had on an individual waiter.

此外，作为高档饭店惯用并正被各类饭店（只要不是脏兮兮的小餐馆）所接受的集中支付小费的做法破坏了顾客通过支付小费对个体侍者本可能产生的任何影响。

结构分析：这是一个主从复合句。主干句的主语是 the practice of tip pooling，谓语是 has ruined，宾语是 whatever 引导的从句，该从句的主语是 whatever effect，谓语是 might have had，effect on.... 是固定搭配，现在分词短语 voting with your tip 是 whatever effect 的定语；主干句的主谓之间出现了 which 引导的定语从句，属于典型的主谓分裂现象，该从句由 and 连接的两部分组成。

Text 14

1 "I promise." "I swear to you it'll never happen again." "I give you my word." "Honestly, believe me." Sure, I trust. Why not? I teach English Composition at a private college. With a certain excitement and intensity, I read my students' essays, hoping to find the person behind the pen. But as each semester progresses, plagiarism appears. Not only is my intelligence insulted as one assumes I won't

1 "我保证。""我向您发誓下不为例。""我向您承诺。""真的，请相信我。"当然，我信。为什么不呢？我在一所私立大学教英文写作，怀着某种兴奋与专注阅读学生们的文章，希望通过文字来认识他们。但是随着每个学期的推移，剽窃现象都会渐渐出现。有人认为我发现不了其优美的散文是

217

detect a polished piece of prose from an otherwise-average writer, but I feel a sadness that a student has resorted to buying a paper from a peer. Writers have styles like fingerprints and after several assignments, I can match a student's work with his or her name even if it's missing from the upper left-hand corner.

2   Why is learning less important than a higher Grade Point Average (GPA)? When we're threatened or sick, we make conditional promises. "If you let me pass math, I will…" "Lord, if you get me over this before the big homecoming game, I'll…" Once the situation is behind us, so are the promises. Human nature? Perhaps, but we do use that cliché (陈词滥调) to get us out of uncomfortable bargains. Divine interference during distress is asked; gratitude is unpaid. After all, few fulfill the contract, so why should anyone be the exception. Why not?

3   Six years ago, I took a student before the dean. He had turned in an essay with the vocabulary and sentence structure of a PhD thesis. Up until that time, both his out-of-class and in-class work were borderline passing. I questioned the person regarding his essay and he swore it was his own work. I gave him the identical assignment and told him to write it in class, and that I'd understand this copy would not have the time and attention an out-of-class paper is given, but he had already a finished piece so he understood what was asked. He sat one hour, then turned in part of a page of unskilled writing and

出自他人之笔，这是对我智慧的侮辱；不仅如此，我还感到十分痛心：有一个学生竟然向同学购买论文。作者的写作风格就如同其指纹一样独一无二。即使左上角的名字不见了，我还是能将学生的文章跟其名字对上号。

2   为什么学习没有高分重要？当我们受到威胁或感到不舒服时，就会做出有条件的承诺。"如果您让我通过数学考试，我就……""上帝，如果在大型校友日前您让我通过，我就……"而一旦时过境迁，承诺也就随风而逝了。这是人的本性吗？也许吧，但我们的确是用那些陈词滥调来摆脱困境。危险的时候求神拜佛，感激不需报酬。毕竟，几乎没人能够遵守承诺，所以为什么要求有人例外？何必呢？

3   六年前，我把一个学生带到系主任那里。他提交的文章中含有博士论文的词汇和句式结构。在那之前，他的课后、课堂作业成绩都处于及格边缘。我就他的文章提问，他发誓文章是自己写的。我给他同一份作业，让他当堂重写。我还告诉他，我知道这份作业不能像课外论文那样被投入更多的时间和精力；但他已经有了成文，所以应该明白我的要求。他坐了一个小时，然后交了半页毫无写作技巧、满是逻辑错误的文章。我让

faulty logic. I confronted him with both essays. "I promise..., I'm not lying. I swear to you that I wrote the essay. I'm just nervous today."

4 The head of the English department agreed with my findings, and the meeting with the dean had the boy's parents present. After an hour of discussion, touching on eight of the boy's previous essays and his Grade Point Average, which indicated he was already on academic probation (留校察看), the dean agreed that the student had plagiarized. His parents protested, "He's only a child" and we instructors are wiser and should be compassionate. College people are not really children and most times would resent being labeled as such... except in this uncomfortable circumstance.

他看着这两篇文章。"我保证……我没撒谎。我向您发誓那篇文章是我写的，只是我今天有点儿紧张。"

4 英语系的领导认同我的观点，系主任请来了这个孩子的父母。经过一小时的讨论，根据该学生以前的八篇文章和平均成绩（这些都表明他已该留校察看），系主任也认定了他的剽窃行为。他的父母抗议道："他只是个孩子，作为老师，你们应该更加明理而富有同情心。"大学生已经不再是孩子了，而且大多数情况下他们也不愿被当成孩子……除了在这种令人尴尬的情形下。

1. According to the author, students commit plagiarism mainly for _____.

    [A] money

    [B] degree

    [C] higher GPA

    [D] reputation

2. The sentence "Once the situation is behind us, so are the promises" implies that _____.

    [A] students usually keep their promises

    [B] some students tend to break their promises

    [C] the promises are always behind the situation

    [D] we cannot judge the situation in advance, as we do to the promises

3. The phrase "borderline passing" (Line 5, Para. 3) probably means _____.

    [A] fairly good

    [B] extremely poor

    [C] above average

    [D] below average

4. The boy's parents thought their son should be excused mainly because _____.

   [A] teachers should be compassionate

   [B] he was only a child

   [C] instructors were wiser

   [D] he was threatened

5. Which of the following might serve as the title of this passage?

   [A] Human Nature

   [B] Conditional Promises

   [C] How to Detect Cheating

   [D] The Sadness of Plagiarism

➡️ 解题之路 ⬅️

1. 【答案】**C** 【题型】细节题。

   【思路】根据题干的关键词plagiarism可定位到原文的第一段，作者一直在谈自己学生剽窃的普遍性。随后作者在第二段第一句话用一个设问句引出了这种做法的根本原因，即为了获得更高的GPA。选项[A]、[B]、[D]均属无中生有。

2. 【答案】**B** 【题型】推理判断题。

   【思路】根据题干的引用内容可定位到第二段的后半部分。题干实际是作者对plagiarism现象的评论。选项[B]中的tend to break对应第二段末句的few fulfill, their promises对应the contract。选项[A]与原文观点矛盾；[D]属于无中生有；而[C]的理解过于肤浅、表面化，属于常规排除项。

3. 【答案】**D** 【题型】词汇题。

   【思路】从词面上看，我们并不太好判断所考查词汇准确的含义。但是根据题干的提示，可以定位到第三段。我们发现，这个学生的成绩很糟糕，但是却交了一份具有博士水平的论文。而且在第四段提到这个学生因为成绩糟糕，已经要被留校查看了。很显然，这里要强调的是该学生学习成绩和最后的论文之间的巨大差异。因此选项[D]是正确的。

4. 【答案】**B** 【题型】细节题。

   【思路】根据题干的关键词The boy's parents定位在原文的第四段。题干中的should be executed是原文protested的同义转述，而[B]是原文protested的内容重现。[A]和[C]虽然也是对原文的内容重现，但均是家长对老师提出的要求，并非真正的理由；[D]属于无中生有。

5.【答案】**D** 【题型】主旨大意题。

【思路】全文都在谈学生的剽窃问题,以及任课教师心中的悲哀,所以中心词plagiarism应在标题中有所体现,所以[D]是正确选项。[A]过于宽泛;[B]和[C]均是论述plagiarism时的具体细节,属于以偏概全。

词汇精解

1. swear [sweə(r)] v. 发誓;诅咒	18. divine [dɪˈvaɪn] a. 神的,神圣的
2. composition [ˌkɒmpəˈzɪʃn] n. 作文;创作	19. distress [dɪˈstres] n. 沮丧,忧伤
3. intensity [ɪnˈtensəti] n. 紧张;强烈	20. gratitude [ˈgrætɪtjuːd] n. 感谢,感激
4. semester [sɪˈmestə(r)] n. 学期	21. dean [diːn] n. 系主任
5. plagiarism [ˈpleɪdʒərɪzəm] n. 剽窃	22. thesis [ˈθiːsɪs] n. 论文,论点
6. insult [ɪnˈsʌlt] v. 侮辱	23. borderline [ˈbɔːdəlaɪn] n. 边界,边缘
7. assume [əˈsjuːm] v. 假定,认为	24. regarding [rɪˈgɑːdɪŋ] prep. 关于
8. detect [dɪˈtekt] v. 发现;侦探	25. identical [aɪˈdentɪkl] a. 相同的,同一的
9. polished [ˈpɒlɪʃt] a. 抛光的;润色的	26. confront [kənˈfrʌnt] v. 面对
10. prose [prəʊz] n. 文章,散文	27. academic [ˌækəˈdemɪk] a. 学业的;学术的
11. resort [rɪˈzɔːt] v. 求助	28. probation [prəˈbeɪʃn] n. 考察期
12. resort to... 求助于……	29. plagiarize [ˈpleɪdʒəraɪz] v. 剽窃
13. peer [pɪə(r)] n. 同龄人,同辈	30. protest [prəˈtest] v. 抗议
14. assignment [əˈsaɪnmənt] n. 任务;作业	31. compassionate [kəmˈpæʃənət] a. 同情的,有同情心的
15. lord [lɔːd] n. 上帝;贵族	32. resent [rɪˈzent] v. 痛恨,憎恨
16. cliché [ˈkliːʃeɪ] n. 陈词滥调	33. circumstance [ˈsɜːkəmstəns] n. 环境,情况
17. bargain [ˈbɑːgən] n. 谈判,谈判的条件	

难句解析

1. With a certain excitement and intensity, I read my students' essays, hoping to find the person behind the pen.	我怀着某种兴奋与专注阅读学生们的文章,希望通过文字来认识他们。

<u>结构分析</u>:双逗号之间的是句子主干,现在分词 hoping 是伴随状语,修饰 read;句首的介词短语 With... intensity 是方式状语。

2. Not only is my intelligence insulted as one assumes I won't detect a polished piece of prose from an otherwise-average writer, but I feel a sadness that a student has resorted to buying a paper from a peer.

有人认为我发现不了其优美的散文是出自他人之笔,这是对我智慧的侮辱;不仅如此,我还感到十分痛心:有一个学生竟然向同学购买论文。

结构分析:该句子是由Not only... but...连接的两个分句组成,由于Not only属于否定性短语,置于句首时句子要进行部分倒装,即:Not only+助动词+主语+实意动词;第一个分句的主干复原后是 my intelligence is not only insulted,as 引导的是方式状语从句,该从句的主语是 one,谓语是 assumes,宾语是省略引导词 that 的一个从句:I won't detect... writer;第二个分句的主干是 I feel a sadness,之后的 that 引导的是 a sadness 的同位语从句。

3. Once the situation is behind us, so are the promises.

而一旦时过境迁,承诺也就随风而逝了。

结构分析:这是一个主从复合句。Once 引导的是条件状语从句;so 引导的是主句,使用了倒装形式,复原后是 the promises are so,这里的 so 指代前半句中的 behind us。

4. After an hour of discussion, touching on eight of the boy's previous essays and his Grade Point Average, which indicated he was already on academic probation, the dean agreed that the student had plagiarized.

经过一小时的讨论,根据该学生以前的八篇文章和平均成绩(这些都表明他已该留校察看),系主任也认定了他的剽窃行为。

结构分析:这是一个主从复合句。主句在句末:the dean agreed that the student had plagiarized,其中 that 引导的从句是 agreed 的宾语;现在分词短语 touching... Average 是伴随状语,之后的 which 引导的是 Grade Point Average 的定语从句。

Text 15

1 Last weekend Kyle MacDonald in Montreal threw a party to celebrate the fact that he got his new home in exchange for a red paper clip. Starting a year ago, MacDonald bartered the clip for increasingly valuable stuff, including a camp stove and free rent

1 上周末,蒙特利尔市的凯尔·麦克唐纳举办了一场聚会,庆祝他用一枚红色回形针换到了一套新房子。从一年前开始,麦克唐纳用这枚回形针换来了越来越值钱的物品,包括

in a Phoenix flat. Having announced his aim (the house) in advance, MacDonald likely got a boost from techies eager to see the Internet pass this daring test of its networking power. "My whole motto (座右铭) was 'Start small, think big, and have fun,'" says MacDonald, 26, "I really kept my effort on the creative side rather than the business side."

2 Yet as odd as the MacDonald exchange was, barter is now big business on the Net. This year more than 400,000 companies worldwide will exchange some $10 billion worth of goods and services on a growing number of barter sites. These Web sites allow companies to trade products for a virtual currency, which they can use to buy goods from other members. In Iceland, garment-maker Kapusalan sells a third of its output on the booming Vidskiptanetid exchange, earning virtual money that it uses to buy machinery and pay part of employee salaries. The Troc-services exchange in France offers more than 4,600 services, from math lessons to ironing.

3 This is not a primitive barter system. By creating currencies, the Internet removes a major barrier—what Bob Meyer, publisher of BarterNews, calls "the double coincidence of wants." That is, two

parties once not only had to find each other, but also an exchange of goods that both desired. Now, they can price the deal in virtual currency.

4   Barter also helps firms make use of idle capacity. For example, advertising is "hugely bartered" because many media, particularly on the Web can supply new ad space at little cost. Moreover, Internet ads don't register in industry-growth statistics, because many exchanges are arranged outside the formal exchanges.

5   Like eBay, most barter sites allow members to "grade" trading partners for honesty, quality and so on. Barter exchanges can allow firms in countries with hyperinflation or nontradable currencies to enter global trades. Next year, a nonprofit exchange called Quick Lift Two (QL2) plans to open in Nairobi, offering barter deals to 38,000 Kenyan farmers in remote areas. Two small planes will deliver the goods. QL2 director Gacii Waciuma says the farmers are excited to be "liberated from corrupt middlemen." For them, barter evokes a bright future, not a precapitalist past.

不仅要寻找到彼此，而且还要交换能同时满足两人需求的物品。现在，他们可以用虚拟货币为交易定价。

4   易货贸易还可以帮助公司利用其闲散的生产能力。比如，广告可用来进行"大量交易"，因为许多媒体，尤其是网络媒体可以用很低的成本提供新的广告位。并且，由于很多交易是在正式的交易平台之外进行的，网络广告并不登记在工业发展的统计数据中。

5   和易趣网一样，多数易货网站允许会员对交易伙伴的诚信度、商品质量等进行评级。以物易物可以让处于恶性通货膨胀或非流通货币国家的公司进行国际贸易。明年，一个名为QL2的非营利性交易网站计划在内罗毕开业，该网站将为肯尼亚偏远地区的38 000位农民提供实物交易。两架小型飞机负责运输货物。QL2主任Gacii Waciuma称，农民对于能够"摆脱舞弊的中间商"感到十分兴奋。对他们而言，易货唤起的是一个光明的未来，而不是前资本主义的过去。

1. The word "techies" (Line 8, Para. 1) probably refers to those who are _____.

    [A] afraid of technology

    [B] skilled in technology

    [C] ignorant of technology

    [D] incompetent in technology

2. Many people may have deliberately helped Kyle because they _____.

[A] were impressed by his creativity

[B] were eager to identify with his motto

[C] liked his goal announced in advance

[D] hoped to prove the power of the Internet

3. The Internet barter system relies heavily on _____.

[A] the size of barter sites

[B] the use of virtual currency

[C] the quality of goods or services

[D] the location of trading companies

4. It is implied that Internet advertisements can help _____.

[A] companies make more profit

[B] companies do formal exchanges

[C] media register in statistics

[D] media grade barter sites

5. Which of the follow is true of QL2 according to the author?

[A] It is criticized for doing business in a primitive way.

[B] It aims to deal with hyperinflation in some countries.

[C] It helps get rid of middlemen in trade and exchange.

[D] It is intended to evaluate the performance of trading partners.

◆ 解题之路 ◆

1. 【答案】B 【题型】词汇题。

   【思路】从techies的构成看，它包含"tech"，与"技术"有关。再根据题干信息，在原文中看到techies前面出现了got a boost from...（从……获得推动力），可大致判断该词具有褒义性，所以[A]、[C]、[D]皆可排除，正确答案为[B]。

2. 【答案】D 【题型】细节题。

   【思路】根据题干关键词Kyle和另一信息may have deliberately helped可定位到首段第三句MacDonald likely got a boost from techies，Kyle对应MacDonald，have deliberately helped对应got a boost from techies，而该句后半部分则解释了原因to see... networking power，因此可知答案为[D]。[A]、[B]、[C]三个选项中的关键词impressed，eager to identify with和liked均属无中生有。

3. 【答案】B 【题型】细节题。

【思路】根据题干的关键词barter system，并依据出题顺序原则，定位到原文第二段、第三段。第二段出现barter system的近义表达barter sites，指出这些易货网站允许将公司产品换作虚拟货币，并使用虚拟货币来购买其他会员的产品；第三段阐述了使用虚拟货币的优势，因此[B]为正确选项。[A]中的size和[D]中的location属于无中生有；[C]中的quality出现在末段，属于出处错位。

4. 【答案】A 【题型】推理判断题。

【思路】根据题干的关键词Internet advertisements可定位到原文第四段的举例处。该例子说明网络能以低廉的成本提供新的广告空间。由于成本降低，公司可获得更高利润，所以[A]为正确选项。[B]和[C]均与原文论述矛盾；[D]中的grade出现在末段，属于出处错位，且按照文章说法，是易货网站的会员为贸易伙伴评级而不是媒体为易货网站评级，犯了偷梁换柱的错误。

5. 【答案】C 【题型】推理判断题。

【思路】根据题干的关键词QL2可定位到原文末段结尾处，引用QL2主管的话说明易货贸易的另一好处，即有助于摆脱贸易和交换过程中的舞弊行为，即为选项[C]的内容。[A]中的primitive出现在原文的第三段，属于出处错位；[B]中的hyperinflation虽然定位在末段，但并不是要deal with恶性通胀，属于偷梁换柱的错误；[D]中的内容表示的是QL2交易的一种方式，而非目的，与原文矛盾。

词汇精解

1. Montreal [ˌmɒntrɪˈɔːl] n. 蒙特利尔（加拿大城市）	11. motto [ˈmɒtəʊ] n. 座右铭
2. throw [θrəʊ] v. 举办（晚会、活动等）；扔	12. odd [ɒd] a. 奇怪的，怪异的
3. barter [ˈbɑːtə] v. 交易，交换	13. virtual [ˈvɜːtʃʊəl] a. 虚拟的
4. camp [kæmp] n. 宿营，野营	14. garment [ˈɡɑːmənt] n. 衣服，外套
5. stove [stəʊv] n. 炉子	15. output [ˈaʊtpʊt] n. 产量
6. rent [rent] n. 租金	16. booming [buːmɪŋ] a. 繁荣的
7. flat [flæt] n. 公寓	17. primitive [ˈprɪmətɪv] a. 原始的
8. boost [buːst] n. 刺激，推动	18. barrier [ˈbærɪə(r)] n. 障碍
9. techie [ˈtekɪ] n. 技术熟练的人	19. coincidence [kəʊˈɪnsɪdəns] n. 巧合
10. daring [ˈdeərɪŋ] a. 有胆量的，大胆的	20. idle [ˈaɪdl] a. 闲置的；闲散的
	21. capacity [kəˈpæsɪtɪ] n. 能力；容量

22. statistics [stəˈtɪstɪks] *n.* 数据，数字	25. corrupt [kəˈrʌpt] *a.* 腐败的
23. hyperinflation [ˌhaɪpərɪnˈfleɪʃn] *n.* 恶性通货膨胀	26. evoke [ɪˈvəʊk] *v.* 唤起，激发
24. liberate [ˈlɪbəreɪt] *v.* 解放，解脱	27. precapitalist [ˌpriːˈkæpɪtəlɪst] *a.* 前资本主义的

◆ 难句解析 ◆

1. Having announced his aim (the house) in advance, MacDonald likely got a boost from techies eager to see the Internet pass this daring test of its networking power.	由于事先宣称过自己的目标是一套房子，麦克唐纳很可能得到了技术高手们的支持与帮助，这些人渴望在互联网上看到这一大胆的尝试，以验证网络的力量。

结构分析：这个句子的主谓宾是 MacDonald... got a boost...；形容词短语 eager to... power 是 techies 的后置定语，其中使用了 see sb. do sth. 的固定结构；句首的现在分词结构是原因状语，括号中的 the house 是 his aim 的同位语。

2. By creating currencies, the Internet removes a major barrier—what Bob Meyer, publisher of *BarterNews*, calls "the double coincidence of wants."	互联网通过创立虚拟货币清除了一个主要障碍，《易物新闻》的发行人鲍勃·梅耶将这一障碍称为"需求的双重巧合"。

结构分析：这个句子的主干是 the Internet removes a major barrier；what 引导的从句是 major barrier 的同位语，其中的 publisher of *BarterNews* 是 Bob Meyer 的同位语；句首的 By creating currencies 是方式状语。

3. Next year, a nonprofit exchange called Quick Lift Two (QL2) plans to open in Nairobi, offering barter deals to 38,000 Kenyan farmers in remote areas.	明年，一个名为 QL2 的非营利性交易网站计划在内罗毕开业，该网站将为肯尼亚偏远地区的 38 000 位农民提供实物交易。

结构分析：该句子的主语是 a nonprofit exchange，过去分词短语 called Quick Lift Two (QL2) 是其定语，谓语是 plans to open，现在分词 offering 引导的是结果状语。

第五章 阅读理解（B 部分）

第一节 最新大纲解读与命题趋势

（一）大纲要求

考研英语（二）大纲从 2010 年开始在阅读理解部分增加了新题型，即 Part B。新题型主要考查考生对诸如连贯性、一致性、逻辑关系等语段乃至语篇整体特征的理解，即要求考生在理解全文的基础上弄清文章的整体和微观结构。2010 年大纲修订之后，规定本部分有三种备选题型：正误判断题、7 选 5 小标题对应题和 7 选 5 多项对应题。2010 年的新题型是正误判断题，即阅读完一篇 450～550 词的文章后，要求根据文章内容对 5 个论述句判断正误。该种题型在 2011 年新大纲中即遭废止，原因是过于简单。所以最新大纲中 Part B 部分减为两种备选题型：7 选 5 小标题对应题和 7 选 5 多项对应题。每次考试从这两种题型中选择其中一种形式，或者两种形式的组合进行考查。本部分文章设 5 小题，每小题 2 分，共 10 分。

（二）命题趋势

考研英语（二）阅读理解 Part B 有两种备选题型，一种是多项对应，另一种是小标题对应。多项对应部分给出一篇 450～550 词的文章，试题内容分为左右两栏，左侧一栏为 5 道题目，右侧一栏为 7 个选项。此部分要求考生在阅读后根据文章内容和左侧一栏中提供的信息从右侧一栏中的 7 个选项中选出对应的 5 项相关信息。这种题型通常也被称为连线题。而小标题对应是在一篇长度为 450～550 词的文章前有 7 个概括句或者小标题。这些文字或标题分别是对文章中某一部分内容的概括或阐述，要求考生根据文字内容和篇章结构从这 7 个选项中选出最恰当的 5 个概括句或小标题填入文章空白处。

多项对应题考查的是考生迅速查找信息、理解信息的能力。其解题思路类似于普通的细节题。一般来讲，首先应该阅读左边 5 个题干，标出其中的重点信息，然后带着这些题干中的重点信息回到原文中精确定位，查找含有相关信息的句子。最后把相关句子的内容和右边选项进行比对，意思吻合的为该题的正确答案。考试时一定要先看题干，根据题干内容去查找信息。这是快速解题的关键所在。

如果说多项对应考查查找信息的能力，那么小标题对应更多是考查考生通过略读概括段意的能力。本题型要求在 7 个选项中为 5 个命题段落选出相应的小标题，其解题思路类似于传统阅读中的主旨大意题，只是主旨大意题是选择全文标题，而小标题对应题是选择文章中某些段落的标题而已。

简而言之，多项对应的解题类似于阅读 A 节中的细节题，最重要的是将题干中的信息精确定位到原文中的位置，而小标题对应的解题关键在于找到段落的主旨，大致概括段落的大意。

（三）备考指南

新题型与传统阅读最大的区别在于，前者共有 7 个选项，工作量和出错的概率要大得多。而且因为这些选项是 5 个题目共用的，一旦前面的题目做错，后面的题目很可能同时错选，从而导致连环错误。考生即使在后面的解题中发现了前面的错误，往往也要再次审视前面的题目，会处于循环求解的困境。

面对这些问题，考生要努力做到两点：一是要保证前面解题的正确率，这样不仅能树立信心，而且有助于排除后面题目中的干扰项；二是做题可以由易到难，难解的题目先放弃，先做简单的，再去面对难题，这样难题的干扰项也会减少，从而无形中降低解题的难度。

做这种题目的时候，可以先理解备选标题的意义，而且在做题中需要反复看这些标题，然后回到文章中总结各段落的内容，并与给出的小标题一一比对，选择最相近的标题。小标题的内容应该体现一个段落的主旨，而段落的主旨通常出现在段落的首尾或者强转折之后，掌握这样的规律就为解题提供了一定的便利。

第二节　题型分类与解题技巧

（一）题型分类

1. 小标题对应

在一篇长度为 450～550 词的文章前有 7 个概括句或小标题。这些文字或标题分别是对文章中某一部分的概括或阐述，要求考生根据文章内容和篇章结构从这 7 个选项中选出最恰当的 5 个概括句或小标题填入文章空白处。

2. 多项对应

本部分为一篇长度为 450～550 词的文章，试题内容分为左右两栏，左侧一栏为 5 道题目，右侧一栏为 7 个选项，要求考生在阅读后根据文章内容和左侧一栏中提供的信息从右侧一栏中的 7 个选项中选出对应的 5 项相关信息。

（二）解题技巧

1. 小标题对应

这种题型侧重考查段落的一致性特征，就是要求考生寻找段落的核心信息，然后进行概括，再与选项中的小标题进行匹配。解题过程类似于传统阅读中的段落主旨题。针对小标题对应题型，解题方法是：

（1）划出选项关键词。重点找名词，因为文章的话题词一般都用名词。

（2）读段落。这一步又分为 4 个步骤：

① 先看每段的首句、第二句。因为一般文章的首句和第二句会概括该段的中心思想，这叫作演绎型的写法；如果无法推导出主旨含义，再看该段的末句，这叫作归纳型的写法。

② 找转折句。若此段落有转折句就一定是关键所在。分析归纳找出关键名词，与选项进行对比。

③ 找总结性的句子。若此段有总结性句子，一般在段落结尾。一般有 so、hence、therefore 等词出现，这句话就是答案所在。

④ 如果主题句比较复杂，先看主句部分：如出现 Although...、If...、Because... 等，要先看主句部分。

（3）细节非解：选项如果描述的是某个细节，且在原文中出现过，但不能直接选为答案。

（4）同义替换为解：只要选项和所读段落有同义替换，则为解。

（5）通读原文，复核检查。

标题初步选定后，将其套入原文进行通读，体会每个初选的主题或段落大意与下面段落中的事例或细节描述是否吻合、贴切。考察所选的各个段落主题与全文的主题和发展脉络是否一致，是否符合逻辑顺序。

2. 多项对应

考生做这种题型时，也是要把握文章的写作结构和脉络层次，了解作者的写作意图和态度，概括文章的主旨。另外，这种题型更趋近于传统阅读的事实细节题，文章的主题有助于解题，但真正解题时还是要根据题干和选项回文定位，然后对定位信息处进行简单的推理或概括，再和选项比对。以下是常用的解题技巧：

（1）一般按文章段落顺序出题。

（2）寻找题干关键词——

近几年多项对应多是专家、学者对应其观点的题型，即左栏是专家、学者，要在右栏中找到其观点。具体做法是：在原文中快速找到所考的所有人名，然后再具体研读他们所说的话。往往在右栏考题的题干中有个别关键词或有文中原词再现，这就是寻找答案的突破口。

（3）一般不需通读全文，按照左栏所给的定位词直接回文寻找信息即可。

（三）真题精讲

2016 真题

Part B

Directions: Read the following text and answer the questions by choosing the most suitable subheading from the list A–G for each of the numbered paragraphs (41–45). There are two extra subheadings which you do not need to use. Mark your answers on the ANSWER SHEET. (10 points)

[A] Be silly

[B] Have fun

[C] Express your emotions

[D] Don't overthink it

[E] Be easily pleased

[F] Notice things

[G] Ask for help

1 As adults, it seems that we are constantly pursuing happiness, often with mixed results. Yet children appear to have it down to an art—and for the most part they don't need self-help books or therapy. Instead, they look after their wellbeing instinctively, and usually more effectively than we do as grownups. Perhaps it's time to learn a few lessons from them.

2 41._____

3 What does a child do when he's sad? He cries. When he's angry? He shouts. Scared? Probably a bit of both. As we grow up, we learn to control our emotions so they are manageable and don't dictate our behaviours, which is in many ways a good thing. But too often we take this process too far and end up suppressing emotions, especially negative ones. That's about as effective as brushing dirt under a carpet and can even make us ill. What we need to do is find a way to acknowledge and express what we feel appropriately, and then—again, like children—move on.

4 42._____

5 A couple of Christmases ago, my youngest stepdaughter, who was nine years old at the time, got a Superman T-shirt for Christmas. It cost less than a fiver but she was overjoyed, and couldn't stop talking about it. Too often we believe that a new job, bigger house or better car will be the magic silver bullet that

will allow us to finally be content, but the reality is these things have very little lasting impact on our happiness levels. Instead, being grateful for small things every day is a much better way to improve wellbeing.

6 43._____

7 Have you ever noticed how much children laugh? If we adults could indulge in a bit of silliness and giggling, we would reduce the stress hormones in our bodies, increase good hormones like endorphins, improve blood flow to our hearts and even have a greater chance of fighting off infection. All of which would, of course, have a positive effect on happiness levels.

8 44._____

9 The problem with being a grownup is that there's an awful lot of serious stuff to deal with—work, mortgage payments, figuring out what to cook for dinner. But as adults we also have the luxury of being able to control our own diaries and it's important that we schedule in time to enjoy the things we love. Those things might be social, sporting, creative or completely random (dancing around the living room, anyone?)—it doesn't matter, so long as they're enjoyable, and not likely to have negative side effects, such as drinking too much alcohol or going on a wild spending spree if you're on a tight budget.

10 45._____

11 Having said all of the above, it's important to add that we shouldn't try too hard to be happy.

最终获得满足的灵丹妙药，但事实上这些东西对于我们的幸福水平影响甚微。相反，对日常琐事充满感恩之情才是提升幸福的更好途径。

6 43._____

7 你曾注意过孩子有多爱笑吗？如果我们成年人能够"愚蠢"一点，时而傻笑，就可以减少体内的压力荷尔蒙，增加诸如内啡肽等良性荷尔蒙，提高心脏血流量，甚至提高抵御传染病的可能性，所有这一切当然会对幸福水平有积极的作用。

8 44._____

9 成年人要面对的问题是有太多严肃的事情要去处理——工作、按揭付款、思考晚餐做什么菜。但是作为成年人，我们的好处是能够把控自己的日程簿，规划好时间享受做喜欢的事情，这一点很重要。那些事情或许是社交应酬、体育运动、新的创意或完全随机的事情（在客厅起舞，有人做过吗？）——这没关系，只要那些事情能让你开心，并且不会带来负面影响，如酗酒或者囊中羞涩还要疯狂购物。

10 45._____

11 综上所述，还有一点有必要补充，那就是我们不必过分刻意追求

Scientists tell us this can backfire and actually have a negative impact on our wellbeing. As the Chinese philosopher Chuang Tzu is reported to have said: "Happiness is the absence of striving for happiness." And in that, once more, we need to look to the example of our children, to whom happiness is not a goal but a natural byproduct of the way they live.

幸福。科学家们说这会适得其反，实际上对我们的幸福产生负面影响。正如中国哲人庄子所言："至乐无乐"。在这一点上，我们应再次以子女为榜样，对他们来说，幸福不是目标，而只是生活方式的自然额外收获。

◆ 解题之路 ◆

41.【答案】[C]表达情绪

【思路】第三段通过描述孩子们悲伤、生气和害怕时的表现来说明我们要学会表达情绪。段落中control our emotions，suppressing emotions和express what we feel都是选项C的同义替换。

42.【答案】[E]容易满足

【思路】第五段主要讲要对小事心存感激，这样也可以提升幸福感。段落中being grateful和选项E中Be easily pleased是同义替换。

43.【答案】[A]愚蠢一点

【思路】第七段主要讲留意孩子们有多爱笑，我们大人也要学会傻傻地笑，这样也可以提升幸福水平。段落中a bit of silliness 和选项A中Be silly是同义替换。

44.【答案】[B]享受快乐

【思路】第九段主要讲成年人有太多严肃的事情要去处理，但是我们可以规划好时间享受做喜欢的事情，接下来举各种具体事例说明那些我们可以做的可以享受的事情，并且最后说明它们的好处。剩余的可选择的选项中只有[B]have fun比较合适。

45.【答案】[D]别想太多

【思路】第十一段主要讲不要去想怎样才可以幸福，并引用了哲人的一句话来说明这个道理，旨在告诉大家享受过程就是幸福的。最后可以用排除法，[G]寻求帮助，文中没有提及；[F]留心事物，文中也未提及。而选项D对应原文句子：we shouldn't try too hard to be happy和happiness is not a goal but a natural byproduct of the way they live。

2017 真题

Part B

Directions: Read the following text and match each of the numbered items in the left column to its corresponding information in the right column. There are two extra choices in the right column. Mark your answers on the ANSWER SHEET. (10 points)

1 The decline in American manufacturing is a common refrain, particularly from Donald Trump. "We don't make anything anymore," he told Fox News, while defending his own made-in-Mexico clothing line.

2 Without question, manufacturing has taken a significant hit during recent decades, and further trade deals raise questions about whether new shocks could hit manufacturing.

3 But there is also a different way to look at the data.

4 Across the country, factory owners are now grappling with a new challenge: Instead of having too many workers, they may end up with too few. Despite trade competition and outsourcing, American manufacturing still needs to replace tens of thousands of retiring boomers every year. Millennials may not be that interested in taking their place. Other industries are recruiting them with similar or better pay.

5 For factory owners, it all adds up to stiff competition for workers—and upward pressure on wages. "They're harder to find and they have job offers," says Jay Dunwell, president of Wolverine Coil Spring, a family-owned firm, "They may be

1 美国制造业的衰败已是千夫所指，尤其被唐纳德·特朗普所诟病。"我们已不再制造任何东西。"他对福克斯新闻这样说，但同时又为自己在墨西哥的服装系列辩解。

2 毋庸置疑，制造业近几十年来遭受了重创，且进一步的贸易协定也对新冲击是否会打击制造业提出了了质疑。

3 但是还可以从一种不同的角度来审视这些数据。

4 全国的工厂老板们现在都在努力应对一项新挑战：庞大的工人数量最终会变得寥寥无几。尽管存在贸易竞争和工程外包，美国制造业每年仍需替换掉数万名即将退休的婴儿潮一代的工人。千禧一代的工人可能对填补他们的职位空缺不那么感兴趣。其他行业正以相近或更高的薪水招聘他们。

5 对工厂老板们而言，所有这一切都加剧了招聘工人的残酷竞争——以及工资上涨的压力。"工人更难找了，而且他们有多个工作机会，"一家名为"金钢狼螺旋弹簧"的家族

coming [into the workforce], but they've been plucked by other industries that are also doing as well as manufacturing," Mr. Dunwell has begun bringing high school juniors to the factory so they can get exposed to its culture.

6   At RoMan Manufacturing, a maker of electrical transformers and welding equipment that his father cofounded in 1980, Robert Roth keeps a close eye on the age of his nearly 200 workers. Five are retiring this year. Mr. Roth has three community-college students enrolled in a work-placement program, with a starting wage of $13 an hour that rises to $17 after two years.

7   At a worktable inside the transformer plant, young Jason Stenquist looks flustered by the copper coils he's trying to assemble and the arrival of two visitors. It's his first week on the job. Asked about his choice of career, he says at high school he considered medical school before switching to electrical engineering. "I love working with tools. I love creating," he says.

8   But to win over these young workers, manufacturers have to clear another major hurdle: parents, who lived through the worst US economic downturn since the Great Depression, telling them to avoid the factory. Millennials "remember their father and mother both were laid off. They blame it on the manufacturing recession," says Birgit Klohs, chief executive of The Right Place, a business development agency for western Michigan.

9 These concerns aren't misplaced: Employment in manufacturing has fallen from 17 million in 1970 to 12 million in 2015. When the recovery began, worker shortages first appeared in the high-skilled trades. Now shortages are appearing at the mid-skill levels.

10 "The gap is between the jobs that take no skills and those that require a lot of skill," says Rob Spohr, a business professor at Montcalm Community College. "There're enough people to fill the jobs at McDonalds and other places where you don't need to have much skill. It's that gap in between, and that's where the problem is."

11 Julie Parks of Grand Rapids Community College points to another key to luring Millennials into manufacturing: a work/life balance. While their parents were content to work long hours, young people value flexibility. "Overtime is not attractive to this generation. They really want to live their lives," she says.

9 这些担忧并非不合时宜：制造业的就业人数已从1970年的1 700万降到了2015年的1 200万。经济开始复苏时，工人短缺现象首先出现在高技能行业。如今工人短缺现象正出现在中级技能行业。

10 "缺口存在于无需任何技能的工作与需要大量技能的工作之间，"蒙特卡姆社区大学的商务学教授罗伯·斯波尔说道，"在麦当劳和其他不需要太多技能的企业，有大量富余人员去填充空缺岗位。那中间存在缺口，那也是问题的症结所在。"

11 大急流社区学院的朱莉·帕克斯提到了吸引千禧一代进入制造业的另一个重要因素：工作与生活达成平衡。他们的父母乐于长时间工作，而年轻人看重灵活性。"加班对年轻一代没有吸引力，他们想过自己的生活。"她说道。

	[A] says that he switched to electrical engineering because he loves working with tools.
41. Jay Dunwell	[B] points out that there are enough people to fill the jobs that don't need much skill.
42. Jason Stenquist	[C] points out that the US doesn't manufacture anything anymore.
43. Birgit Klohs	[D] believes that it is important to keep a close eye on the age of his workers.

44. Rob Spohr	[E] says that for factory owners, workers are harder to find because of stiff competition.
45. Julie Parks	[F] points out that a work/life balance can attract young people into manufacturing.
	[G] says that the manufacturing recession is to blame for the lay-off of the young people's parents.

解题之路

41.【答案】E

【思路】根据Jay Dunwell定位到第五段 "For factory owners, it all adds up to stiff competition for workers—and upward pressure on wages. 'They're harder to find and they have job offers,' says Jay Dunwell, president of Wolverine Coil Spring…"。其中stiff competition for workers对应选项E中的 stiff competition；they're harder to find对应选项E中的workers are harder to find。

42.【答案】A

【思路】根据 Jason Stenquist定位到第七段 "Asked about his choice of career, he says at high school he considered medical school before switching to electrical engineering. 'I love working with tools. I love creating,' he says."。其中he considered medical school before switching to electrical engineering对应选项A中的he switched to electrical engineering；I love working with tools对应选项A中的because he loves working with tools。

43.【答案】G

【思路】根据Birgit Klohs定位到第八段，其中They blame it on the manufacturing recession对应选项G中的the manufacturing recession is to blame for the lay-off of the young people's parents。

44.【答案】B

【思路】根据Rob Spohr定位到第十段 "There're enough people to fill the jobs at McDonalds and other places where you don't need to have much skill. It's that gap in between, and that's where the problem is."。其中There're enough people to fill the jobs对应选项B中的there are enough people to fill the jobs；where you don't need to have much skill对应选项B中的that don't need much skill。

45.【答案】F

【思路】根据 Julie Parks定位到 "Julie Parks of Grand Rapids Community College points to another key to luring Millennials into manufacturing: a work/life balance."。其中luring Millennials into manufacturing: a work/life balance对应选项F中的a work/life balance can attract young people into manufacturing。

第三节　真题同源实战

（一）小标题对应

Text 1

Directions: Read the following text. For Questions 1–5, choose the most suitable subtitle from the list A–G to fit into each of the numbered blanks. There are two extra choices, which do not fit in any of the blanks. (10 points)

[A] Copy the best stuff around, and make it my own

[B] Recite numerous passages

[C] Learn to be observative

[D] Read through the whole night

[E] Learn structure from software and business writing

[F] Understand and nurture my creative process

[G] Take a hacksaw to sentences, paragraphs, and words

1　How does one become a better writer? Happy to answer this but be aware, my writing abilities are quite limited. I am an essayist, an article writer of short, pithy, vignettes. That's it.

2　I cannot write novels, or extremely persuasive pieces, nor can I distill massively complex issues to a single truth. But, for my writing style, this is what has helped me:

> 1　如何变成一个更好的写作者？很高兴能够回答这个问题，但是请注意，我的写作能力是有限的。我是一位散文作者，一位写简短、精练的小文章的作者。仅此而已。
>
> 2　我写不了小说，或者极有说服力的短文，我也不能将大量复杂的论点提炼成一个简短的中心论点。但是就我的写作风格来说，以下这几点

1. _____

Consulting is the art of condensing massive amounts of information into a visual medium. To be effective, PPS must be well-organized. They have main topics, sub-topics, supporting evidence, conclusions, and excellent flow. I learned this structure in consulting and I apply it to my writing. As well as numbers, bold, italics and other visual aids.

2. _____

Original sentence: *I have a tendency to make sentences overly complicated by adding more and more words until the meaning of the sentence is obfuscated under the weight of so many superfluous words.*

Post-edit: *I'm verbose.*

I edit. I reduce. Tighten. Improve.

3. _____

Some mild plagiarism is common in my more humorous writings. Well, not plagiarism, more like mild flirtation with plagiarism under the guise of "inspired by..."

I read a lot and watch good TV. I copy what interests me. I use similes, like my favorite TV comedy writer Ben Elton, and I pilfer silly words from my favorite humor author, P.G. Wodehouse. I also copy the intimate conversational style of David

对我很有帮助：

1. _____

查阅是一种将大量的信息浓缩成可见媒介的艺术。为了更加有效，PPS肯定是经过精心编排的。它们都有主要的主题、次主题、支持的理据、结论以及良好的流程。在查阅中，我学到了这种结构上的技巧，并且把它应用在写作当中。除此之外还有数据、加粗体、斜体以及其他可见的辅助手法。

2. _____

原句：我倾向于添加更多用词来让一个句子变得非常复杂，直到整个句子的意思因为相当多的多余的词而变得模糊不清。

修改注释：我太啰唆了。

我修改，我缩短句子并提炼，提高我的写作水平。

3. _____

某种轻度的抄袭在我幽默的句子中是非常普遍的。好吧，并不是抄袭，更像是一种在"由……所激发灵感"的伪装下与"抄袭"这两个字所进行的小小的挑逗。

我阅读大量的材料，并且看不错的电视节目。我记录能引起我兴趣的东西。我用了比喻，就像我最喜欢的电视喜剧作家本·埃尔顿那样。而且我从我最喜欢的喜剧作家P·G·沃德

Sedaris, Bill Bryson and Tina Fey.

12 4. _____

13 This was very difficult. It took me a while to realize I needed it. I'd sit and sit but no words would come. Finally, I read *Becoming a Writer*, by Dorothea Brande (written in 1934, but timeless). She discusses psychological blocks that writers face and how to overcome them.

14 What I learned was in order to write, you have to open your mind and let your unconscious— your creativity—flow freely. I have an organized mind and desire for control so this is difficult. I have found ways to do this now, but only recently. Practice helps.

15 5. _____

16 Observing comes naturally to me. Because I'm introverted. I'd rather watch the play than act in it. Yes, stuff has happened to me. Yes, I have a never-ending string of eccentric people around me who stuff also happens to. But I pay attention, I watch, I listen, and I notice things. The obvious, the subtext, and the sub-subtext. I think my observational abilities are unique.

17 Besides, I write for hours, every day. Most of it I'll never use, but it gets easier, faster, better. First thing I do in a.m. is exercising my brain with 20 minutes of writing nonsense. Through practice I've honed my voice and I know what feels like me. That is most important; have confidence in your words, your style, and your tone. You find it through practice.

17 此外，我每天都写作几个小时。我写作的内容大多数从来没用过，但是我的写作变得更加简单、快速，也变得更好。在早上，我做的第一件事情是用20分钟没有意义的写作锻炼我的大脑。通过练习，我磨炼了我的观点，而且我知道什么样的写作方式更为符合真正的我。这是最重要的。对你的文字、风格和语调要有自信。你会发现，通过练习，这些都能够锻炼出来。

解题之路

1. 【答案】E

   【思路】从第四段第二句中PPS must be well-organized和第四句I learned this structure…可知选项[E]为正确答案。

2. 【答案】G

   【思路】第六、七、八段中对句子的删减对应，选项[G]中的hacksaw，故为正确答案。

3. 【答案】A

   【思路】第十段首句Some mild plagiarism is common in my more humorous writings（某种轻度的抄袭在我幽默的句子中是非常普遍的）的关键词是plagiarism，选项[A]中的Copy替换了plagiarism，由此推断选项[A]是正确答案。

4. 【答案】F

   【思路】结合第十三段第二句It took me a while to realize…以及第十四段首句中的your creativity，可知选项[F]为正确答案，Understand和creative process分别替换了realize和creativity。

5. 【答案】C

   【思路】根据第十六段首句中的Observing可知选项[C]为正确答案，observative对应文中的observing。

Text 2

Directions: Read the following text. For Questions 1–5, choose the most suitable subtitle from the list A–G to fit into each of the numbered blanks. There are two extra choices, which do not fit in any of the blanks. (10 points)

[A] Make work inspiring and fun

[B] Planning makes perfect

[C] Trust people to do their jobs

[D] Treating people well is a requirement

[E] Reward success

[F] Having a vision is awesome, communicating it

[G] Punishment is necessary

1　One of the top complaints of successful business owners is that it's hard to keep good people. That revolving door of mediocre help is taking precious time and money and it's frustrating as Hell. Especially when there isn't extra time and money just laying around, begging to be thrown at another person who will probably just quit or have to be fired in six months.

2　In both my business and in my corporate experience, I've hired for some very successful people, some of whom keep teams around for a long time and some of whom go through employees faster than green grass through a goose.

3　The most successful business owners and managers understand that their team is a tool that helps get them to where they want to go. Take care of your tools and they take care of you.

4　1._____

1　对成功的企业主来说，很难留住人才可谓是最头疼的问题之一，庸才可谓费时、费财又累心。当企业并没有多余的时间及金钱可供挥霍，却不得已雇用那些"跳槽达人"或者"被炒天王"时，这种情况尤为让企业主烦心。

2　从我的从业及公司经历来看，我雇用过很多非常成功的人。有些人长时间维系一个团队，有的人则如流水线般更换员工。

3　成功的企业主和领导者很清楚他们的团队是他们征程的航船，他们对待员工的态度会反映到员工对工作的回报中去。

4　1._____

5 You may have the best intentions and goals and dreams, but if you aren't sharing them with your team, how can they help you reach them?

6 2. _____

7 When I interview potential contractors and employees, the top answer to the question "What qualities about a boss drive you crazy", the top answer is micro management. If you've shared your vision, a clear job description and you're communicating regularly, you have to trust that people are doing their best. If they still aren't, there's an underlying issue.

8 3. _____

9 Some of the most successful people I've ever met plan for that success. It doesn't just happen. They have weekly or daily team meetings, yearly meetings, they plan their marketing, their offers, their launches... and they include their team in that process.

10 4. _____

11 There's a reason people stay with companies long term. A lot of it is about relationships and feeling like a part of something but rewarding a job well done is helpful too, especially for people who would be hard to replace. Having a compensation plan and bonuses with specific goals that your team can aspire to is one Hell of a motivator. Paid days off, gift cards, hand written cards and letters of appreciation are great ways to reward your team if money is tight.

5 你可能胸怀大志，志存高远，但假如不与下属分享的话，到头来也只是一纸空谈。

6 2. _____

7 从我面试承包商及员工的经验来看，他们对"雇主的什么品质会使你抓狂"这一问题最大的抱怨便是监视性管理（微观管理）。如果你能做到分享你的计划，落实工作内容，并定期与员工交流的话，那你便要相信自己的员工已经尽他们所能做好工作了。如果员工仍没有尽职尽责的话，那应该是有隐藏的原因。

8 3. _____

9 我见过的许多成功人士都会未雨绸缪，从不打无准备之仗。他们会组织每日例会、周例会、年会来跟进进度，制定营销、报价、发行计划……并把团队包含在计划内。

10 4. _____

11 员工的稳定性是有原因可循的。除了良好的人际关系以及归属感外，奖励也尤为重要，对于那些身居要职、无可替代的人来说更是如此。所以，制定一个薪酬计划和奖励机制可以非常有效地激励整个团队，让团队有所期待。当团队资金紧张时，带薪休假、礼品卡、亲笔感谢信等都是不错的选择。

12 5. _____

13 No one wants to work for a Debbie Downer. It sucks. Brainstorm ways to make the job that you're all doing a bit more inspired and fun. Chances are it will boost your bottom line in the process and stave off burnout for you and everyone around you.

14 Do you have a great team? What do you do to make sure they stick around long term?

12 5. _____

13 没有人想为苦瓜脸工作，这样确实不招人待见。集思广益以寻找方法使工作任务变得有趣，比如在工作过程中适当提高要求并注意劳逸结合。

14 你有优秀的团队吗？你用什么方法留住人才？

● 解题之路 ●

1. 【答案】F

【思路】第五段的意思是："你可能胸怀大志，志存高远，但假如不与下属分享的话，到头来也只是一纸空谈。"可以看出，其中的重要信息有：best intentions、goals、dreams和sharing them。选项[F]包含了以上内容：a vision替换了best intentions、goals和dreams，而communicating替换了sharing，故为正确选项。

2. 【答案】C

【思路】第七段首句是一个例子，本身并不重要。因此至少从第二句寻找核心内容：If you've shared your vision, a clear job description and you're communicating regularly, you have to trust that people are doing their best。该句是一个主从复合句，主句应该是核心，其中出现了trust，因此可知选项[C]是正确答案。

3. 【答案】B

【思路】第九段首句Some of the most successful people I've ever met plan for that success中出现了plan for that success，可断定选项[B]是正确答案，makes perfect是对success的改写。

4. 【答案】E

【思路】第十一段首句没有对应的选项，所以应该接着从下文寻找信息。第二句A lot of it is about relationships and feeling like a part of something but rewarding a job well done is helpful too（除了良好的人际关系以及归属感外，奖励也尤为重要）中出现了关键词rewarding，选项[E]包含了该词，因此正确答案为选项[E]。

5. 【答案】A

【思路】第十三段前两句"No one wants to work for a Debbie Downer. It sucks.（没有人想为苦瓜脸工作，这样确实不招人待见。）"谈到了工作不愉快的感受，接着第三句Brainstorm ways to make the job that you're all doing a bit more inspired and fun中出现了关键词inspired and fun，选项[A]符合此意，故为正确选项。

245

Text 3

Directions: Read the following text. For Questions 1–5, choose the most suitable subtitle from the list A–G to fit into each of the numbered blanks. There are two extra choices, which do not fit in any of the blanks. (10 points)

[A] You prove worthy of other people's energy

[B] Criticism has two categories

[C] The person shows you who they really are

[D] It means you are doing something

[E] Critics reassure us that we are on the right track

[F] It teaches you about yourself

[G] It can make you better

1 There are two types of critics. One comes from a place of love, another from a place of fear or envy. To receive positive criticism is one thing, but to suffer negative criticism is another. To be criticized with negative intention means that you have aroused something within someone else such as jealousy or a feeling of inadequacy. In order for the critic to feel better and elevated somehow, they need to put other people down. When someone condemns our work, comments unkindly on our appearance, judges our parenting style or disapproves of any of our actions, it is a pure and total reflection of them, not us. Take relief and comfort that a critic's words actually have nothing to do with you at all.

2 Here are five reasons to welcome critics in your life:

3 1. _____

4 When criticism is positively-fueled and

1 批评有两种形式：一种是出于爱，另一种是出于恐惧和嫉妒。得到正面的批评是一回事，承受负面的批评是另外一回事。被人带着负面意图指摘代表你激起了别人某方面的不快，比如嫉妒或缺乏自信。批评者为了设法获得优越感，就批评别人。当有人责备我们的工作，令人不快地评价我们的相貌，评判我们的教育方式或不认可我们的某些行为时，这只是纯粹在折射他们自己，而不是我们。放宽心，批评者的话语其实和你毫不相干。

2 以下是乐于接受生活中的批评者的5个原因：

3 1. _____

4 当我们接受充满善意的、有

constructive, we can improve, learn and grow. I love hearing thoughtful and useful feedback about my writing and coaching style. I take it all on board and use what works for me. Constructive criticism can express a great form of people's love for you. It can give you great insight and direction if your heart is open and the energy behind the feedback is well-meaning, considered and kind.

5 2. _____

6 Anais Nin wisely said, "We don't see things as they are, we see them as we are." Negatively-fueled critics therefore show us who they really are—often unfulfilled people who are therefore naturally unsupportive of your success. The way they react to what you are doing is a reflection of how they feel about their own lives. You can make a judgment call early on at how exposed you want to be to these people in your life.

7 3. _____

8 The further you get in your life, the more critics you can expect. It means that people are paying attention to you. Steven Pressfield said that criticism is what you really want as a creative person; he calls it "the supreme compliment". A public figure once told me that the more critics she gets, the more popular she knows she is becoming. What a great way to look at it!

9 4. _____

10 When a critic, in person or online or

whatever form they take, makes the effort to write or comment about you, it means you are affecting people somehow. They are using their time and attention to talk about you. You are not being ignored. Funnily enough, being the subject of someone's criticism is a flattering thing.

11 5. _____

12 I was so sensitive when I first started blogging. I was shocked at the venom of online commenters. It still isn't nice when I receive harsh comments but over time I have really learned to let go of it and understand that is not about me at all. As Gabby Bernstein says, "Forgive and delete!" Sometimes some responses can be helpful as they point out something that I never considered or they highlight a different way of looking at something. But in the end, I have to approve of my work and trust that I am always learning and improving. The more confident I feel in who I am, the less influenced I am by negativity. The way you let criticism impact you is a great barometer of how strong you are becoming.

13 My mom always told me that you can't please everyone, so please yourself. There will always be people who disagree with you or who dislike your ideas and actions—whether or not these people are coming from a positive or a negative place. Appreciate and accept them for being different than you and forgive them if they upset you. Remember that the road to success invites a lot of

critics so the sooner you know what to take on board and what to release, the better. The fact that criticism exists at all also reminds us that all we can do is our best—speak our truth, deliver our best work and surrender the rest.

14 And as one of my favorite books, *The Magic of Thinking Big*, says, "Expect critics, it's proof you are growing." And on the ladder of growth is the only place to be.

或舍弃什么，就会做得越好。事实上批评总是存在，这也提醒我们，我们的所作所为就是最好的回应——说真话，交出最好的作品并让别人信服。

14 正如我喜欢的一本书《大思想的神奇》中所说："期待批评者们，这证明你在成长。"而只有在成长的阶梯上才是你的归处。

解题之路

1. 【答案】G

   【思路】第四段首句When criticism is positively-fueled and constructive, we can improve, learn and grow（当我们接受充满善意的、有建设性的批评时，我们能获得提升、学到东西并成长）中的关键词是improve, learn and grow，选项[G]中的make you better恰好是对这几个词的浓缩提炼，故答案为选项[G]。

2. 【答案】C

   【思路】依据第六段首句We don't see things as they are, we see them as we are（我们眼中的事物往往不是它们本身，而是在折射我们自己），以及第三句The way they react to what you are doing is a reflection of how they feel about their own lives（他们对你所做之事的反应就是他们对自己生活的感触），可以推断选项[C]"批评别人，折射自己"是对以上内容的综合和提炼，故为正确答案。

3. 【答案】E

   【思路】第八段前两句The further you get in your life, the more critics you can expect（你在生活中走得越远，就会遇到越多的批评者）和It means that people are paying attention to you（这意味着人们正在关注着你）表明：生活中遭遇批评再自然不过，并非坏事。由此断定选项[E] Critics reassure us that we are on the right track是对这些内容的合理改写，故为正确答案。

4. 【答案】A

   【思路】从第十段首句中it means you are affecting people somehow（这意味着你正在以某种方式影响别人）和第二句They are using their time and attention to talk about you（他们在花时间和精力来谈论你），可以推断选项[A]是正确答案。

5. 【答案】F

【思路】第十二段前四句都是讲述作者本人以前的经历，可视作例子。真正重要的信息是从第五句开始的：Sometimes some responses can be helpful as they point out something that I never considered or they highlight a different way of looking at something（有时有些评论还是很有益的，因为它们能指出我没有考虑到的东西，或是使我学会了从不同角度看待事物），由此可知选项[F]符合此意，故为正确选项。

Text 4

Directions: Read the following text. For Questions 1–5, choose the most suitable subtitle from the list A–G to fit into each of the numbered blanks. There are two extra choices, which do not fit in any of the blanks. (10 points)

[A] High-paying job is preferred

[B] Cyber-loafing your way to the top

[C] Waiting loses opportunity

[D] Appear hard at work

[E] Laziness is contempted

[F] Technology: blessing or curse?

[G] Low-pressure work is desirable

1　The best way to understand a system is to look at it from the point of view of people who want to subvert it. Sensible bosses try to view their companies through the eyes of corporate raiders. Serious-minded politicians make a point of putting themselves in their opponents' shoes. The same is true of the world of work in general: the best way to understand a company's "human resources" is not to consult the department that bears that ugly name but to study the basic principles of one of the world's most popular, if unrecognized, sciences: skiving.

2　1. _____

3　To skive (or shirk, as Americans call it),

1　熟悉一个系统的最好方法是从那些想要颠覆这个系统的人的视角来审视。明智的老板通过有意破坏公司者的视角了解自己的公司。严谨的政治家也会站在对手的角度看问题。职场大体上都是一样的：了解公司"人力资源"的最好方式不是去咨询那个挂着丑陋牌子的人力部门，而是去了解也许不被认可、却最热门的其中一门学科——怠工学——的基本原则。

2　1. _____

3　要怠工，你得看似非常专注

you are supposed to be seemingly preoccupied. This is the ancient jacket-on-the-back-of-the-chair trick: leave a coat permanently on display so that a casual observer—a CEO practising "managing by walking around," for example—will assume that you are the first to arrive and the last to leave. The skill of skiving is subtle: ensure you are somewhere else when the work is being allocated. Successful skivers never visibly shy away from work: confronted with the inevitable they make a point of looking extremely eager. This "theatre of enthusiasm" has fooled almost everyone. But as Roland Paulsen, of Sweden's Lund University, explains in *Empty Labour*, an example-packed new book, innumerable studies suggest that the average worker devotes between one-and-a-half and three hours a day to loafing.

2. _____

Information technology is both the slacker's best friend and his deadliest enemy. The PC is custom-made for the indolent: you can give every impression of being hard at work when in fact you are doing your shopping, booking a holiday or otherwise frolicking in the cyber-waves. And thanks to mobile technology you can now continue to frolic while putting in face time in meetings. There is also a high-tech version of the jacket trick: program your e-mails to send themselves at half past midnight or 5:30 a.m. to give your managers the impression that you are a Stakhanovite.

But there is a dark side to IT: one estimate

suggests that 27m employees around the world have their internet use monitored. Dealing with this threat requires vigilance: do everything you can to hide your browsing history. It may also require something that does not come naturally to skivers: political activism. Make a huge fuss about how even the smallest concessions on the principle of absolute data privacy will create a slippery slope to a totalitarian society. Skiving is like liberty: it can flourish only if Big Brother is kept at bay.

3. _____

You should always try to get a job where there is no clear relation between input and output. The public sector is obviously a skiver's paradise. In 2004 it took two days for anyone to notice that a Finnish tax inspector had died at his desk. In 2009 the Swedish Civil Aviation Administration discovered that some of its employees had spent three-quarters of their working hours watching internet pornography. In 2012 a German civil servant wrote a farewell message to his colleagues, on his retirement, confessing that he hadn't done a stroke of work for the past 14 years. And even if managers can find people who are failing on the "input" side it is almost impossible to sack them.

Big private-sector organisations can be almost as fertile skiving grounds as public ones. In *The Living Dead* (2005), his memoir of life as an office worker, David Bolchover says that the amount of work he had to do was inversely related to the size of the company that he worked for. He started his career in a small firm where he had to work hard for no title and low pay. He ended working for a big company where he had a grand title and a fat pay packet but did almost nothing. Mr Bolchover was not a member of the brotherhood: he asked his bosses for more work and, when they failed to oblige, filled his idle hours by writing a management book. But millions of others are perfectly happy to devote their lives to firm-financed leisure.

10 4._____

11 The clever clerks are exploring the rich opportunities provided by the new economy. The likes of Google and Facebook make a great fuss about installing the adult equivalent of children's playgrounds—everything from massage rooms to sleep pods and pinball machines—to provide their employees with an opportunity for relaxation between intense bursts of toil. But now that these companies are becoming bloated monopolists there is a perfect opportunity for canny skivers to take advantage of the nap pods without bothering with the frantic work. New-economy companies have even provided a handy way to discover if they are ripe for exploitation: if employees have titles such as "director of visioning" or "vice-chairman of big-data analytics" then you know that it is time to start geekifying your CV.

12 5._____

13 You should not allow your preference for

企业工作，他必须非常努力，却没有职称，薪水也很低。最后他为一家大公司工作，拥有重要的头衔和丰厚的薪水，但是几乎什么都不用做。鲍乔弗先生并不是兄弟会的成员：他跟老板要求更多的工作，在没有得到同意后，他便利用他的闲暇时间写了一本管理学书籍。但是其他的几百万人则十分开心地将自己的生命花费在公司资助的安逸中。

10 4._____

11 聪明的怠工者开始寻求新兴经济体里的大量机会。比如谷歌和脸书网这类公司都大张旗鼓地为他们的职员能在紧张的工作之余得到放松而建立了娱乐场所，包括按摩房、睡眠舱、弹球台等。但如今这些公司都成了膨胀的垄断者，这就给了精明的怠工者们一个不用紧张工作就能享受娱乐工具的完美机会。新兴经济体的公司甚至为他们提供了一个检测自己是否够格享乐的便捷方法：如果员工们拥有了诸如"愿景总监"或是"大数据分析部副主席"的头衔，那么他们就可以对自己的简历嗤之以鼻了。

12 5._____

13 你不该让对于闲暇的喜好阻

leisure to limit your ambition. Too many skivers are still bewitched by the old myth that there is a connection between effort and reward. There are inevitably few quantitative studies of skiving. But the ones that exist suggest it is most prevalent at the very top and bottom of the pay scale. A Finnish study in 2010 found that the people who reported the most "empty labour" earned more than €80,000 ($112,000) a year while the runners-up earned less than €20,000. It can be hard to begin your climb up the greasy pole without making some effort: the trick is to be brimming over with clever ideas for other people to execute. But when you become a manager your problems are solved: you can simply delegate all your work to other people while you spend your days attending international conferences or "cultivating relationships with investors".

挡了你的野心。太多的怠工者仍然迷信于"回报与努力相关"这种神话。不言而喻，关于怠工的量化分析很少。但现有的研究显示，怠工现象从薪酬的最顶端人群到最低端人群中普遍存在。2010年，芬兰的一份研究显示，报称"空手而归"的人的最高年薪超过8万欧元（合11.2万美元），而第二名只有不足2万欧元。如果不去做些努力，你很难爬到高薪职位：你的聪明才智只能供他人所用。但当你成了管理者，问题就迎刃而解了：你只需把所有工作交给他人，而自己则出席国际会议或去"与投资商拉拢关系"就行了。

解题之路

1. 【答案】D

   【思路】第三段首句出现了be seemingly preoccupied（看似非常专注于工作），下面的内容是对该句的解释，所以可以断定该句是本段的主题思想。对比各个选项，选项[D]的Appear hard at work是be seemingly preoccupied的同义改写，因此该选项就是正确答案。

2. 【答案】F

   【思路】第五段首句Information technology is both the slacker's best friend and his deadliest enemy（信息技术既是懒鬼的好友，也是他的死敌）中的几个关键词是technology、friend和enemy。选项[F]包含了Technology，而且blessing（福）和curse（祸）恰好是friend和enemy的适度改写，所以该选项即是答案。

3. 【答案】G

   【思路】第八段首句出现了try to get a job where there is no clear relation between input and output（努力去找一份投入与产出关系不明确的工作），第二句说The public sector is obviously a skiver's paradise（公共部门显然是怠工者的天堂），随后的内容是对前两句的解释，大致意思是：公共部门的工作效率低下，要求不高。可看出选项[G]是对这些内容的浓缩和提炼，因此该选项即是答案。

4. 【答案】C

【思路】第十一段首句The clever clerks are exploring the rich opportunities provided by the new economy（聪明的怠工者开始寻求新兴经济体里的大量机会），随后举例说明了Google和Facebook等新兴企业为其员工修建了舒适的供娱乐放松的环境和设施，以此建议人们尽可能在这些行业里寻求发展机会。选项[C]的表述Waiting loses opportunity（等待丧失机会）是对这些内容的正话反说，因此为正确答案。

5. 【答案】B

【思路】第十三段首句You should not allow your preference for leisure to limit your ambition（你不该让对于闲暇的喜好阻挡了你的野心）中出现了关键词ambition，接着第六句It can be hard to begin your climb up the greasy pole without making some effort（如果不去做些努力，你很难爬到高薪职位）中出现了begin your climb up the greasy pole。选项[B]中的to the top（攀上顶峰）包含了以上信息，故为正确选项。

Text 5

Directions: Read the following text. For Questions 1–5, choose the most suitable subtitle from the list A–G to fit into each of the numbered blanks. There are two extra choices, which do not fit in any of the blanks. (10 points)

[A] Embrace your inner liking

[B] Say "no" to the Productivity Industrial Complex

[C] Realize the importance of perspective

[D] Stop hiding behind the comfort of stepping stones

[E] Pursue self-development over productivity

[F] Get to "mind like water" the original way

[G] Convert your money back into time

1 Anti-hacks attempt to solve problems by approaching them at a higher level of thinking. For example, while David Allen says that "mind like water" (piece of mind) comes from creating

> 1 颠覆意味着从更高层次解决生活中的问题。例如，戴维·艾伦说过，要达到"心若止水"的境界，必须列出所有要做的事，挖掘头脑深

255

exhaustive to-do lists and getting everything out of your head, an anti-hack might involve meditation, because all the list-making in the world will not bring you to a meditative, mind-like-water state.

2 Please keep in mind some of these "anti-hacks" may not be practicable for you. These aren't "one size fits all" solutions.

3 1. _____

4 So many of us live "stepping stone lives". We spend the majority of our waking hours working for goals that are merely stepping stones to other goals. I realize that not everyone has the luxury of avoiding stepping stones. If your dream requires a medical degree, for example, you'll need to suck it up and stay on those stones.

5 2. _____

6 There is a myth among many productivity evangelists that productivity—or a productivity system—can lead to the meditative state likened to "mind like water".

7 In karate there is an image that's used to define the position of perfect readiness: "mind like water". Imagine throwing a pebble into a still pond. How does the water respond? The answer is, totally appropriately to the force and mass of the input; then it returns to calm. It doesn't overreact or underreact.

8 3. _____

9 The Productivity Industrial Complex is a

层；而颠覆则可能包括冥思，因为任何挖空心思的列表都不能达到冥思和心若止水的境界。

2 下面是我的一些关于颠覆的想法。请注意，其中的一些颠覆行为可能并不适合你，因为它们不是"一人适用，万人皆可"的良方妙计。

3 1. _____

4 很多人都过着这种"为未来打基础"的生活。我们大部分时间都在做一些为追求其他目标作基石的事情。我意识到不是所有的人都能绕过这些准备性的阶段。例如，你如果要拿到一个医学学位，就必须坚持学完所有课程，打好基础。

5 2. _____

6 在鼓吹效率的人中流传着一种神话，即效率或效率系统可通向一种类似于心若止水的禅思状态。

7 空手道中有一种用来描述完全就绪的说法，叫作"心若止水"。设想你将石子扔到静静的池塘中，池水会有什么反应？其反应的程度和范围与受到外力的大小和质量完全对等。然后一切重归平静。池水不会过度反应或反应不足。

8 3. _____

9 行业内的复杂的效率公式往

marriage between corporations and an entire industry of productivity companies, gurus, consultants, and solution-makers who help corporations squeeze every ounce of productivity from their workers. Organizations like The David Allen Company, for example, make the bulk of their income from corporations looking to "maximize their employee output," and it's no surprise that they have a *Fortune* 500-studded client list which includes Lockheed Martin, Deloitte & Touche, and the US Department of Defense.

10 4._____

11 Since World War II, productivity in the US has doubled. So we should be working 20-hour work weeks, right? Well, we're not. We're working more (we've exchanged our extra time for more money). In fact, we're working more than medieval peasants, and the 40-hour work week hasn't changed since 1940 even though productivity levels have been growing steadily since then.

12 5._____

13 Raoul Vaneigem once wrote that "everything has already been said and all our knowledge is essentially banal." And he's right. If you read the profound thoughts of any great teacher or leader, you'll likely find no new knowledge. What you will find, however, is heaps of timeless perspective. You'll find knowledge deeply rooted in perspective and amplified by perspective.

14 Great thinkers and teachers are great because

their perspective forces you to take a second glance at the knowledge you already have. And their perspective is so compelling because it couldn't have come from anywhere except direct experience.

伟大，就在于他们的思想高度迫使你重新审视你现有的知识。其思想高度之所以如此引人入胜，是因为这种思想高度源于直接的经验，而非他处。

→ 解题之路 ←

1. 【答案】D

   【思路】第四段首句出现了关键词stepping stone lives，选项[D]包含了stepping stones这个短语，因此该选项为正确选项。

2. 【答案】F

   【思路】该段首句最后出现了关键词mind like water，在选项[F]中找到了原词，因此该选项是正确答案。

3. 【答案】B

   【思路】第九段首句出现了关键词The Productivity Industrial Complex，选项[B]中原词重现，该选项是正确答案。

4. 【答案】G

   【思路】第十一段第四句We're working more (we've exchanged our extra time for more money)中出现了关键词time和money，选项[G]也包含了这两个词，因此该选项为正确答案。

5. 【答案】C

   【思路】第十三段第四句What you will find, however, is heaps of timeless perspective中出现了重要的逻辑转折词however和关键名词perspective，对比剩余选项，可断定选项[C]是对该句的合理改写，故为正确选项。

（二）多项对应

Text 1

Directions: Read the following text and answer the questions by finding information from the left column that corresponds to each of the marked details given in the right column. There are two extra choices in the right column. (10 points)

1　The Surrealists' ideal state for making art was the twilight between wakefulness and

1　超现实主义者创作艺术品的理想状态是清醒与昏睡之间的蒙眬状

sleep, when they would dredge up images from the murky subconscious and throw them onto the page or canvas. Proposing sleepwalking as an optimal widespread societal condition, André Breton once asked, "When will we have sleeping logicians, sleeping philosophers?" It seems that the Surrealist vision of a dream culture has been fully realized in today's technologies. We are awash in a new, electronic collective unconscious; strapped to several devices, we're half awake, half asleep. We speak on the phone while surfing the Web, partially hearing what's being said to us while simultaneously answering e-mails and checking status updates. We've become very good at being distracted. From a creative point of view, this is reason to celebrate. The vast amount of the Web's language is perfect raw material for literature. Disjunctive, compressed, decontextualized, and, most important, cut-and-pastable, it's easily reassembled into works of art.

2 Come January, fifteen University of Pennsylvania creative-writing students and I will sit silently in a room with nothing more than our devices and a Wi-Fi connection, for three hours a week, in a course called "Wasting Time on the Internet." Although we'll all be in the same room, our communication will happen exclusively through chat rooms and Listservs, or over social media. Distraction and split attention will be mandatory. So will aimless drifting and intuitive surfing. The students will be encouraged to get lost on the Web,

disappearing for three hours in a Situationist-inspired *dérive*, drowsily emerging from the digital haze only when class is over. We will enter a collective dreamspace, an experience out of which the students will be expected to render works of literature. To bolster their practice, they'll explore the long history of the recuperation of boredom and time-wasting, through critical texts by thinkers such as Guy Debord, Mary Kelly, Erving Goffman, Raymond Williams, and John Cage.

3 Nothing is off limits: if it is on the Internet, it is fair play. Students watching three hours of porn can use it as the basis for compelling erotica; they can troll nefarious right-wing sites, scraping hate-filled language for spy thrillers; they can render celebrity Twitter feeds into epic Dadaist poetry; they can recast Facebook feeds as novellas; or they can simply hand in their browser history at the end of a session and present it as a memoir.

4 I've never taught this class before, but I have a hunch that it's going to be a success. For the past decade, I've been teaching a class at Penn called "Uncreative Writing", where students are forced to plagiarize, appropriate, and steal texts that they haven't written and claim them as their own. For a final assignment, I require them to buy a paper from a paper mill, put their name on it, and

情境所激发的氛围里，只有下课时才懒洋洋地从数字化的蒙眬状态中摆脱出来。我们将进入一个集体梦幻地带，根据这样的体验过程，学生将有望创作文学作品。为了支持他们的实践，他们将会阅读一些思想家的批判性作品，如居伊·德波、玛丽·凯利、欧文·戈夫曼、雷蒙德·威廉斯以及约翰·凯奇的文章，以此来探索如何摆脱无聊和避免浪费时间的悠久历史。

3 所有事都不受限制：只要是在网上，那就可以。学生看3个小时的色情作品，可以用它作为创作引人注目的情色作品的基础；他们可以浏览邪恶的右翼网站，搜集充满恨意的语言来为创作间谍惊险小说积累素材；他们可以把名人的博客翻译成史诗般的达达主义诗歌；他们可以将脸书网的内容重新编排成中篇小说；或者更简单，他们可以在课程结束时提交自己的上网浏览记录，把它作为回忆录展示出来。

4 我之前从没教过这样的课，但我有种预感，这会成功的。过去的10年中，我在宾夕法尼亚大学教过一个名为"没有创造性的写作"的课程。学生被强迫剽窃、盗用、抄袭那些并非自己所作的文章，并声称确是自己的作品。最后一项作业，我要求他们从一个造纸厂买文章，并署上自

defend it as their own—surely the most forbidden act in academia. In the class, students are penalized for originality, sincerity, and creativity. What they've been surreptitiously doing throughout their academic career—patchwriting, cutting-and-pasting, lifting—must now be done in the open, where they are accountable for their decisions. Suddenly, new questions arise: What is it that I'm lifting? And why? What do my choices about what to appropriate tell me about myself? My emotions? My history? My biases and passions? The critiques turn toward formal improvement: Could I have swiped better material? Could my methods in constructing these texts have been better? Not surprisingly, they thrive. What I've learned from these years in the classroom is that no matter what we do, we can't help but express ourselves.

	[A] made from Twitter feeds of famous people.
1. The Surrealists' ideal state was	[B] allowed students to do something forbidden in academia.
2. A Situationist-inspired *dérive* was	[C] put on the Internet.
3. Raymond Williams and John Cage were	[D] neither wakeful nor sleeping.
4. Dadaist poetry can be	[E] be presented as a memoir.
5. The course of "Uncreative Writing"	[F] writers of critical writing.
	[G] used as a course setting in University of Pennsylvania.

➡️ 解题之路 ⬅️

1. 【答案】**D**

   【思路】根据左栏题干关键词The Surrealists' ideal state可定位到原文首段第一句：The Surrealists' ideal state for making art was the twilight between wakefulness and sleep，从wakefulness和sleep两词可判断出选项[D]为正确答案。

2. 【答案】**G**

   【思路】根据左栏题干关键词A Situationist-inspired *dérive*可定位到原文第二段第五句：The students will be encouraged to get lost on the Web, disappearing for three hours in a Situationist-inspired *dérive*, drowsily emerging from the digital haze only when class is over。根据该句中when class is over可知，它和某种课程相关，而且地点是某所大学（该段首句）：University of Pennsylvania，两个信息相结合，可推断出选项[G]为正确答案。

3. 【答案】**F**

   【思路】根据左栏题干关键词Raymond Williams and John Cage可定位到原文第二段末句：through critical texts by thinkers such as Guy Debord, Mary Kelly, Erving Goffman, Raymond Williams, and John Cage。从Raymond Williams and John Cage这两个名词前面的信息词critical texts可确定选项[F]为正确答案。

4. 【答案】**A**

   【思路】根据左栏题干关键词Dadaist poetry可定位到原文第三段第二句：they can render celebrity Twitter feeds into epic Dadaist poetry。Dadaist poetry前面的celebrity Twitter feeds就是答案，选项[A]包含了这些信息，famous people是celebrity的同义替换。

5. 【答案】**B**

   【思路】根据左栏题干关键词Uncreative Writing可定位到原文第四段第二句：For the past decade, I've been teaching a class at Penn called "Uncreative Writing"。但答案在下一句的破折号之后：surely the most forbidden act in academia，与选项[B]中信息对应，因此选项[B]为正确答案。

Text 2

Directions: Read the following text and answer the questions by finding information from the left column that corresponds to each of the marked details given in the right column. There are two extra choices in the right column. (10 points)

1 Robin Dunbar came up with his eponymous number almost by accident. The University of Oxford anthropologist and psychologist (then at University College London) was trying to solve the problem of why primates devote so much time and effort to grooming. In the process of figuring out the solution, he chanced upon a potentially far more intriguing application for his research. At the time, in the nineteen-eighties, the Machiavellian Intelligence Hypothesis (now known as the Social Brain Hypothesis) had just been introduced into anthropological and primatology discourse. It held that primates have large brains because they live in socially complex societies: the larger the group, the larger the brain. Thus, from the size of an animal's neocortex, the frontal lobe in particular, you could theoretically predict the group size for that animal.

2 Looking at his grooming data, Dunbar made the mental leap to humans. "We also had humans in our data set so it occurred to me to look to see what size group that relationship might predict for humans," he told me recently. Dunbar did the math, using a ratio of neurotically volume to total brain volume and mean group size, and came up with a number. Judging from the size of an average human brain, the number of people the average person could have in her social group was a hundred and fifty. Anything beyond that would be too complicated to handle at optimal processing levels. For the last twenty-two years, Dunbar has been "unpacking and

1 罗宾·邓巴提出邓巴数字几乎可以说纯属意外。这位牛津大学的人类学家、心理学家（提出邓巴数字时他还在伦敦大学学院）当时想解决的问题是为什么灵长类动物会花那么多的时间和精力梳理毛发。在寻找答案的过程中，邓巴无意中为自己的研究找到了更有意思、更具潜在应用价值的东西。当时是20世纪80年代，马基雅弗利智力假说（就是现在大家知道的社会化大脑假说）刚被引入到人类学和灵长类学的著述当中。这个假说认为灵长类动物的脑子大，是因为他们生活在复杂的、群居活动的社会里：群体越大，脑子就越大。所以，依据一个动物的新大脑皮层的大小，特别是大脑额叶的大小，从理论上讲我们就可以预测这个动物生活的群体的大小了。

2 看着自己收集的灵长类动物梳毛的数据，邓巴的思维跳跃到了人类身上。"我们也有人类的数据库，所以我想到依据这种关系，看看能对人类群体组织的大小做出何种预测，"不久前邓巴对我这样说。他用的是数学方法，使用新皮层容积与总的脑容量和平均群体人数之间的比例，得出一个数字。以人脑的平均大小为标准，一般人的社会群体的人数是150个。超过这个数，群体就过于复杂，超过了大脑最优层面的处理水平。过去22年，邓巴一直在"分析和探究"

exploring" what that number actually means—and whether our ever-expanding social networks have done anything to change it.

3   The Dunbar number is actually a series of them. The best known, a hundred and fifty, is the number of people we call casual friends—the people, say, you'd invite to a large party. (In reality, it's a range: a hundred at the low end and two hundred for the more social of us.) From there, through qualitative interviews coupled with analysis of experimental and survey data, Dunbar discovered that the number grows and decreases according to a precise formula, roughly a "rule of three." The next step down, fifty, is the number of people we call close friends—perhaps the people you'd invite to a group dinner. You see them often, but not so much that you consider them to be true intimates. Then there's the circle of fifteen: the friends that you can turn to for sympathy when you need it, the ones you can confide in about most things. The most intimate Dunbar number, five, is your close support group. These are your best friends (and often family members). On the flipside, groups can extend to five hundred, the acquaintance level, and to fifteen hundred, the absolute limit—the people for whom you can put a name to a face. While the group sizes are relatively stable, their composition can be fluid. Your five today may not be your five next week; people drift among layers and sometimes fall out of them altogether.

3   所谓的邓巴数字实际上是由一系列这样的数字组成的。150人：这个数字最为人所知，指的是我们认为是普通朋友的数量——所谓的普通朋友就是你若开一个盛大晚会要邀请的人。（实际上150只是个范围：低可至100，如果社会交往多一些，可到200人。）以此为发端，通过定性访谈，以及对实验数据和调查数据的分析，邓巴发现这个数据的增减是有一个精确的公式的——大致说来就是"三定律"。150再往下是数字50：就是我们说的亲密朋友的数量——就是你可能会请来一起聚餐的朋友。这些朋友经常碰面，但也达不到知己的程度。再下来就是15人的圈子：是那种有需要时可以一吐苦水的朋友，是你大多数事都可以倾诉的知己。最亲密的关系圈人数是5人，这些人是你紧密的支持团，是你最亲密的朋友（多数情况下是你的家人）。相对应地，群体能扩及500人，这是泛泛之交的标准；再到1500人，这是绝对极限——就是你能把脸和名字对上号的人的数量。虽说群体的大小相对来说是"铁打的营盘"一样固定，但其组成却像"流水的兵"那样会变动。你们今天的5人，到下周可能就不是这些人了；人的层次会有变换，有时会一起失去。

	[A] is not as stable as its size.
1. Robin Dunbar at first	[B] fall out of them altogether.
2. The Social Brain Hypothesis	[C] the number of a group increases and decreases.
3. A human group of 150	[D] focused on the aspect of brain size.
4. According to a "rule of three"	[E] was criticized widely.
5. The composition of a human group	[F] tried to explore why primates groomed so long.
	[G] is ideal in terms of the brain's processing ability.

解题之路

1. 【答案】F

【思路】根据左栏题干关键词Robin Dunbar和出题段落顺序原则，可定位到原文首段。再根据at first可定位到第二句：...was trying to solve the problem of why primates devote so much time and effort to grooming，由此断定选项[F]为正确答案，属于同义转述。

2. 【答案】D

【思路】根据左栏题干关键词The Social Brain Hypothesis可定位到原文第一段第四句：...the Machiavellian Intelligence Hypothesis (now known as the Social Brain Hypothesis) had just been introduced into anthropological and primatology discourse。但答案在下一句：It held that primates have large brains because they live in socially complex societies，其中出现了关键词brain，所以可断定正确答案为选项[D]。

3. 【答案】G

【思路】根据左栏题干关键词human group和数字150可定位到原文第二段第四句和第三段第二句：Judging from the size of an average human brain, the number of people the average person could have in her social group was a hundred and fifty；The best known, a hundred and fifty, is the number of people we call casual friends。对比关键词出现的这两处信息的前后内容，可知选项[G]为正确答案，对应的是第二段第五句：Anything beyond that would be too complicated to handle at optimal processing levels。

4. 【答案】C

【思路】根据左栏题干关键词a "rule of three"可定位到原文第三段第四句：Dunbar discovered that the number grows and decreases according to a precise formula, roughly a "rule of three"，可知选项[C]为正确答案，increases替换了原文的grows。

5. 【答案】A

【思路】根据左栏题干关键词The composition of a human group可定位到原文第三段倒数

第二句：While the group sizes are relatively stable, their composition can be fluid。选项[A]是对该句的正确改写，故为答案。

Text 3

Directions: Read the following text and answer the questions by finding information from the left column that corresponds to each of the marked details given in the right column. There are two extra choices in the right column. (10 points)

1 A study of how older teenagers use social media has found that Facebook is "not just on the slide, it is basically dead and buried" and is being replaced by simpler social networks such as Twitter and Snapchat.

2 Young people now see the site as "uncool" and keep their profiles live purely to stay in touch with older relatives, among whom it remains popular.

3 Professor Daniel Miller of University College London, an anthropologist who worked on the research, wrote in an article for academic news website The Conversation: Mostly they feel embarrassed even to be associated with it.

4 "This year marked the start of what looks likely to be a sustained decline of what had been the most pervasive of all social networking sites. Young people are turning away in their droves and adopting other social networks instead, while the worst people of all, their parents, continue to use the service.

5 "Where once parents worried about their

1 关于年龄较大的青少年使用社交媒体情况的一项研究表明，脸书的受欢迎程度"不仅每况愈下，甚至基本上是明日黄花"了。许多更简单的社交网络如推特和色拉布在逐步取代脸书。

2 现在的年轻人觉得脸书一点都"不酷"，但他们仍然保留着自己的账号，只是为了和长辈保持联系，因为脸书在长辈中依旧风靡。

3 伦敦大学学院的教授丹尼尔·米勒是位人类学家，他也曾参与此项调查研究，并且还为学术研究网站"对话"写了一篇文章，其中提到：和脸书联系在一起通常也会让他们感到尴尬。

4 "今年对于那些过去风靡全球的社交网站来说是惨淡的，呈现出持续下滑的趋势。年轻人开始陆陆续续地转而使用其他社交网络，而他们的父母则还在使用原来的那些服务。

5 "父母们曾经担心他们的孩子

children joining Facebook, the children now say it is their family that insists they stay there to post about their lives. Parents have worked out how to use the site and see it as a way for the family to remain connected. In response, the young are moving on to cooler things.

6 "What appears to be the most seminal moment in a young person's decision to leave Facebook was surely that dreaded day your mum sends you a friend request."

7 The Global Social Media Impact Study, which was funded by the European Union, observed 16- to 18-year-olds in eight countries for 15 months and found that Facebook use was in freefall. Instead, young people are turning to simpler services like Twitter, Instagram, Snapchat and WhatsApp which Professor Miller conceded were "no match" for Facebook in terms of functionality.

8 "Most of the school children in our survey recognized that in many ways, Facebook is technically better than Twitter or Instagram. It is more integrated, better for photo albums, organizing parties and more effective for observing people's relationships," said Professor Miller, adding that "slick isn't always best" in attracting young users.

9 WhatsApp has overtaken Facebook as the number one way to send messages, say the researchers, while Snapchat has gained in popularity in recent months by allowing users to send images

which "self-destruct" after a short period on the recipients phone in order to maintain privacy.

10 Snapchat claims that 350 million images are sent every day, and reportedly recently turned down a $3 billion (£1.8 billion) acquisition offer from Facebook. Co-founder Evan Spiegel, who lives at home with his father despite an estimated net worth of $3 billion, last month told *The Telegraph* that "deleting should be the default".

11 Researchers found that close friends were using Snapchat to communicate, while WhatsApp was used with acquaintances and Twitter broadcasted indiscriminately to anyone who chose to follow that person.

12 The study found that Facebook was now used by teenagers as a way to stay in touch with older members of their family and sibling who have left for university and has "evolved into a very different animal" from its early days as a social network focusing on young users at university.

13 Facebook, which will be a decade old next year, is currently offering 70m shares for sale at $55.05 a share, 41m of which belong to founder Mark Zuckerberg.

14 The stock has climbed well above the $38 price set in Facebook's initial public offering 19 months ago.

图片，以此来保护隐私，而在最近几个月中广受欢迎。

10 色拉布声称人们每天总共会发送3.5亿张图片。据报道，它最近还拒绝了脸书提出的30亿美元（1.8亿英镑）的收购计划。其共同创立者埃文·施皮格尔尽管拥有着价值30亿的网站，可他还是和父亲一起生活，上个月他告诉《电讯报》："色拉布应该默认删除图片。"

11 研究者们还发现密友之间使用色拉布进行交流，而熟人之间使用瓦次普，给关注者一视同仁地发布消息则使用推特。

12 此次研究还发现，青少年现在把脸书作为和家中长辈、毕业分别的同学保持联系的一种方式，已经和其早前将大学在校的年轻用户作为生力军的社交网络宗旨背道而驰。

13 脸书明年就10岁了，目前对外发售7 000万股，每股55.05美元，其中创始人马克·扎克伯格拥有4 100万股。

14 自19个月前最初公开发售38美元每股的股价，脸书的股票上升状况良好。

第五章 阅读理解（B 部分）

	[A] a service provided by Snapchat.
1. Professor Daniel Miller argues	[B] more than half of Facebook's shares.
2. The Global Social Media Impact Study thinks	[C] Facebook is still better in function.
3. "Self-destruct" is	[D] WhatsApp has overtaken Facebook.
4. Evan Spiegel says	[E] Facebook is losing its influence quickly.
5. Mark Zuckerberg claims	[F] more used by close friends.
	[G] deleting should be done automatically.

解题之路

1. 【答案】C

    【思路】根据左栏题干关键词Daniel Miller回看原文，原文共有三处出现该名字。第三段首句：Professor Daniel Miller of University College London, an anthropologist who worked on...；第七段第二句：...which Professor Miller conceded were "no match" for Facebook in terms of functionality；第八段第二句：...said Professor Miller, adding that "slick isn't always best" in attracting young users。通过阅读这三句的信息，可知选项[C]为正确答案，即对第七段第二句Miller的话进行的同义转述。

2. 【答案】E

    【思路】根据左栏题干关键词The Global Social Media Impact Study可定位到原文第七段首句：The Global Social Media Impact Study, which was funded by the European Union, observed 16- to 18-year-olds in eight countries for 15 months and found that Facebook use was in freefall。选项[E]是对该句中Facebook use was in freefall的正确改写，故为正确选项。

3. 【答案】A

    【思路】根据左栏题干关键词"Self-destruct"可定位到原文第九段末句：...which "self-destruct" after a short period on the recipients phone in order to maintain privacy。对整句话进行解读，再对比各个选项可知选项[A]是正确答案。

4. 【答案】G

    【思路】根据左栏题干关键词Evan Spiegel可定位到原文第十段第二句：Co-founder Evan Spiegel, who lives at home with his father despite an estimated net worth of $3 billion, last month told *The Telegraph* that "deleting should be the default"。该句中引号里的内容就是答案所在，选项[G]是对这个内容的同义改写，automatically替换原文的should be the default。

269

5. 【答案】B

【思路】根据左栏题干关键词Mark Zuckerberg可定位到原文倒数第二段。该段主要说：脸书目前的总股是7 000万股，而马克·扎克伯格拥有4 100万股。所以正确答案是选项[B]。

Text 4

Directions: Read the following text and answer the questions by finding information from the left column that corresponds to each of the marked details given in the right column. There are two extra choices in the right column. (10 points)

1 In 1948, two professors at Harvard University published a study of thirty-three hundred men who had recently graduated, looking at whether their names had any bearing on their academic performance. The men with unusual names, the study found, were more likely to have flunked out or to have exhibited symptoms of psychological neurosis than those with more common names. The Mikes were doing just fine, but the Berriens were having trouble. A rare name, the professors surmised, had a negative psychological effect on its bearer.

2 Since then, researchers have continued to study the effects of names, and, in the decades after the 1948 study, these findings have been widely reproduced. Some recent research suggests that names can influence choice of profession, where we live, whom we marry, the grades we earn, the stocks we invest in, whether we're accepted to a school or are hired for a particular job, and the quality of our work in a group setting. Our names can even determine whether we give money to disaster victims: if we share an initial with the name of a

1 1948年，两位哈佛大学教授发表了对当时毕业的3 300名男生的研究成果，研究内容是他们的名字是否对学术表现产生影响。研究发现，名字特别的人相对于名字普通的人更倾向于退学或者表现出心理神经征兆。叫迈克的人表现良好，但是叫贝里恩的人就麻烦了。教授们推测，特殊的名字会对此人的心理产生负面影响。

2 从那以后，探究者们又继续研究了名字的影响。在1948年研究成果发表之后的几十年里，这些成果被广泛使用。一些最近的研究表明，名字能够对人们选择职业、选择家庭住址、择偶对象、取得的成绩、股票投资、是否被学校录取或公司录用以及在团队中的工作质量这些方面产生影响。我们的名字甚至可以决定我们是否会把钱财捐给灾民：研究显示，如果我们的名字首字母和飓风名字的首

hurricane, according to one study, we are far more likely to donate to relief funds after it hits.

3   Much of the apparent influence of names on behavior has been attributed to what's known as the implicit-egotism effect: we are generally drawn to the things and people that most resemble us. Because we value and identify with our own names, and initials, the logic goes, we prefer things that have something in common with them. For instance, if I'm choosing between two brands of cars, all things being equal, I'd prefer a Mazda or a Kia.

4   That view, however, may not withstand closer scrutiny. The psychologist Uri Simonsohn, from the University of Pennsylvania, has questioned many of the studies that purport to demonstrate the implicit-egotism effect, arguing that the findings are statistical flukes that arise from poor methodology. "It's like a magician," Simonsohn told me. "He shows you a trick, and you say, 'I know it's not real, but how did he pull it off?' It's all in the methodology." A problem that he cites in some of these studies is an ignorance of base rates—the overall frequency with which something, like a name, occurs in the population at large. It may be appealing to think that someone named Dan would prefer to be a doctor, but we have to ask whether there are so many doctor Dans simply because Dan is a common name, well-represented in many professions. If that's the case, the implicit-egotism effect is no longer

valid.

5 There are also researchers who have been more measured in their assessments of the link between name and life outcome. In 1984, the psychologist Debra Crisp and her colleagues found that though more common names were better liked, they had no impact on a person's educational achievement. In 2012, the psychologists Hui Bai and Kathleen Briggs concluded that "the name initial is at best a very limited unconscious prime, if any." While a person's name may unconsciously influence his or her thinking, its effects on decision-making are limited. Follow-up studies have also questioned the link between names and longevity, career choice and success, geographic and marriage preferences, and academic achievement.

5 也有研究者已对名字和成就之间的关系进行了慎重的探究。1984年，心理学家黛布拉·克里斯普和她的同事们发现，虽然更常用的名字会更受人们的青睐，但名字对于一个人的教育成就并没有影响。2012年，心理学家胡伊·鲍伊和凯瑟琳·布里格斯总结道："名字首字母的作用充其量就是非常有限的无意识优势罢了。"一个人的名字也许在无意间会影响他或她的想法，但名字对决策的影响十分有限。后续的研究也同样对名字与寿命、与职业选择和成就、与地理位置和婚姻的选择以及与学业成就之间的联系提出了质疑。

	[A] names can influence many aspects of our life.
1. A study by Harvard University found	[B] the name initial has very small function.
2. Some recent research suggests	[C] names are vital for longevity.
3. Uri Simonsohn claims	[D] implicit-egotism effect may be groundless.
4. Debra Crisp found	[E] names are not cared by older people.
5. Hui Bai and Kathleen Briggs think	[F] people with strange names are more inclined to quit school.
	[G] common names had no relation to academic achievement.

解题之路

1. **【答案】** F

   【思路】 根据左栏题干关键词A study 和Harvard University可定位到原文首段。出题点在第二句：The men with unusual names, the study found, were more likely to have flunked out or to have exhibited symptoms of psychological neurosis than those with more common names，对比各个选项，选项[F]是对这句话的同义改写，strange替换了原文的unusual，are more inclined to替换了were more likely to，quit school替换了flunked out。

2. **【答案】** A

   【思路】 根据左栏题干关键词Some recent research可定位到原文第二段第二句。出题点就在suggests之后的内容：names can influence choice of profession, where we live, whom we marry, the grades we earn, the stocks we invest in, whether we're accepted to a school or are hired for a particular job, and the quality of our work in a group setting，因此可断定正确答案为选项[A]。

3. **【答案】** D

   【思路】 根据左栏题干关键词Uri Simonsohn可定位到原文第四段第二句。出题点是：has questioned many of the studies that purport to demonstrate the implicit-egotism effect，由此可知选项[D]为正确答案，groundless是对原文questioned的改写。

4. **【答案】** G

   【思路】 根据左栏题干关键词Debra Crisp可定位到原文第五段第二句。出题点在found之后：though more common names were better liked, they had no impact on a person's educational achievement，由此可知选项[G]为正确答案，had no relation to替换了原文的had no impact on。

5. **【答案】** B

   【思路】 根据左栏题干关键词Hui Bai and Kathleen Briggs可定位到原文第五段第三句。出题点在concluded之后：the name initial is at best a very limited unconscious prime, if any。选项[B]是对该句的正确改写，故为答案。

Text 5

Directions: Read the following text and answer the questions by finding information from the left column that corresponds to each of the marked details given in the right column. There are two extra choices in the right column. (10 points)

1 In interviews, famous people often say that the key to becoming both happy and successful is	1 在采访中，名人们常说他们之所以能够同时收获快乐和成功，秘

to "do what you love." But mastering a skill, even one that you deeply love, requires a huge amount of drudgery. Any challenging activity—from computer programming to playing a musical instrument to athletics—requires focused and concentrated practice. A perfect golf swing or flawless butterfly stroke takes untold hours of practice (actually around 10,000 hours, according to Malcolm Gladwell) and countless repetitions to perfect.

2 Anyone who wants to master a skill must run through the cycle of practice, critical feedback, modification, and incremental improvement again, again, and again. Some people seem able to concentrate on practicing an activity like this for years and take pleasure in their gradual improvement. Yet others find this kind of focused, time-intensive work to be frustrating or boring. Why?

3 The difference may turn on the ability to enter into a state of "flow," the feeling of being completely involved in what you are doing. Whether you call it being "in the zone," "in a groove," or something else, a flow state is a special experience. Since Mihaly Csikszentmihalyi developed the concept of flow in the 1970's, it has been a mainstay of positive-psychology research. Flow states can happen in the course of any activity, and they are

诀就在于"做自己爱做的事"。但是要掌握一门技能，即使你再深爱它，也需要做大量苦工。任何具有挑战性的活动——不管是电脑编程，还是弹奏乐器，还是体育竞技——都需要专心致志、心无旁骛地练习。无论是一个完美的高尔夫挥杆动作，或是一个无可挑剔的蝶泳泳姿，都需要花费数不清的时间去练习（马尔科姆·格拉德威尔说实际上大约需要10 000小时），进行无数次反复练习才能达到完美无缺的境界。

2 对于任何人而言，若想掌握一门技能，都必须一遍一遍又一遍地经历"练习——批评性反馈——修改——渐进式改进"这一循环过程。有些人似乎能够这样几十年如一日专注于一项活动，并且在逐步提高的过程中获得乐趣。然而其他人却发现这种需要专心而且耗费大量时间的工作让人感到沮丧和无聊。为什么呢？

3 差异可能反映在人们进入"心流"（flow）这种状态的能力上，这是在你完全投入到所做之事时产生的感觉。不管你把它称为"专心致志""得心应手"，还是别的什么，心流状态都是一种特殊的体验。自从20世纪70年代米哈伊·奇克森特米哈伊提出"心流"这一概念以来，它已成为积极心理学研究的主流思想。心

most common when a task has well-defined goals and is at an appropriate skill level, and where the individual is able to adjust their performance to clear and immediate feedback.

4 Flow states turn the drudgery of practice into an autotelic activity—that is, one that can be enjoyed for its own sake, rather than as a means to an end or for attaining some external reward. That raises the question of how we can turn this to our advantage: How can we get into a flow state for an activity that we want to master, so that we enjoy both the process of improving skills and the rewards that some with being a master?

5 Csikszentmihalyi suggested that those who most readily entered into flow states had an "autotelic personality"—a disposition to seek out challenges and get into a state of flow. While those without such a personality see difficulties, autotelic individuals see opportunities to build skills. Autotelic individuals are receptive and open to new challenges. They are also persistent and have low levels of self-centeredness. Such people, with their capacity for "disinterested interest" (an ability to focus on tasks rather than rewards) have a great advantage over others in developing their innate abilities.

6 Fortunately for those of us who aren't necessarily blessed with an autotelic personality, there is evidence that flow states can be facilitated by environmental factors. In particular, the learning

流状态可以发生在任何活动中；当一项任务目标明确并且技能水平要求得当时，当一个人能够根据清晰及时的反馈调整自己的表现时，这种状态最容易出现。

4 心流状态把练习这个苦力活变成了本身有目的的活动——也就是说，人们可以单纯地享受这一活动，而不是把它作为达到某一目的、获得某些外在回报的方式。接下来的问题是我们如何把它变成优势：怎样才能在自己想要掌握的活动中进入心流状态，以让我们既能享受提升技能的过程，同时又能享受成为大师的回报呢？

5 奇克森特米哈伊认为，那些随时都有可能进入心流状态的人都有"自带目的性人格"——这种性情的人会主动迎接挑战，然后进入心流状态。非此人格的人看到的是困难，而此人格的人看到的却是增强技能的机会。自带目的性人格的人乐于接受新的挑战。他们也会做到持之以恒，并且不太会以自我为中心。这样的人有能力去追求"不为功利的兴趣"（关注任务本身而非回报），因此在挖掘自身天赋方面优于他人。

6 幸运的是，对于我们这些并非天生自带目的性人格的人而言，有证据证实心流状态可以由一些环境因素促成。尤其值得注意的是，蒙特梭

framework prescribed by Montessori schools seems to encourage flow states. A comparison of Montessori middle schools with traditional middle schools (co-written by Csikszentmihalyi) found that the Montessori students showed greater affect, higher intrinsic motivation, and more frequent flow experiences than their counterparts in traditional schools. In Montessori schools, learning comes through discovery rather than direct instruction, students are encouraged to develop individual interests, and a great deal of unstructured time is built into the day so that they can pursue these interests. Competition is discouraged and grading is de-emphasized, taking the focus off of external rewards. Students are grouped together according to shared interests, rather than segregated by ability.

利学校规定的学习架构似乎有利于心流状态的形成。一项针对蒙特梭利中学和传统中学的比较研究（奇克森特米哈伊参与写作）发现，相比于传统中学的学生，蒙特梭利中学的同年级学生展现出的情感更多、内在动力更强、心流经历更加频繁。在蒙特梭利学校，学生习得是通过自己去发现，而非直接教学，学校鼓励学生发展个人兴趣，学校还会留出大量自由时间给学生，这样他们就可以追求自己的兴趣。这里不鼓励竞争，不强调分数，也不关注外在回报。有着相同兴趣的学生被分到一组，而不是按照能力水平把他们分开。

	[A] well ready for new challenges.
1. Malcolm Gladwell argues	[B] total involvement in what one is doing.
2. A state of "flow" means	[C] people focus on "disinterested interest."
3. Csikszentmihalyi proposes	[D] "autotelic personality" is common in young people.
4. Autotelic individuals are	[E] students' initiative rather than instruction.
5. Montessori schools emphasize	[F] people with autotelic personality can be easier to enter into a state of flow.
	[G] practice makes perfect.

→ 解题之路 ←

1. 【答案】G

   【思路】根据左栏题干关键词Malcolm Gladwell可定位到原文首段末句：A perfect golf swing or flawless butterfly stroke takes untold hours of practice (actually around 10,000 hours, according to Malcolm Gladwell) and countless repetitions to perfect。由10,000 hours和

countless repetitions可知选项[G]是正确答案。

2. 【答案】B

   【思路】根据左栏题干关键词A state of "flow"可定位到原文第三段首句：...a state of "flow," the feeling of being completely involved in what you are doing。选项[B]是对该句的同义改写，因此为正确答案。

3. 【答案】F

   【思路】左栏题干关键词Csikszentmihalyi在原文共出现三次，分别是第三段第三句：Since Mihaly Csikszentmihalyi developed the concept of flow in the 1970's, it has been a mainstay of positive-psychology research；第五段首句：Csikszentmihalyi suggested that those who most readily entered into flow states had an "autotelic personality"；第六段第三句：A comparison of Montessori middle schools with traditional middle schools (co-written by Csikszentmihalyi) found that the Montessori students showed greater affect...。对比这三处信息点，可看出选项[F]是对第二处信息点（第五段首句）的同义改写，故为正确答案。

4. 【答案】A

   【思路】根据左栏题干关键词Autotelic可先定位到原文第五段首句：...an "autotelic personality"—a disposition to seek out challenges and get into a state of flow，再往下找，即可发现在该段第三句出现了Autotelic individuals：Autotelic individuals are receptive and open to new challenges。由此可知选项[A]为正确答案，well ready for替换了原文的receptive and open to。

5. 【答案】E

   【思路】根据左栏题干关键词Montessori schools可定位到原文末段第二句及以下内容：In particular, the learning framework prescribed by Montessori schools seems to encourage flow states...。出题点在第三句、第四句：A comparison of Montessori middle schools... found that the Montessori students showed greater affect, higher intrinsic motivation, and more frequent flow experiences than their counterparts in traditional schools. In Montessori schools, learning comes through discovery rather than direct instruction, students are encouraged to develop individual interests。选项[E]是对这两句内容的提炼和浓缩，故为正确答案。

第六章 英译汉

第一节 大纲解读与应试策略

（一）大纲要求

考查考生理解所给英语语言材料并将其译成汉语的能力。要求译文准确、完整、通顺。要求考生阅读、理解约150词的一个或几个英语段落，并将其全部译成汉语。共15分。

（二）命题趋势

2008年考研英语（二）大纲做了修订，翻译题型由翻译五个句子改为翻译一段或几段文字。测试点仍在于考生对常规句子结构和一些特殊结构的分析能力，因此仍然强调基本功。考生要学会在分析句子结构时化繁为简，学会抓住句子的核心主干，即主谓宾；在理解句子结构之后，落笔进行语言表达时，只要基本意思正确严谨即可。

（三）评分标准说明

翻译流畅，意思准确，特别是关键词要翻译出来；有一定文采，语句不死板，得分就会高。

主要是抓住主旨，语义通顺，前后连贯。

英译汉评分标准

档次分类	对应分值	评分要求
第五档	14~15分	很好地完成了试题规定的任务。理解准确无误；表达通顺清楚；没有错译、漏译。

第四档	11~13 分	较好地完成了试题规定的任务。理解准确无误；表达通顺清楚；没有错译、漏译。
第三档	8~10 分	基本完成了试题规定的任务。理解基本准确；表达比较通顺；没有重大错译、漏译。
第二档	4~7 分	未能按要求完成试题规定的任务。理解不够准确；表达欠通顺；有明显错译、漏译。
第一档	0~3 分	未完成试题规定的任务。不能理解原文；表达不通顺；文字支离破碎。

五个档次的译文对比原文

Many Americans regard the jury system as a concrete expression of crucial democratic values, including the principles that all citizens who meet minimal qualifications of age and literacy are equally competent to serve on juries; that jurors should be selected randomly from a representative cross section of the community; that no citizen should be denied the right to serve on a jury on account of race, religion, sex, or national origin; that defendants are entitled to trial by their peers; and that verdicts should represent the conscience of the community and not just the letter of the law. The jury is also said to be the best surviving example of direct rather than representative democracy. In a direct democracy, citizens take turns governing themselves, rather than electing representatives to govern for them.

第五档（14～15 分）：很好地完成了试题规定的任务。理解准确无误；表达通顺清楚；没有错译、漏译。

译文

许多美国人将陪审团制度视为是重要民主价值观的直接体现。更具体地说，陪审团制度应该包括下列原则：一、所有达到年龄和认知最低标准的公民均可担当陪审员；二、陪审员应从整个社会中随机挑选且能代表社会各阶层；三、所有公民，无论其种族、信仰、性别和国籍如何，都有权在陪审团中担当陪审员；四、被告有权要求接受同龄人的审判；五，判决不仅应该依据法律条款，也应代表社会良知。陪审团也被认为是现存的直接式而非代表式民主的典范。即，在一种直接式民主中，公民轮流执政而非选举代表替其执政。

第四档（11～13 分）：较好地完成了试题规定的任务。理解准确无误；表达通顺清楚；没有错译、漏译。

译文

很多美国人把陪审团制度（陪审制）看作是其民主价值观的重要体现，具体包括以下原则：任何达到最低年龄和文化程度限制的公民都有资格参与审判；陪审员应该在社区代表中随机挑选；任何人不得由于种族、宗教、性别或民族原因被拒绝参与陪审团；被告人有权接受同龄人的审判；判决应该代表良知而不仅仅代表法律条文。在一个直接民主制度中，公民轮流管理自己，而不是选出一名代表来管理他们。

第三档（8~10分）：基本完成了试题规定的任务。理解基本准确；表达比较通顺；没有重大错译、漏译。

译文

许多美国人认为陪审团制度是一个具体的民主价值观，包括所有公民满足最低资格的年龄和文化也可在陪审团中。陪审员应该选择随机从社区挑选。不应该以种族、宗教、性别或国籍而拒绝公民权利担任陪审员。同龄人可以审判被告。判决应该不仅仅代表社会的良心，也要代表法律条文。陪审团也被认为是最好的存在的例子比起代表式民主。在一个直接民主中，公民轮流管理自己，而不是为他们选出一名代表来管理他们。

第二档（4~7分）：未能按要求完成试题规定的任务。理解不够准确；表达欠通顺；有明显错译、漏译。

译文

许多美国人认为陪审团制度是一个具体的表达至关重要的民主价值观，包括所有公民的原则满足最低资格的年龄和文化也同样主管陪审团服务。陪审员应该选择随机从社区的代表截面。不应该剥夺公民权利在担任陪审员的种族、宗教、性别或国籍。同龄人，被告有权审判。判决应该不仅仅代表社会的良心和法律条文。陪审团也被认为是最好的生存直接而不是代议制民主的例子。在一个直接民主，公民轮流管理自己，而不是为他们选出一名代表来管理。

第一档（0~4分）：未完成试题规定的任务。不能理解原文；表达不通顺；译文支离破碎。

译文

许多美国人认为jury是一个具体的表达至关重要的democratic价值，包括所有公民的原则满足最低资格的年龄和文化也competent jury服务。陪审员应该选择随机代表穿越社区。不应该拒绝公民权利在担任陪审员的种族、宗教、性别或国籍。被告trialed entitled peers。verdicts应该不仅仅代表社会的conscience和法律书信。陪审团也被说是最好的生存直接而不是代表民主的例子。在一个直接民主，公民换着政府自己，而不是为他们选出代表政府为他们。

（四）考查重点与解题策略

1. 词义选择与语序调整

考研翻译重点考查学生在不同语境中对词义的理解，以及语义组合和语言表达的准确性和通顺性。因此在翻译时，考生要注意不同语境中词义的选择，译文表达要符合汉语的表达习惯和中国人的逻辑思维习惯。在做题时，可运用词义引申，词类转换的方法结合上下文语境确定词义，并且注意英语中的定语结构、状语结构、被动语态、代词、动宾结构在汉语中的表达顺序和表达习惯的区别。

2. 专有名词、词组和多义词的翻译

专有名词、词组和多义词是翻译中对单词考查的重要内容。翻译时，高频专有名词，要按照约定俗成、广为接受的方法翻译；非著名的专有名词，采取音译或音译加括号英文的方法翻译；不熟悉的专有名词，直接照抄英文即可。词组的翻译需要考生注意平时的积累，要做到理解和熟记词组。多义词词义的选择可根据语境联系上下文猜测词义，根据词根词缀选择猜测生词的词义，或者根据汉语的习惯搭配来翻译。

3. 特殊句型和特殊结构的翻译

被动语态、定语从句、同位语从句、it 作形式主语句、倒装结构、比较结构为翻译考查的重点内容。考生应在掌握以上考点的语法知识的前提下，运用各考点相对应的翻译方法，通过真题翻译的练习达到准确、通顺的翻译。

4. 语篇衔接

英语（二）的翻译部分考查考生对一个包含若干段落的篇章进行翻译的能力，所以译文语篇的完整性和语义、段落之间的衔接也是考查的重点内容之一。翻译时，不仅要对每个句子进行理解和表达，而且还要注意到整个语篇的结构和完整性。语篇衔接要侧重于句间不同成分之间的语义联系，其中包括照应、替代、省略、连接和词汇衔接。

汉语错别字不单独扣分，按整篇累计的方式扣分。在不影响意思的前提下，满三个错别字扣 0.5 分。

（五）复习备考指南

翻译是一个考查基本功的题型，考查词汇、语法等基本要素。应当将翻译部分的复习与练

习融会贯通，将要点与技巧谙熟于心。

1. 词汇

要加强考研英语高频词汇的复习与巩固。考研翻译的单词基本都出现在高频词里，而高频词的问题在考研英语（二）里更为明显。一旦不认识高频词，而该高频词又是主题词的话，考生就会在翻译时出现连带性错误。考前一个月应当反复练习高频词，不能出现任何纰漏。

2. 句法

英语（二）考试大纲明确列出了考查的语法知识点：（1）名词、代词的数和格的构成及其用法；（2）动词时态、语态的构成及其用法；（3）形容词与副词的比较级和最高级的构成和使用；（4）常用连词的词义及其用法；（5）非谓语动词的构成及其用法；（6）虚拟语气的构成及其用法；（7）各类从句（定语从句、主语从句、表语从句等）及其强调句型的结构及其用法；（8）倒装句、插入语的结构及其用法。考生要熟练掌握以上知识点，做到举一反三、运用自如。

3. 翻译的基本方法

考生在掌握以上语法知识点、准确理解句子之后，应当掌握一些基础考点的翻译方法，否则很难用汉语进行通顺流畅的表达。因此，考生应当熟悉和掌握英汉语言的主要差异，学习基本的翻译方法，比如定语从句等各种从句的翻译方法、非谓语动词的翻译方法，以及插入语的翻译、被动语态的表达、语序的调整等等。这样才能使表达符合汉语语言习惯，才能使译文流畅，达到大纲"准确、完整、通顺"的要求。具体方法和技巧会在下文详细介绍。

第二节　英译汉技巧

翻译本身是一个复杂的心理活动过程，任何从事翻译的人都会感到艰巨和耗时。"一名之立，踌躇旬月"，就是说要找到一个贴切的词来翻译，常常需要花费数月功夫。由于时间限制和紧张心理，考研英语翻译由不得考生字斟句酌。在翻译的整个基本过程"理解——表述——检查"这三个环节中，大多数初学翻译的人感觉最明显的问题是：英语理解不容易，汉语表达不轻松。

要真正掌握英译汉的技巧并非易事，会遇到各种各样的困难。一是英文理解难。这是学习、使用英文的人的共同感觉，由于中西方历史、文化、风俗习惯的不同，一句英文在英美人士看来顺理成章，而在中国人看来却是颠三倒四、凌乱不堪。二是中文表达难。为了找到一个合适的对等词汇，考生往往绞尽脑汁却一无所获。另外，英译汉对掌握各种文化知识的要求很高，因为我们所翻译的文章内容可能涉及极为广博的知识领域，而这些知识领域多半是我们不大熟悉的异域文化，如果不具备相应的文化知识储备，难免会出现一些翻译上的差错或笑话。正是因为英译汉时会遇到诸多困难，所以必须通过翻译实践，对英汉两种不同语言的特点加以对比、概括和总结，找出一般的表达规律，避免不该出现的翻译错误。这些表达的规律就是所谓的翻译技巧。

（一）词汇处理

1. 词义选择

大多数英语词汇具有多义性，翻译时必须选择正确的词义。词义选择的方法是：根据上下文和词组搭配选择、根据词类选择。

2. 词义转换

在理解英文词汇原始意义的基础上，翻译时可根据汉语的习惯按引申含义译出；或用反义词语译出，即所谓的正说反译、反说正译。

3. 词类转换

词本无义，义由境生。翻译时还需要注意词性的转化。由于英汉两种语言在语法和习惯上存在差异，在描述同一事物时，两种语言会使用不同的词性。因此在翻译过程中，有时需要变换原词的词性，来有效地传达原文的信息。英语中有很多由动词转化而成的名词、动名词以及非谓语动词等，汉译时可将它们转换成动词。以下是几种常用的词类转化法：

（1）英语名词→汉语动词

英语中具有动作意义或由动词转化过来的名词，汉译时往往转化为动词。

【例1】His arrival at this conclusion was the result of much thought.

【译文】他得出这结论是深思熟虑的结果。

【例2】The government called for the establishment of more key universities.

【译文】政府号召建立更多的重点大学。

【例3】The prolongation of life and the search for perfect health (beauty, youth, happiness) are inherently self-defeating.

【译文】延长寿命、追求完美的健康（美貌、青春、幸福）本质上都是自拆台脚。

（2）英语动词→汉语名词

有些英语动词在汉语里虽有相对应的动词词义，但在某种特定的语言环境下不能使用该动词词义，或者需要选择另一种更好的词义，因而将其转化为汉语的名词。

【例1】Judgment should be based on facts, not on hearsay.

【译文】判断应该以事实为依据，而不应该道听途说。

【例2】The man I saw at the party looked and talked like an American.

【译文】我在晚会上看到的那个人，外表和谈吐都像美国人。

【例3】The electronic computer is chiefly characterized by its accurate and rapid computation.

【译文】电子计算机的主要特点是计算准确迅速。

（3）英语名词→汉语形容词

英语原文中有形容词加后缀构成的名词，翻译时可转化为汉语的形容词。

【例1】Scientists are no strangers to politics.

【译文】科学家对政治并不陌生。

【例2】We found difficulty in solving the complicated problem.

【译文】我们发现解决这个复杂的问题是很困难的。

（4）英语介词或副词→汉语动词

【例1】He came to my home for help.

【译文】他来到我家请求帮助。

【例2】I love having Friday off.

【译文】我喜欢周五休息。

【例3】I am for the former.

【译文】我支持前者。

【例4】I am against the latter.

【译文】我反对后者。

（5）英语副词→汉语名词

【例1】It was officially announced that Paris is invited to the meeting.

【译文】官方宣布，巴黎应邀出席会议。

（6）英语副词→汉语短语或句子

【例1】Globally, this phenomenon has aroused considerable concern.

【译文】从全世界来看，这个现象已经引起了极大关注。

【例2】Wisely, you made no attempt to have this question discussed by the General Assembly.

【译文】明智的地方在于，你没有试图让大会讨论这个问题。

4. 增词

指原文已有某种含义但未用词汇直接表达，翻译时需将这些含义补充进去，这样译文才更通顺易读，如：英语中数词与名词之间没有量词，而译成汉语时可酌情增加。由于英汉两种语言的差异，在英文看上去比较正常的句子，译成汉语时，如果不增加一些词可能无法把英文的原意表达出来，这样就需要适当地运用增词法。例：

【例1】After the footfall match, he has got an important meeting.

【译文】看完足球赛之后，他有一个重要的会议要去参加。

【例2】The latest type of TVR system is light, inexpensive and easy to manipulate.

【译文】这种最新型的电视录像装置很轻便，价格低，而且操作简便。

【例3】This aircraft is small, cheap, and pilotless.

【译文】这种飞机体积小，价格低，不需要人驾驶。

5. 省词

由于英汉在用词和语法结构上的差异，英文中的某些词如果直译出来会使译文变得累赘，不符合汉语的表达习惯。在这种情况下，就要将一些冠词、代词、介词或连词等省去不译，但是又不影响原文的意思。例：

【例1】We live and learn.

【译文】（我们）活到老，学到老。

【例2】If winter comes, can spring be far behind?

【译文】（如果）冬天来临，春天还会远吗？

【例3】It must be snowing, for it is so bright outside.

【译文】（因为）外面这么亮，一定在下雪。

【例4】Smoking is prohibited in public places.

【译文】（在）公共场所不能吸烟。

6. 并列与重复

避免重复是英语的一大特色。为了达到简明扼要、富于变化的目的，在表达重复含义的并列结构中通常采用共享、替代、转换等形式来避免重复。而喜欢重复则是汉语的特点。英语中经常省略前面出现过的名词，或使用代词代替，在翻译时则尽量把这些代词恢复成汉语的名词。例：

【例1】We have to analyze and solve problems.

【译文】我们要分析问题，解决问题。

【例2】He opened his eyes and they were filled with tears.

【译文】他睁开双眼，眼里噙满了泪水。

【例3】Big powers have their strategies while small countries have their own lines.

【译文】大国有大国的策略，小国有小国的路线。

（二）句子结构

长句、难句、复杂句，句句难懂，这是每一个考生都非常清楚的。用汉语清楚地表达出来，则难上加难。看懂句子，并且最快地把译文写出来以提高分数，就成了迫在眉睫的任务。

首先，在翻译之前必须要把英语原文看懂。理解原文是整个翻译过程的第一步，这也是最关键、最容易出问题的一步。许多考生在复习的时候发现自己的译文含糊不清、语言表述不准确，原因正是没有透彻理解原文。大部分的翻译错误都源于考生理解错误。没有做到正确地理解，考生传达的内容就不是原文的意思，由此可能扭曲原文，造成严重的扣分现象，甚至不得分。

由于英语具有"形合"的特点，也就是说，英语的句子无论多么复杂，都是通过一些语法手段和逻辑手段连接起来的"葡萄藤"结构。所以在理解英语句子的时候，理解并拆分句子的语法结构和逻辑结构就自然而然成了解题的突破口。考研英语翻译中的所有句子基本上都是结构复杂的长难句，因此理清句子结构层次至关重要。在翻译句子之前，先通读全句，注意一边读一边拆分句子的语法结构。

由以上分析可以看出，考研翻译中的长难句可以通过简单的"拆分与组合"得出汉语译文。但是也不要忽略汉语译文的检查工作。最有效的译文检查方式是阅读汉语译文，通过阅读就可以知道自己的译文表达是不是准确、通顺。如果不通顺，我们可以比对英语原文，通过仔细分析句子结构，选择合适的单词意思来翻译。简单来说，考研翻译中长难句的翻译法则是，先把这个长难句分为几个部分，每个部分都短小精悍，也就比较容易理解和翻译。这时候，我们再把一个个小的翻译单位，组合成准确而又通顺的汉语即可。

英语语法结构和逻辑结构比较明显，在理解时，可以把主句和从句拆分出来，或者把主干部分和修饰部分拆分出来。说得更具体一点，可以根据下面一些"信号词"来对英语句子进行拆分，进而更加有效地理解英语原文。

1. 基本原则

把主句和从句拆分出来，把主干部分和修饰部分拆分出来。

（1）连词：如 and，or，but，yet，for 等并列连词连接着并列句；还有连接状语从句的连接词，如：when，as，since，until，before，after，where，because，since，though，although，so that 等；它们是英语句子的拆分点。

（2）关系词：如连接名词性从句的 who，whom，whose，what，which，whatever，whichever 等关系代词和 when，where，how，why 等关系副词；还有连接定语从句的关系代词，如 who，which，that，whom，whose 等；它们也是英语句子的拆分点。

（3）介词：如 on，in，with，at，of，to 等介词常常引导介词短语作修饰语，所以它们也是英语句子的拆分点。

（4）不定式符号 to：不定式常常组成不定式短语做定语或者状语修饰语，所以也可以是拆分点。

（5）分词：过去分词和现在分词可以构成分词短语作修饰语，所以可以是拆分点。

（6）标点符号：标点符号常常断开句子的主干和修饰部分，也是一个明显的拆分点。

以上列举的这些"信号词"只是在拆分英语原文时可能断开句子的地方，但并不是绝对的。它们有助于我们看清句子结构，进而更好地理解英语原文。但是，在拆分长难句的过程中，最好不要把单独的一个英语单词拆分出来，因为如果单词都一个一个地被拆分出来的话，整个英语句子就可能会无限制地被拆分下去了。

2. 基于原文，多种组合

句子拆分后必然有一个如何排列各分句或句子的问题。为了不歪曲或者削弱原句各个成分之间的逻辑联系，同时又照顾到汉语的思维与表达习惯，拆分后的分句或者句子常常必须打乱原来英语句子的语序，然后重新组合。究竟该如何改变原文顺序，完全要根据汉语习惯来安排，不过也是有一定的规律可以遵循的。比如：

（1）顺译法

顾名思义，顺译法就是按原文句子结构的排列顺序进行翻译的方法，这种译法适合于原文叙述层次与汉语表达相近的长句翻译，比如只含名词性从句的复合句、前置的状语从句或从句在后的长复合句等。如果名词（短语）的定语（从句）很长，则可以放在名词（短语）之后，按原句的顺序翻译，译成汉语的平行并列结构。有时英语的定语从句或同位语从句比较复杂，翻译时如果放在所修饰的名词前，汉语句子会很不通顺，这时就可以把定语从句或同位语从句放在所修饰的名词后面来翻译，独立成为一句话。例：

【例1】As an obedient son, I had to accept my parents' decision that I was to be a doctor, though the prospect interested me not at all.

【译文】作为一个孝顺的儿子，我不得不接受父母的意见去当大夫，虽然我对这样的前途毫无兴趣。

【例2】They see a day in the not-too-distant future when all autos will be abandoned and allowed to rust.

【译文】他们预见到不久的将来，所有汽车将被遗弃，任其生锈。

【例3】When the auto enters the highway system, a retractable arm will drop from the auto and make contact with a rail, which is similar to those powering subway trains electrically.

【译文】当汽车进入公路系统，一只伸缩臂从车上落下与铁轨接触，这种铁轨同给地下列车供电的铁轨相似。

【例4】It is only now that we have reached the level of technology where we can make a determined attempt to search all nearby stars for any sign of life.

【译文】只是到今天我们才达到了如此高的技术水平，可以坚持不懈地在附近所有的恒星上搜寻生命迹象。

【例5】The majority of students believe that part-time jobs will provide them with more opportunities to develop their interpersonal skills, which may put them in a favorable position in the future job markets.

【译文】大多数学生认为兼职工作会有更多机会培养人际交往的能力，这将使他们在未来的就业市场处于有利位置。

【例6】Perhaps the most commonly voiced objection to volunteer participation during the undergraduate years is that it consumes time and energy that the students might otherwise devote to "academic" pursuits.

【译文】对大学期间从事义工最强烈的反对观点或许是这会浪费时间和精力，而学生本可以将这些时间和精力用于学习。

【例7】Others have attributed increased cheating to the fact that today's youth are far more pragmatic than their more idealistic predecessors.

【译文】其他人将愈演愈烈的作弊现象归结于如今的年轻一代比他们理想化的前辈更加务实（注重实际）。

【例8】There is little evidence that traditional efforts to boost financial know-how help students make better decisions outside the classroom.

【译文】很少有证据显示，注重金融专业知识的传统教学能够帮助学生走出课堂之后做出更加明智的选择。

【例9】Plato expressed the idea that humor is simply a delighted feeling of superiority over others.

【译文】柏拉图的观点是：幽默只不过是自认为比他人优越的一种愉悦感罢了。

【例10】These leaders are living proof that prevention works and that we can manage the health problems that come naturally with age.

【译文】这些领导者都是活生生的例子，他们证明了预防是有效的，而且我们能够应对因自然衰老而产生的健康问题。

【例11】A century ago, Freud formulated his revolutionary theory that dreams were the disguised shadows of our unconscious desires and fears.

【译文】一个世纪以前，弗洛伊德创建了其革命性的理论：梦是人类无意识的欲望和恐惧的深层的反映。

【例12】There was a time not long ago when new science Ph.D.s in the United States were expected to pursue a career path in academia.

【译文】就在不久前，美国刚刚毕业的理科博士们还被指望着能够走上学术研究的道路。

【例13】Countries with the highest scores tend to be clustered in the West, where gender discrimination is against the law, and equal rights are constitutionally enshrined.

【译文】得分最高的国家集中在西方，（因为）在那里性别歧视被视为非法，而且宪法规定男女平等神圣不可侵犯。

【例 14】Many in the medical community acknowledge that the assisted-suicide debate has been fueled in part by the despair of patients for whom modern medicine has prolonged the physical agony of dying.

【译文】许多医学界人士都承认，关于安乐死争论升温的部分原因是病人的绝望情绪，现代医学延长了其死亡时遭受的身体痛苦。

【例 15】In early 1976, Mau Pialug, a freshman, led an expedition in which he sailed a traditional Polynesian boat across 2,500 miles of ocean from Hawaii to Tahiti.

【译文】1976年年初，一位名叫Mau Pialug的新手率领一支远征队，驾驶一只传统的波利尼西亚小船从夏威夷出发，航行了2 500英里，最终到达塔希提岛。

【例 16】He had at last been allowed to send a fax in which he informed the editor that he had been arrested while counting the 1,084 steps leading to the 15-foot wall which surrounded the president's palace.

【译文】最终他被允许发一封传真。在传真里他告知编辑，当他数着通往总统官邸15英尺高墙的1 084个台阶时，被当场逮捕。

【例 17】While there is evidence that instructors must work harder to run a distance learning course for a variety of reasons, they won't be paid more, and might well be paid less.

【译文】虽然有证据显示，因为各种原因老师在开设远程教育课程时要更加尽心，但他们由此获得的报酬不是更多，而是可能更少。

【例 18】The same abundance of theory that allowed Walt Whitman to fill out his poetry with philosophical road signs of American optimism allows a president to make pious references to God as an American tradition—references which, despite their somewhat mechanical quality, are not only sincere but which, to most Americans, express the reality of America.（2003年阅读真题）

【译文】丰富的理论使沃尔特·惠特曼用美国乐观主义的哲学路标填写诗词，也同样使美国总统把对上帝虔诚的提及作为一种美国传统。尽管这种提及有些机械呆板，但是这不仅是真诚的，而且对于大多数美国人而言，还代表了美国的现实。

【例 19】But there's never been definitive proof that treatment with very bright lights makes a difference.

【译文】从未有确凿证据表明亮光治疗法会有差别。

【例20】Midcareer executives, forced by a takeover or a restructuring to quit the corporation and find another way to support themselves, may savor the idea of being their own boss but may forget that entrepreneurs must also, at least for a while, be bookkeepers and receptionists, too.（2003年真题）

【译文】中层管理者由于公司并购或重组被迫离职只能自谋生路，（他们）或许想自己做老板，但也许忘记了企业家也必须做至少一段时间的记账员和接待员。

【例21】As a boy, he spent time in the larger cities of Italy, France and Switzerland, where bottled water is consumed daily.

【译文】在他还是个小男孩的时候，他曾在意大利、法国和瑞士的大城市生活过，那里的人们日常都喝瓶装水。

【例22】Imagine a person who is about the right weight, but does not eat very nutritious foods, who feels OK but exercises only occasionally, who goes to work every day, but is not an outstanding worker, who drinks a few beers at home most nights but does not drive while drunk, and who has no chest pains or abnormal blood counts, but sleeps a lot and often feels tired.

【译文】想象这样一个人：体重刚好但不吃营养食物，感觉良好但只是偶尔锻炼，每天上班但工作并不出色，总是晚上在家饮酒但不会酒驾，没有胸痛或血压异常的现象，但很嗜睡并且感觉疲惫。

【例23】I had an experience some years ago which taught me something about the ways in which people make a bad situation worse by blaming themselves.

【译文】几年前我经历了一件事，让我了解了自责可以让情况变得更糟。

【例24】Very often, we do not completely outgrow that infantile notion that our wishes cause things to happen.

【译文】经常的情况是，我们不能彻底摆脱某种年幼时的想法：愿望总会成真。

【例25】Happiness without meaning characterizes a relatively shallow, self-absorbed or even selfish life, in which things go well, needs and desires are easily satisfied, and complicated relationships are avoided.

【译文】虚无的幸福表现为一种相对肤浅、孤芳自赏甚至自私自利的生活状态：一切顺风顺水，需求和愿望轻易得到满足，复杂的人际关系都得以避免。

【例26】Silicon Valley is a magnet to which numerous talented engineers, scientists and entre-preneurs from overseas flock in search of fame, fast money and to participate in a technological revolution whose impact on mankind will surely surpass the epoch-making European Renaissance and Industrial Revolution of the bygone age.

【译文】硅谷就是一块磁石,众多富有才华的工程师、科学家和企业家从海外汇聚于此,他们渴望出人头地、一夜暴富,并且参与一场技术革命,这场革命对人类的影响势必超越昔日具有划时代意义的欧洲文艺复兴和工业革命。

【例 27】To snatch opportunity, you must spot the signals that it is time to conquer the new markets, add products or perhaps franchise your hot ideas.(2003 年真题)

【译文】若要得到机会,你就必须发现一些节点,比如何时占领新市场,何时增加新产品,或者何时兜售你的好想法。

【例 28】One major problem, experts say, is that the Social Security Number (SSN)—originally meant only for retirement benefit and tax purposes—has become the universal way to identify people. (2004 年真题)

【译文】专家说,一个主要问题就是社保号(SSN)已经成为身份识别的普遍方式——该号码最初只用于退休福利和纳税。

【例 29】For instance, a capable corporate manager might see an alarming rise in local housing prices that could affect the availability of skilled workers in the region.(2005 年真题)

【译文】比如,一位能干的公司经理或许会发现当地房价飙升,这可能影响到该地区可用的熟练工人的数量。

【例 30】It was not until the mid-1980s, when amplifying age and sex differences became a dominant children's marketing strategy, that pink fully came into its own, when it began to seem inherently attractive to girls.(2012 年阅读真题)

【译文】直到20世纪80年代中期,夸大年龄和性别差异成为儿童市场主导性的营销策略,粉色才真正登台亮相,大受女孩青睐。

(2)逆译法

逆译法就是颠倒原文句子结构的排列顺序来进行翻译的方法。汉语喜欢先说原因、条件、方式等内容,然后才是结果、结论、观点等内容,即先"因"后"果";英语则没有这么严格,往往将原因、条件、方式等内容放在结果、结论、观点的后面,信息排列顺序与汉语思维相反,即先"主"后"次"。英译汉时应尽量按照汉语的习惯处理,先把原因、条件、让步等细节译出,再把结论性、态度性的内容译出,即把状语(从句)放在所修饰的主句或内容前面。另外,英语中较短的限定性定语从句、表身份特征等的同位语在译成汉语时,往往可以提到先行词(中心词)的前面。

【例1】The moon is completely empty of water because the gravity on the moon is much less than on the earth.

【译文】因为月球的引力比地球小得多，所以月球上根本没有水。

【例2】The football students can be removed from the university if they fail to pass their examination.

【译文】如果考试不及格，参与足球运动的学生就会被开除。

【例3】People in less developed countries often imagine that they can become rich simply by emigrating to America.

【译文】发展中国家的民众经常幻想（认为），只要移民美国就能发家致富。

【例4】Cognitive psychologists assert that our behavior is influenced by our values, by the way in which we interpret our situations and by choice.

【译文】认知心理学家断言（认为），我们的价值观、我们对所处环境的理解方式以及我们的选择影响着我们的行为。

【例5】The reader's hair stands on end when he reads in the final pages of the novel that the heroine, a dear old lady who had always been so kind to everybody, had, in her youth, poisoned every one of her five husbands.

【译文】当读者读到小说最后几页，了解到书中女主人公——那位一向待大家很好的可爱的老妇人却在年轻时一连毒死了五任丈夫的时候，不禁会毛骨悚然。

【例6】Atomic power is associated in the public mind with the destructive force of atom bombs and partly for this reason, though it is claimed that there is no danger to be associated with atomic power stations, they are being sited away from populous centres.

【译文】尽管据称原子能电站不具有危险性，然而在公众心目中，原子能是和原子弹的破坏力密切相连的；部分由于这个原因，原子能电站的选址要远离人口密集的地区。

【例7】While you need to employ both thoughts to get to a finished result, they cannot work in parallel no matter how much we might like to think so.

【译文】虽然你需要使用两种思维来实现既定目标，然而无论我们多么渴望，它们都无法同时运行。

【例8】Even people who have a physical disease or handicap may be "well" in this new sense, if they make an effort to maintain the best possible health they can in the face of their physical limitations.

【译文】如果身患疾病或残疾的人们仍能克服身体局限，最大限度地维持自身健康，他们就给"健康"这个词赋予了新的含义。

【例9】You must learn to create first and then criticize <u>if you want to make writing the tool for thinking that it is.</u>

【译文】<u>如果你想得心应手、驾轻就熟地写作，就首先要学会写作，然后再去批判。</u>

【例10】If you think you'll abandon meat and become a vegetarian, you have the choice of very expensive organically-grown vegetables or a steady diet of pesticides <u>every time you think you're eating fresh salads and vegetables!</u>

【译文】如果你想放弃肉类而变成一位素食主义者，那么你可以两者择一：或是选用价格昂贵、有机培育的蔬菜；或是<u>每次想当然地认为在享用新鲜沙拉和蔬菜，而实际上却在不断地吃进杀虫剂。</u>

【例11】Parents would be greatly surprised and deeply touched, <u>if they realized how much belief their children usually have in their character and infallibility, and how much this faith means to a child.</u>

【译文】<u>如果家长意识到孩子通常是多么相信家长品行端正、完美无缺，意识到这种信念对于孩子而言多么重要，</u>那么家长会大为吃惊、深受触动的。

【例12】Anthropology was by definition impossible <u>as long as these distinctions between ourselves and the primitive, ourselves and the barbarian, ourselves and the pagan, held sway over people's minds.</u>

【译文】<u>只要我们与原始人、我们与野蛮人、我们与异教徒之间的差异依旧在人们的头脑中占主导地位，</u>那么人类学按其定义就无法存在。

【例13】There is a virtual limit on how long we can hope to remain alive, <u>however lucky and robust we are.</u>

【译文】<u>不管我们多么幸运，多么健壮，</u>我们所希望的长寿年龄实际上是有限度的。

【例14】It is always wiser and safer to face up to reality, <u>however painful it may be at the moment.</u>

【译文】<u>尽管会有暂时的痛苦，</u>遇事采取面对现实的态度总是比较明智和稳妥的。

【例15】Most children have such a high ideal of their parents, <u>unless the parents themselves have been unsatisfactory,</u> that it can hardly hope to stand up to a realistic evaluation.

【译文】<u>除非父母自身不能令人满意，</u>大多数孩子对父母期待过高，以致这种期待很难经受住现实的考验。

【例 16】The futurists recognized that the future world is continuous with the present world, so we can learn a great deal about what may happen in the future <u>by looking systematically at what is happening now.</u>（2005 年真题）

【译文】未来主义学家认识到未来世界与当前世界是连为一体的，因此<u>通过系统地观察当前发生的一切</u>，就可以了解到许多未来可能发生的事情。

【例 17】Once again, the space agency has been forced to put off the flight <u>until it can find a solution to the problem,</u> and no one seems willing to guess how that may take.（2006 年真题）

【译文】<u>在解决问题之前</u>，航天局再次被迫推迟飞行，没人愿意猜测这次推迟会持续多久。

【例 18】Space officials were justifiably happy that so much had gone well, <u>despite daily worries over possible risks.</u>（2006 年真题）

【译文】<u>尽管每天都在担心可能出现的险情</u>，但一切进展顺利，航天局的官员们还是有理由感到高兴。

【例 19】The term "business model" first came into widespread use <u>with the invention the personal computer and the spreadsheet.</u>（2008 年真题）

【译文】<u>随着个人电脑和电子制表软件的问世</u>，"商业模式"这个术语第一次被广泛使用。

（3）分译法

有些句子由于有"联系词"的关系，虽在形式上是一个句子，但句子中许多成分的意义是独立的，将它们断开分成短句是完全可以的。断开的位置一般可选在这些联系词处。联系词通常为关系代词、关系副词、独立副词、伴随动词等。从被分译成分的结构而言，分译大致可以分为单词的分译、短语的分译和从句的分译三种。

单词的分译即拆词，将难译的词从句子主干中拆离出来，另做处理。这种方法常常引起句式上的调整，英译汉中要拆译的词常常是形容词和副词。

【例 1】He <u>unnecessarily</u> spent a lot of time introducing his book, which the student are familiar with.

【译文】他花了很长时间介绍这本书，<u>其实没有必要</u>，因为学生们对它已经很熟悉了。

【例 2】They, <u>not surprisingly</u>, did not respond at all.

【译文】他们根本没有答复，<u>这完全是意料之中的事</u>。

短语的分译是指将英语的某个短语单独拿出来译成一个独立成分、从句或并列句。

【例1】We tried in vain to persuade him to give up his wrong belief.

【译文】我们尽力劝说他放弃错误的信念,但没有成功。

【例2】The professor entered the laboratory followed by his graduate students.

【译文】教授走进试验室,后面跟着他的研究生。

从句的分译则是根据译文需要打散句子,重新组织。英语的长句主要由主从复合句构成,结构严谨,只要明确主从关系,就能正确分译。

【例1】He told me such experience as I had never heard of before.

【译文】他给我讲述了他的经历,那些经历是我以前从未听说过的。

【例2】He did not remember his father who died when he was three years old.

【译文】他三岁丧父,所以记不起父亲了。

【例3】Strange enough they were the same age to the day.

【译文】说来也巧,他俩年纪一样大,而且还是同日的。

（4）合译法

合译法是将原文的两个或多个分开叙述的意思或层次合并重组的译法,如同一主语的简单句、并列句可合成一个句子的并列成分,较短的定语从句、状语从句可由从句缩成主句的修饰成分,从而使全句的结构更加紧凑,语句更加通顺。

【例1】There are men here from all over the country. Many of them are from the north.

【译文】从全国各地来的人中有许多是北方人。

【例2】There are many people who want to see the film.

【译文】许多人想看这部电影。

【例3】The time was 10:30, and traffic on the street was light.

【译文】10点30分的时候,街上来往的车辆很少了。

（三）语法功能

英语中某些具有语法功能和意义的句子,如主语从句、定语从句、同位语从句、状语从句等,在翻译时该如何准确恰当地转换为对应的汉语句子呢?

1. it 形式主语句的译法

通常而言,以 what, who, whether, how 等特殊引导词引导的主语从句放在句首时,按照正常语序翻译即可。但主语从句结构冗长时往往会用 it 作形式主语放在句首,而将真正主语后置,即形成"It + 系动词 + 真正主语"的结构,以免整个句子看起来头重脚轻。

在翻译时,要尽可能将作真正主语的从句或不定式连同后面的内容提前至主语的位置上。

【例1】It has long been proved that the creative power of the people knows no limits.

【译文】人民的创造力是无穷的,这一点早已得到证实。

【例2】It doesn't make much difference whether he attends the meeting or not.

【译文】他参不参加会议没有多大关系。

当然,如果按照正常顺序翻译没有问题,主语从句也可以不提前。

【例3】It is strange that she did not see her own shortcomings.

【译文】真奇怪,她竟然没看出自己的缺点。

2. 定语从句、同位语从句的译法
（1）前置法

一般而言,在汉语表达中定语往往置于所修饰的名词或代词的前面,而在英语中修饰语往往后置。下面我们通过一个例句看看汉英这两种语言在这方面的差异。

【例】蜂鸟翅膀振动的速度极为惊人。

①速度极为惊人。	① The rapidity is remarkable.
②振动速度极为惊人。	② The rapidity of the motion is remarkable.
③翅膀振动的速度极为惊人。	③ The rapidity of the motion of the wing is remarkable.
④蜂鸟翅膀振动的速度极为惊人。	④ The rapidity of the motion of the wing of the hummingbird is remarkable.

通过例句①~④,可以看到中文例句中"速度"的修饰语无论多么冗长复杂,都是放置在前面的;而从英文例句中可以看出,"The rapidity"的修饰语都是放置在其后的。

定语从句的翻译涉及限定性定语从句和非限定性定语从句。限定性定语从句对所修饰的先行词起限制作用,与先行词关系密切,不用逗号隔开;当从句结构和意义比较简单,不会对主句部分造成理解上的困难时,翻译这类句子多使用前置法。可翻译成"……的"的定语词组,放在被修饰词的前面,将英语的复合句翻译成汉语的简单句。

【例1】The house whose roof was damaged has now been repaired.

【译文】屋顶坏了的房子现在已经修葺好了。

【例2】Anyone who has not attended a large college football game has missed one of the most colorful aspects of American college life.

【译文】任何一个没有参加过学校大型橄榄球比赛的人，都会错过美国大学生活中最为精彩的一面。

【例3】Whether such a sense of fairness stems from the common ancestor that the species had 35 millions years ago is as yet, an unanswered question.

【译文】这种公平感是否源于（人与猴这两个物种）3 500万年前的共同祖先，目前尚无定论。

【例4】Anthropologists wondered where the remote ancestors of the Polynesian peoples now living in the Pacific Islands came from.

【译文】人类学家们想知道目前生活在太平洋诸岛上的波利尼西亚各民族遥远的祖先从何而来。

【例5】It is critical that our nation and the world base important policies on the best judgments that science can provide concerning the future consequences of present actions.

【译文】我们的国家及世界各国应该把科学能提供的、关于当前行动对未来产生的影响的最好判断作为制定重大政策的基础，这一点很关键。

【例6】The majority of the patients attending the medical out-patients departments of our hospitals feel that they have not received adequate treatment unless they are able to carry home with them some tangible remedy.

【译文】来我们医院门诊部就诊的多数病人觉得，除非能带回家一些实实在在的药物，否则治疗就没达到效果。

【例7】The blunt truth of the matter is that human beings are not designed for tasks which require relentless vigilance: for the sophisticated human brain these are fatiguing and boring.

【译文】此事说明了一个真切的道理：人类并不是生来就适合做不间断的、高度警觉的工作。对于复杂的人类大脑来说，这些工作太乏倦无味了。

【例8】Most foods that we consume on a daily basis like potatoes and rice are loaded with carbohydrates.

【译文】我们每天所吃的大多数食物，像土豆和大米，都含有大量的碳水化合物。

【例9】The age at which young people are allowed to drive any vehicle should be raised to at least 21.

【译文】年轻人驾驶机动车的法定年龄应该至少提高到21岁。

【例10】Most credited their success in large part to having picked a business they already were comfortable in.（2003年真题）

【译文】大多数人把他们的成功归因于选择了一个自己过去已经很熟练的行业。

【例11】An investigator for a bank was on the line, asking in a severe voice why Collins, a university physicist, was late on payments for a $27,000 car, bought in Virginia the previous year.（2004年真题）

【译文】打电话的是一家银行的调查员，他以严厉的口吻质问柯林斯——一位大学物理学家为何去年在弗吉尼亚州购买了一辆价值27 000美元的汽车，至今仍拖欠车款。

【例12】The mechanism by which brain cells store memories is not clearly understood.

【译文】脑细胞储存记忆的机制还不是很清楚。

【例13】"Any student who combines an expert knowledge in gerontology with, say, an MBA or law degree will have a license to print money," one professor says.

【译文】"拥有老年学专业知识并且能获得工商管理或法律学位的任何学生都能赚到大钱。"一位教授说。

【例14】"Slowly, you recognize that the things that matter are those that can't be bought."

【译文】"渐渐地你会意识到，真正重要的东西是金钱买不到的（东西）"。

【例15】In a 2010 poll of Americans, loss of morality topped the list of the biggest problems facing the US.

【译文】根据2010年对美国人所做的一次调查，美国所面临的最大问题中，道德标准下滑位列首位。

【例16】In recent years, however, some health specialists have begun to apply the terms "well" and "wellness" only to those who are actively striving to maintain and improve their health.

【译文】然而近年来，某些健康专家仅仅将"健康的"和"健康"这两个概念赋予那些积极努力保持和提升自身健康的人们。

【例17】It's not clear whether the organism, first engineered by a German institute for biotechnology, is still in use.

【译文】由德国一家生物科技研究所率先研制的这种有机体是否还在使用尚不清楚。

【例18】Then she read about seasonal affective disorder, a form of depression that occurs in fall and winter.

【译文】随后她了解到了季节性情绪紊乱——一种发生在秋季和冬季的抑郁症。

【例19】And it happens very easily because every identification number you have—Social Security, credit card, driver's license, telephone—"is a key that unlocks some storage of money or goods", says a fraud program manager of the US Postal Service.（2004年真题）

【译文】这种事极易发生，因为你拥有的每个身份号码——社保号、信用卡号、驾驶证号、电话号码"都是打开财物的钥匙"，美国邮政局的一位反诈骗项目经理说。

【例20】That means getting a police report and copy of the erroneous contract, and then using them to clear the fraud from your credit report, which is held by a credit bureau.（2004年真题）

【译文】也就是说，先拿到警方的调查报告和假合同的副本，然后再从信用卡发卡机构持有的信用卡报告中消除诈骗记录。

【例21】They replaced a broken device, repaired another and carted away a load of rubbish that had been left on the station, showing the shuttle can bring full loads back down from space.（2006年真题）

【译文】他们换掉了故障设备，修理了另一个设备，并且运走了遗留在空间站的垃圾，这表明飞船能将所有物品从太空运送回来。

【例22】The flood of images and the openness in discussing its uncertainties about potential hazards sometimes made it appear that the shuttle was about to fall apart.（2006年真题）

【译文】大量图片和讨论飞船潜在危险不确定性时的透明程度，都似乎在说这艘飞船会立刻解体。

（2）后置法

如果定语从句结构复杂，译成汉语前置定语显得太长而不符合汉语表达习惯时，往往可以将其译成后置的并列分句。此时把定语从句单独翻译成一个句子，放在原来它所修饰的词的后面，关系代词可以翻译为先行词，或者与先行词相对应的代词。

【例1】They are striving for the ideal which is close to the heart of every Chinese and for which, in the past, many Chinese has laid down their lives.

【译文】他们正在为实现一个理想而努力，这个理想是每个中国人所珍爱的，在过去，许多中国人曾为了这个理想而牺牲了性命。

【例2】Electronic computers, which make it possible to free man from the labor of complex measurements and computation, have found wide application in engineering.

【译文】电子计算机在工程技术上已获得广泛应用，它使人可能摆脱复杂的测量和计算工作。

【例3】He had talked to vice-president Nixon, who assured him that everything that could be done would be done.

【译文】他和副总统尼克松谈过话，副总统向他保证，凡是能够做到的都将竭尽全力去做。

【例4】We will put off the party until next week, when we won't be so busy.

【译文】我们把聚会推迟到下周，那时我们就不会这么忙了。

同位语从句的翻译原理与定语从句基本类似，前置或后置可根据具体情况做相应处理。

【例1】But I knew I couldn't trust him. There was always the possibility that he was a political swindler.

【译文】但我知道不能轻信他。他是政治骗子，这种可能性总是存在的。

【例2】The fact that a woman has had an education may simply indicate her family's wealth or that it values its children more highly.

【译文】一个女人受过教育这个事实只是表明她家境殷实或她的家庭对孩子更加重视。

【例3】He expressed the hope that he would come over to visit China again.

【译文】他表示希望再次到中国访问。

或者增加"即"（或"就是"），或用冒号、破折号与主句分开。

【例】But considered realistically, we had to face the fact that our prospects were less than good.

【译文】但是考虑一下现实，我们不得不面对这样的现实，那就是我们的前景并不乐观。

3. 状语从句的译法

状语从句较为简单，位置也较为灵活，翻译时一般按照正常语序处理即可。但由 because，since，for，if，while，however 等引导的原因、条件或让步状语从句通常放在主句前面为宜。

4. 语态的转换

英语中多使用被动句，而汉语中则多使用主动句，所以翻译的时候可以少用"被"字句，用别的词来代替"被"字或者将被动句转化成主动句。一些被动语态的句子可以按顺译法直译，但大多数被动语态的句子翻译时需要做一番转换才能使译文更加符合汉语习惯，这是因为汉语较少使用被动语态。

被动语态的翻译常有三种方法。①还原成主动句：将 by 后的动作发出者还原成主语，或增加"人们""我们"等原文省略的动作发出者还原成主动句。②构造成主动句：使用"把、由、使、让、给"等词译成主动句。③转化成自动句：通过选择汉语译文的动词，将原文动词的承受者（即主语）转变成汉语中那个动词动作的发出者（仍然作主语）。下面这些英文被动句常常译成汉语主动句：

It is said that... 据说……

It is reported that... 据报道……

It is estimated that... 据估计……

It is believed that... 人们认为……

It is known that... 人人皆知……

It must be pointed out that... 必须指出的是……

【例1】Much has been said about the necessity of introducing foreign funds into Chinese enterprises.

【译文】有关中国企业引进外资的必要性已经谈了很多。

英文中的被动语态也可以通过汉语中的"由、受、遭到、让、要、得到、得以、可以、加以"等词语来表示。

【例2】If the stability can be maintained, one of the worst features of the cycle will have been removed.

【译文】如果这种稳定状态得以保持下去，商业周期最坏的一个特征将被消除。

英文中的被动语态还可以译成汉语中的无主句，或者译成泛指主语。

【例3】You are required to return all the books you borrowed from the library by the end of this month.

【译文】要求大家在月底前把从图书馆借的书全部归还。

【例4】It is generally accepted that the experiences of the child in his first years largely determines his character and later personality.

【译文】人们普遍认为,儿童早年的经历很大程度决定着其性格和今后的人格发展。

【例5】From what is stated above, it is learned that the sun's heat can pass through the empty space between the sun and the atmosphere that surrounds the earth.

【译文】从以上所述可知,太阳的热量可以穿越太阳与围绕地球的大气之间的广阔空间。

【例6】It may also be said that rational, industrious, useful human beings are divided into classes.

【译文】或许可以说,理性的、勤奋的、有用的人可以分为两类。

【例7】It has never been explained why university students seem to enjoy practical jokes more than anyone else.

【译文】无人能说清为何大学生似乎比别人更爱搞恶作剧。

【例8】It is commonly thought that our society had been dramatically changed by modern science and technology, and that humans had made extraordinary progress in knowledge and technology over the recent decades.

【译文】人们普遍认为,现代科技给我们的社会带来巨变,近些年来人类在知识和科技方面取得了非凡的进步。

【例9】It is estimated that an automated highway will be able to handle 10,000 vehicles per hour, compared with the 1,500 to 2,000 vehicles that can be carried by a present-day highway.

【译文】据估计,相比于目前高速公路每小时通过1 500至2 000辆机动车,自动化高速公路将能每小时通过1万辆。

【例10】Raised in an era of privatization and increased consumer choice, today's tech-savvy workers have embraced a free market in love as well as economics.

【译文】今天的技术熟练工在私有化和消费者选择增多的时代中成长起来,他们喜欢自由化的经济和市场。

【例11】Reports came into London Zoo that a wild puma had been spotted forty-five miles south of London.

【译文】伦敦动物园接到报告,说在伦敦以南45英里处发现一只野生美洲狮。

（四）直译与意译

直译，即忠于原文意思又保留原文形式；意译，即不受原文词语的限制，不拘泥于原文句子的结构，用不同于原文的表达方式，把原文意思表达出来。在考研英语翻译中，我们应遵循的方法是：直译为先，意译补后，必要时直译与意译相结合。

直译指基本保留原有句子结构，照字面意思翻译；意译是在不损害原文内容和精神的前提下，为了表达的需要，对原文做相应的调整。

【例1】Good marriages doesn't just happen. They take a lot of love and a lot of work.

【直译】好的婚姻不会仅仅发生——它们需要大量的爱和大量的工作。

【意译】幸福的婚姻不是凭空发生的——需要你为它付出大量的爱和做大量的工作。

（美满的婚姻不会从天上掉下来——你必须为它付出大量的爱，做大量的工作。）

很显然，本句话意译要比直译更符合汉语表达习惯。当然，一句话并不限于一种译法，要根据具体需要而定。一般来说，在英汉翻译考试中，如果直译能达意就用直译，如果直译效果不好，就应该考虑意译。只要译文内容忠实于原文，意思明白即可。

翻译大师严复曾提出翻译学的三大原则"信、达、雅"，已成为该领域的尺度和标杆。"信"即忠实于原文；"达"即通顺自然；"雅"即精雕细琢，语言臻美。

【例1】I was playing with my pet dog, which was 4 years old, on the grassland on that sunny day.

【译文】我在和爱犬玩耍，它四岁了，在草地上，一个阳光灿烂的日子。（信）

通过研读，我们发现该句只达到了"信"的原则，但言语艰涩拗口，因此需要略微调整。

【例2】I was playing with my pet dog, which was 4 years old, on the grassland on that sunny day.

【译文】一个阳光灿烂的日子，我和四岁的爱犬在草地上戏耍。（达）

【例3】I'm here today and gone tomorrow.

【译文1】我今天在这儿，明天就走了。（信）

【译文2】人生苦短。（达+雅）

【例4】One boy is a boy, two boys half a boy, three boys no boy.

【译文1】一个男孩是男孩，两个男孩是半个男孩，三个男孩不是男孩。（信）

【译文2】一个和尚挑水吃，两个和尚抬水吃，三个和尚没水吃。（达+雅）

【例5】She is a very pretty girl.

【译文1】她是个漂亮女孩儿。（信）

【译文2】她相貌出众。（达）

【译文3】她貌若天仙。/她有沉鱼落雁之美，闭月羞花之貌。（雅）

（五）插入语、同位语以及特殊结构的处理

对于特殊结构，比如倒装结构，分隔结构，应对策略在于调整原文的顺序，找到成分搭配关系。考研英语中的成分分隔主要有两种：一种是成分插入，即所谓的插入语；另一种是顺序调整，即宾语后置。前者主要是指介词短语、分词短语、独立主格等置于主谓之间或主从之间，往往前后都加逗号；后者主要是指紧挨在动词之后的宾语后置到其他成分之后。成分插入结构往往可以直接翻译，而宾语后置需要把宾语还原到原先的位置再进行翻译。总之，成分隔离结构翻译的关键是识别出隔离的具体内容。

插入语和同位语一般是对一个事物或一句话做一些附加解释，位置十分灵活，译成汉语时，有时要做相应的调整以合乎汉语的表达习惯。

【例1】There are, to be exact, only two choices.

【译文】准确而言，只有两种选择。

上面提到的成分分隔结构中，由于插入语通常都位于标志性的双逗号之间，因而比较容易辨别；而宾语后置则需要较强的语法能力，花费一定时间才能辨别。英文句子中之所以存在宾语后置的现象，是因为当动宾结构中的宾语过长或者过于复杂，且宾语后紧跟的补语或状语（多为介词短语）相对较短小或简单时，为了保持句子的平衡和信息的可读性，往往将宾语后置到这些补语或状语之后，构成宾语后置。下面通过例句进行简单解析。

【例2】I shall define him as an individual who has elected as his primary duty and pleasure in life the activity of thinking in Socratic way about moral problems.

例句中的 elect 是及物动词，而出现在它后面的是介词短语 as his primary duty and pleasure in life，由此判断发生了宾语后置。句中 elected 的真正宾语是这个介词短语后面的 the activity of thinking in Socratic way about moral problems，由于成分复杂、结构冗长，故被后置，以免句子头重脚轻。判断出宾语后置后就可以着手翻译。

【译文】我把他（知识分子）定义为这样的人：他们把以苏格拉底的方式来思考道德问题作为自己人生的主要责任和乐趣。

【例3】On the other hand, he did not accept as well founded the charge made by some of his critics that, while he was a good observer, he had no power of reasoning .

例句中的 accept 也是及物动词，但是紧跟其后的并不是它的宾语，而是 as well founded，由此也可判断发生了宾语后置，即 accept 的真正宾语是 the charge。宾语之所以后置是因为有一个过去分词短语 made by some of his critics 作其后置定语，同时被一个 that 引导的同位语从句修饰。与此同时，这个 that 同位语从句中还嵌套了一个 while 引导的让步状语从句。这个宾语的复杂程度可见一斑。

【译文】另一方面，某些人批评他虽然善于观察，却不具备推理能力，而他认为这种说法也是缺乏根据的。

（六）核校、调整、成文

组合成汉语之后，一定要再检查一遍，做出相应的调整，最终成文。核校主要有三个方面：一是检查译文是否忠于原文，通过对照译文和原文往往能发现问题；二是检查译文本身是否通顺、表达是否清楚，通读译文，如果读起来拗口或者有歧义，很有可能是翻译不准确或表达不清晰，就要通过适当增减词语或调整语序来解决；三是检查译文是否有笔误，是否有漏洞，时态是否译出，数字、日期是否译错，标点符号是否用错等。

（七）指导方法与建议

相对而言，考生对考研英语翻译的重视程度不及阅读或写作等题型，前期投入不够，最后只能仓促应战。所以建议大家每天坚持四件事，从小入手、日积月累，才能实现量变到质变的飞跃。

（1）每天磨炼

一定要动手做题。坚持练习，每天磨炼。可以利用考研翻译近十年的真题或阅读文章中结构复杂的句子进行练习，每天一个长难句，最终就会有长足进步。

（2）修改译文

翻译之后不要马上比对参考答案。首先要自我检查。检查、修改译文的过程就是真正提高翻译能力和技巧的过程。然后再看参考译文，或许某些地方略有差异，只要自己在语法和句法上没有出错，而且自己的译文通畅自如，就不必苛求和参考答案完全一致。条条大路通罗马，千人千面，千人千译。

（3）分析错误

分析错误就是要找到译错的地方，分析错误原因。或是词汇问题，或是短语问题，或是结构问题。大多数情况是由两个方面造成的：单词不认识，结构没看懂。

（4）每天精译

刚才提到，翻译素材可以选用考研英语阅读文章，每天一个长难句，加大阅读量。做精读，做精译，逐字逐句理解透彻，翻译到位准确，最后势必收获满满。

第三节　精讲精练

（一）真题精讲

2016年考研英语（二）翻译真题

The supermarket is designed to lure customers into spending as much time as possible within its doors. The reason for this is simple: The longer you stay in the store, the more stuff you'll see, and the more stuff you see, the more you'll buy. And supermarkets contain a lot of stuff. The average supermarket, according to the Food Marketing Institute, carries some 44,000 different items, and many carry tens of thousands more. The sheer volume of available choice is enough to send shoppers into a state of information overload. According to brain-scan experiments, the demands of so much decision-making quickly become too much for us. After about 40 minutes of shopping, most people stop struggling to be rationally selective, and instead

超市设计的目的就是为了诱使消费者花尽可能多的时间在店内逛。理由很简单：你在店里待的时间越长，你看到的东西就越多；你看到的东西越多，你买的东西就越多。超市中有各种各样的商品。根据食品营销研究所的调查，普通超市约有44 000种不同种类的商品，许多超市甚至还要多出成千上万种商品。单是可供选择的货品数量就足以让顾客眼花缭乱。根据脑部扫描实验，迅速做出决定对我们来说实在太难。购物约40分钟后，大多数人已不再是理性选择，而是开始感性消费了。这就是为什么购物车里的商品会有50%是我们本没打算买的。

begin shopping emotionally—which is the point at which we accumulate the 50 percent of stuff in our cart that we never intended buying.

语篇分析

该段主要讲述了超市的设计宗旨：尽可能让顾客在店里长时间驻足停留。超市通常在货架上陈列大量商品，使顾客眼花瞭乱。根据脑部扫描实验，面对大量要处理的信息，消费者迅速做出的决定往往都是感性的。这样的结果就是最后购买了许多本没打算买的商品。

必背词汇

1. lure [lʊə(r)] v. 诱惑，诱使	10. decision-making 决策，做决定
2. lure sb. into doing sth. 引诱某人做某事	11. struggle ['strʌgl] v. 挣扎，争斗
3. stuff [stʌf] n. 物品，商品	12. rationally ['ræʃnəli] ad. 理性地，合理地
4. contain [kən'teɪn] v. 包含，容纳	13. selective [sɪ'lektɪv] a. 选择的
5. average ['ævərɪdʒ] a. 普通的，一般的	14. emotionally [ɪ'məʊʃənəli] ad. 情感地，感性地
6. sheer [ʃɪə(r)] a. 绝对的，纯粹的	
7. volume ['vɒljuːm] n. 数量	15. accumulate [ə'kjuːmjəleɪt] v. 积累
8. available [ə'veɪləbl] a. 可提供的，可利用的	16. cart [kɑːt] n. 小推车
9. overload [ˌəʊvə'ləʊd] n. 超载，超量	17. intend [ɪn'tend] v. 打算

难句解析

1. The supermarket is designed <u>to lure customers</u> *into spending as much time as possible within its doors.* 下划线的不定式短语作目的状语；斜体部分是介词短语作宾语customers的补足语；within its doors作地点状语。

2. <u>The longer</u> you stay in the store, <u>the more stuff</u> you'll see, and <u>the more stuff</u> you see, <u>the more</u> you'll buy. 下划线部分是"the+比较级，the+比较级"结构，即"越……，越……"；其中and之前的部分为一个整体，前半句表条件，后半句表结果；and之后的部分为一个整体，前半句表条件，后半句表结果。

3. The average supermarket, <u>according to the Food Marketing Institute</u>, carries some 44,000 different items, and many (supermarkets) carry tens of thousands more (items). 下划线部分是介词短语作方式状语；and后面的句子承前省略了supermarkets和items。

4. The sheer volume of available choice is enough <u>to send shoppers</u> *into a state of information overload.* 下划线的不定式短语作结果状语，斜体的介词短语作宾语shoppers的补足语。

5. After about 40 minutes of shopping, most people stop struggling to be rationally selective, and instead begin shopping emotionally—<u>which is the point (at which we accumulate the 50 percent of stuff in our cart *that we never intended buying*)</u>. 下划线部分是which引导的非限定性定语从句修饰主句，括号里是"介词+关系代词"即at+which引导的定语从句，which指代the point；最后的斜体部分是that引导的从句，作the 50 percent of stuff 的定语。

2017年考研英语（二）翻译真题

My dream has always been to work somewhere in an area between fashion and publishing. Two years before graduating from secondary school, I took a sewing and design course thinking that I would move on to a fashion design course. However, during that course I realised I was not good enough in this area to compete with other creative personalities in the future, so I decided that it was not the right path for me. Before applying for university I told everyone that I would study journalism, because writing was, and still is, one of my favourite activities. But, to be honest, I said it, because I thought that fashion and me together was just a dream—I knew that no one could imagine me in the fashion industry at all! So I decided to look for some fashion-related courses that included writing. This is when I noticed the course "Fashion Media & Promotion."

我一直梦想能在一个与时尚和出版相关的领域工作。中学毕业前两年，我选修了缝纫和设计课程，心想自己以后会继续选修时尚设计课程。然而在此期间，我意识到自己在该领域不够优秀，在未来不足以与其他富有创造力的人竞争，因此我认定：这条路不适合我。在申请大学之前，我告诉所有人我会选择新闻专业，因为写作一直都是我最喜欢的事情之一。但是说实话，当时这样说是因为我认为时尚于我而言就只是个梦想。我知道，根本没有人能想象我会进入时尚这一行！因此我决定去寻找一些既与时尚相关又涉及写作的课程。就在这时，我注意到了"时尚媒体与营销"这门课程。

必背词汇

1. somewhere [ˈsʌmweə(r)] ad. 在某处，大约
2. publishing [ˈpʌblɪʃɪŋ] n. 出版，出版业
3. graduate [ˈɡrædʒuət] v. 毕业
4. secondary [ˈsekəndri] a. 中等教育的
5. sewing [ˈsəʊɪŋ] n. 缝纫
6. compete with sb. 与某人竞争
7. creative [kriˈeɪtɪv] a. 创造性的
8. personality [ˌpɜːsəˈnæləti] n. 个性，人才
9. apply for sth. 申请……
10. journalism [ˈdʒɜːnəlɪzəm] n. 新闻业
11. favourite [ˈfeɪvərɪt] a. 最喜爱的
12. to be honest 坦率而言，说实话
13. promotion [prəˈməʊʃn] n. 促销，推动

难句解析

1. Two years before graduating from secondary school, I took a sewing and design course <u>thinking that I would move on to a fashion design course</u>. 下划线部分是现在分词短语作伴随状语，修饰took a sewing and design course。

2. However, during that course I realised I was not good enough in this area <u>to compete with other creative personalities in the future</u>, so I decided <u>that it was not the right path for me</u>. 第一个下划线部分是不定式短语作结果状语；第二个下划线部分是that引导的从句作decided的宾语。

3. Before applying for university I told everyone <u>that I would study journalism</u>, because writing was (one of my favourite activities), and still is, one of my favourite activities. 下划线部分是that引导的从句作told的宾语；括号里是省略的内容。

4. But, to be honest, I said it, *because I thought that fashion and me together was just a dream*—<u>I knew that no one could imagine me in the fashion industry at all</u>! 斜体部分是原因状语从句，对前面的I said it进行解释；后面下划线部分和I said it是并列关系。

（二）题源实战

经典短文 1

The old lady had always been proud of the great rose-tree in her garden, and was fond of telling how it had grown from a cutting she had brought years before from Italy, when she was first married. She and her husband had been

老太太总以自家花园里那棵高大的玫瑰树为荣。她总乐于告诉别人，数年前她初婚时从意大利带回来的枝条是如何长成如今这般高大的。那

traveling back in their carriage from Rome (it was before the time of railways) and on a bad piece of road south of Siena the carriage had broken down, and had been forced to pass the night in a little house by the road-side. The accommodation was wretched of course; she had spent a sleepless night, and rising early had stood, wrapped up, at her window, with the cool air blowing on her face, to watch the dawn. She could still, after all these years, remember the blue mountains with the bright moon above them, and how a far-off town on one of the peaks had gradually grown whiter and whiter.

时，她与丈夫乘马车从罗马旅行归来（那时还没有火车），途经锡耶纳南部的崎岖路段时，马车坏了，他们被迫寄宿于路边的小屋。住宿条件当然非常差，她一夜未眠，一早便起身穿好衣服，立于窗前，感受着扑面而来的习习凉风，等待着黎明的到来。事隔多年，她仍然记得当时的情景：明月高悬在青山群峦之上，远处山峰上的小镇逐渐明亮起来。

语篇分析

该段的主要内容是：一位老太太讲述了自家花园里的一棵让她引以为豪的玫瑰树，以及早年和丈夫初婚时的一段难忘旅程。这段旅程之所以难忘，是因为那些景物虽历经岁月，仍历历在目。

必背词汇

1. be proud of... 以……为荣	5. sleepless ['sli:pləs] a. 无眠的；失眠的
2. break down 出故障；抛锚	6. wrap [ræp] v. 包裹
3. accommodation [əˌkɒməˈdeɪʃn] n. 住宿；住宿条件	7. dawn [dɔːn] n. 黎明；破晓
	8. far-off a. 遥远的；久远的
4. wretched [ˈretʃɪd] a. 悲惨的；破旧的	

难句解析

1. The old lady had always been proud of the great rose-tree in her garden, // and was fond of telling how it had grown from a cutting (that she had brought years before from Italy), *when she was first married.*

"//"分隔的是由 and 连接的两个并列分句；下划线部分是 was fond of 的宾语，括号里省略引导词 that 的从句作 a cutting 的定语，斜体部分 when 引导的从句作 years before 的定语。

2. She and her husband had been traveling back in their carriage from Rome (it was before the time of railways) // and (on a bad piece of road south of Siena) the carriage had broken down, // and had been forced to pass the night in a little house by the road-side.

两个"//"分隔的是由 and 连接的三个并列分句，第二个分句中的括号里 on a bad piece of...Siena 是介词短语，作地点状语。

3. She had spent a sleepless night, // and (rising early) had stood, (wrapped up), at her window, (with the cool air blowing on her face), to watch the dawn.

"//"分隔的是两个并列分句；第二个分句中第一个括号里的内容是现在分词短语，作伴随状语；第二个括号里的内容是过去分词短语，作方式状语；第三个括号里的内容是独立主格结构，作伴随状语；最后的不定式 to watch the dawn 作 had stood 的目的状语。

4. She could still, (after all these years), remember <u>the blue mountains *with the bright moon above them*, and how a far-off town on one of the peaks had gradually grown whiter and whiter</u>.

括号里是时间状语，将助动词 could 和实意动词 remember 分隔，目的是突出强调时间概念；下划线部分是 remember 的宾语，其中 how 引导的是一个宾语从句，斜体部分是独立主格结构，即 with+ 名词 +介词短语，作伴随状语。

经典短文 2

1 My mom always told me that you can't please everyone, so please yourself. There will always be people who disagree with you or who dislike your ideas and actions—whether or not these people are coming from a positive or a negative place. Appreciate and accept them for being different than you and forgive them if they upset you. Remember that the road to success invites a lot of critics so the sooner you know what to take on board and what to release, the better. The fact that criticism exists at all also reminds us that all we can do is

1 我的母亲曾说："你不能取悦所有人，就取悦自己。"总有人会不认可你或不喜欢你的想法和行为——不管这些人是出于善意或恶意。因为他们和你不同，所以请感激并接受他们，并在他们令你痛苦时原谅他们。记住，成功路上会有许多批评者，因此你越早明白需要接受什么或舍弃什么，就会做得更好。事实上批评总是存在，也提醒我们，做到最好就是最好的回应——说真话，交出最好的作

our best—speak our truth, deliver our best work and surrender the rest.

2　And as one of my favorite books, *The Magic of Thinking Big*, says, "Expect critics, its proof you are growing." And on the ladder of growth is the only place to be.

品并让别人信服。

2　正如我喜欢的一本书《远大理想的神奇》中所说，"期待批评者们，这证明你在成长"。而只有在成长的阶梯上你才能期盼到。

➡️ 语篇分析 ⬅️

第一段讲述了"我"借用母亲的一句话来告诫自己：对于持有不同意见者，要勇于原谅并心怀感激，只有做到最好，才能令人信服。

第二段讲述了"我"借用《远大理想的神奇》中的句子来勉励自己：批评者助"我"成长。

➡️ 必背词汇 ⬅️

1. please [pliːz] *v.* 取悦	11. release [rɪˈliːs] *v.* 放手；释放
2. disagree with... 不赞同……	12. criticism [ˈkrɪtɪsɪzəm] *n.* 批评
3. positive [ˈpɒzətɪv] *a.* 积极的；肯定的	13. remind [rɪˈmaɪnd] *v.* 提醒
4. negative [ˈneɡətɪv] *a.* 消极的；否定的	14. deliver [dɪˈlɪvə(r)] *v.* 交出；运送；传达
5. appreciate [əˈpriːʃieɪt] *v.* 欣赏；感激	15. surrender [səˈrendə(r)] *v.* 征服；使屈服
6. be different than... 与……不同	16. rest [rest] *n.* 其余的人
7. forgive [fəˈɡɪv] *v.* 原谅	17. favorite [ˈfeɪvərɪt] *a.* 最喜爱的
8. upset [ʌpˈset] *v.* 使……难过；使沮丧	18. magic [ˈmædʒɪk] *n.* 魔力；魔术
9. invite [ɪnˈvaɪt] *v.* 招致；导致	19. proof [pruːf] *n.* 证明；证据
10. critic [ˈkrɪtɪk] *n.* 批评者	20. ladder [ˈlædə(r)] *n.* 阶梯；梯子

➡️ 难句解析 ⬅️

1. There will always be people (who disagree with you or who dislike your ideas and actions)— whether or not these people are coming from a positive or a negative place.

括号里是 or 连接的两个 who 引导的从句作 people 的定语；下划线部分 whether 引导的是让步状语从句。

2. Appreciate (them) and accept them for being different than you and forgive them if they upset you.

这是由两个 and 连接的三个并列分句，都是原形动词开头，称为祈使句；第一个分句省略了 them；第一个下划线部分作原因状语，修饰前两个分句；第二个下划线部分 if 引导的条件状语从句修饰第三个分句。

3. Remember (that the road to success invites a lot of critics) // so <u>the sooner</u> you know what to take on board and what to release, <u>the better</u>.

"//" 之前是一个祈使句，括号里 that 引导的从句作宾语；"//" 之后的下划线部分是 "the + 比较级，the + 比较级" 结构，即"越……，越……"。

4. The fact (that criticism exists at all) also reminds us (that all we can do is our best)—speak our truth, deliver our best work and surrender the rest.

第一个括号里 that 引导的从句作 fact 的同位语；第二个括号里 that 引导的从句作 reminds 的宾语；破折号后面的 speak，deliver 和 surrender 是并列结构，进一步解释前面的 all we can do。

5. And on the ladder of growth is the only place to be.

这是一个特殊倒装句，自然语序是：And the only place is to be on the ladder of growth. 倒装的目的是突出强调 on the ladder of growth 这个介词短语。

经典短文 3

1 A study of how older teenagers use social media has found that *Facebook* is "not just on the slide, it is basically dead and buried" and is being replaced by simpler social networks such as *Twitter* and *Snapchat*.

2 Young people now see the site as "uncool" and keep their profiles live purely to stay in touch with older relatives, among whom it remains popular.

3 Professor Daniel Miller of University College London, an anthropologist who worked on the research, wrote in an article for academic news website *The Conversation*: "Mostly they feel

1 一项关于年龄较大的青少年使用社交媒体的研究表明，脸书的受欢迎程度"不仅每况愈下，甚至基本上是明日黄花了"。许多更简单的社交网络如推特和色拉布在逐步取代脸书。

2 现在的年轻人觉得脸书一点都不酷，但他们仍然保留着自己的账号，只是为了和长辈保持联系，脸书在长辈中依旧风靡。

3 伦敦大学学院的教授丹尼尔·米勒是人类学家，他也曾参与此项调查研究。并且还在学术研究网站 The Conversation 上发表的一篇文章中称：

embarrassed even to be associated with it."

4 "This year marked the start of what looks likely to be a sustained decline of what had been the most pervasive of all social networking sites. Young people are turning away in their droves and adopting other social networks instead, while the worst people of all, their parents, continue to use the service."

"就连和脸书联系在一起通常都会让他们感到尴尬。"

4 "今年对于那些过去风靡全球的社交网站来说是惨淡的，开始呈现出持续下滑的趋势。年轻人开始陆陆续续地转而使用其他社交网络，而他们的父母则还在使用原来的那些服务。"

语篇分析

第一段讲述了根据一项研究的调查结果，脸书的受欢迎程度正每况愈下，有被对手超越的危险。

第二段讲述了脸书在年轻人中的地位一落千丈，只充当了与长辈保持联系的一种方式。

第三段提及伦敦大学学院的一位教授，他参与了此项调查研究，谈到脸书的没落。

第四段讲述了年轻人开始转向其他社交网络，而其父母则还在使用原来的那些服务。

必背词汇

1. teenager ['ti:neɪdʒə(r)] n. 青少年
2. social media 社交媒体
3. on the slide 下滑
4. basically ['beɪsɪklɪ] ad. 基本上
5. replace [rɪ'pleɪs] v. 替代
6. see... as... 把……视作……
7. site [saɪt] n. 网址；地址
8. uncool [ˌʌn'kuːl] a. 不酷的；不流行的
9. profile ['prəʊfaɪl] n. 简介；轮廓
10. purely ['pjʊəlɪ] ad. 纯粹地
11. live [laɪv] a. 活跃的；现场的
12. stay in touch with sb. 与某人保持联系
13. relative ['relətɪv] n. 亲戚
14. anthropologist [ˌænθrə'pɒlədʒɪst] n. 人类学家
15. work on sth 从事某事
16. academic [ˌækə'demɪk] a. 学术的
17. website ['websaɪt] n. 网址
18. embarrassed [ɪm'bærəst] a. 尴尬的
19. be associated with... 与……有联系
20. mark [mɑːk] v. 标志着；意味着
21. sustained [səs'teɪnd] a. 持续的
22. decline [dɪ'klaɪn] n. 下滑；下降
23. pervasive [pə'veɪsɪv] a. 流行的；普及的
24. in droves 成群地
25. adopt [ə'dɒpt] v. 采纳；采取
26. instead [ɪn'sted] ad. 代替；反而

难句解析

1. A study of (how older teenagers use social media) has found that *Facebook* is "not just on the slide, (and also) it is basically dead and buried" and is being replaced by simpler social networks such as *Twitter* and *Snapchat*.

第一个括号里 how 引导的从句作 of 的宾语；下划线 that 引导的从句作 has found 的宾语，其中括号里的 and also 是省略成分，与 not just 构成整体，即"不仅……而且……"。

2. Young people now see the site as "uncool" and keep their profiles live *purely to stay in touch with older relatives*, (among whom it remains popular).

第一个下划线使用了 see...as... 结构，即"把……视作……"；第二个下划线使用了 keep sth. *adj.* 结构，live 在这里是形容词，意思为"活跃的；现场的"；斜体部分是不定式短语，作目的状语；括号里是"介词＋关系代词（among whom）"引导的定语从句，修饰 older relatives。

3. Professor Daniel Miller of University College London, an anthropologist (who worked on the research), wrote in an article (for academic news website *The Conversation*): "Mostly they feel embarrassed even to be associated with it."

下划线部分是一个名词短语，作 Daniel Miller 的同位语，其中括号里 who 引导的是 anthropologist 的定语从句；后面一个括号里的介词短语作 article 的后置定语。

4. This year marked the start of what looks likely to be a sustained decline of *what had been the most pervasive of all social networking sites*.

下划线部分 what 引导的从句作 of 的宾语，其中的斜体部分也是 what 引导的从句作 of 的宾语。

5. Young people are turning away in their droves and adopting other social networks instead, // while the worst people of all, their parents, continue to use the service.

"//"之前是由 and 连接的两个分句构成，下划线部分的介词短语作方式状语；"//"之后是由 while 连接的一个并列句，下划线部分的名词短语是 the worst people of all 的同位语。

经典短文 4

1 In interviews, famous people often say that the key to becoming both happy and successful is to "do what you love." But mastering a skill, even one that you deeply love, requires a huge amount of

1 在采访中，名人们常说他们之所以能够同时收获快乐和成功，秘诀就在于"做自己爱做的事"。但是要掌握一门技能，即使你再深爱它，

drudgery. Any challenging activity—from computer programming to playing a musical instrument to athletics—requires focused and concentrated practice. A perfect golf swing or flawless butterfly stroke takes untold hours of practice and countless repetitions to perfect.

2 Anyone who wants to master a skill must run through the cycle of practice, critical feedback, modification, and incremental improvement again, again, and again. Some people seem able to concentrate on practicing an activity like this for years and take pleasure in their gradual improvement. Yet others find this kind of focused, time-intensive work to be frustrating or boring.

也需要下大量功夫。任何具有挑战性的活动——从电脑编程、弹奏乐器到体育竞技——都需要专心致志、心无旁骛地练习。无论是一个完美的高尔夫挥杆动作或是一个标准的蝶泳泳姿，都需要花费大量的时间、进行无数次重复练习才能达到完美无缺的境界。

2 对于任何人而言，若想掌握一门技能，都必须一遍一遍又一遍地经历"练习——批评性反馈——修改——渐进式改进"这一循环过程。有些人似乎能够这样几十年如一日专注于一项活动，并且在逐渐的改进过程中获得乐趣。然而另一些人却发现这种需要专心而且时间密集的工作让人感到沮丧和无聊。

语篇分析

第一段讲述了名人们获取快乐和成功的秘诀在于"做自己爱做的事"。但是要掌握一门技能，即使再深爱它，也需要花费大量的时间和精力、进行无数次重复练习才能达到完美无缺的境界。

第二段讲述了对于任何人而言，若想掌握一门技能，都必须长年累月专注于它，并且从中取乐。然而另一些人却发现这种需要专心而且时间密集的工作让人感到沮丧和无聊。

必背词汇

1. interview [ˈɪntəvjuː] n. 采访
2. master [ˈmɑːstə(r)] v. 掌握
3. drudgery [ˈdrʌdʒərɪ] n. 苦力活
4. challenging [ˈtʃælɪndʒɪŋ] a. 挑战的
5. programming [ˈprəʊgræmɪŋ] n. 编程
6. musical [ˈmjuːzɪkl] a. 音乐的
7. instrument [ˈɪnstrəmənt] n. 乐器；仪器
8. athletics [æθˈletɪks] n. 体育运动
9. focused [ˈfəʊkəst] a. 专注的；专心的
10. concentrated [ˈkɒnsntreɪtɪd] a. 专注的；集中的
11. swing [swɪŋ] n. 摆动；摇摆

12. flawless [ˈflɔːləs] *a.* 完美的；无瑕的	19. critical [ˈkrɪtɪkl] *a.* 批判性的
13. butterfly stroke 蝶泳中的一次挥臂	20. feedback [ˈfiːdbæk] *n.* 反馈
14. untold [ˌʌnˈtəʊld] *a.* 数不清的；不计其数的	21. modification [ˌmɒdɪfɪˈkeɪʃn] *n.* 改进
	22. incremental [ˌɪŋkrəˈmentl] *a.* 提高的
15. countless [ˈkaʊntləs] *a.* 数不清的；不计其数的	23. concentrate on sth. 专注于某事
	24. take pleasure in sth. 以……为乐
16. repetition [ˌrepəˈtɪʃn] *n.* 重复	25. gradual [ˈɡrædʒuəl] *a.* 逐渐的
17. run through sth. 经历某事	26. time-intensive 时间密集的
18. cycle [ˈsaɪkl] *n.* 周期	27. frustrating [frʌˈstreɪtɪŋ] *a.* 令人沮丧的

◆ 难句解析 ◆

1. In interviews, famous people often say <u>that the key (to becoming both happy and successful) is to "do what you love."</u>

下划线部分 that 引导的从句作 say 的宾语，其中括号里的介词短语作 the key 的后置定语，is 后面的不定式作表语。

2. But mastering a skill, <u>even one (that you deeply love)</u>, requires a huge amount of drudgery.

这句话的主语是动名词短语 mastering a skill，谓语是 requires，宾语是 a huge amount of drudgery；下划线部分是一个名词短语，one 指代 a skill，括号里 that 引导的从句作 one 的定语。

3. A perfect golf swing or flawless butterfly stroke <u>takes untold hours of practice and countless repetition to perfect</u>.

下划线部分使用了 take some time to do sth. 结构，即：花费时间做某事。

4. Some people seem able to concentrate on practicing an activity (like this) for years and take pleasure in their gradual improvement.

这是由 and 连接的两个分句组成的并列句，括号里的介词短语作 activity 的后置定语。

5. Yet others find this kind of focused, time-intensive work <u>to be frustrating or boring</u>.

下划线部分的不定式短语作宾语 this kind of focused, time-intensive work 的补足语。

经典短文 5

1 Climate change is the greatest challenge facing humanity: drastic reduction of carbon emissions

1 气候变化是人类面临的最大挑战：如果要避免一场对于世界大部

is vital if we are to avoid a catastrophe that devastates large parts of the world. Governments and businesses have been slow to act and individuals now need to take the lead.

2   The Earth can absorb no more than 3 tons of carbon dioxide emissions each year for every person on the planet if we are to keep temperature and rainfall change within tolerable limits. Yet from cars and holiday flights to household appliances and the food on our plates, Western consumer lifestyles leave each of us responsible for over 12 tons of carbon dioxide a year—four times what the Earth can handle.

3   Individual action is essential if we want to avoid climate chaos. *How to Live a Low-Carbon Life* shows how easy it is to take responsibility, providing the first comprehensive, one-stop reference guide to calculating your CO_2 emissions and reducing them to a sustainable 3 tons a year

分地区的灭顶之灾，大幅度减少碳排放非常关键。政府和企业一直以来都行动迟缓，所以现在我们个人应该积极行动起来。

2   如果要把气温和降水量的变化保持在可控范围内，地球上每个人每年产生的二氧化碳排放量就不能超过3吨，然而，由于使用汽车、假日乘坐航班、使用家用电器以及消耗食物，西方人的生活方式使得我们每年产生12吨的二氧化碳排放，是地球承受力的四倍。

3   如果想避免气候灾难，个人行为至关重要。《如何低碳生活》一书表明承担责任非常容易，它给我们提供了综合性的、一站式的参考指南，告诉我们如何计算个人的二氧化碳排放量，并且将其控制在每年3吨的可持续发展的水平之内。

语篇分析

第一段讲述了气候变化是人类面临的最大挑战，大幅度减少碳排放非常关键。政府和企业一直以来都行动迟缓，我们个人应该积极行动起来。

第二段讲述了如果要把气温和降水量的变化保持在可控范围内，就要大幅降低二氧化碳的排放量。然而，现代人的生活方式使得排放量远远超出了标准。

第三段讲述了如果想避免气候灾难，个人行为至关重要。《如何低碳生活》一书给我们提供了综合性的、一站式的参考指南，告诉我们如何计算二氧化碳的排放量，并且将其控制在可持续发展的范围之内。

必背词汇

1. climate [ˈklaɪmət] n. 气候
2. challenge [ˈtʃæləndʒ] n. 挑战
3. humanity [hjuːˈmænəti] n. 人类
4. drastic [ˈdræstɪk] a. 剧烈的；显著的
5. reduction [rɪˈdʌkʃn] n. 减少
6. carbon [ˈkɑːbən] n. 碳
7. emission [ɪˈmɪʃn] n. 排放；释放
8. vital [ˈvaɪtl] a. 关键的；重要的
9. avoid [əˈvɔɪd] v. 避免
10. catastrophe [kəˈtæstrəfi] n. 灾难
11. devastate [ˈdevəsteɪt] v. 破坏；毁灭
12. take the lead 带头；起模范作用
13. absorb [əbˈsɔːb] v. 吸收
14. no more than 不超过；仅仅
15. carbon dioxide 二氧化碳
16. rainfall [ˈreɪnfɔːl] n. 降雨；降水
17. tolerable [ˈtɒlərəbl] a. 可容忍的
18. household [ˈhaʊshəʊld] n. 家庭
19. appliance [əˈplaɪəns] n. (家用)电器；设备
20. handle [ˈhændl] v. 处理
21. essential [ɪˈsenʃl] a. 必要的；重要的
22. chaos [ˈkeɪɒs] n. 混乱
23. take responsibility 承担责任
24. comprehensive [ˌkɒmprɪˈhensɪv] a. 综合的；广泛的
25. one-stop a. 一站式的
26. reference [ˈrefrəns] n. 参考；参照
27. calculate [ˈkælkjʊleɪt] v. 计算
28. sustainable [səˈsteɪnəbl] a. 可持续的

难句解析

1. Climate change is the greatest challenge (facing humanity).

括号里的现在分词短语作 challenge 的后置定语。

2. Drastic reduction of carbon emissions is vital // if we are to avoid a catastrophe (that devastates large parts of the world).

"//" 将主句和条件状语从句隔开，括号里 that 引导的从句作 catastrophe 的后置定语。

3. Yet from cars and holiday flights to household appliances and the food on our plates, Western consumer lifestyles leave each of us *responsible for over 12 tons of carbon dioxide a year*—four times (what the Earth can handle).

下划线部分是一个介词短语：from...to...，意思是"从……到……"，作范围状语；斜体部分是一个形容词短语，作宾语 each of us 的补足语；最后括号里 what 引导的从句作 four times 的后置定语。

4. *How to Live a Low-Carbon Life* shows how easy it is to take responsibility, (providing the first

comprehensive, one-stop reference guide *to calculating your* CO_2 *emissions and reducing them to a sustainable 3 tons a year*).

下划线 how 引导的从句作 shows 的宾语，其中的 it 指代后面的不定式 to take responsibility；括号里现在分词短语作伴随状语，其中斜体部分是介词短语，作 guide 的后置定语。

经典短文 6

1　When I reached the age of twelve I left the school forever and got my first full-time job, as a grocer's boy. I spent my days carrying heavy loads, but I enjoyed it. It was only my capacity for hard work that saved me from early dismissal, for I could never stomach speaking to my "betters" with the deference my employer thought I should assume.

2　But the limit was reached one Tuesday—my half holiday. On my way home on that day I used to carry a large basket of provisions to the home of my employer's sister-in-law. As her house was on my way home I never objected to this.

3　On this particular Tuesday, however, just as we were putting the shutters up, a load of smoked hams was delivered at the shop. "Wait a minute," said the boss, and he opened the load and took out a ham, which he started to bone and string up.

1　我十二岁时永远地离开了学校，同时得到了第一份全职工作，给一家杂货店打工。我每天都要搬重物，不过干得倒也带劲。要不是我能干重活，早就被辞退了，因为老板要我毕恭毕敬地给那些上等人说话，这样干，我实在受不了。

2　但是某个星期二，到了我的忍耐极限——这是我歇半天的假日。那天在回家的路上，我又像往常一样替老板捎了一大篮子吃的东西给他嫂子送去。因为顺路，我也从没说过不乐意。

3　然而，就在这个特别的星期二，我们正要关门的时候，一大批熏火腿送到了店里。"等一下。"老板说，他打开包裹，拿出一只火腿，开始剔骨头，然后用绳子绑起来。

语篇分析

第一段讲述了"我"年纪很小就辍学，给一家杂货店打工。"我"不愿卑躬屈膝，但因为每天都干重活，才得以保住工作。

第二段讲述了某天"我"遇到一件不顺心的事，几乎到了"我"的忍耐极限。

第三段讲述了就在这个特别的日子，正当关门之时，一大批熏火腿送到了店里。然后老板开始收拾这批火腿。

必背词汇

1. grocer ['grəʊsə(r)] *n.* 杂货店
2. load [ləʊd] *n.* 货物;装载
3. capacity [kə'pæsəti] *n.* 能力
4. dismissal [dɪs'mɪsl] *n.* 开除;解散
5. stomach ['stʌmək] *v.* 容忍
6. deference ['defərəns] *n.* 恭敬;尊重
7. employer [ɪm'plɔɪə(r)] *n.* 老板;雇主
8. assume [ə'sjuːm] *v.* 承担;肩负
9. used to do sth. 过去常做某事
10. provision [prə'vɪʒn] *n.* 生活物品
11. sister-in-law 嫂子;弟媳;夫或妻的姐妹
12. objected to sth./sb. 反对某事/某人
13. particular [pə'tɪkjələ(r)] *a.* 特殊的;特定的
14. deliver [dɪ'lɪvə(r)] *v.* 运送
15. bone [bəʊn] *v.* 剔骨
16. string up 捆绑

难句解析

1. When I reached the age of twelve // I left the school forever and got my first full-time job, <u>as a grocer's boy</u>.

"//"将时间状语从句和主句分隔,下划线是一个介词短语,作方式状语。

2. <u>It was</u> only my capacity for hard work <u>that</u> saved me from early dismissal, // for I could never stomach speaking to my "betters" with the deference (that *my employer thought* I should assume).

"//"将主句和原因状语从句分隔,主句使用了 It was...that... 的强调句结构,强调的是句子主语;for 引导的原因状语从句中,括号里是省略了引导词 that 的从句,作 deference 的后置定语,斜体部分可看作是插入语。

3. <u>On my way home</u> on that day I used to carry a large basket of provisions to the home of my employer's sister-in-law.

下划线部分是一个介词短语,作方向状语。

4. "Wait a minute," <u>said the boss</u>, and he opened the load and took out a ham, (which he started to bone and string up).

下划线部分使用了倒装语序,自然语序是 the boss said。一般而言,如果引言在前面,都可以使用这种主谓倒装结构,但主语必须是名词,不能是代词。括号里 which 引导的从句作 ham 的定语。

第七章　英文写作

第一节　英文写作大纲解读与应试策略

（一）大纲要求和命题趋势

1. 大纲要求

考生应能根据所给的提纲、情景或要求完成相应的短文写作。短文应中心思想明确、切中题意、结构清晰、条理清楚、用词恰当、无明显语言错误。

该部分由 A、B 两节组成，主要考查考生的书面表达能力。共 2 题，25 分。

A 节

考生根据所给情景写出一篇约 100 词（标点符号不计算在内）的应用性短文，包括私人和公务信函、备忘录、报告等。共 10 分。

B 节

要求考生根据所给定的情景或给出的提纲，写出一篇约 150 词的英语说明文或议论文。提供情景的形式为图画、图表或文字。共 15 分。

2. 命题趋势

以下是 2010—2019 年英语（二）写作的考查类型：

2010—2019年考研英语（二）小作文考查类型

年份	考研英语（二）小作文主题	考查形式
2010	感谢＋邀请	书信

2011	祝贺 + 建议	书信
2012	投诉 + 要求	电子邮件
2013	通知 + 邀请	电子邮件
2014	告知 + 询问	电子邮件
2015	介绍 + 号召	通知
2016	感谢 + 建议	电子邮件
2017	感谢 + 介绍	书信
2018	道歉 + 建议	电子邮件
2019	建议 + 介绍	电子邮件

从上表中不难看出，英语（二）的小作文写作倾向于综合体，即考查内容要涉及考试指令（Directions）中所要求的两点，缺一不可，这也是阅卷过程中的一个重要采分点。因此，在应用性小作文写作准备阶段一定要兼顾各种形式，这样才能真正做到知己知彼、百战不殆。

2010—2019年考研英语（二）大作文考查类型

年份	考研英语（二）大作文主题	考查形式	图表类型
2010	发达国家与发展中国家手机用户数量的变化	柱状图	动态图表
2011	2008—2009年国产、日系、美系品牌汽车销售情况	柱状图	动态图表
2012	某公司员工工作满意度调查	表格	静态图表
2013	某高校学生大一到大四兼职情况	柱状图	静态图表
2014	20年间中国城镇人口、乡村人口变化图	柱状图	动态图表
2015	我国某市居民春节假期花销比例	饼状图	静态图表
2016	某高校学生旅行目的调查	饼状图	静态图表
2017	2013—2015年我国博物馆数量和参观人数	曲线图	动态图表
2018	2017年某市消费者选择餐厅时的关注因素	饼状图	静态图表
2019	某高校2013年和2018年本科毕业生去向统计	柱状图	动态图表

从上表中不难看出，英语（二）的大作文写作基本都是图表形式，大致分为四种：柱状图、饼状图、曲线图、表格。柱状图出现的频率最高，饼状图其次，曲线图和表格出现的频率较低。考生在备考阶段对这四种形式都要加强练习，可以适当侧重曲线图和表格。

（二）评分标准

小作文评分标准

档次分类	对应分值	评分要求（各档可酌情加减1分）
第五档	9~10分	使用丰富的语法结构和词汇；语言自然流畅，语法错误极少；有效地采用了多种衔接手法，内容连贯，层次清晰。
第四档	7~8分	使用较丰富的语法结构和词汇；语言基本准确，只有在试图使用较复杂结构或较高级词汇时才有个别错误；采用了恰当的衔接手法，层次清晰，组织较严密。
第三档	5~6分	有一些语法错误及词汇错误，但不影响理解；采用了简单的衔接手法，内容较连贯，层次较清晰。
第二档	3~4分	语法结构单调，词汇有限；有较多语法或词汇错误，影响了内容的理解；未采用恰当的衔接手法，内容缺乏连贯。
第一档	0~2分	语法结构和词汇单调、重复；语言错误多，有碍对内容的理解，语言运用能力差；未采用任何衔接手法，内容不连贯，缺乏组织，未分段。

大作文评分标准

档次分类	对应分值	评分要求（各档可酌情加减1分）
第五档	14~15分	使用丰富的语法结构和词汇；语言自然流畅，语法错误极少；有效地采用了多种衔接手法，内容连贯，层次清晰。
第四档	11~13分	使用较丰富的语法结构和词汇；语言基本准确，只有在试图使用较复杂结构或较高级词汇时才有个别错误；采用了适当的衔接手法，层次清晰，组织较严密。
第三档	8~10分	有一些语法错误及词汇错误，但不影响理解；采用了简单的衔接手法，内容较连贯，层次较清晰。
第二档	4~7分	语法结构单调，词汇有限；有较多语法或词汇错误，影响了内容的理解；未采用恰当的衔接手法，内容不连贯。
第一档	0~3分	语法结构和词汇单调、重复；语言错误多，有碍对内容的理解，语言运用能力差；未采用任何衔接手法，内容不连贯，缺乏组织，未分段。

（三）考查重点与应试策略

考研英语（二）小作文一般以书信居多，写作时要注意两点：

第一，严格按照书信的格式写作。阅卷老师最先注意到的就是格式，其次才通过阅读看内容是否符合要求。

第二，仔细审题。要抓住关键词，然后围绕场景和关键词进行扩展。

具体写作一般分为三段。第一段简单说明事由，第二段具体叙述内容，第三段根据题目要求可以提出建议、祝贺等，这样给人的印象是重点突出、条理清晰。

考研英语（二）大作文近几年都是图表类作文，要求描述、分析原因和总结建议。其实也是三段式，第一段简单描述图表内容，如果试卷提供的是英文注释，则可以摘抄，再写上一些语句加以丰富即可；如果提供的是汉语注释，则要翻译成对应的英文。第二段是原因分析，针对图表所描述的现象、问题等给出自己的观点和看法，基本可以归结为教育、人口、经济等方面。原因具体可以分为两类：宏观上主要表现为国家政策、经济发展、教育发展、收入提高、国家地位增强等；微观上主要表现与人们的日常生活相关的事，如人们意识提高（下降），空闲时间多了，精力、金钱多了，自己的偏好等。同时，一定要注意连接词的运用，这一点是非常关键的。诸如 At the top of the list，In addition，Last but not the least 等，复习时要注意多加积累和练习。第三段一般是展望、建议或提供解决方案，可以根据具体话题加以对应。

（四）复习备考指南

首先，写作不仅要多看，而且一定要花时间自己动手写作文。会写作文与真正答题是两回事。同时，练习时应该尽量按照正式考试的要求来做，无论是考试时间、写作字数、语言规范、卷面整洁度等。

从9月到12月，每周练习写两篇小作文、一篇大作文。语法应该尽可能正确，规避常见的语言表达失误，如句子成分残缺、主谓不一致、时态语态不正确、句子累赘等。词汇、句式尽可能多变，适当写几个长句。句子之间的衔接一定要用连接词，比如递进关系、因果关系、转折关系等。完成后放一下，第二天再自行修改，第三天做最后定稿，然后对比范文，看看哪里有欠缺，哪里需要完善。有意识地背诵并运用一些优美实用的模板句型，并尽量在练习过程中增加使用频率，达到熟能生巧的效果。

其次，鉴于近些年英语（二）作文平稳中有提升，对于小作文而言，综合型考点（如欢迎、建议等元素）有所增加。因此，自己在练习过程中要按照题目要求写，不要遗漏。

第三，考研英语（二）写作是语言考试而非思维考试，更多是针对内容评分。在考试评分中，语言第一位，结构第二位，内容第三位。所以阅卷更多关注的不是写作内容，而是语言表达，所以要注意优化自己的语言表达。

第二节 写作高分要素与谋篇布局原则

一、高分五要素

关于英语作文这个环节，很多考生觉得有话可说、能写够要求的字数即能拿到理想分数。这个认识非常片面。首先有必要了解考试的目的、考试评分要点等，才能做到有的放矢、心中有数，写起来也会相对轻松自如。

大体而言，考研作文就是语言考试。换句话说，重点不是考查分析判断和逻辑推理能力，而是重点针对语言表达本身进行评分。所以考生要关注的重心不是写作内容，而是语言表达。语言顺畅自如，内容相对空洞，分数不会太差，反之，内容较为庞杂，文章却词不达意，分数一般不会高。说得更加直白一些，礼品包装大于礼品内容。所以，应当考虑如何运用已有的语言知识和能力，提升表达的欣赏度和美感才是王道。

（一）语法正确

影响分数的一个重要因素是：错误，错误，错误。这里的错误包括多个方面，如拼写错误，语法错误，逻辑错误等；语法错误又包括主谓一致问题，单复数问题，时态问题等。

（二）拼写无误

拼写无误主要指单词方面。获取高分的基本要素就是不能出错，这就包括单词拼写环节。如果使用高级或复杂词汇，一定做到精确无误。如果拿不准，则退而求其次，宁可使用简单词汇，这样至少保证获得基本分数。

（三）书写工整

此外，字迹书写也是影响最后分数的重要因素。因为字迹如外表，颜值高一定会有吸引力。阅卷人在时间紧迫、高度紧张的状态下，看到字迹清晰整洁、书写漂亮的卷面，会顿时产生好感。即使你的作文其他方面有问题和缺陷，同情心也会影响阅卷人的给分心理。因此，从你看到这本书的一刻起，就着手练字吧。可以买一本字帖，每天坚持临摹，最后的改变会令人刮目相看的。

(四)语言流畅

语言流畅指的是语法层面准确无误,如保持主谓一致,分词短语与主句合理的逻辑关系,以及句间使用正确的连接词,等等。

这四个因素放在一起讲解是因为它们基本属于同一层面、密不可分。前两种都是基本且不可原谅的错误。有些考生过分专注于内容的充实和句子的美丽,或者套用很多大词难句,但忘了一个前提,错误的多少决定了你是否及格。边际成本和机会成本的产生是不必要的,你需要的是过关,拿高分冲难度往往会留下很多不可饶恕的错误。是要过关,还是要高分,这是进入考场前事先想好的,如果是二选一的话。分数高低伴随风险高低,这成正比。你的能力极限是什么,哪些难句和词语是超出自己能力范围的。最后,到底是要过关还是要高分,这是需要慎重思考的问题。

以下的每个语法标题下都提供了 a) 和 b) 两个例句,其中的 a) 都出现了语法错误,而 b) 句是正确的。通过对比分析,希望考生们能够在语法这个环节上有质的提高和进步。

1. 动词谓语的时态是否有错

【例句】

a) We college students had enough time to take a part-time job, no matter how busy we were.

b) We college students have enough time to take a part-time job, no matter how busy we are.

【解析】这里描述的是一般情况,所以动词时态应使用一般现在时,因此 a) 句错误。

【例句】

a) Riding bicycles had more advantages than taking a bus.

b) Riding bicycles has more advantages than taking a bus.

【解析】同理,这里描述的也是一般情况,所以动词时态应使用一般现在时,因此 a) 句错误;而且动名词短语作主语应作为单数看待,所以动词谓语用单数形式。

【例句】

a) There are so many countries using English that it had been regarded as an international language.

b) There are so many countries using English that it has been regarded as an international language.

【解析】这里描述的也是一般情况,所以动词时态应使用一般现在时,因此 a) 句错误。

2. 主语和谓语，名词和代词，以及人称是否保持一致

【例句】

a) The eating habit of Chinese people have changed in the past decade.

b) The eating habit of Chinese people has changed in the past decade.

【解析】这里主语是 The eating habit of Chinese people，一个名词短语，表示单数，所以动词谓语用单数形式，因此 a) 句错误。

【例句】

a) Now fruits and vegetables can be seen everywhere when it is in season.

b) Now fruits and vegetables can be seen everywhere when they are in season.

【解析】这里 when 从句的主语 it 指主句的主语 fruits and vegetables，应使用 they，谓语用 are，因此 a) 句错误。

【例句】

a) I feel proud to come to our university.

b) I feel proud to come to this university.

【解析】这里主语是 I，university 的修饰词应是对应的 my，或者 this 也可，因此 a) 句错误。

3. 修饰语是否放在正确的位置上

【例句】

a) Without television, people can't get information which comes from other parts of the world immediately.

b) Without television, people can't immediately get information which comes from other parts of the world.

【解析】一般而言，副词修饰动词或形容词时应尽可能挨近后者。这里 immediately 本是修饰 get，应紧贴该词，所以 b) 句正确。a) 句中 immediately 置于句尾，可能被误解为修饰距离更近的 comes，因此 a) 句错误。

【例句】

a) At the age of six, my father began to give me English lessons.

b) When I was five years old, my father began to give me English lessons.

【解析】这里主语是 My father，a) 句句首的 At the age of six 逻辑上是修饰主语的，这是明显的语病，因此 a) 句错误。

329

【例句】

a) To improve one's writing skill, regular practice is necessary.

b) To improve one's writing skill, one must make regular practice.

【解析】a) 句主语是 regular practice，而不定式 To improve one's writing skill 的逻辑主语应该是人，因此 a) 句错误。

4. 表示相同的意思，是否用了平行语法结构

【例句】

a) With the computer, one can do shopping, banking and read at home.

b) With the computer, one can do shopping, banking and reading at home.

【解析】a) 句中 shopping，banking and read 应该是平行并列关系，read 应改为 reading，因此 a) 句错误。

【例句】

a) Nowadays, people not only eat enough food, but also eat better.

b) Nowadays, people not only eat more, but also eat better.

【解析】a) 句中的 not only...but also 是平行并列关系，前后内容应该结构等同。enough food 是名词短语，而 eat better 是动词短语，因此 a) 句错误。

【例句】

a) Participating in sports is good for our physical health, and through it we can also train our character.

b) Participating in sports is good for our physical health, and it is also beneficial to our character-training.

【解析】a) 句中的 and 表并列关系，前后内容应该结构等同。前面是主系表结构：Participating in sports is good for our physical health，而后面是动宾结构：train our character，因此 a) 句错误。

5. 用代词时，指代是否清楚

【例句】

a) Sometimes teachers will inform students of the heavy burden they have to bear.

b) Sometimes a teacher will inform students of the heavy burden he has to bear.

【解析】a) 句中的代词 they 可以指代 teachers，也可以指代 students，会造成歧义，因此 a)

句错误，而 b) 句的 he 只能指代 a teacher，所以很明确。

【例句】

a) Someone believes that the teacher's task is to give students knowledge, which may not be true.

b) Someone believes that the teacher's task is to give students knowledge, a notion which may not be true.

【解析】a) 句中的关系代词 which 可以指代 knowledge，也可以指代前面整句话，会造成歧义，因此 a) 句错误，而 b) 句添加了 a notion，which 就只能明确指代 a notion，意思明确清晰。

【例句】

a) People have been fighting against the influence of TV commercials, but it often proves useless.

b) People have been fighting against the influence of TV commercials, but the effort often proves useless.

【解析】a) 句中的代词 it 可以指代 the influence，也可以指代前面整句话，会造成歧义，因此 a) 句错误，而 b) 句将 it 改成 the effort，则 the effort 只能指代前面一句话，意思明确清晰。

6. 相邻的句子，是否避免了不必要的结构转变

【例句】

a) While we reduce the number of vehicles, the speed of traffic can be increased.

b) While the number of vehicles is reduced, the speed of traffic is increased.

【解析】a) 句中 While 从句和主句的主语分别是 we 和 the speed，显得没有关联性和逻辑性；而 b) 句中的 the number 和 the speed 则表明了类似主题。

【例句】

a) Each of us may take a part-time job to help support ourselves, but if you spend too much time on it, your study will be affected.

b) Each of us may take a part-time job to help support ourselves, but if too much time spent on it, our studies will be affected.

【解析】a) 句中的 each of us、you 和 your 论述的不是同一对象，逻辑混乱；而 b) 句中的 each of us 和 our 则指明了同一对象，逻辑清晰。

331

7. 可数名词与不可数名词是否用得正确

【例句】

a) TV presents us with many useful informations.

b) TV presents us with a lot of useful information.

【解析】information 是不可数名词，a) 句中用错了 many 和 informations；b) 句中的 a lot of 既可修饰不可数名词，也可修饰可数名词的复数形式。

【例句】

a) Making our cities greener is not an easy work.

b) Making our cities greener is not an easy job.

【解析】a) 句中的 work 是不可数名词，不能用 an/a 来修饰；b) 句中的 job 是可数名词，因此 b) 句正确。

【例句】

a) Each people has his own opportunities.

b) Each person has his own opportunities.

【解析】a) 句中的 people 是复数形式，不能用 each 来修饰；b) 句中的 person 是单数形式，因此 b) 正确。

8. 冠词是否用得正确

【例句】

a) Book knowledge is important, but we should also learn something in the society.

b) Book knowledge is important, but we should also learn something in society.

【解析】society 意思是"社会"，如果加 the 则表示"社团、协会"，因此 a) 句错误。

【例句】

a) If there were no electric power, we would have to do everything by the hands.

b) If there were no electric power, we would have to do everything by hand.

【解析】by hand 是固定搭配，表示"用手"，因此 b) 句正确。

【例句】

a) If there were no electric power, factory would stop producing goods, car, bus and train would stop running.

b) If there were no electric power, factories would stop producing goods; cars, buses and trains would stop running.

【解析】factory，car，bus 和 train 都是可数名词，使用时前面要加冠词或定冠词，或者采用复数形式，因此 b) 句正确。

9. 句子的主谓宾是否齐全

【例句】

a) TV now plays an important role in our daily life. Because we cannot live without it.

b) TV now plays an important role in our daily life, because we cannot live without it.

【解析】一般而言，状语从句和主句之间可以不加标点，也可用逗号间隔，但不能用句号，因此 b) 句正确。

【例句】

a) There are many ways to contact with society. For example, joining clubs, taking part-time jobs and helping the poor.

b) There are many ways to contact with society, for example, joining clubs, taking part-time jobs and helping the poor.

【解析】一般而言，插入语和主干之间要用双逗号间隔，但不能用句号，因此 b) 句正确。

【例句】

a) If no electricity, all activities such as watching TV and seeing movies will be impossible.

b) If there is no electricity, all activities such as watching TV and seeing movies will be impossible.

【解析】状语从句也是句子，因此要有完整的语言成分，比如主谓宾或主系表。a) 句中 If 从句不是成分完整的句子，因此是错句。

10. 过渡词是否用得合适

【例句】

a) Because some college graduates could not find a better job, so they decided to continue to read for a second degree.

b) As some college graduates could not find a better job, they decided to continue to read for a second degree.

【解析】一般而言，两个单句中间只需要一个连词进行连接，a) 句中的 Because 和 so 功能重叠，因此是错句，去掉其中一个即可，或者改写成 b) 句也可。

【例句】

a) Although an opportunity is rare, but we must be ready to seize it.

b) Although an opportunity is rare, we must be ready to seize it.

【解析】同理，a) 句中的 Although 和 but 功能重叠，因此是错句，去掉其中一个即可。

11. 词语的搭配是否正确

【例句】

a) We students should learn/study as much knowledge as possible.

b) We students should acquire/obtain as much knowledge as possible.

【解析】knowledge 搭配的动词不能用 learn 或 study，这与汉语思维有所冲突，因此 a) 句是错句；可用 b) 句中的 acquire 或 obtain。

【例句】

a) With a rise in the number of cars and buses, traffic in Shanghai has become more and more crowded.

b) With a rise in the number of cars and buses, traffic in Shanghai has become increasingly heavier.

【解析】traffic 的修饰词不能用 crowded，这与汉语思维有所冲突，因此 a) 句是错句；可用 heavy 来修饰，因此 b) 句正确。

【例句】

a) People begin to eat more vice food.

b) People begin to eat more non-staple foodstuffs.

【解析】汉语的"副食"对应的是 non-staple foodstuffs，a) 句中的 vice 表示"副职的"，因此 b) 句正确。

12. 词语是否用得得当

【例句】

a) Actually, traffic jams have effected our daily life.

b) Actually, traffic jams have affected our daily life.

【解析】effect 通常作名词使用，而 affect 通常作动词，因此 b) 句正确。

【例句】

a) When old problems are solved, new problems will rise.

b) When old problems are solved, new problems will arise.

【解析】rise 意思是"升起，上升"，而 arise 意思是"出现，发生"，problem 的搭配应该是 arise，因此 b) 句正确。

【例句】

a) There are many factors leading to changes in people's diet. At first, people can afford expensive food.

b) There are many factors leading to changes in people's diet. First, people can afford expensive food.

【解析】At first 通常表时间概念"最初"，而 First 则表顺序关系"首先"，因此 b) 句正确。

13. 是否重复使用了表示相同意思的词语

【例句】

a) In my opinion, I believe the present educational system is in need of reform.

b) In my opinion, the present education system is in need of reform.

【解析】a) 句中的 In my opinion 和 I believe 属于重复表达，去掉其中一个即可。

【例句】

a) The reason why people choose to live in the country is because there is no pollution nor noise there.

b) The reason why people choose to live in the country is that there is no pollution nor noise there.

【解析】reason 后面一般不能接 because，而要用 that，因此 b) 句正确。

【例句】

a) People try to find a solution to solve the problem.

b) People try to find a solution to the problem.

【解析】solution 后面的 to 是介词，要接名词形式，不是不定式中的 to，因此 a) 句错误。

14. 介词 / 副词是否用得正确

【例句】

a) After four years, we all graduated from college and entered society.

b) Four years later, we all graduated from college and entered society.

【解析】这里描述的是过去情形，而 After 一般和将来有关，later 则用于描述过去的场景，因此 b) 句正确。

【例句】

a) Many college students have a strong desire to be independent on their parents.

b) Many college students have a strong desire to be independent of their parents.

【解析】independent 搭配的介词是 of 而不是 on，dependent 才与 on 搭配，因此 b) 句正确。

15. 词性是否用得正确

【例句】

a) The computer like TV, it has both advantages and disadvantages.

b) Like TV, the computer has both advantages and disadvantages.

【解析】like TV 在这里是插入语，在句子中间时使用双逗号间隔，或置于句首时用一个逗号，而且 like 做介词使用，a) 句中直接和 The computer 连接，like 则表"喜欢"的意思，因此 a) 句错误。

【例句】

a) Obviously, our country would stop develop if no electricity.

b) Obviously, our country would stop developing if there were no electricity.

【解析】stop 做动词后接的内容要用不定式或动名词形式，因此 b) 句正确。

【例句】

a) Riding bicycles conveniences my work.

b) Riding bicycles is convenient to my work.

【解析】convenience 一般不做动词使用，因此 a) 句错误，b) 句采用了形容词用法是可以的。

16. 句子是否有明确的主语

【例句】

a) Unlike the movie, TV shows on continuously, and doesn't need to pay extra money.

b) Unlike the movie, TV shows on continuously, and one doesn't need to pay extra money.

【解析】a) 句中 doesn't need to pay extra money 的主语是 TV，逻辑不通；而 b) 句中加了 one，则符合逻辑。

【例句】

a) Too easy or too difficult is no good for us.

b) The books which are too easy or too difficult are no good for us.

【解析】easy 和 difficult 都是形容词，而形容词不能做主语，因此 a) 句错误。

【例句】

a) Reading books can acquire knowledge.

b) Through reading one can acquire knowledge.

【解析】a) 句的主语是动名词短语 Reading books，和谓语及宾语 can acquire knowledge 逻辑不通；而 b) 句中的主语是 one，符合常规逻辑。

17. 一个句子是否确保只有一个动词

【例句】

a) People think go to the movies will cost a lot of money.

b) People think that going to the movies will cost them a lot of money.

【解析】一般而言，一个单句只能有一个动词谓语，a) 句中出现了 think 和 cost 两个动词，语法上是错误的；b) 句中包含了一个 that 宾语从句，think 属于主句的动词，而 cost 则属于从句的动词，语法合乎要求。

【例句】

a) There are many people take part in sports and games now.

b) Many people take part in sports and games now.

【解析】a) 句中出现了 are 和 take part in 两个动词（短语），语法上是错误的；b) 句中只包含 take part in 一个动词短语，语法合乎要求。

【例句】

a) Although difficulty is exist, but we can overcome it.

b) Although difficulty does exist, we can overcome it.

【解析】a) 句中出现了 is 和 exist 两个动词，语法上是错误的；b) 句中 does 是助动词，是为了强调 exist 而加的，语法合乎要求。

（五）逻辑严密

最后再谈谈逻辑表达。在尽力做好以上环节的同时，可以培养逻辑思维的拓展能力。要做到这一点，可以通过大量阅读英文杂志或期刊上的文章或考研历年真题中的阅读文章来加以提高，尤其是对评论性文章多加重视，因为其中的论点提出、论据补充、结论归纳等环节都值得借鉴并灵活运用。

此外，汉语被称为意合语，也可理解为平行语，即构成一句话的各个部分呈平行排列，没有主次之分，形似竹子结构，句子之间一般没有连词，句间逻辑主要是一种意会和内含关系；英语则是形合语，或称层次语，即一句话的各个组成部分有主次之分，呈树形排列。句间关系主要是通过连词来实现的，比如并列关系、因果关系、递进关系、转折关系等。下面用一个例句加以说明。

【例句】海内存知己，天涯若比邻。

If /As you have a friend who knows your heart, distance can not take you two apart.

汉语的两个单句表面看是并列关系。但经过仔细阅读和理解，实际两者之间存在着条件——结果或原因——结果的逻辑关系，因此在译成英文时必须添加连词，即 if 或 as。当然 As 也可以用 because 替代。

以下是英文写作表示起承转合以及其他逻辑关系的常见关联词或短语，希望大家熟用牢记。

起：In general / Generally speaking / On the whole。

承：Moreover / Also / Furthermore / Meanwhile / What is more。

转：Nevertheless / However / On the other hand / Unfortunately。

合：As a result / Consequently / Thus / Therefore / Hence / In brief / In conclusion。

列举常用的表达方法有：first, second, in the first place, first of all, to begin with, in the second place, next, also, besides, furthermore, moreover, in addition, what is more, beyond that, for one thing, for another, finally。

举例常用的表达方法有：for example, for instance, as an example, as a case in point, as an illustration, such as, namely, that is, like, say。

原因与结果常用的表达方法有：because, because of, as, since, for, owing to, due to, on account of, on the ground of, as a result of, thus, so, consequently, hence, therefore, accordingly, as a result, for this reason, as a consequence, on that account, it follows that 等。

对比或比较常用的表达方法有：similarly, likewise, in the same way, equally important, like, both, the same as, in common, on the contrary, on the other hand, otherwise, unlike, in contrast, whereas, rather than, conversely, instead, by contrast 等。

二、谋篇五原则

（一）以读带写原则

这个原则上面提到过。就是通过阅读英文杂志或期刊上登载的文章，或者考研历年真题中的阅读文章来提升分析和批判能力。要进行定量要求，比如每天阅读两篇文章。而且关注重点不仅是作者如何遣词造句，而且是如何进行逻辑延展、归纳总结等，而文章后面的题目分析则不是重点。

（二）短语优先原则

使用英文写作时，非母语者较多使用单词而非短语。究其原因大致有两点：一是单词记忆得相对牢靠，用起来有把握；二是短语平时积累得较少，在时间紧迫、心理紧张的前提下无法有效地调动使用资源。但是，建议大家在写作时有意识地多尝试使用名词短语、动词短语、介词短语等，这样既能起到独树一帜的效果，也能适当增加作文的字数，一箭双雕，何乐而不为呢？在平时阅读时，可以把文中出现的短语尽量全部记录下来，并加大记忆的频率和重复率，日积月累，最后就会起到事半功倍的效果。以下列举了一些单词以及与之对应的短语表达，通过比较加强记忆。

【例】

know/realize → be aware of/be conscious of 知道，意识到

expect → look forward to 期望

bear/tolerate → put up with 忍受

dislike → be fed up with 不喜欢，讨厌，厌倦

（三）词汇替换原则

词汇替换也是提高写作的一大利器。在用词方面，相对而言，汉语多重复，英语多变化。汉语通过重复来加以突出强调，英语则通过变化来实现色彩多姿。语言的变化是高分的重要条件。英语讲究变化，如"满意"这个词可以用 satisfied，content，be happy with 等。用词用句的难易不是关键，重要的是变化。这一点是大多以语言为主的考试中比较看重的。从西方人的日常着装也可看出变化的基本特点。在西方人的衣柜中，男士至少拥有多件颜色、款式各异的衬

衫和领带，而女士则拥有不同风格样式的裙子。在记忆单词时，可以有意识地把意思相近的词归纳到一起进行整体记忆，可以适当忽略词义的细微差别。

词汇替换大致分为五类：代词、同义词、上义词、下义词和统称词。上义词是对事物的概括性、抽象性说明；下义词是事物的具体表现形式，或更为具体的说明。例如动物和鸟，其中，动物是上义词，而鸟是下义词。所谓下义关系，亦称种属关系，就是指几个单词的词义属于另一个词的词义范畴。现以 color 为例，其下义词有：white、black、red、green、yellow、blue、brown、orange、gray 等；又如 subject 的下义词有：maths、physics、chemistry、politics、Chinese、biology 等。统称词就是具有同类特点的词概括起来的最大称谓。比如 man，woman，sheep 的统称词就是 creature。下面通过实例来具体解释以上的理论原则。

例句

①在科技界、医学界和体育界，存在同样的情况，这种情况相当糟糕。这种情况一直到九十年代初才有所改变。

【译文】A similar story has been told in science, medicine and sports circles. The situation was so grim. It didn't change much until the early 1990.

【解析】汉语句子重复使用"情况"一词，而英文译文却使用了 story 和 situation 两个同义词，以及代词 it 的不同表达。

②人们常把闯红灯看成小错，不当一回事，然而闯红灯一旦形成习惯，则问题远非是违反交通规则。

【译文】Red-light running has always been regarded as a minor wrong, and so it has never been taken seriously. When the violation becomes habitual, however, a great deal more than a traffic problem is involved.

【解析】汉语句子重复使用"闯红灯"一词，而英文译文使用了 Red-light running 及其上义词 the violation 两个不同的表达。

③I turned to the ascent to the peak—it/the climb/the task/the thing is very easy.

【译文】我走向通往顶峰之路——攀登还是很轻松的。

【解析】该句中的 it，the climb，the task，the thing 均是 the ascent 的替换表达，分别使用了

代词、同义词、上义词和统称词的方法。

④The telephone rang; he returned to reach for it/the instrument/the thing.

【译文】 电话响了,他转身去拿电话。

【解析】该句中的 it,the instrument,the thing 均是 the telephone 的替换表达,分别使用了代词、上义词和统称词的方法。

⑤When reports came into London Zoo that a wild puma had been spotted forty-five miles south of London, they were not taken seriously. However, as the evidence began to accumulate, experts from the Zoo felt obliged to investigate, for the descriptions given by people who claimed to have seen the puma were extraordinarily similar.

【译文】 伦敦动物园接到了报告,报告称伦敦以南45英里发现了一只野生美洲狮,但这一消息并未受到重视。然而,随着证据越来越多,动物园的专家们感到有必要开展调查,因为声称见过该狮子的人们所描述的内容非常相似。

【解析】该段中的 reports,they,the evidence,the descriptions 均表同一个意思;spotted 和 seen 也属于替换形式。

⑥Anthropologists wondered where the remote ancestors of the Polynesian peoples now living in the Pacific Islands came from. The sagas of these people explain that some of them came from Indonesia about 2,000 years ago.

But the first people who were like ourselves lived so long ago that even their sagas are forgotten. So archaeologists have neither history nor legends to help them to find out where the first "modern men" came from. Fortunately, however, ancient men made tools of stone, especially flint.

【译文】 人类学家们想知道现在居住在太平洋诸岛的波利尼西亚民族的古老祖先来自何方。这些民族的英雄故事解释了其中一些人大约2 000年前来自印度尼西亚。

但是,与现代人相像的最早人类生活的时代太久远,即使有英雄故事也都被人遗忘了。因此,考古学家既没有历史也没有传奇来了解最早的现代人来自何方。然而,幸运的是,古人制造石器,尤其是用燧石制造工具。

【解析】这两段中画线部分的名词短语都属于替换表达。

⑦As is often pointed out, television <u>keeps one better informed about the current events</u>, <u>allows one to follow the latest developments</u> in politics and science, and offers endless series of programs which are both instructive and stimulating. The most distant countries, the strangest customs and attractive scenes of nature are brought right into one's room. Yet here again, there is danger. The main problem with TV has been its <u>negative</u> effect on people in general. For example, <u>rubbishy</u> commercials and <u>harmful</u> programs contribute to the rise in violence and crime in the streets.

【译文】 人们常说，看电视可以了解时事、了解政治和科学的最新动态；电视还提供了既有教育意义、又让人刺激的系列节目。最遥远的国度、最奇特的风俗和大自然的美景都可以在室内欣赏。然而这里也隐藏着危险。电视的主要问题是对大众产生的负面影响。比如，垃圾广告和不良节目会导致街头暴力和犯罪的增加。

【解析】该段中的 keeps one better informed about the current events 和 allows one to follow the latest developments 属于替换关系；negative，rubbishy，harmful 也属于不同的替换表达。

下面给大家总结了一些常见的替换表达：

如要表示"使"，不要仅依靠 make：

【例句】

a) This society still makes women unable to enjoy equal rights.

b) Women are still denied equal rights.

【解析】b) 句中的 are denied 表"使失去"，比 a) 句中的 makes...unable to 更地道简练。

【例句】

a) The incident made me recall one of my past experiences.

b) The incident reminded me of one of my past experiences.

【解析】b) 句中的 reminded me of 表"使我想起"，比 a) 句中的 made me recall 更地道规范。

如要表达"越来越……"，不要只使用 more and more：

【例句】

a) More and more students find learning English has become more and more difficult.

b) Students in growing numbers find learning English has become increasingly difficult.

【解析】b) 句中的 in growing numbers 表"越来越多"，比 a) 句中的 more and more 更高雅正式。

【例句】

a) More and more teenagers smoke cigarettes in recent years.

b) Teenage smoking is on the rise in recent years.

【解析】b) 句中的 on the rise 表"越来越多",比 a) 句中的 more and more 更高雅正式。

【例句】

a) More and more teachers are demanded with the development of economy.

b) There is an increasing demand for teachers with the development of economy.

【解析】b) 句中的 an increasing demand 表"越来越多",比 a) 句中的 more and more 更高雅正式。

如要表达"大多数",不要一味用 most:

【例句】

a) Most students take a part-time job after class.

b) The vast majority of students take a part-time job after class.

【解析】b) 句中的 The vast majority of 表"大多数",比 a) 句中的 Most 更正式高级。

【例句】

a) Most people take part in sports of different kinds.

b) The considerable proportion of people take part in sports of different kinds.

【解析】b) 句中的 The considerable proportion of 表"大多数",比 a) 句中的 Most 更正式高级。

【例句】

a) Most college students take a negative attitude towards smoking.

b) The large percentage of college population take a negative attitude towards smoking.

【解析】b) 句中的 The large percentage of 表"大多数",比 a) 句中的 Most 更正式高级。

如要表达"不仅……而且……",不要只用 not only...but also...。

【例句】

a) The factors for a rise in teenage smoking are not only social but also psychological.

b) The factors for a rise in teenage smoking are psychological as well as social.

【解析】一说到"不仅……,而且……",多数人脑海里浮现的就是 not only...but also...,但 b) 句中的 as well as 明显给人眼前一亮的感觉。

【例句】

a) Taking a part-time job can not only earn a little money, but also have an opportunity to contact with society.

b) Taking a part-time job means more than a little money you can earn. It also means an opportunity to contact with society.

【解析】b) 句中的 also 也有"而且"的含义，并且富有新意。

【例句】

a) Old people go to park not only to do exercise but also to make friends.

b) Old people go to park as much for companionship as for exercise.

【解析】b) 句中的 as much...as 表"和……一样"，包含了"不仅……而且"之意。

（四）层次句原则

刚才谈到，汉语被称为意合语，也可理解为平行语，即构成一句话的各个部分呈平行排列，没有主次之分，形似竹子结构；英语则是形合语，或称层次语，即一句话的各个组成部分有主次之分，呈树形排列。

【例1】孔乙己着了慌，伸开五指将碟子罩住，弯腰下去说道："不多了，我已经不多了。"

【中式思维】Kong Yiji grew flushed, stretched his fingers, covered the dish, bent forward from his waist, and would say: "There aren't many left, not many at all."

从汉语结构看，该句的五个动词（画线部分）是平行关系，即 $S+V_1+V_2+V_3+V_4+V_5$，但译成英文时，则必须分出主次，可以灵活处理。

【改进版本】Kong Yiji grew flushed, covering the dish with his hand, bending forward from his waist, and would say, "There aren't many left, not many at all."

【解析】英文结构转化为 $S + V_1 +Ving+Ving+ V_4$，强化了"着了慌""说道"两个动作，淡化了"罩住""弯腰"两个行为，省掉"伸开"，主次分明，重点突出。了解了英汉之间的这种本质差别，对于突破英语写作是很有帮助的。

【例2】他一看表，才一点钟，可是那钟一连敲了13下才停。

【中式思维】He looked at his watch, and it was one o'clock, but the bell struck thirteen times and then it stopped.

【改进版本】Looking at his watch, it was one o'clock, but the bell struck thirteen times before it stopped.

【解析】按照中式思维写成的句子称为流水账句，没有主次之分；而改进版本将"看"写成现在分词形式，将"13下才停"写成时间状语从句，突出了"才一点钟"和"敲"两个动作，整个句子显得主次分明，层次有致。

【例3】我在地毯上跳过来蹦过去，扭曲身子，摆出各种姿势，弄得浑身不舒服，然后坐到桌边吃早饭，看上去一副筋疲力尽的样子。

【中式思维】I jumped about on the carpet, twisted, made various poses, and felt very uncomfortable. Then I sat down, had my breakfast and felt very exhausted.

【改进版本】After jumping about on the carpet and twisting the human frame into uncomfortable positions, I sat down at the breakfast table in an exhausted condition.

【解析】该句原理如同上句。按照中式思维写成的句子中几个动词并列出现，没有主次之分；而改进版本将"跳""扭曲"和"看上去一副筋疲力尽的样子"均写成介词短语形式，从而突出强调了"坐到"这个动作，整个句子显得主次分明，层次有致。

（五）长短句原则

这是相对高级的一条写作原则，涉及形式美观、结构对称等方面。下面这段文字选自《新概念英语》第三册，其中包括四句话，分别以 a)、b)、c)、d) 表示。通过观察可以看出，a) 句较短，b) 句较长，c) 句较短，d) 句较长，整段文字排列工整，结构对称，给读者带来赏心悦目的形式美和视觉美。

a) Antique shops exert a peculiar fascination on a great many people. b) The more expensive kind of antique shop where rare objects are beautifully displayed in glass cases to keep them free from dust is usually a forbidding place. c) But no one has to muster up courage to enter a less pretentious antique shop. d) There is always hope that in its labyrinth of musty, dark, disordered rooms a real rarity will be found amongst the piles of assorted junk that litter the floors.

以下两段文字同样选自《新概念英语》第三册，也运用了类似的长短句排列技巧。

a) The river which forms the eastern boundary of our farm has always played an important part in our lives. b) Without it, we could not make a living. c) There is only enough spring water to supply the needs of the house, so we have to pump from the river for farm use. d) We tell the river all our secrets. e) We know instinctively, just as beekeepers with their bees, that misfortune might overtake us if the important events of our lives were not related to it.

a) We often read in novels how a seemingly respectable person or family has some terrible secret which has been concealed from strangers for years. b) The English language possesses a vivid saying to describe this sort of situation. c) The terrible secret is called "a skeleton in the cupboard". d) At some dramatic moment in the story the terrible secret becomes known and a reputation is ruined. e) The reader's hair stands on end when he reads in the final pages of the novel that the heroine, a dear old lady who had always been so kind to everybody, had, in her youth, poisoned every one of her five husbands.

第三节 应用文（小作文）高分指南

一、考查题型

上面谈到，最新大纲对小作文的要求是：应用性短文，包括私人和公务信函、备忘录、报告等。纵观历年真题，考查内容基本集中在这样一些类型：推荐信、申请信、请求信、求职信、邀请信、感谢信、祝贺信、建议信、投诉信、道歉信、辞职信、介绍信、询问信、通知等，或其中两种的组合。以下是 2010—2017 年英语（二）小作文题目，可以从中看到考查的基本内容和大致规律。

2010 年小作文（感谢＋邀请）：

You have just come back from the U.S. as a member of a Sino-American cultural exchange program. Write a letter to your American colleague to

1) express your thanks for his/her warm reception;

2) welcome him/her to visit China in due course.

You should write about 100 words on ANSWER SHEET 2.

Do not sign your own name at the end of the letter. Use "Zhang Wei" instead.

Do not write your address. (10 points)

2011 年小作文（祝贺＋建议）：

Suppose your cousin Li Ming has just been admitted to a university. Write him/her a letter to

1) congratulate him/her, and

2) give him/her suggestions on how to get prepared for university life.

You should write about 100 words on ANSWER SHEET 2.

Do not sign your own name at the end of the letter. Use "Zhang Wei" instead.

Do not write the address. (10 points)

2012 年小作文（投诉＋要求）：

Suppose you have found something wrong with the electronic dictionary that you bought from an online store the other day. Write an email to the customer service center to

1) make a complaint, and

2) demand a prompt solution.

You should write about 100 words on ANSWER SHEET 2.

Do not sign your own name at the end of the letter. Use "Zhang Wei" instead.

Do not write the address. (10 points)

2013 年小作文（通知 + 邀请）：

Suppose your class is to hold a charity sale for kids in need of help. Write your classmates an email to

1) inform them about the details, and

2) encourage them to participate.

You should write about 100 words on the ANSWER SHEET.

Do not use your own name. Use "Li Ming" instead.

Do not write your address. (10 points)

2014 年小作文（告知 + 询问）：

Suppose you are going to study abroad and share an apartment with John, a local student. Write him an email to

1) tell him about your living habits, and

2) ask for advice about living there.

You should write about 100 words on the ANSWER SHEET.

Do not use your own name. Use "Li Ming" instead.

Do not write your address. (10 points)

2015 年小作文（介绍 + 号召）：

Suppose your university is going to host a summer camp for high school students. Write a notice to

1) briefly introduce the camp activities, and

2) call for volunteers.

You should write about 100 words on the ANSWER SHEET.

Do not use your own name. Use "Li Ming" instead.

Do not write your address. (10 points)

2016 年小作文（感谢 + 建议）：

Suppose you won a translation contest and your friend, Jack, wrote an email to congratulate you and ask for advice on translation. Write him a reply to

1) thank him, and

2) give your advice.

You should write about 100 words on the ANSWER SHEET.

Do not use your own name. Use "Li Ming" instead.

Do not write your address. (10 points)

2017 年小作文（感谢 + 介绍）：

Suppose you are invited by Professor Williams to give a presentation about Chinese culture to a group of international students. Write a reply to

1) accept the invitation, and

2) introduce the key points of your presentation.

You should write about 100 words on the ANSWER SHEET.

Do not use your own name. Use "Li Ming" instead.

Do not write your address. (10 points)

二、文体格式

小作文通常是书信形式，所以一定要按照书信的格式进行写作。阅卷人最先注意到的就是格式，其次才通过阅读看看内容是否符合要求。不注意格式，肯定被扣分。下面列举了格式中比较重要的几个部分。

（一）称呼

该部分所有实词首字母全部大写，而且后面要用逗号，不能写成冒号，如 Dear Professor，Dear Smith，To Whom It May Concern 等。

（二）正文

正文一般分两段或三段。每段开头可顶格，也可空四个字母。顶格的话每段空一行。

（三）署名

一般用 Yours truly，Truly yours，Yours sincerely 或 Sincerely yours，表达尊敬时用 Yours respectfully 或 Respectfully yours，写在正文下面的最右端或最左端。注意第一个单词的首字母要大写，第二个单词首字母不大写，末尾用逗号。署名另起一行，写在 Yours truly 等的下方即可，不需加标点。一般用 Li Ming 或 Zhang Wei，或按照考试的要求署名，切记不能写自己的真名。

书信格式的展示样本：

Dear _____,

　　..........................

　　..........................

Yours sincerely,
XXX

备忘录格式的展示样本：

Date:

From:

To:

Subject:

　　..........................

　　..........................

报告格式的展示样本：

Report on _____

　　..........................

　　..........................

　　其内容一般包括：(1) Title（标题）；(2) Introduction（介绍）；(3) Method（方法）；(4) Result（结果）；(5) Discussion（讨论）；(6) Conclusion（结论）。

通知格式的展示样本：

NOTICE

　　..........................

　　..........................

XXX（人名/机构名）
XXXX（日期）

三、经典模板

（一）投诉信

Dear _____,

　　I am _____ (写信人身份). I venture to write you a letter about _____ (投诉内容).

　　The focus of the complaint is _____ (投诉内容的核心). For one thing, _____ (投诉内容的一个方面). For another, _____ (投诉内容的另一方面). Honestly speaking, _____ (客观的评价). But _____ (抱怨产生的原因).

　　All in all, there is much room for improvement. Before I take any further action, I do hope _____ (表达本人的愿望). Thank you for your time and kind consideration.

Yours sincerely,
Li Ming

（二）求职信

Dear Sir/Madam,

　　I write this letter to apply for the position that you have advertised in _____ (报纸/杂志名称) of _____ (广告发布时间).

　　Not only do I have the qualifications for this job, but I also have the right personality for a _____ (工作名称). On the one hand, _____ (第一个原因). On the other, _____ (另一个原因).

　　Should you grant me a personal interview, I would be most grateful. If you need to know more about me, please feel free to contact me at any time at _____ (电话号码).

　　Thank you for considering my application, and I am looking forward to your early reply.

Yours sincerely,
Li Ming

（三）建议信

Dear _____,

You have asked me for my advice with regard to _____ (咨询的内容), and I will try to make some feasible suggestions here.

In my humble opinion, you would be wise to take the following actions: _____ (建议的内容).

I hope you will find these proposals useful, and I would be ready to discuss this matter with you in further detail.

Yours sincerely,
Li Ming

（四）请求信

Dear _____,

I am writing to formally request to _____ (请求的内容).

The reasons for my urgent need are as follows: 1) _____; 2) _____; 3) _____ (陈述请求的原因).

Therefore, I will be much obliged if you can help me _____ (对收信人的期望). Please feel free to contact me at any time at _____ (电话号码).

Thank you for your time and patience, and I am looking forward to your prompt reply.

Yours respectfully,
Li Ming

（五）邀请信

Dear _____,

There will be a(n) _____ (内容) at/in _____ (地点) on _____ (时间). We would be honored to have you there with us.

The occasion will start at _____ (具体时间). This will be followed by a _____ (进一

步的安排). At around _____ (时间), _____ (另一个安排).

I really hope you can make it. RSVP before _____ (你要求的最后期限).

Yours respectfully,
Li Ming

(六) 道歉信

Dear _____,

I am writing this letter to apologize to you for my failing to _____ (直接说出道歉理由).

The reason is that _____ (过失的原因). I am sorry for any inconvenience caused, but is it possible that it makes up the loss by _____ (补救措施)? If so, I will put everything else aside to _____ (表决心).

I do hope you can understand my situation and accept my apology.

Yours sincerely,
Li Ming

(七) 感谢信

Dear _____,

I am writing to extend my sincere gratitude for _____ (感谢的原因). If it had not been for your timely assistance in _____ (对方给予的具体帮助), I fear that would have been _____ (没有对方帮助的后果).

Again, I would like to express my warm thanks to you. Please accept my gratitude.

Yours sincerely,
Li Ming

(八) 推荐信

Dear _____,

I am writing this letter to recommend _____ (被推荐人) to you. During his/her graduate years he/she was my _____ (学生等).

His/Her performance in the school years was outstanding. First, he/she showed great talents in _____. In addition, he/she has a very pleasant personality. He/She has developed a strong sense of _____, and working with him/her is a happy and easy thing.

Therefore, I here recommend him/her to you with all my heart. I am sure that his/her future conduct/academic work will prove worthy of your confidence.

Yours sincerely,
Li Ming

（九）祝贺信

Dear _____,

Good news travels fast! It is delightful for me to hear that _____ (祝贺理由).

Please accept my sincere congratulations to you.

I have been watching your progress with admiration all these years, and I know more than anyone else how much effort you have put in. Now you prove to be very mature and well-rounded in every aspect.

May you have a brighter future and more success!

Yours sincerely,
Li Ming

（十）问询信

To Whom It May Concern,

I would be grateful if it's so kind of you to give me some essential information about ____ (问询的大致内容). As a(n) _____ (自己身份介绍), I would like to receive information regarding _____ (问询内容的延伸). For one thing, I wonder whether it is possible for me to _____ (问询的目的一). For another, _____ (问询的目的二). If possible, please show me what procedures I should go through.

Would you please send me all the information and other materials as soon as possible? I would be much obliged to you for all your consideration and attention.

Yours respectfully,
Li Ming

（十一）备忘录

Date: Feb. 10, 2019

From: Zhang Wei

To: All teachers

Subject: New Syllabus for 2020

As informed earlier this week, all teaching staff of Foreign Languages Department are required to attend a plenary session on New Syllabus for 2020 at 4pm in Room 314, Teaching Building. Considering some revisions have been made about textbooks for junior and senior students, this conference is organized quite out of necessity and urgency. All of you are requested to write a brief report on your own ideas about the new versions of textbooks and share them with other colleagues during the conference. In addition, do not feel hesitant to submit any suggestion on the feasibility and applicability of the new syllabus.

（十二）报告（Report）

(1) Title（标题）

(2) Introduction（介绍）：Aim/Objective/Background等

(3) Method（方法）

(4) Result（结果）

(5) Discussion（讨论）

(6) Conclusion（结论）

Report on Charity Donation

This report focuses on the progress of a charity donation organized by Huadong Univiersity. The activity is aimed at offering assistance to those in need in economically and culturally backward regions.

The organizers issued a call on the web to all students on campus to make a contribution to this action. Plus, they spread the information among their schoolmates and classmates. Positive response was tremendous. Clothes, shoes, books, stationeries and schoolbags flooded in.

Judging from the current development of this donation, students show considerable enthusiasm in and passion for helping others. So to achieve bigger success in this field, we should make more detailed and careful plans and call for large-scale involvement of the general public.

四、真题精练（2015—2019 年）

2015 年

Suppose your university is going to host a summer camp for high school students. Write a notice to

1) briefly introduce the camp activities, and

2) call for volunteers.

You should write about 100 words on the ANSWER SHEET.

Do not use your own name.Use "Li Ming" instead.

Do not write your address. (10 points)

NOTICE

Since our university is going to organize a camp for high school students during this summer vacation, the Students' Union is now recruiting volunteers to <u>make the camp a complete success</u>.

As a cultural exchange program, this camp is scheduled to be held from July 20 to August 10, aiming to promote the understanding of American culture among high school students. Students will visit a high school in Chicago and exchange ideas with students there. After that, they will have a tour to major American universities and famous tourist spots. Those who would like to volunteer for this activity must possess fluent communication skills in English. All the transportation and accommodation expenses are covered.

Anyone who is interested in international communication is encouraged to apply. The applicants may download the application form from the university website and send it to 9865321@163.com.

The Students' Union
May 27th, 2014

◆ 亮点解析 ◆

第一段使用了主从复合句，有加分的概率，Since 引导的是原因状语从句。最后的下划线部分也是一个亮点短语。

第二段第一句中使用了现在分词短语 aiming to...，为目的状语，这种方法建议多加尝试。第四句是主从复合句，增加了语言的复杂度和多样性。

第三段第一句是主从复合句，同时主句使用了被动语态，显得层次多样，表达丰富。

妙词佳句

1. make sth. a complete success 使某事大获成功
2. be scheduled to do sth. 预定做某事
3. aim to do sth. 力争做某事
4. would like to do sth. 想做某事
5. be interested in sth. 对某事感兴趣

2016 年

Suppose you won a translation contest and your friend, Jack, wrote an email to congratulate you and ask for advice on translation. Write him a reply to

1) thank him, and
2) give your advice.

You should write about 100 words on the ANSWER SHEET.

Do not use your own name. Use "Li Ming" instead.

Do not write your address. (10 points)

Dear Jack,

I'm writing to express my gratitude for your congratulation on my success in the translation contest.

As regard to my experience, I would like to offer you some proposals in this part. First, I strongly suggest you that you need to practice with painstaking effort in this field. What's more, you had better have more communication with foreigners, which guarantees that you will have a deeper understanding of foreign culture. Last but not least, you are supposed to participate in some international events to accumulate a wealth of practical experience.

I do hope you could take my suggestions into consideration. I wish you have good luck and make great success in your future study.

Yours sincerely,

Li Ming

亮点解析

第一段使用了经典短语 express one's gratitude for sth. 和高级词汇 gratitude，要加强背诵和熟练应用。

第二段使用了表达顺接关系的短语或词汇：First，What's more，Last but not least，层次清晰，要点分明。开头的 As regard to 和最后的 a wealth of 都是高级短语，值得借鉴。

第三段 I do hope 是一种强调谓语动词的用法，后面的 wish 和 hope 属于同义词，词汇多变也是写作的提分利器。

妙词佳句

1. express one's gratitude for sth. 为某事表达感谢
2. congratulation on sth. 对某事的祝贺
3. as regard to sth. 关于某事
4. be supposed to do sth. 应该做某事
5. a wealth of... 大量的……
6. take sth. into consideration 把某事考虑在内
7. make great success in sth. 在某事上取得巨大成功

2017 年

Suppose you are invited by Professor Williams to give a presentation about Chinese culture to a group of international students. Write a reply to

1) accept the invitation, and

2) introduce the key points of your presentation.

You should write about 100 words on the ANSWER SHEET.

Do not use your own name. Use "Li Ming" instead.

Do not write your address. (10 points)

Dear Professor Williams,

I felt much honored when I received your invitation to give a presentation about Chinese culture to the international students of your college. I am writing to tell you something about the presentation to be given.

The focus of my presentation will be Chinese traditional festivals, such as the Spring Festival and the Mid-autumn Day. In the speech, I will introduce the origin and conventions of these festivals. For example, the Mid-Autumn Day, falling on the 15th of August in the Chinese lunar calendar, is a traditional Chinese holiday for family members and loved ones to gather together. In addition to enjoying the glorious full moon on this day, Chinese people will also eat festival moon cakes, recite ancient Chinese poems as well as guess lantern riddles. I believe the knowledge will help the foreign students obtain a deeper understanding of Chinese culture.

I am looking forward to sharing these with all of the international students.

Yours respectfully,

Li Ming

亮点解析

第一段第一句是主从复合句，主句使用了 felt much honored 的经典表达，when 引导的是时间状语从句。

第二段第三句使用了分裂结构，将主语 the Mid-Autumn Day 和谓语 is 分隔，富于变化。falling on the 15th of August 也是英文的经典表达。In addition to 表递进关系，起到了承上启下的作用。

第三段是表达期望的经典句型，要熟练应用。

妙词佳句

1. feel much honored 倍感荣幸
2. fall on 适逢（后接具体日期）
3. in addition to sth. 除了某事之外
4. look forward to sth./doing sth. 期望某事/做某事

2018 年

Suppose you have to cancel your travel plan and will not be able to visit Professor Smith. Write him an email to

1) apologize and explain the situation, and

2) suggest a future meeting.

You should write about 100 words on the ANSWER SHEET.

Do not use your own name. Use "Li Ming" instead.

Do not write your address. (10 points)

参考范文

Respectable Prof. Smith,

I hereby make a sincere apology for my failing to keep the appointment with you. As scheduled, I would pay you a visit in your office next Friday, but much to my regret, I have to cancel this arrangement.

On that day, I will sign for an important job interview, which is extremely important for my future. As a result, I am compelled to make an adjustment to my previous plan and cannot keep my word. I feel terribly sorry for missing the precious opportunity to get some enlightenment from you.

Is it possible that we meet at another time when both of us are available? Please let me know your preferable date. I am looking forward to having a pleasant time with you. Please allow me to say sorry again for my absence.

Yours respectfully,
Li Ming

亮点解析

称呼语使用 respectable，以示敬意。

第一段首句使用 hereby（在此 / 特此）表达正式程度。As scheduled 是 As it is scheduled 的省略形式，起到了简明扼要的作用。

第二段首句使用 which 引导定语从句，第二句使用 As a result 进行自然过渡，都是增加语言变化的常用技巧。

第三段首句使用一般疑问句的形式表达礼貌客气。

最后的落款使用 respectfully 也是显示对长者的敬意。

妙词佳句

1. hereby [ˌhɪəˈbaɪ] ad. 在此，特此
2. make a sincere apology for sth. 为某事真诚道歉
3. fail to do sth. 无法做某事，不能做某事
4. keep the appointment with sb. 和某人约定
5. schedule [ˈʃedjuːl] v. 安排，约定
6. pay sb. a visit 造访某人
7. be compelled to do sth. 被迫做某事
8. adjustment [əˈdʒʌstmənt] n. 调整，调节
9. previous [ˈpriːviəs] a. 先前的，之前的
10. keep one's word 信守承诺
11. enlightenment [ɪnˈlaɪtnmənt] n. 启迪，启蒙
12. available [əˈveɪləbl] a. 可提供的，可利用的
13. to one's regret 令某人遗憾
14. cancel [ˈkænsl] v. 取消

> 15. sign for sth. 注册登记做某事
> 16. as a result 因此
> 17. preferable [ˈprefrəbl] a. 更喜欢的
> 18. look forward to sth./doing sth. 期望某事/做某事
> 19. absence [ˈæbsəns] n. 缺席

2019 年

Suppose Professor Smith asked you to plan a debate on the theme of city traffic. Write him an email to

1) suggest a specific topic with your reasons, and

2) tell him about your arrangements.

You should write about 100 words on the ANWSER SHEET.

Do not use your own name. Use "Li Ming" instead. (10 points)

Respectable Prof. Smith,

  I feel fairly honored and pleased to plan a debate on the theme of city traffic. Here are some of my humble ideas.

  No one can doubt the fact that in recent years the traffic problem in many cities has caused wide public concern. There are several reasons for this problem. For one thing, the number of vehicles is increasing much more rapidly than building of roads. For another, public transport services like subways and buses are still inadequate. Hence, "Green Commuting" is a more reasonable choice, namely, riding bicycles or choosing public transport instead of driving private vehicles. Meanwhile, the government is expected to invest more on public transport and road construction. Furthermore, to heighten the awareness of local residents is equally essential.

  This is my brief illustration of the above-mentioned topic. If possible, please offer me some constructive suggestions.

Yours respectfully,
Li Ming

◆ 亮点解析 ◆

  第一段使用了表达客套礼貌的常用句型：I feel fairly honored and pleased（我倍感荣幸和高兴）；以及表示列举的常用句型：Here are...（如下是……）。

  第二段开头使用了表示双重否定的句型：No one can doubt...（没有人会怀疑……），具有标新立异的效果。然后使用了表达顺接关系的短语和词汇：For one thing, For another, Hence, Meanwhile, Furthermore，层次清晰，要点分明。

第三段首句是对上文的概括总结，第二句寻求建议，使用了 If possible 这个表达礼貌客气的句型。

妙词佳句

1. feel fairly honored and pleased to do sth. 对做某事倍感荣幸和高兴
2. No one can doubt... 没有人能怀疑……
3. cause wide public concern 引起广泛的公众关注
4. for one thing 其一
5. for another 其二
6. inadequate [ɪnˈædɪkwət] a. 不充足的
7. hence [hens] ad. 因此
8. green commuting 绿色出行
9. namely [ˈneɪmlɪ] ad. 即，也就是
10. heighten the awareness of sb. 提高某人的意识
11. essential [ɪˈsenʃl] a. 必要的，重要的
12. illustration [ˌɪləˈstreɪʃn] n. 阐述，说明
13. constructive [kənˈstrʌktɪv] a. 建设性的

第四节 图表作文（大作文）高分指南

（一）考查题型

前面谈到，考研英语（二）的大作文主要形式是根据所规定的情景或给出的提纲，写出一篇 150 词左右的英语说明文或议论文，提供情景的形式为图画、图表或文字。纵观近年来的题目和类型，基本以图表作文为主，偶尔出现提纲作文，但没有出现过图画作文。

具体而言，图表作文大致分为 4 种：曲线图（line chart），柱状图（bar chart），饼状图（pie chart），表格（table）。以下是 2010—2017 年考研英语（二）大作文的题目和类型，从中可以发现出题的大致要求和一般规律。

（二）写作步骤

分析数据不要面面俱到，找最高、最低数据描述即可。一般分三段来写：首段综述最高、最低点；第二段分析原因：2～3 点；第三段建议、号召、解决措施等。

1. 曲线图

1）首段交代"四要素"（描述对象、数据内容、时间和地点）。

2）曲线图的描写要点是"趋势描述"（将曲线分段，分别描述各段上升、下降、保持不变的趋势，用关联词将这些线段连接起来）和"数据支持"（写出趋势变化关键点的数值）。

3）多条曲线组成的曲线图，除了描述各条线的特点以外，重点描写两条线的相似点和差异。

2. 柱状图

1）首段交代"四要素"（描述对象、数据内容、时间和地点）。

2）注意柱与柱之间的落差，突出落差的极值。

3）柱状图也可以转化为曲线图（把每根柱子的顶端连接起来就是一根曲线），然后再进行"趋势描述"和"数据支持"。

3. 饼状图

1）首段交代"四要素"（描述对象、数据内容、时间和地点）。

2）介绍各扇面及总体的关系。

3）重点突出特点最明显的扇面：最大、最小。

4. 表格

1）首段交代"四要素"（描述对象、数据内容、时间和地点）。

2）横向比较：介绍横向各个数据的区别、变化和趋势。

3）纵向比较：介绍纵向各个数据的区别、变化和趋势。

4）不需要将每个数据分别说明，突出数值最大值和最小值，对比时总结出数据对比最悬殊和最小的。

提纲作文是前些年考研英语（二）的考查重点，近年来没有出现过，作为一般性知识了解即可。下面是 2002 年的真题：

In this diction, you are asked to write a composition entitled Is Failure a Bad Thing or a Good Thing? You composition should be based on the Answer Sheet.

Outline:

1. Failure is what often happens.

2. Different attitudes towards failure.

3. Your attitude.

图画作文是考研英语（一）的考查重点，但在考研英语（二）中还未出现过，作为一般知识了解即可。其主要形式为图画或漫画，如下图所示，要求考生对该图画或漫画进行解读并阐述可能引申的社会意义。通常可以分为五个步骤来写：图画描述段，寓意阐释段，解决问题段，发扬展望段，举例段。前两段为必有段，后面三段可选择其一。

养老"足球赛"

（三）高频词汇、短语

1）图表内容：figure; statistic; number; percentage; proportion。

2）描述（用 v.）：show; describe; depict; illustrate; present; indicate; reveal。

① illustrate：表明，show/demonstrate/give information on/about/of... 与其同义。

② 趋势（增、减、上下浮动、持平）：increase, soar, rocket, ascend, mount, climb, jump, rise, grow; fall, drop, decline, reduce, decrease, descend, go down; fluctuate; remain steady/stable, stay the same, keep to the same level, little/hardly any/no change。

rise：上升；increase：增长；climb：爬升；jump：激增。

sth. climbed from 小数量 to 大数量 during the period from 年 to 年。

sth. jumped from 小数量 to 大数量 during the period from 年 to 年。

蹿升：rocket；降：fall/decrease/decline/drop；猛降：plummet。

【例句】The consumption of beef experienced a dramatic drop from 2000 to 2014.

时间段 +witnessed/saw a sharp+ 上升 / 下降 +in + 某事。

【例句】The following decade witnessed a sharp increase in the consumption of beef.

跌：decrease。

sth. experienced a ____ decrease 某事经历了……的下降。

sharp/dramatic 剧烈的；slight 轻微的；gradual 逐渐的；significant 显著的。

sth. decreased dramatically/sharply/slightly/gradually。

大约：approximately；数字 + or so；about 大约。

over 超过

more than 超过

less than 不到

overtake 超过（overtook；overtaken）

outnumber 数量上超过

outweigh 超过

fluctuate 上下波动

sth. experienced a slight fluctuation 某事经历了一次轻微的波动

sth. remained stable 某事保持稳定

=sth. climbed steadily

sth. remained the same 某事保持不变

be similar to 相似的

be the same as 一模一样

=be identical to

be different from... 与……不同

=be in contrast with...

account for 占……

=occupy

=take up

=make up

占 + 百分比 + of sth.

【例句】Boys account for 40% of the total students in this school.

③ 最值（用 v.）：reach/arrive at the bottom/peak/highest point/lowest point。

最大、最少（用短语）

The most popular...

The least popular...

The second popular...

Sth. dominated sth.

reach the peak

fall to the lowest point

④ 变化程度（用 *adj./adv.*）：noticeable, considerable, suddenly, rapidly, dramatically, significantly, sharply, steeply, steadily, gradually, slowly, slightly, stably, considerably, substantially。

程度（用 *adv.*）：almost, nearly, approximately, about, just over, over, exactly, precisely。just over 刚刚超过，more than 超过，less than 不足，a little bit less than 差一点儿到……。

（用 *v.*）：change/expand from...to..., range from...to..., range between...and...。

⑤ 倍数表达

as...as...；

the same as；

倍数 + 形容词比较级 +than；

倍数 +the+ 计量名词（length, width, height, weight, size）+of。

⑥ 时间

a century=100 年

half a century=50 年

decade=10 年

a quarter of century = 25 年

⑦ 数字

hundred 百

thousand 千

million 百万

billion 十亿

hundreds of 成百上千的

thousands of 成千上万的

millions of 成百上千万的

billions of 几十亿的

a few 一些 + 可数名词复数

few 几乎没有

quite a few 很多

few/fewer/fewest

a little 一些 + 不可数名词

little 几乎没有

quite a little 很多

（四）图表作文常用句型

According to the figures shown in the table/graph we can see/conclude that...

【例句】 According to the figures shown in the table, we can see that great changes have been taking place in people's diet over the period from 2004 to 2013.

We can see/We have noted/It can be seen from the table/chart/graph that...

【例句】 We have noted from the graph that there is a wide gap between the top ten universities both of China and of the world.

The graph/table/chart shows/indicates/reveals/points out that...

【例句】 The chart reveals that the number of road accidents is spiraling upward every year as more and more highways are constructed all over China.

As is shown/can be seen in the chart/graph/diagram released by the government...

【例句】 As can be seen in the diagram released by the government, the rapid growth of population has resulted in the extinction of many wildlife species.

After considering the information in the graph/table/chart, we might conclude that...

【例句】 After considering the information in the graph, we might conclude that the energy structure in rural areas has been greatly improved over the past 15 years.

The chart/graph/table shows a minimal/slight/slow/steady/marked/dramatic/sharp/sudden increase/rise/decline/reduction/fall/drop in...compared with those of last year/10 years ago/last century...

【例句】 The graph shows a marked decline in the number of wildlife species compared with that of last century.

This year, the products of...dropped to half/was cut in half/doubled/tripled.

【例句】 This year, the products of cotton doubled.

The number of...grew/rose/dropped from...to...

【例句】 The number of car accidents grew from 3,691 in 2003 to 8,245 in 2013.

No increase is shown in...; then came a sharp increase of...

【例句】 No increase is shown in 2004; then came a sharp increase of 8 million.

Sth. is twice/three/half as large/high/much as sth. else.

【例句】 This house is three times as large as that one.

The table/chart/graph represents the development and changes in...

【例句】 The table represents the development and changes in agriculture structure in the past 30 years.

By comparison with..., it dropped/fell/decreased from...to.../by...

【例句】 By comparison with 2004, it dropped by 15 percent.

There appeared an even more stable/consistent/steady tendency to rise/drop.

【例句】 There appeared an even more stable tendency to rise for 2 years.

（五）经典模板

1. 整体模板

From the chart, we know that _____ (图表内容总概括). On the one hand, _____ (情况一). On the other hand, _____ (情况二).

There are many reasons to explain the effect/phenomenon/case/instance. The most contributing one is that _____ (理由一). What is more, _____ (理由二). _____ (理由三) also plays a role in this case.

In my opinion, the proper attitude towards/suggestion for _____ (主题) is that _____ (我的态度/观点/建议). For one thing, we should _____ (方法一). For another, _____ (方法二). Only in this way can _____ (总结句).

2. 分段模板

（1）描述段

【示例一】

① From the chart, we know that _____ (图表内容总概括). ② On the one hand, _____ (情况一). ③ On the other hand, _____ (情况二). ④ It can easily be seen that _____ (揭示图表含义).

【示例二】

① As is shown/described/depicted in the chart, _____（图表内容总概括）. ② In the chart, _____（描述图表内容）. ③ It is safe to draw the conclusion that _____（揭示含义，或主题句）.

（2）意义阐述段

【示例一】

① Judging from the chart, we can clearly infer that _____（主题句）. ② _____（扩展句）. ③ For one thing/First of all/Firstly, _____（第一个层面）. ④ For another/Besides/Moreover/In addition/Secondly, _____（第二个层面）. ⑤ Thus/As a result/Therefore/Finally, _____（总结句）.

【示例二】

① To begin with, the chart shows us that _____（主题句）. ② _____（扩展句）is naturally associated with, to be specific, _____（第一个层面）. ③ Besides/Moreover/In addition, _____（第二个层面）. ④ As a result/Therefore, _____（总结句）.

（3）原因阐释段

【示例一】

① There are many reasons responsible for this phenomenon/case/instance and the following are the typical ones. ② The first reason is that _____（理由一）. ③ The second reason is that _____（理由二）. ④ The third reason is that/A case in point is that/The typical example is that _____（理由三）.

【示例二】

① There are many reasons to explain/explaining the effect/phenomenon/case/instance. ② The most contributing one is/the main reason is no other than _____（理由一）. ③ What is more, _____（理由二）. ④ _____（理由三）also plays a role in this case.

（4）建议措施段

【示例一】

① Considering all these reasons/this situation/Confronted with such a problem, I think we need to take more positive measures. ② On the one hand, _____（方法/建议一）. ③ On the other hand, it is necessary for us to _____（方法/建议二）. ④ Thus/Only in this way can _____（总结自己的观点/建议/态度）.

【示例二】

① In order to improve the situation/To sum up the above argument/Confronted with such an issue/problem, we should find several solutions to it/need to take some positive measures. ② On the one hand/For one thing, we should _____ （方法/建议一）. ③ On the other hand/For another, _____ （方法/建议二）. ④ Therefore/Thus/Only in this way, can _____ （段落总结句）.

（5）趋势预测段

【示例一】

① Accordingly, it is vital for us to derive positive implications from the chart. ② On the one hand, we can frequently use them to enlighten that _____ （主题）. ③ On the other hand, we should be sensible enough to _____ （观点/态度）. ④ Only by _____ （段落总结句）, and only in this way can we have a brilliant future.

【示例二】

① The effects of which has produced on can be boiled down to two major ones. ② First, _____ （影响一）. ③ More importantly, _____ （影响二）. ④ Hence, I believe that we will see a _____ （提出展望）. Nevertheless, I do not think we will see a _____ （或反面展望）.

（六）真题精炼

2015 年：

Write an essay based on the following chart. In your writing, you should

1) interpret the chart, and

2) give your comments.

You should write about 150 words on the ANSWER SHEET. (15 points)

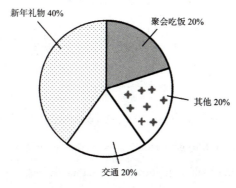

我国某市居民春节假期花销比例

The pie chart above clearly illustrates the percentage of the residents' spending during the Spring Festival Vacation in a certain city of China. From the statistics given, we may draw the conclusion that the percentage of New Year presents is highest among all the four categories, at approximately 40%, whereas the data of transport, gathering and dining, as well as others account for about 20% respectively.

The fundamental factors that contribute to the aforementioned tendency may be summarized as follows. To start with, a New Year gift might be memorable because of the special occasion when people give it to you. If the present is something that only your best friend knows you want, you will never forget it in that it shows the closeness of your relationship with that friend. In addition, festival presents might be unforgettable since they are related to significant events in your life. For instance, I still remember the first New Year gift my best friend Simon gave me.

In summary, people spend a lot on Spring Festival presents for a large number of reasons. Some gifts might be memorable owing to the special person who gave the gift. Others are unforgettable due to the significance of the event. Most of all, it is easy to remember special presents as they give you a significant sense of personal worth.

亮点解析

第一段注意该段中的一些固定表达，如 draw the conclusion, at + 百分比，account for 等。

第二段使用了比较新颖的衔接过渡表达，To start with, In addition, in that 等；还有高级词汇 aforementioned 等。

第三段使用 In summary 表明这是结论段，owing to 和 due to 属于同义替换，增加语言表达的丰富多样性。

妙词佳句

1. draw the conclusion 得出结论	知，某物是所有类型中数据最高的。
2. at approximately+百分比 达到……比例	6. fundamental [ˌfʌndə'mentl] a. 重要的；基础的
3. account for 占……（比例）	
4. respectively 分别地	7. contribute to sth. 导致某事
5. From the statistics given, we may draw the conclusion that the percentage of sth. is highest among all the categories. 从如上数据我们可	8. to start with 首先
	9. in that 由于
	10. be related to sth./sb. 与某事/某人相关

11. The fundamental factors that contribute to the aforementioned tendency may be summarized as follows. 导致如上趋势的重要因素可归纳如下。	12. in summary 总而言之 13. owing to sth. 由于 14. due to sth. 由于

2016年：

Write an essay based on the chart below. In your writing, you should

1) interpret the chart, and

2) give your comments.

You should write about 150 words on the ANSWER SHEET. (15 points)

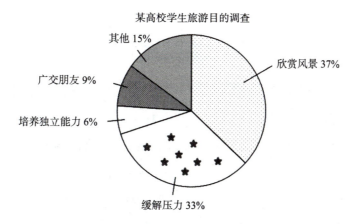

As is clearly reflected in the above pie chart, the purpose of students traveling abroad demonstrates obvious differences in one college of China. According to the data given, the purpose of enjoying the beautiful landscape <u>takes a</u> comparatively <u>large share</u>, <u>accounting for</u> 37%, while that of relieving pressure also <u>takes away</u> 20% of the whole proportion.

What triggers this phenomenon? It is not difficult to put forward several factors responsible for this phenomenon. To start with, with the rapid development of economy, people, including college students, are becoming increasingly wealthy, which enables them to afford the once-deemed-expensive oversea traveling. In order to enjoy the charming landscape all around the world, a large proportion of students choose to travel abroad. What's more, along with the ever-accelerating improvement of economy and society is also the ever-increasing work and life pressure. Consequently, the purpose of relieving pressure ranks the second among all the purposes for folks to travel around the world.

In view of the arguments above, we can conclude that the current phenomenon is of no surprise. And therefore, it can be predicted that <u>admiring the scenery and alleviating pressure</u> will still be the main purpose for people to arrange a traveling to other countries.

◆ 亮点解析 ◆

第一段第一句是总述句，后面是展开的具体细节。下划线部分使用了同义替换：take a large share，account for, take away。

第二段使用了明显的衔接过渡的表达：To start with，What's more，Consequently；其他需关注的是一些经典表达：a large proportion of，ranks the second 等。

第三段 In view of 一般用作表达关注或态度；下划线部分使用了动名词短语充当句子主语，也是一种变化的手段。

◆ 妙词佳句 ◆

1. take a large share 占很大份额	富裕，使得他们能够做某事。
2. account for 占……（比例）	9. It is not difficult to put forward several factors responsible for this phenomenon. 很容易找到导致这种现象的几个因素。
3. take away 占……（比例）	
4. to start with 首先	
5. a large proportion of 大量的	10. in view of 鉴于
6. what's more 而且	11. In view of the arguments above, we can conclude that the current phenomenon is of no surprise. 鉴于以上观点，我可以断言当前这种趋势不足为奇。
7. consequently [ˈkɒnsɪkwəntlɪ] ad. 因此	
8. people are becoming increasingly wealthy, which enables them to do sth. 人们变得越来越	

2017 年：

Write an essay based on the chart below. In your writing, you should

1) interpret the chart, and

2) give your comments.

You should write about 150 words on the ANSWER SHEET. (15 points)

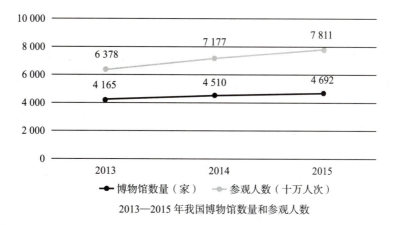

2013—2015年我国博物馆数量和参观人数

Reflected in the chart given above are the respective changes in the numbers of museums and their visitors in China from the year 2013 to 2015. It can be clearly seen that the number of museums was on a continuous rise from 4,165 to 4,692 in the two years, up more than 12%, and so was that of the visitors, with an increase of over 22% from 6,378 to 7,811.

What might account for the notable growth? Reasons are many, but the most important one, as far as I am concerned, is that with the boom of Chinese economy in recent years, our government has been placing an increasingly high value on the inheritance of traditional culture, which connects modern people with the historical past, allowing them to acquire a cultural and historical identity. What's more, more attention is paid to touring Chinese traditional culture since the Chinese have improved living standards.

With the development of China, the increasing trend is bound to continue for some time in the future. From my perspective, it is a positive trend and should be encouraged, for it is not only beneficial for the preservation and rejuvenation of our ancestral heritages but also conducive to the cultural diversity of the world.

亮点解析

第一段第一句使用了倒装结构，即过去分词Reflected提到句首，这是一种求新求变的方法；最后一句的 so was that... 也采用了此法。

第二段开篇使用了问句形式，目的是起到引人耳目的效果。然后通过 but 和 as far as I am concerned 引出个人看法，再通过 What's more 引出更多的观点，思路清晰，脉络严谨。

第三段通过 From my perspective 引出个人观点，再通过 positive 和 encouraged 表达了自己的鲜明立场，最后通过 for 引导的从句进行原因佐证。

妙词佳句

1. on a continuous rise 持续增长	多，但我认为最重要的是……
2. so is sth. 某事也是如此	7. be bound to do sth. 注定做某事
3. boom [bu:m] n. 繁荣	8. perspective [pəˈspektɪv] n. 角度；视角
4. inheritance [ɪnˈherɪtəns] n. 传统；遗产	9. be beneficial for... 对……有利
5. What might account for the notable growth? 什么可以解释这种显著增长呢？	10. preservation [ˌprezəˈveɪʃn] n. 保护
	11. rejuvenation [rɪˌdʒuːvəˈneɪʃn] n. 振兴；复活
6. Reasons are many, but the most important one, as far as I am concerned, is that... 原因众	12. be conducive to... 对……有益

2018年：

Write an essay based on the chart below. In your writing, you should

1) interpret the chart, and

2) give your comments.

You should write about 150 words on the ANSWER SHEET. (15 points)

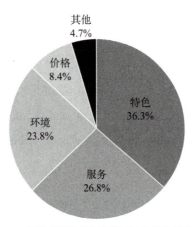

2017年某市消费者选择餐厅时的关注因素

The pie chart illustrates consumers' concerns about selecting a restaurant for dinner in a certain city in 2017. Specifically, the features of the restaurants account for the largest proportion of 36.3%. Then the service and the environment of the restaurants constitute 26.8% and 23.8% respectively. Next comes the price, with only 8.4%, while other unmentioned factors take up the least proportion of 4.7%.

Not surprisingly, nowadays consumers pay more attention to the features of restaurants rather than the price of the dinner. What has caused this phenomenon? On the one hand, the rise in income boosts consumers' buying power, so lower price becomes less of an advantage for restaurants in attracting customers. On the other hand, with the development of economy, an increasing number of dining options are made available to customers, so more attention has been paid to the specialties of the restaurants.

To sum up, as people's living conditions have been significantly improved, this trend is likely to maintain for quite a long time in the future: The features of the restaurants, namely the taste of food, is always on the top of consumers' priority list.

亮点解析

第一段第一句是总述概括，第二句使用 Specifically 进行分述，描述了图中的不同数据，层次分明，逻辑严谨。

第二段论述上文提及的现象所产生的原因，使用 On the one hand, On the other hand 进行自然衔接，环环相扣。

第三段是概括段，使用 To sum up 进行归纳总结，this trend is likely to maintain for quite a long time in the future 是对未来的预测和展望。

妙词佳句

1. illustrate ['ɪləstreɪt] v. 阐述，阐明	10. boost [buːst] v. 促进，提升
2. concern [kən'sɜːn] n. 关注，关心	11. buying power 购买力
3. specifically [spə'sɪfɪklɪ] ad. 具体地，具体而言	12. advantage [əd'vɑːntɪdʒ] n. 优势，优点
4. feature ['fiːtʃə(r)] n. 特色，特点	13. option ['ɒpʃn] n. 选择
5. account for sth. 占据（份额/比例等）	14. specialty ['speʃəltɪ] n. 特色，特点
6. proportion [prə'pɔːʃn] n. 比例	15. sum up 总而言之
7. constitute ['kɒnstɪtjuːt] v. 构成，组成	16. significantly [sɪg'nɪfɪkəntlɪ] ad. 显著地，明显地
8. respectively [rɪ'spektɪvlɪ] ad. 分别地，各自地	17. namely ['neɪmlɪ] ad. 即，也就是
9. take up sth. 占据（份额/比例等）	18. priority [praɪ'ɒrətɪ] n. 优先，优先权

2019 年：

Write an essay based on the chart below. In your writing, you should

1) interpret the chart, and
2) give your comments.

You should write about 150 words on the ANSWER SHEET. (15 points)

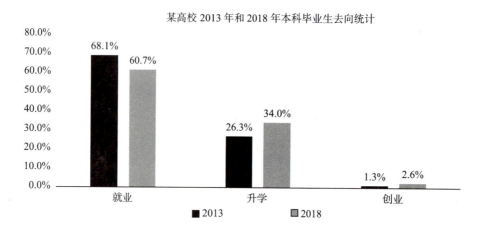

某高校 2013 年和 2018 年本科毕业生去向统计

The bar chart reveals the various career options of graduates of a certain university between 2013 and 2018. During this period, job-seekers saw a downward trend from 68.1% to 60.7%, while those who registered for the postgraduate entrance examination and started a business experienced a gradual rise, from 26.3% to 34.0% and from 1.3% to 2.6% respectively.

The reasons are obvious why an increasing number of students withdraw from the job market to choose further studies. For one thing, with the overall improvement of literacy of the public, the competition of the job market is sure to become fiercer, higher standards and stricter qualifications are required, hence a higher academic degree is a must. For another, further studies will provide a bigger platform and brighter prospect for future development. The fact that relatively few students establish their own companies is complicated. Two important reasons may be lack of fund and insufficiency of a set of favorable policies.

The multiple career choices of college graduates, to some degree, should be encouraged, which means they show a tendency to have a final say in their future.

亮点解析

第一段第一句是总述概括，第二句使用 During this period, job-seekers..., while... 结构表达了不同群体的特点，层次分明，逻辑严谨。

第二段第一句是总体概括，然后使用 For one thing, hence, For another 和 Two important reasons 表达了不同层次的观点。

第三段是概括总结段，运用被动语态来突出主题 The multiple career choices of college graduates，其中的 to some degree 将主语和谓语部分分隔，再加上最后 which 引导的定语从句，都是增加分数常用的手段和技巧。

妙词佳句

1. career option 职业选择
2. job-seeker *n.* 求职者
3. downward ['daʊnwəd] *a.* 下降的，下行的
4. register for sth. 注册登记某事
5. the postgraduate entrance examination 研究生入学考试
6. start a business 创业
7. respectively [rɪ'spektɪvlɪ] *ad.* 分别地，各自地
8. withdraw from... 从某处撤离（from 后接地点名词）
9. literacy ['lɪtərəsɪ] *n.* 有知识，有文化
10. fierce [fɪəs] *a.* 激烈的，残酷的
11. qualification [ˌkwɒlɪfɪ'keɪʃn] *n.* 资格，要求
12. must [mʌst] *n.* 必须，必要
13. platform ['plætfɔːm] *n.* 平台
14. prospect ['prɒspekt] *n.* 前景
15. establish one's own company 创业
16. complicated ['kɒmplɪkeɪtɪd] *a.* 复杂的
17. insufficiency [ˌɪnsə'fɪʃənsɪ] *n.* 不充足
18. a set of 一系列
19. favorable ['feɪvərəbl] *a.* 有利的，优惠的
20. multiple ['mʌltɪpl] *a.* 多重的，多种的
21. say [seɪ] *n.* 话语权

（七）同源实战与参考范文

练习 1

Directions:

In this section, you are asked to write an essay based on the following chart. In your writing, you should

1) interpret the chart, and

2) give your comments.

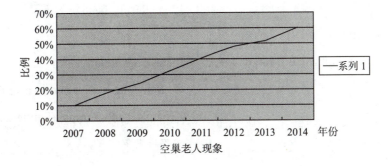

空巢老人现象

The curve chart describes the statistic changes of empty-nest elders from 2007 to 2014. The general trend witnessed an upward rise from 10% to 60%.

More than one reason is attributable to the growing severity of neglect of senior citizens. For one thing, with the full implementation of single-child policy, nuclear families have become the dominant social units in China. So the only child, as he/she grows into adulthood, has to maintain balance between supporting himself/herself and his/her ever-older parents, thus inevitably resulting in the empty-nest phenomenon. For another, with life-supporting costs soaring and work pressure turning heavier, young people cannot afford to give full attention and care to their older generation, at least in financial terms.

To reverse the current situation, on the one hand, the younger generation is expected to take the initiative to shoulder more responsibilities. On the other hand, the government and society should map out relevant policies to safeguard the rights and benefits of senior citizens. (161 words)

亮点解析

第一段第二句是亮点句，谓语 witnessed 和宾语 an upward rise 都是经典表达。

第二段第一句是表多重原因的经典句型，可作为模板使用。For one thing 和 For another 是衔接过渡的短语，起到了承上启下的作用。For another 后面的下划线部分使用了独立主格结构，也是一种高级语法的表达形式。

第三段的 on the one hand 和 on the other hand 是衔接过渡短语，起到了承上启下的作用。take the initiative 是经典短语，须熟练掌握。

妙词佳句

1. empty-nest elder 空巢老人
2. witness ['wɪtnəs] v. 见证，目睹
3. upward rise 上升
4. The general trend witnessed an upward rise. 总趋势呈上升态势。
5. severity [sɪ'verɪti] n. 严重性
6. implementation [ˌɪmplɪmen'teɪʃ(ə)n] n. 实施，执行
7. for one thing 其一
8. for another 其二
9. give full attention and care to sth./sb. 对某事/某人予以全面关注和呵护
10. in...terms 就……而言
11. reverse [rɪ'vɜːs] v. 逆转，改变
12. on the one hand 一方面
13. on the other hand 另一方面
14. take the initiative 采取主动
15. Someone is expected to take the initiative to shoulder more responsibilities. 某人应该主动担当更多责任。

练习 2

Directions:

In this section, you are asked to write an essay based on the following chart. In your writing, you should

1) interpret the chart, and

2) give your comments.

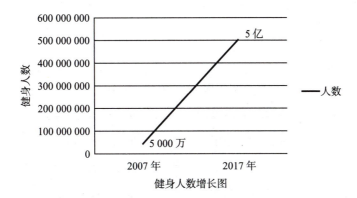

健身人数增长图

As is revealed in the above line chart, the number of fitness enthusiasts has witnessed an incredible increase from 50 million in 2007 to 500 million in 2017, an encouraging issue worthy of close attention.

Why has fitness attained such popularity nowadays? Several reasons contribute to this phenomenon. Above all, exponential growth of economy makes increase in wealth possible for more people, which allows them to seek extra enjoyment beyond material needs, like sightseeing, fitness activities, etc. What's more, heightened awareness for health prompts more people to go into gyms. They are fully convinced that health is wealth and better health can produce bigger wealth. One more noticeable reason is that the engagement in fitness offers an excellent opportunity for alleviating pressure.

With more and more people attaching importance to health and stronger consuming power becoming possible, it is predictable that in years to come fitness will greet a brighter tomorrow. (151 words)

亮点解析

第一段使用了图表作文的经典句型：has witnessed an incredible increase，最后使用了同位语结构，与前面的内容构成一个有机整体。

第二段以问句开头，起到了引人入胜的作用，然后是总述句，接着使用 Above all，What's more 和 One more noticeable reason 进行了条理有序的分步阐述。

第三段开头使用了 With 引导的独立主格结构，这是高级语法的经典用法，须熟练掌握，后面的主句也是常用的写作模板。

妙词佳句

1. witness an incredible increase 见证了非凡增长
2. sth. is worthy of close attention 某事值得密切关注
3. contribute to sth. 导致某事
4. sb. is/are fully convinced that... 某人深信……
5. alleviate pressure 减压
6. attach importance to sth. 对某事重视
7. consuming power 消费能力
8. It is predictable that in years to come... 未来可预见的是……

练习 3

Directions:

In this section, you are asked to write an essay based on the following chart. In your writing, you should

1) interpret the chart, and
2) give your comments.

大学生消费态度对比图

The pie chart demonstrates different attitudes of university students towards consumption. One third of them show little care about how much they spend. One third make a careful plan for expenditure, while the rest exercise considerable thrift in their daily life.

The following factors contribute to this phenomenon. As the only child of their families, many students are the apples of their parents' eyes and are naturally invested with more care and pocket money. Some are even spoiled and take spending money from their parents for granted. In addition, with the improvement of living standards, parents can afford higher expenditure of their children. Some students like to pursue fashion and trends, which can be quite costly. Finally, love on campus is another possible factor causing too much spending.

University students should learn to be thrifty, with expenditure being put on daily necessities instead of luxuries. This healthful habit is surely favorable to their future development. (154 words)

亮点解析

第一段第一句是总述概括，然后使用 One third..., One third..., while the rest... 结构表达了不同群体的特点，层次分明，逻辑严谨。

第二段第一句是总体概括，然后使用 In addition 和 Finally 表达了不同层次的观点。

第三段运用了独立主格结构：with expenditure being put on daily necessities instead of luxuries，这是高级语法结构，是增加分数常用的手段和技巧。

妙词佳句

1. demonstrate ['demənstreɪt] v. 展示，显示	8. pocket money 零花钱
2. one third of sb. ……的三分之一	9. take sth. for granted 把某事认为理所当然
3. the rest 其余的部分	10. thrifty ['θrɪftɪ] a. 节俭的
4. exercise considerable thrift 非常节俭	11. daily necessities 日常用品
5. contribute to sth. 导致某事	12. This healthful habit is surely favorable to their future development. 这种健康的习惯势必会对其未来成长大有裨益。
6. the apple of one's eyes 某人的掌上明珠	
7. be invested with sth. 被赋予某物	

练习 4

Directions:

In this section, you are asked to write an essay based on the following chart. In your writing, you should

1) interpret the chart, and

2) give your comments.

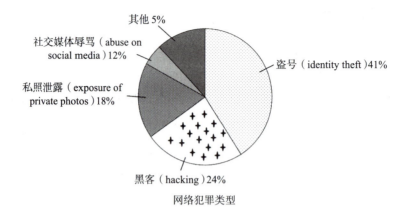

网络犯罪类型

The pie chart shows the various cybercrime categories, with identity theft, hacking, exposure of private photos, abuse on social media and others accounting for 41%, 24%, 18%, 12% and 5% respectively.

Cybercrime is a relatively new form of violation, whose impact may be severer than ordinary crimes. The fact that identity theft and hacking rank the first two places leaves little doubt. Leakage of personal information may mean loss of money, which is surely the primary goal of online crime practitioners. The motives of exposure of private photos can be profit-driven or curiosity-driven. Abuse on social media may be out of hype, a commonly employed trick of drawing attention of the public.

We can take simple steps to protect ourselves, including putting a password on your computer or mobile device, never clicking on a link sent by a stranger, using strong passwords and always logging off from an account or website when you are finished. In addition, a joint partnership between the government, law enforcement bodies and relevant operators is required. (171 words)

亮点解析

第一段下划线部分使用了独立主格结构，作伴随状语。独立主格是一种比较复杂和高级的语法结构，希望熟练掌握并加以应用。

第二段使用了两个定语从句和一个同位语从句：whose..., which..., that..., 使得句子层面增加了广度和厚度；最后使用了同位语结构，进一步解释阐述 hype，起到了烘托主题词的功效。

第三段使用了平行并列结构：putting..., never clicking..., using..., 呈现一种形式上的对称美；通过 In addition 又将论点推向更高的层次。

妙词佳句

1. category [ˈkætəɡərɪ] n. 类型；范畴
2. account for 占……（比例）
3. respectively [rɪˈspektɪvlɪ] ad. 分别地
4. identity theft 盗号
5. leave little doubt 几乎没有疑问
6. primary goal 主要目标
7. profit-driven 趋利的
8. hype [haɪp] n. 炒作
9. take simple steps to do sth. 采取简单步骤做某事
10. in addition 此外
11. A joint partnership between the government, law enforcement bodies and relevant operators is required. 需要政府、执法机构和相关部门协同努力。

练习 5

Directions:

In this section, you are asked to write an essay based on the following chart. In your writing, you should

1) interpret the chart, and
2) give your comments.

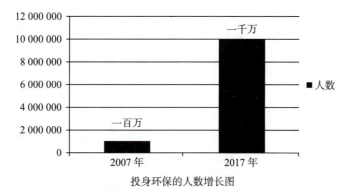

投身环保的人数增长图

The bar chart indicates the big jump of the number of environmental volunteers from 1 million in 2007 to 10 million in 2017.

It is no difficulty to come up with some possible reasons for this significant rise. At the top of the list is the ever-clearer consciousness on the part of some volunteers of the deteriorating natural environment. Fast economic growth has no doubt positive effects, but in the meantime resulted in immeasurable destruction to the nature, like air pollution, soil erosion, and deforestation. In addition, real experience of the destroyed environment has urged some responsible people to devote themselves to the great cause of environmental protection. For example, in the past several years citizens of the northern part of China have suffered tremendously from the suffocating smog. One more factor may be the power of the press, whose wide coverage on environmental destruction sounds an alarm to whole society.

As conscientious earth-dwellers, we desire not only material wealth but clearer rivers and bluer sky. (166 words)

亮点解析

第一段的 big jump 表示"巨大增长"，是一个比较鲜活生动的表达。

第二段第一句是总体概括，然后使用 In addition 和 One more factor 表达了不同层次的观点。第二句运用了完全倒装结构：At the top of the list is...；第三句使用了分裂结构：...has (no doubt) positive effects，尽量使句式呈现多种多样、富于变化的特点。

第三段使用了高级表达 conscientious earth-dwellers（负责任的地球居民），以及 not only...but...（不仅……而且……）的经典搭配。

妙词佳句

1. big jump 巨大增长	8. immeasurable [ɪˈmeʒərəbl] a. 不可估量的
2. environmental volunteer 环保志愿者	9. devote oneself to sth. 致力于某事
3. It is no difficulty to come up with some possible reasons for sth. 很容易为某事找到一些可能的原因。	10. suffocating [ˈsʌfəkeɪtɪŋ] a. 窒息的
	11. coverage [ˈkʌvərɪdʒ] n. 报道
4. consciousness [ˈkɒnʃəsnəs] n. 意识	12. sound an alarm to whole society 给整个社会敲响警钟
5. on the part of sb. 就某人而言	13. conscientious [ˌkɒnʃiˈenʃəs] a. 负责任的，有良知的
6. in the meantime 同时	
7. result in sth. 导致某事	14. earth-dweller n. 地球居民

练习 6

Directions:

In this section, you are asked to write an essay based on the following chart. In your writing, you should

1) interpret the chart, and
2) give your comments.

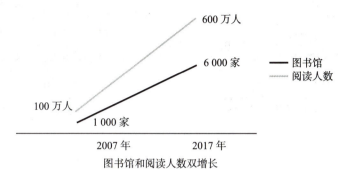

图书馆和阅读人数双增长

The line chart demonstrates the increase in numbers of libraries and readers from 2007 to 2017. During that period, the former witnessed an increase of 5,000 while the latter experienced a sharp rise from 1 million to 6 million.

A good many factors can expound the increase and the major ones are as follows. To begin with, with the speedy development of economy, more funds have been put into the construction of libraries. In addition, along with the good performance of economy comes the rise of people's income, which not only meets material needs but triggers a craving for spiritual enjoyment, so reading in libraries becomes a trend. Finally, it is needless to say that today's people live under greater pressure and are faced with severer competition, therefore visiting libraries for reading is a good choice for relaxation on one hand and for self-enrichment on the other.

As a famous saying goes, "Reading is profitable". Don't hesitate. Spare some time to read more in the library and a more magnificent world is awaiting you. (174 words)

亮点解析

第一段使用了 the former 和 the latter 将对比对象清晰地呈现出来，并且使用近义词 witnessed 和 experienced 增加了语言表达的色彩和变化。

第二段第一句是总述句，然后通过 To begin with, In addition 和 Finally 将分论点有机结合起来，论述严谨，一气呵成。此外，一些高级表达如 expound, it is needless to say that... 也给本文增色不少。

第三段开头使用了人人熟知的谚语，起到了引人入胜的效果。后两句运用祈使句，起到了鼓舞人心、令人奋进的作用。

> 妙词佳句

1. the former 前者
2. the latter 后者
3. witness ['wɪtnəs] n. 见证，目睹
4. a sharp rise 显著增长
5. expound [ɪk'spaʊnd] n. 解释；阐述
6. along with sth. 除了……之外
7. It is needless to say that... 毋庸置疑的是……
8. As a famous saying goes 俗话说
9. Reading is profitable. 开卷有益。
10. A more magnificent world is awaiting you. 更灿烂辉煌的世界迎候着你。

练习 7

Directions:

In this section, you are asked to write an essay based on the following chart. In your writing, you should

1) interpret the chart, and
2) give your comments.

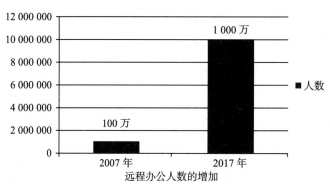

远程办公人数的增加

As is revealed in the bar chart, noticeable increase is seen in the number of people involved in telecommuting. In 2007 it was merely 1 million whereas it surged to ten million in 2017.

Positive effects of the new trend are obvious. For workers, it promises freedom from the office, less time wasted in traffic, and help with child-care conflicts. For management, it helps keep high performers on board, minimizes tardiness and absenteeism by eliminating commutes, allows periods of solitude for high-concentration tasks, and provides scheduling flexibility. In some areas, local governments are encouraging companies to start telecommuting programs in order to reduce rush-hour congestion and improve air quality. Besides, this new work mode can largely reduce the cost for both employees and their employers.

But these benefits do not come easily. Making a telecommuting program work requires careful planning and an understanding of the differences between telecommuting realities and popular images. (152 words)

亮点解析

第一段第一句连续使用了两个被动句 As is revealed in the bar chart 和 noticeable increase is seen，体现了句式结构的灵活变化。第二句使用 whereas 进行对比，显得自然顺畅。

第二段第一句是总体概括，然后使用 For workers 和 For management 分别对两个群体的不同特点进行描述。

第三段开头使用 But 与上文构成自然过渡，第二句使用动名词短语 Making a telecommuting program work 作主语是一种灵活的表达形式。

妙词佳句

1. reveal [rɪ'vi:l] v. 揭示，显示
2. noticeable ['nəʊtɪsəbl] a. 显著的，明显的
3. merely ['mɪəli] ad. 仅仅
4. surge [sɜ:dʒ] v. 上升
5. minimize ['mɪnɪmaɪz] v. 最小化
6. tardiness ['tɑ:dɪnəs] n. 迟缓，缓慢
7. absenteeism [ˌæbsən'ti:ɪzəm] n. 旷工，旷课
8. This new work mode can largely reduce the cost for both employees and their employers. 这种新工作模式可以很大程度降低员工和其雇主的成本。

练习 8

Directions:

In this section, you are asked to write an essay based on the following chart. In your writing, you should

1) interpret the chart, and
2) give your comments.

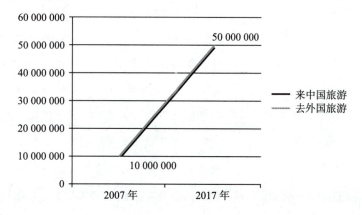

As the line chart demonstrates, the decade from 2007 to 2017 has witnessed a tremendous increase in the number of both foreign travellers to China and outbound Chinese travellers. In 2007, the two numbers were only 10 million; however, they soared to 50 million in 2017.

At least three factors contribute to the boom of travelling. For one thing, China has in recent years made enormous efforts in publicizing its dazzling achievements in various aspects and in upgrading the facilities and service of its scenic spots, which definitely become an irresistible temptation for foreign tourists. For another, the growing economy and enhanced consuming power over the period made it possible for Chinese citizens to travel abroad. In addition, the simplification of applying procedures is no doubt a promoting element for visitors coming into or going out of China.

Travelling has many positive effects, so the upward trend is desirable for both individuals and society. (154 words)

亮点解析

第一段第一句使用了非人称主语 the decade，是一种很有创新的表达形式。

第二段第一句是总体概括，然后使用 For one thing, For another 和 In addition 对三个因素分别阐述，形成逻辑严谨的衔接过渡。

第三段使用 so 得出结论，是一种常用的总结手段。

妙词佳句

1. demonstrate ['demənstreɪt] v. 展示，显示	9. China has in recent years made enormous efforts in publicizing its dazzling achievements in various aspects and in upgrading the facilities and service of its scenic spots, which definitely become an irresistible temptation for foreign tourists. 近年来，中国在宣传诸多方面取得的瞩目成就以及改善景点的设施和服务方面做出了巨大努力，这对国外游客绝对是一个不可抗拒的诱惑。
2. witness ['wɪtnəs] v. 见证，目睹	
3. tremendous [trə'mendəs] a. 巨大的	
4. outbound ['aʊtbaʊnd] a. 出境的	
5. soar [sɔː(r)] v. 高飞，飙升	
6. boom [buːm] n. 繁荣	
7. enormous [ɪ'nɔːməs] a. 巨大的	10. irresistible [ˌɪrɪ'zɪstəbl] a. 不可抗拒的
8. in various aspects 在许多方面	11. desirable [dɪ'zaɪərəbl] a. 可取的，令人满意的

练习 9

Directions:

In this section, you are asked to write an essay based on the following chart. In your writing, you should

1) interpret the chart, and

2) give your comments.

不同年龄群体获取信息的渠道

年龄 \ 渠道	电视、报纸	电脑上网	微信、微博
≤ 30 岁	7%	62%	91%
30~50 岁	41%	79%	68%
≥ 50 岁	82%	33%	34%

This table reveals different channels for people of various ages to seek information. WeChat and Microblog are most popular among those under 30, reaching 91%; surfing the Internet is more attractive to those between 30 and 50, occupying 79%, while TV and newspapers are preferred by those beyond 50, at 82%.

What has possibly contributed to the differences as described above? Some driving factors can be summarised as follows. For one thing, mastery of technology varies. Younger people are better at new technology, hence such newly-developed tools as WeChat and Microblog become their favorites. For another, views on what is important in information differ. Generally speaking, reports on TV and newspapers are more conventional and thus formal in style, to the taste of older people.

To sum up, which channel to choose is dependent to some extent on the mastery of technology, content of information and other factors, and may mirror people's different daily habits.

亮点解析

第一段使用了 are most popular, is more attractive 和 are preferred，不同的词汇表达了类似的内容，这是英语写作的重要特点之一。

第二段使用特殊疑问句开头，既新颖独特，又自然过渡到下文，然后使用 For one thing, For

another 和 Generally speaking 进行有机而紧凑的逻辑延伸。

第三段使用 To sum up 进行归纳总结，在 is dependent on 中间使用 to some extent 进行分裂，既起到突出强调的作用，又富于变化。

妙词佳句

1. surf [sɜːf] v. （网上）冲浪
2. occupy [ˈɒkjupaɪ] v. 占据
3. contribute to sth. 导致某事
4. driving factor 驱动因素
5. for one thing 其一
6. summarise [ˈsʌməraɪz] v. 总结
7. mastery [ˈmɑːstəri] n. 掌握
8. vary [ˈveəri] v. 不同，变化
9. Mastery of technology varies. 对技术的掌握程度各不相同。
10. for another 其二
11. to some extent 某种程度上
12. Views on what is important in information differ. 对于信息中哪些内容才重要，观点各异。
13. To sum up, which channel to choose is dependent to some extent on the mastery of technology, content of information and other factors. 总而言之，选择哪种渠道某种程度上取决于对技术的掌握程度、信息的内容以及其他因素。

第五节 高分范文与热点话题预测

（一）高分范文（图表作文）

预测 1 中国贸易

For many countries around the world, China is rapidly becoming their most important bilateral trade partner. However, there have been concerns over large trade imbalances between China and the rest of the world. The U.S. in particular has the largest trade deficit in the world with China at $315 billion, more than three times what it was a decade ago. There have also been a growing number of trade disputes brought against, mainly for dumping, intellectual property and the valuation of the *yuan*.

【译文】对于世界上很多国家来说，中国正迅速成为他们最重要的双边（bilateral）贸易伙伴。然而，中国和世界其他国家之间贸易不平衡的问题已经引发了关注。尤其是美国对中国的贸易赤字是最大的，达到了3 150亿美元，这个数字是十年前的三倍还多。贸易纠纷也越来越多，主要是关于倾销、知识产权和人民币的估价。

预测2　毕业生过剩

The 2008 global recession resulted in a significant drop in the job market for China's new graduates. Students graduating in 2009 will join around three million students who graduated in 2008 and are still seeking job opportunities. The graduate glut can also be attributed to a rise in the number of college enrollments and educational institutions. Although the number of college students has increased, there has not been any significant improvement in their quality. In most cases, graduates were unable to find suitable employment in 2008 because they did not have the skills required by the industry.

【译文】2008全球经济衰退导致中国的新毕业生的就业市场显著下降。2009年毕业的学生将加入2008年毕业仍在找工作的300万学生之中。毕业生过剩（glut）也可以归因于大学入学率的提高和教育机构的增加。虽然大学的学生人数增加了，但是他们的质量并没有明显地提高。在大多数情况下，毕业生无法在2008年找到合适的就业机会是因为他们没有行业所需的技能。

预测3　对代沟的看法

When it comes to the problem of generation gap, people's ideas are not cut from the same cloth. Most of the old argue that young people should be responsible for the problem. They base their argument on the ground that young people either turn a deaf ear to the elders' experience-based advice or set themselves against what the elders have been proud of. Yet the younger generation reacts to the problem the other way around and holds that the opposite is just reasonable. From their angle of view, the older generation is too conservative to accept anything new, as a result of which, their voices are not taken into account, and their efforts are far from the requirements set by the elders. I am of the opinion that both generations should take the responsibility for the problem. Much evidence proves that the generation gap results just when the two generations miss connecting or understanding with each other. As long as both sides keep their minds open to each other's outlooks on the world and get ready for adjustment of their own ideas to the social needs, the gap between them will be narrowed down in time.

【译文】谈到代沟问题，人们的看法不尽相同。多数老者认为责任在年轻人。其理由是，年轻人要么对其经验之谈充耳不闻，要么对其引以为豪之事嗤之以鼻。但是年轻人却持有相反观点。他们认为老一代太保守而不愿接受任何新事物，他们的观点从不受重视，付出的努力也远达不到老者的要求。我认为双方都有责任。很多证据表明，两代人无法沟通或无法相互理解时就会产生代沟。只要双方敞开胸怀，接受彼此的世界观，并随时调整自己的想法以适应社会需求，代沟会随着时光流逝而日渐缩小。

预测 4　戒烟

If you find it hard to get rid of your bad habit of smoking, you are not alone, for quite a few smokers have tried to break with it but in vain. Like other bad habits, smoking, once you have become addicted to it, is very hard to break. For instance, one friend of mine, a chain smoker, has done everything he could to give up smoking but now he is still living with it.

But if there is every reason for you to rid yourself of it, here is how: Build up your will to abandon it by frequently reminding yourself of its harmfulness. Replace your bad habit with a good one, such as coffee drinking or bubble-gum chewing. And listen to the regret the victims of smoking express from the bottom of their hearts. As long as you cling to the steps as mentioned above, you will be amazed at how effective they are.

【译文】如果你觉得很难改掉吸烟的恶习，你并不孤单，因为很多吸烟者试图戒掉但都是徒劳。吸烟如同其他恶习一样，一旦染上就很难摆脱。比如，我的一位朋友是大烟鬼，曾努力戒烟，但现在还是与烟为伴。

但是如果你觉得非常有必要戒烟，方法如下：不断提醒自己吸烟的危害，增强戒烟的毅力。用好习惯代替恶习，比如喝咖啡或嚼口香糖。倾听吸烟受害者发自内心的忏悔。只要坚持以上提及的步骤，你会惊叹这些步骤多么有效。

预测5　对待金钱的态度

With the arrival of market-based economy, money is becoming more and more important in our life. Hit with this trend, many people come to believe that money is above everything else in their life. But their belief could not arouse any echo in my mind.

It is true that money is a key ingredient in one's struggle towards happiness, without which, for example, there would be no way to go to college or form a family. On any scale of one's daily worry, in fact, there is almost nothing heavier than money. If we see it in its true colors, however, money is nothing but a means to an end. Money can buy us food, but not appetite; medicine, but not health; diplomas, but not knowledge; and days of joy, but not the whole life of happiness. And moreover, laying any undue stress on money may lead one to stop at nothing in making it, as can be easily seen in the cases of most corrupt officials.

Therefore, it is necessary to take a correct attitude towards money. On the one hand, money is vital to our daily life, in which case, it is wise of you to spend not where you may save. On the other hand, money is something to be plowed into something more important, so it is better to spare not where you must spend. In sum, money means something but not everything to our life.

【译文】随着市场经济的到来，金钱在我们生活中的作用愈加重要。在此趋势的影响下，许多人开始相信金钱至高无上。但是他们的观点无法引发我内心的共鸣。

诚然，金钱是我们获取幸福的重要因素，没有金钱就无法上大学或组建家庭。在每日的种种忧愁中，几乎没有什么比金钱更令人忧愁。但从本质上看，金钱不过是实现目标的某种手段。金钱可以买来食物，却买不来食欲；能买来药物，却买不来健康。能买来文凭，却买不来知识；能买来一些快乐日子，却买不来一生的幸福。而且，过分重视金钱会令人不择手段去获取，这很容易从多数腐败官员的案例中找到答案。

因此，有必要对金钱采取正确的态度。一方面，金钱对于日常生活非常重要，花在该花的地方是明智的。另一方面，可以利用金钱实现追求更重要的事情，该花钱时别节省。总而言之，金钱固然重要，但绝非一切。

预测 6　锻炼的益处

As is known to all, exercise does bring a lot of benefits to our health. First, it can greatly strengthen our hearts, lungs, bones and muscles, thereby changing our whole health for the better. Besides, it can make our brains better able to react to what is going on around us. And best of all, it can help us breed optimism about our tough life.

But all the above does not mean that we can turn a blind eye to the negative effects exercise brings about. If you are normally inactive and then, contrary to your usual habit, start a program of undue exercise, as a succession of scientific studies reveals, there are more chances that you have yourself injured. In addition, the more exercise those on a fat-reducing diet take, the more loss of iron they will suffer and the worse their health will get. And worst of all, continual as well as excessive exercise can result in sudden death.

Therefore, a scientific approach must be adopted to solve the problem of exercise. On the one hand, our physical exercise must be based on both progressiveness and regularity. On the other, we must go in for physical exercise according to local as well as health conditions of our own. In sum, exercise can do us good or harm, all depending on how we make use of it.

【译文】众所周知，锻炼对于健康益处多多。首先，锻炼可以增强心肺、骨骼和肌肉功能，改善整体健康状况。此外，锻炼可以使大脑对周围事物更加应对自如。最重要的是，锻炼有助于让我们面对困境时培养乐观心态。

但是，以上诸多好处并不意味着我们对锻炼的负面影响视而不见。如果你不爱运动，但是却违背常规习惯进行不正确的身体锻炼，正如一系列的科学研究所表明，你受伤的概率更大。此外，正在减肥的人如果锻炼越多，就会流失更多铁元素，健康状况也会更差。最糟的是，持续且过度锻炼可能导致猝死。

因此，必须采取科学方法解决锻炼的问题。一方面，锻炼必须要循序渐进、遵照规律。另一方面，从事锻炼要根据身体局部和整体状况。总而言之，锻炼利弊兼有，一切取决于如何利用。

预测 7　我的生活观

Life may be different things to different people. Some may regard it as building up as much material wealth as possible while others may view it as enjoying to the fullest the pleasures each day offers. As far as I am concerned, however, I would prefer to value it as my sole chance to enrich myself with knowledge first, then to serve the society with all my heart, and finally to leave the world without any regrets.

My outlook on life is bound up with three major factors. Primarily, life is so wondrous that I am eager to explore it. Set your heart on a mystery and you can find something new; attach more of your mind to a challenge and you can get a sense of success, all of which, however, depends on how much knowledge you have equipped yourself with first. Secondly, life is also short to any individual like me. The flower you have just kissed for the first time is now fading away while the love from others you have come to cherish more is already on the wane. And most of all, both wonderfulness and shortness of life push me to seize every golden minute and every golden chance. Once I idle away the time I am supposed to grasp to study or work for the people, there will be no more hope of making up for it.

I have much option in this matter, but I have never found any other way of seeing life more reasonable and acceptable than mine. Thus, I will leave no stone untuned during the course of my college studies in order to pave the way for my meaningful and colorful life.

【译文】每个人眼中的生命不尽相同。有人认为生命就是积累足够多的财富，有人认为生命就是最大程度享受每天的乐趣。就我而言，我认为生命就是先用知识充实自己、然后全心全意服务社会、最后离开尘世时无怨无悔的唯一机会。

我的生命观与三个因素相关。首先，生命如此美妙，我渴望去探索。用心专注于某个奥秘，就会发现新事物；让思想接受挑战，就会获得成就感。然而，这一切起初都要基于你拥有的知识储备。其次，生命如此短暂。你初吻过的花儿正在凋零，你所珍视的人给予你的爱正在消退。最重要的是，生命之美妙和生命之短暂促使我要抓住每个宝贵时刻和机会。一旦我把本该用于学习和为他人服务的时光荒废，就更希望将其弥补。

关于这个问题我有多个选择。但是尚未发现看待生活的其他方式比我的更合理和让人接受。因此，为了给富有内涵、灿烂绚丽的生命铺就道路，我会在大学期间会不遗余力，刻苦学习。

预测 8　做慈善

Nowadays, it is universally acknowledged that charity plays a more and more important role in our lives and society. The number of people who make donations to charity has been increasing at a high speed in the past years.

It goes without saying that this change can only be better understood by associating with the social reality and living situation. Actually, some factors stand out on top of others, if we take a closer look into the phenomenon. First of all, people's living standard is increasingly better off and they are now having enough money to do something for charity. Furthermore, this trend is enhanced and promoted by the better government's policies, and there are many convenient channels in the charity field. Last but not least, the trend has a lot to do with the turning of people's attitude towards and outlook on life. People are more willing to help others with nothing to ask for.

With the development of our society, this change is bound to continue for a few years in the future. As far as I am concerned, this rise in charity is a positive trend and should be encouraged since it is beneficial not merely to individuals but to the whole society.

【译文】众所周知，慈善如今在我们生活和社会中的作用日益重要。从事慈善捐款的人数在过去几年快速增长。

毋庸置疑，将社会现状和生活环境结合起来才能更好地了解这种变化。事实上，如果我们仔细研究这一现象就会发现，某些因素相比其他因素还是比较突出的。首先，人们的生活水平日益提高，可以有足够的钱财从事慈善。而且，这种趋势得到政府更好政策的鼓励和推动，从事慈善有了更加便捷的渠道。最后，这种趋势也与人们对生活的态度和观念转变有关。人们更乐意帮助他人而别无所求。

随着社会发展，这种变化注定会在未来几年持续。就我而言，慈善的兴起是一种积极趋势，不仅利于个人，也利于整个社会，应该加以鼓励。

预测9　留守儿童问题

Along with the rapid development of society and improvement of people's living standard, more and more people are coming to realize the serious problem of the left-behind children. So it is of great importance for us to pay attention to this phenomenon.

It goes without saying that this increase of left-behind children can only be better understood by associating with the social reality and living situation. Actually, some factors stand out on top of others, if we take a closer look into the phenomenon. First of all, social transition is an important driving factor in our country, our society is transforming from a developing country into a developed one, many things, including left-behind children, have been forced upon us. More people leave their homes to hunt for jobs, and tend to leave their children to their grandparents in hometown. Furthermore, there are not enough regulations and instructions to guide people to avoid this problem. Last but not least, lack of government policies and supervisions has definitely exerted some negative influences, because children can't receive proper education in new places.

There is no doubt that attention must be paid to the solution of this problem, and efforts must be taken. In this aspect, everyone should make a special effort to avoid this problem, and government ought to spare no effort to achieve the goal. As long as we combine our efforts, there will be a greater chance that we can solve it.

【译文】随着社会的快速发展和生活水平的提高，越来越多的人意识到了留守儿童问题的严重性。因此，对我们来说关注该现象至关重要。

毋庸置疑，将社会现状和生活环境结合起来才能更好了解这种变化。实际上，仔细研究这一问题就会发现，某些因素还是比较突出的。首先，社会转型是一个重要驱动力。我国正从发展中国家向发达国家过渡，许多事情，包括留守儿童，都是我们面临的问题。更多人离家寻找工作，将子女留给家中的祖辈照看。而且，尚未制定足够的规则和指令来引导人们避免这一问题。最后，国家政策和监管的缺失无疑带来负面影响，因为孩子们无法在新地方接受适龄教育。

毫无疑问，一定要重视该问题，并采取相应措施。在这方面，人人都要付出特别努力避免该问题，政府要不余遗力实现既定目标。只要齐心协力，就有更大机会解决这个问题。

预测 10　老龄化问题

Along with the rapid development of society and improvement of people's living standard, more and more people are coming to realize the serious problem of the Aging Population. So it is of great importance for us to pay attention to this phenomenon.

It goes without saying that this change can only be better understood by associating with the social reality and living situation. Actually, some factors stand out on top of others, if we take a closer look into the issue. First of all, social transition is an important driving factor in our country, and our society is transforming from a developing country into a developed one, many things, including Aging Population, have been forced upon us. Furthermore, thanks to the policy of reform and opening up, the national economy has been developing at a considerably high speed in the past years, which contributes to this change.

With the development of society, this change is bound to continue for a few years in the future. As far as I am concerned, it is a negative trend and should be reversed since it is a threat not merely to economic development but to the whole society.

【译文】随着社会的快速发展和生活水平的提高，越来越多的人意识到了老龄化问题。因此，对我们来说关注该现象至关重要。

毋庸置疑，将社会现状和生活环境结合起来才能更好了解这种变化。实际上，仔细研究这一问题就会发现，某些因素还是比较突出的。首先，社会转型是一个重要驱动力。我国正从发展中国家向发达国家过渡，许多事情，包括老龄化，都是我们面临的问题。而且，由于改革开放政策，我国经济在过去几年高速发展，造成了这种变化。

随着社会发展，这种变化注定会在未来几年持续。就我而言，这种变化是一种负面趋势，不仅威胁经济发展，也威胁整个社会，应予以扭转。

（二）热点话题

话题1　一带一路

The China-proposed Belt and Road Initiative (BRI) can be a very important instrument to meet the UN 2030 Agenda for Sustainable Development.

Multilateralism is the solution to global problems. And China has been a strong pillar of multilateralism. When we look at BRI, we see a very important contribution to this solidarity in addressing global problems with international cooperation, where China plays a very central role.

We need an initiative of international solidarity to make people believe there's better globalization, to make people believe there's free trade that can benefit people overall, and to make people believe that it's possible not to leave anyone behind.

China's Belt and Road Initiative provides valuable opportunities for bilateral and multilateral cooperation. These have to be realized case by case to ensure mutual benefits are delivered.

【译文】由中国提出的"一带一路"倡议对联合国《2030年可持续发展议程》的推进有重要作用。

多边主义是解决国际问题的良方，而中国已经成为多边主义的中坚力量。"一带一路"让我们看到中国担起核心重任，通过国际合作解决全球问题，为多边力量的团结一致做出了重要贡献。

我们现在需要一个能将国际社会团结起来的倡议，以此来让人们相信全球化正朝着更好的方向发展，自由贸易能够给全体人类带来福祉，让人们相信没有人会被落下。

中国的"一带一路"倡议为双边和多边合作提供了宝贵机遇。必须依次实现双边、多边合作，以确保互利共赢。

话题2　成功的要素

Some people say the most important element to success is luck, while others claim it is hard work. There is no doubt that successful people take advantage of opportunities. But if a man does nothing but wait for the chance to come, he will achieve anything but success.

【译文】有人说成功最重要的因素是运气，而别人却说是努力。毫无疑问，成功者善于抓住机会。但是如果一个人无所事事，只是等待机会来临，他将一事无成。

话题3　新技术带来的问题

1）One of the basic questions facing our society today is: What promise or threat does new technology hold for our global future? Since the decision our society makes about technological development will undoubtedly have tremendous consequences in the years to come, it is urgently necessary to explore this question, especially by examining science and technology in their relationship to the development of humanity.

【译文】今天我们的社会面临的一个基本问题是：新技术对于全球的未来有何利弊呢？由于对技术进步的决策将毫无疑问在未来产生巨大影响，很有必要研究这一问题，尤其是研究科技与人类发展之间的关系。

2）No invention has received more praise and abuse than the Internet.

【译文】没有一项发明比互联网受到更多的赞扬和批评。

3）People equate success in life with the ability of operating computers.

【译文】人们把会使用计算机的能力与人生成功相提并论。

4）People believe that computer skills will enhance their job opportunities or promotion opportunities.

【译文】人们相信拥有计算机技术可以获得更多工作或提升的机会。

话题 4　环境污染

1）The problem of development vs. environment has now been in the limelight. Nowhere is the clash more visible than in China, where the world's largest population faces pollution, deforestation and acid rain on a large scale.

【译文】发展与环境的问题如今备受关注。中国在这方面的矛盾最为明显：拥有世界最多人口的国家面临大规模的污染、森林破坏和酸雨等问题。

2）There is no denying the fact that air pollution is an extremely serious problem: the city authorities should take strong measures to deal with it.

【译文】无可否认，空气污染是一个极其严重的问题：城市当局应该采取有力措施来解决它。

3）Environmental experts point out that increasing pollution not only causes serious problems such as global warming but also could threaten to end human life on our planet.

【译文】环境学家指出：持续增加的污染不仅会导致像全球变暖这样严重的问题，而且还将威胁到人类在这个星球的生存。

4）We should spare no effort to beautify our environment.

【译文】我们应该不遗余力地美化我们的环境。

话题 5　经济发展与环境

There is much discussion today about whether fast economic growth is desirable. Those who criticize economic growth argue that we must slow down. They believe that society is approaching certain limits on growth. These include the fixed supply of natural resources, and the possible negative effects of industry on the natural environment. People who want more economic growth, on the other hand, argue that even at the present growth rate there are still many poor people.

【译文】如今，关于经济高速发展是否可取讨论颇多。反对经济高速发展的人认为必须降速,因为社会已接近发展的极限,这些极限包括有限的自然资源,以及工业对自然环境潜在的负面影响。而另一方面,赞成高速发展的人认为,即便在当前的发展态势下,穷人数量还是很庞大。

话题6 青少年吸烟

The factors for a big rise in the teenage smoking are complex. Some attribute it to the increased standard of living which enables kids to have more pocket money than ever before. Others place the blame on the neglectful parents who tolerate and sometimes even encourage their kids smoking. Still others complain of the sharp increase in cigarette advertising and tobacco imports which give young people easy access to Marlboro, Kent and Parliament.

【译文】造成青少年吸烟快速增长的因素很复杂。有人归因于生活水平的提高使得孩子拥有了比以前更多零花钱。有人认为应该批评粗心的父母,他们容忍甚至有时鼓励孩子吸烟。还有人抱怨香烟广告的大量出现和进口香烟的大幅增长使得年轻人很容易买到诸如万宝路、健牌、百乐门等国外品牌的香烟。

话题7 教育

1) People seem to fail to take into account the fact that education does not end with graduation.

【译文】人们似乎忽视了教育不应该随着毕业而结束这一事实。

2) An increasing number of people are beginning to realize that education is not complete with graduation.

【译文】越来越多的人开始意识到教育不能随着毕业而结束。

3) When it comes to education, the majority of people believe that education is a lifetime study.

【译文】说到教育,大部分人认为其是一个终生的学习。

4) No one can deny the fact that a person's education is the most important aspect of his life.

【译文】没有人可以否认这个事实:教育是人生最重要的一方面。

5) There is a growing tendency for parents to ask their children to accept extra educational programs over the recent years.

【译文】近些年,父母要求他们的孩子接受额外的教育呈增长的势头。

6) This phenomenon has caused wide public concern in many places of the world.

【译文】这一现象在全世界许多地方已经引起了广泛公众关注。

7) Many parents believe that additional educational activities enjoy obvious advantage. By extra studies, they maintain, their children are able to obtain many kinds of practical skills and useful knowledge, which will put them in a beneficial position in the future job markets when they grow up.

【译文】许多家长相信额外的教育活动有许多优点,通过额外的学习,他们的孩子可以获得很多实践技能和有用的知识,当他们长大后,这些对他们就业是大有好处的。

8) In the first place, extra studies bring about unhealthy impacts on physical growth of children. Educational experts point out that, it is equally important to take some sport activities instead of extra studies when children have spent the whole day in a boring classroom.

【译文】首先,额外的学习对孩子们的身体发育是有不健康影响的。教育专家指出,孩子们在枯燥的教室里待了一整天后,从事一些体育活动,而不是额外的学习,是非常重要的。

9) Children are undergoing fast physical development; lack of physical exercise may produce disastrous influence on their later life.

【译文】孩子们正处于身体快速发育时期,缺乏体育锻炼可能会对他们未来的生活造成灾难性的影响。

10) In the second place, from psychological aspect, the majority of children seem to tend to have an unfavorable attitude toward additional educational activities.

【译文】第二,从心理上讲,大部分孩子似乎对额外的学习没有什么好感。

11) It is hard to imagine a student focusing their energy on textbook while other children are playing.

【译文】当别的孩子在玩耍的时候，很难想象一个学生能集中精力在课本上。

12) Moreover, children will have less time to play and communicate with their peers due to extra studies, consequently, it is difficult to develop and cultivate their character and interpersonal skills. They may become more solitary and even suffer from certain mental illness.

【译文】而且，由于要额外地学习，孩子们没有多少时间和同龄的孩子玩耍和交流，很难培养和发展他们的个性和交际能力。他们可能变得更孤僻甚至产生某些心理疾病。

13) From what has been discussed above, we may safely draw the conclusion that, although extra studies indeed enjoy many obvious advantages, its disadvantages shouldn't be ignored and far outweigh its advantages. It is absurd to force children to take extra studies after school.

【译文】通过以上讨论，我们可以得出结论：尽管额外学习的确有很多显而易见的优点，但它的缺点不可忽视，且远大于它的优点。因此放学后强迫孩子额外学习是不明智的。

14) Any parents should place considerable emphasis on their children to keep the balance between play and study. As an old saying goes：All work and no play makes Jack a dull boy.

【译文】任何家长都应非常重视保持孩子在学习与玩耍的平衡，正如那句老话：只工作，不玩耍，聪明的孩子会变傻。

话题8　旅游发展

1) With the opening and reform policy being carried out, thousands upon thousands of foreign visitors are crowding into China. They are eager to see this old mysterious land with a splendid culture of more than 5,000 years.

【译文】随着改革开放政策的贯彻执行，数以万计的外国游人涌入中国。他们渴望参观这个有着5 000多年灿烂文化的神秘古国。

2) Tourism brings China a lot of benefits. First, it enables the Chinese people to know more

about the outside world and promotes friendship and understanding. Second, it is financially beneficial to China, which needs more foreign currencies for its modernization program.

【译文】旅游业给中国带来许多好处。首先，它使中国人更加了解外界，并有助于促进友谊和理解。其次，在经济上也有利于我国，因为中国现代化建设需要更多的外汇。

3）Tourism, however, gives rise to a number of problems. For instance, it becomes a burden to inefficient transportation system.

【译文】旅游业也引起许多问题。例如，它成了我国本来效率不高的运输系统的负担。

4）Besides, the living standard of the average Chinese is still not high enough to be able to afford the many different sorts of expense during long distance travels.

【译文】此外，平均每个中国人民的生活水平还没有高到足以有钱支付长途旅行的各种开支。

第六节 提纲作文或图表作文句型

一、简单型开篇句

1. Many nations are faced with the problem of...

2. Recently the problem has been brought into focus.

3. Recently the phenomenon has become a heated topic.

4. Recently the issue has aroused great concern among...

5. Nowadays there is a growing concern over...

6. Never in our history has the idea that...been so popular.

7. Faced with..., many people argue that...

8. According to recent survey...

9. With the rapid development of...

二、复杂型开篇句

1. The human race has entered a completely new stage in its history, along with the advance of the society and the increasingly rapid economic globalization and urbanization, more problems are brought to our attention, one of which is that...

2. Recently, the phenomenon has aroused wide concern, some people are in alarm that...

3. ...plays such an important role that it undeniably becomes a widespread concern of the present-day world, so there comes a question, is it a blessing or a curse?

4. As society develops, there is a widespread concern over...

5. As to whether it is a blessing or a curse, people take different attitudes.

6. As to whether it is worthwhile..., there is a long-term debate. As an old saying goes, "Every coin has two sides." People from various backgrounds have different attitudes towards it.

7. In the process of modern urbanization, we often find ourselves in a dilemma.

8. People are attaching growing importance to...

9. An increasing number of people appreciate...

三、引言段开头语句

1. A proverb says, "..."

2. An old saying goes, "..."

3. As the proverb says, "..."

4. Generally speaking, ...

5. As we all know, ...

6. It goes without saying that ...

7. It is (quite) clear that... because...

8. It is often said that...

9. Many people often ask this question, "...?"

10. When asked about..., many people say that...

引言段写法举例

1. An English proverb says, "Early to bed and early to rise makes a man healthy, wealthy and wise." This saying is indeed full of truth. We should regard it as our motto.

2. It goes without saying that a firm resolution is the important element of success. In other words, a successful man must possess a firm resolution and an inflexible spirit. On the contrary, a man without a firm resolution will not succeed all his life.

3. It is quite clear that English has become an international language because it has been used by most of the nations in the world. In other words, you may make a trip around the world without being misunderstood if you know English.

4. Generally speaking, men who possess knowledge are more powerful than those without knowledge. In other words, the educated class always plays a more important role than ignorant people in society. This is an unchangeable truth.

5. When asked about the biggest problem today, many people say that it is the serious energy crisis. They are afraid that the world will soon run out of oil and run short of food. But other people hold different views. They regard it as a natural result of the economic development and believe it will be only solved with further advances in economy and technology.

6. There is a general debate on campus today over the phenomenon of college students' doing a part-time job. Those who object to it argue that students should not spend their precious time in this way. But people who advocate it, on the other hand, claim that by taking a major-related part-time job or summer job, students can not only improve their academic studies, but gain much experience, which they can not get from the textbooks.

四、第一个推展段落开头语句

1. Everybody knows that...

2. It can be easily seen that...

3. It is true that...

4. No one can deny that...

5. One thing which is equally important to the above mentioned is...

6. The chief reason why... is that...

7. We must recognize that...

8. There is no doubt that...

9. I am of the opinion that...

10. This can be expressed as follows.

11. To take...for an example...

12. Therefore, we should realize that...

13. We have reason to believe that...

14. (Now that) we know that...

15. What is more serious is that...

16. When it comes to..., some people think/believe that... Others argue/claim that the opposite is true. There is probably some truth in both arguments/statements, but...

17. We are often told these days that... But is this really the case?

18. In recent years, many cities/countries have been faced with the serious problem of...

19. One of the biggest issues many people talk about now is...

20. With the rapid development/improvement of..., more and more...

21. People used to think/It was thought that... In the past/old days, ... But things are quite different/But few people now share this view now.

五、第二个推展段落开头语句

1. Another special consideration in this case is that...

2. Besides, we should not neglect that...

3. But it is a pity that...

4. But the problem is not so simple. Therefore, ...

5. However, ...

6. Others may find this to be true, but I do not. I believe that...

7. On the other hand, ...

8. Perhaps you'll question why...

9. There is a certain amount of truth in this, but we still have a problem with regard to...

10. Though we are in basic agreement with...

11. What seems to be the trouble is...

12. Yet differences will be found, that's why I feel that...

13. So long as you regard this as reasonable, you may...

六、结尾句

1. From what has been discussed above, we can draw the conclusion that...

2. It is high time that strict measures should be taken to stop...

3. It is necessary that effective steps should be taken to...

4. In conclusion, it is imperative that...

5. There is no easy method, but...may be of some help.

6. To solve the above-mentioned problems, we must...

7. In summary, if we continue to ignore the above-mentioned issue, more problems will crop up.

8. With the efforts of all parties concerned, the problem will be solved thoroughly.

9. Whether it is good/positive/negative or not, one thing is clear/certain...

10. From this point of view, ...

11. In a word, ...

12. In conclusion, ...

13. On account of this we can find that ...

14. The result is dependent on ...

15. Therefore, these findings reveal the following information.

16. Thus, this is the reason why we must ...

17. To sum up, ...

18. In summary, it is important/essential/vital/necessary/urgent that we should/must...

19. From what has been discussed/mentioned above, we may safely/reasonably arrive at/come to reach/draw the conclusion that...

20. Taking into account all these factors, we can say...

七、关于比较的例句

1. The advantages far outweigh the disadvantages.

2. The advantages of A are much greater than those of B.

3. A may be preferable to B, but A suffers from the disadvantages that...

4. It is reasonable to maintain that..., but it would be foolish to claim that...

5. For all the disadvantages, it has its compensating advantages.

6. Like anything else, it has its faults.

7. A and B have several points in common.

8. However, the same is not applicable to B.

9. A and B differ in several ways.

10. Evidently, it has both positive and negative effects.

八、关于原因的例句

1. A number of factors are accountable for this situation.

2. A number of factors contribute to/lead to this phenomenon/problem.

3. The answer to this problem involves many factors.

4. The phenomenon mainly stems from the fact that...

5. The factors that contribute to the situation include...

6. The change in... largely results from the fact that...

7. We may blame..., but the real causes are...

8. Part of the explanation for it is that...

九、关于后果的例句

1. It may give rise to a host of problems.

2. The immediate result it produces is...

3. It will exert a profound influence upon...

4. Its consequence can be so great that...

十、关于批驳的例句

1. While it is true that..., it is also true that...

2. It is true that..., but one vital point is left out.

3. There is a grain of truth in these statements, but they ignore a more important fact.

4. Some people say, but it does not hold water.

5. Contrary to what is widely accepted, I maintain that...

6. It makes no sense to argue for...

十一、关于举例的例句

1. A good case in point is...

2. As an illustration, we may take...

3. Such examples may be given easily.

4. ...is often cited as an example.

十二、关于证明的例句

1. No one can deny the fact that...

2. The idea is hardly supported by facts that...

3. Unfortunately, none of the available data shows...

4. Recent studies indicate that...

5. There is sufficient evidence to show that...

6. According to statistics proved by..., it can be seen that...

十三、写作常用短语 100 条

1. 随着经济的繁荣 with the booming of the economy

2. 随着人民生活水平的显著提高 with the remarkable improvement of people's living standard

3. 先进的科学技术 advanced science and technology

4. 为我们的日常生活增添了情趣 add much spice/flavor to our daily life

5. 人们普遍认为 it is commonly believed that...

6. 我同意前者 / 后者的观点 I give my vote to the former/latter opinion.

7. 引起了广泛关注 sth. has aroused wide public concern/sth. has drawn great public attention

8. 不可否认 it is undeniable that...

9. 热烈的讨论 / 争论 a heated discussion/debate

10. 有争议性的问题 a controversial issue

11. 就我而言 / 就个人而言 as far as I am concerned/personally

12. 有充分的理由支持 be supported by sound reasons

13. 双方的论点 argument on both sides

14. 发挥日益重要的作用 play an increasingly important role

15. 对……必不可少 be indispensable to...

16. 正如谚语所说 as the proverb goes

17. 对……产生有利 / 不利的影响 exert positive/negative effects on...

18. 利远远大于弊 the advantages far outweigh the disadvantages

19. 导致，引起 lead to/give rise to/contribute to/result in

20. 复杂的社会现象 a complicated social phenomenon

21. 责任感 / 成就感 sense of responsibility/achievement

22. 竞争与合作精神 sense of competition and cooperation

23. 开阔眼界 widen one's horizon/broaden one's vision

24. 学习知识和技能 acquire knowledge and skills

25. 经济 / 心理负担 financial/psychological burden

26. 考虑到诸多因素 take many factors into consideration

27. 从另一个角度 from another perspective

28. 做出共同努力 make joint efforts

29. 对……有益 be beneficial/conducive to...

30. 为社会做贡献 make contributions to the society

31. 为……打下坚实的基础 lay a solid foundation for...

32. 综合素质 comprehensive quality

33. 致力于 / 投身于 be committed/devoted to...

34. 应当承认 admittedly

35. 不可推卸的义务 unshakable duty

36. 满足需求 satisfy/meet the needs of...

37. 可靠的信息源 a reliable source of information

38. 宝贵的自然资源 valuable natural resources

39. 因特网 the Internet（一定要有冠词，字母 I 大写）

40. 方便快捷 convenient and efficient

41. 在人类生活的方方面面 in all aspects of human life

42. 环保的材料 environmentally friendly materials

43. 社会进步的体现 a symbol of society progress

44. ……大大方便了人们的生活 ...has greatly facilitated people's lives

45. 对这一问题持有不同态度 hold different attitudes towards this issue

46. 在一定程度上 to some extent

47. 理论和实践相结合 integrate theory with practice

48. ……的必然趋势 an irresistible trend of...

49. 日益激烈的社会竞争 the increasingly keen social competition

50. 眼前利益 immediate/short-term interest

51. 长远利益 long-term interest

52. ……有其自身的优缺点 ...has its own merits and demerits/pros and cons

53. 对……有害 do harm to.../be harmful to.../be detrimental to...

54. 交流思想 / 情感 / 信息 exchange ideas/emotions/information

55. 跟上……的最新发展 keep pace/abreast with the latest development of...

56. ……的健康发展 the healthy development of...

57. 重视…… attach great importance to...

58. 社会地位 social status

59. 把时间和精力放在……上 focus one's time and energy on...

60. 扩大知识面 expand one's scope of knowledge

61. 身心两方面 both physically and mentally

62. 与……有直接/间接关系 be directly/indirectly related to...

63. 导致很多问题 give rise to/lead to/spell various problems

64. 认为 believe, claim, maintain, argue, insist, hold the opinion/belief/view that

65. 缓解压力/减轻负担 relieve stress/burden

66. 优先考虑/发展…… give (top) priority to...

67. 与……比较 compared with.../ in comparison with...

68. 可降解的/可分解的材料 degradable/decomposable material

69. 代替 replace/substitute/take the place of

70. 提供就业机会 offer job opportunities

71. 反映了社会进步 mirror the social progress/advance

72. 增进相互了解 enhance/promote mutual understanding

73. 充分利用 make full use of/take advantage of

74. 承受更大的工作压力 suffer from heavier work pressure

75. 保障社会稳定和繁荣 guarantee the stability and prosperity of our society

76. 更多地强调…… put more emphasis on...

77. 适应社会发展 adapt oneself to the social development

78. 实现梦想 realize one's dream

79. 主要理由列举如下 the main/leading reasons are listed as follows

80. 我们还有很长的路要走 we still have a long way to go

81. 单独二孩政策 selective two-child policy

82. 中国梦 China's Dream/the Chinese Dream

83. 中国精神 China's Spirit/the Chinese Spirit

84. 从我国国情出发 proceed from our national conditions

85. 以德治国 rule the country by virtue

86. 依法治国 rule the country according to law

87. 法治政府 law-based government

88. 服务型政府 service-oriented government

89. 人性化管理 human-based management

90. 促进社会和谐 promote social harmony

91. 出国热 craze for going abroad

92. 创新型国家 innovation-oriented nation

93. 摆脱贫困 shake off poverty

94. 社会主义荣辱观 Socialist Concept of Honor and Disgrace

95. 八项规定 the Eight-Rule Code

96. 物质社会 materialistic society

97. 温饱问题 subsistence problem

98. 从众心理 group/herd psychology

99. 带薪休假 paid leave

100. 公务车 state-financed vehicle

十四、写作常用句型 150 句

1. According to a recent survey, four million people die each year from diseases linked to smoking.

【译文】依照最近的一项调查，每年有400万人死于与吸烟有关的疾病。

2. The latest surveys show that quite a few children have unpleasant associations with homework.

【译文】最近的调查显示，相当多的孩子对家庭作业没什么好感。

3. No invention has received more praise and abuse than the Internet.

【译文】没有一项发明像互联网一样同时受到如此多的赞扬和批评。

4. People seem to fail to take into account the fact that education does not end with graduation.

【译文】人们似乎忽视了教育不应该随着毕业而结束这一事实。

5. An increasing number of people are beginning to realize that education is not complete with graduation.

【译文】越来越多的人开始意识到教育不能随着毕业而结束。

6. When it comes to education, the majority of people believe that education is a lifetime study.

【译文】说到教育，大部分人认为其是一个终生的学习。

7. Many experts point out that physical exercise contributes directly to a person's physical fitness.

【译文】许多专家指出体育锻炼直接有助于身体健康。

8. Proper measures must be taken to limit the number of foreign tourists and the great efforts should be made to protect local environment and history from the harmful effects of international tourism.

【译文】应该采取适当的措施限制外国旅游者的数量，努力保护当地环境和历史不受国际旅游业的不利影响。

9. An increasing number of experts believe that migrants will exert positive effects on construction of city. However, this opinion is now being questioned by more and more city residents, who complain that the migrants have brought many serious problems like crime and prostitution.

【译文】越来越多的专家相信移民对城市的建设起到积极作用。然而，越来越多的城市居民却怀疑这种说法，他们抱怨移民给城市带来了许多严重的问题，像犯罪和卖淫。

10. Many city residents complain that it is so few buses in their city that they have to spend much more time waiting for a bus, which is usually crowded with a large number of passengers.

【译文】许多市民抱怨城市的公交车太少,以至于他们要花很长时间等一辆公交车,而车上可能已满载乘客。

11. There is no denying the fact that air pollution is an extremely serious problem: the city authorities should take strong measures to deal with it.

【译文】无可否认,空气污染是一个极其严重的问题:城市当局应该采取有力措施来解决它。

12. An investigation shows that female workers tend to have a favorable attitude toward retirement.

【译文】一项调查显示妇女欢迎退休。

13. A proper part-time job does not occupy students too much time. In fact, it is unhealthy for them to spend all of time on their study. As an old saying goes, "All work and no play makes Jack a dull boy."

【译文】一份适当的业余工作并不会占用学生太多的时间,事实上,把全部的时间都用到学习上并不健康,正如那句老话:"只工作,不玩耍,聪明的孩子会变傻。"

14. Any government, which is blind to this point, may pay a heavy price.

【译文】任何政府忽视这一点都将付出巨大的代价。

15. Nowadays, many students always go into raptures at the mere mention of the coming life of high school or college they will begin. Unfortunately, for most young people, it is not pleasant experience on their first days on campus.

【译文】当前,一提到即将开始的学校生活,许多学生都会兴高采烈。然而,对多数年轻人来说,校园生活刚开始的日子并不是什么愉快的经历。

16. In view of the seriousness of this problem, effective measures should be taken before things get worse.

【译文】考虑到问题的严重性,在事态进一步恶化之前,必须采取有效的措施。

17. The majority of students believe that part-time job will provide them with more opportunities to develop their interpersonal skills, which may put them in a favorable position in

the future job markets.

【译文】大部分学生相信业余工作会使他们有更多机会发展人际交往能力，而这对他们未来找工作是非常有好处的。

18. It is indisputable that there are millions of people who still have a miserable life and have to face the dangers of starvation and exposure.

【译文】无可争辩，现在有成千上万的人仍过着挨饿受冻的痛苦生活。

19. Although this view is wildly held, there is little evidence that education can be obtained at any age and at any place.

【译文】尽管这一观点被广泛接受，很少有证据表明教育能够在任何地点、任何年龄进行。

20. No one can deny the fact that a person's education is the most important aspect of his life.

【译文】没有人能否认：教育是人生最重要的一方面。

21. People equate success in life with the ability of operating computer.

【译文】人们把会使用计算机与人生成功相提并论。

22. In the last decades, advances in medical technology have made it possible for people to live longer than in the past.

【译文】在过去的几十年，医疗技术的进步已经使得人们比过去活的时间更长成为可能。

23. In fact, we have to admit the fact that the quality of life is as important as life itself.

【译文】事实上，我们必须承认生命的质量和生命本身一样重要。

24. We should spare no effort to beautify our environment.

【译文】我们应该不遗余力地美化我们的环境。

25. People believe that computer skills will enhance their job opportunities or promotion opportunities.

【译文】人们相信拥有计算机技术可以获得更多工作或提升的机会。

26. The information I have collected over last few years leads me to believe that these knowledge may be less useful than most people think.

【译文】从这几年我搜集的信息来看，这些知识并没有人们想象的那么有用。

27. Now, it is generally accepted that no college or university can teach its students all the knowledge by the time they graduation.

【译文】现在，人们普遍认为没有一所大学能够在毕业时候教给学生所有的知识。

28. This is a matter of life and death—a matter no country can afford to ignore.

【译文】这是一个关系到生死的问题，任何国家都不能忽视。

29. For my part, I agree with the latter opinion for the following reasons.

【译文】我同意后者，有如下理由。

30. Before giving my opinion, I think it is important to look at the arguments on both sides.

【译文】在给出我的观点之前，我想看看双方的观点，这很重要。

31. This view is now being questioned by more and more people.

【译文】这一观点正受到越来越多人的质疑。

32. Although many people claim that, along with the rapidly economic development, the number of people who use bicycle are decreasing and bicycle is bound to die out. The information I've collected over the recent years leads me to believe that bicycle will continue to play extremely important roles in modern society.

【译文】尽管许多人认为随着经济的高速发展，用自行车的人数会减少，自行车可能会消亡，然而，这几年我收集的一些信息让我相信自行车仍然会继续在现代社会发挥极其重要的作用。

33. Environmental experts point out that increasing pollution not only causes serious problems such as global warming but also could threaten to end human life on our planet.

【译文】环境学家指出：持续增加的污染不仅会导致像全球变暖这样严重的问题，而且还将威胁到人类在这个星球的生存。

34. In view of such serious situation, environmental tools of transportation like bicycle are more important than any time before.

【译文】考虑到这些严重的状况，我们比以往任何时候更需要像自行车这样的环保型交通工具。

35. Using bicycle contributes greatly to peoples physical fitness as well as easing traffic jams.

【译文】使用自行车有助于人们的身体健康，并极大地缓解了交通阻塞。

36. There is a general discussion these days over education in many colleges and institutes. One of the questions under debate is whether education is a lifetime study.

【译文】当前在高校和研究机构对教育存在着大量争论，其中一个问题就是教育是否是个终身学习的过程。

37. This issue has caused wide public concern.

【译文】这个问题已经引起了广泛关注。

38. It must be noted that learning must be done by a person himself.

【译文】必须指出学习只能靠自己。

39. A large number of people tend to live under the illusion that they had completed their education when they finished their schooling. Obviously, they seem to fail to take into account the basic fact that a person's education is a most important aspect of his life.

【译文】许多人存在这样的误解，认为离开学校就意味着结束了他们的教育。显然，他们忽视了教育是人生的重要部分这一基本事实。

40. As for me, I'm in favor of the opinion that education is not complete with graduation, for the following reasons.

【译文】就我而言，我同意教育不应该随着毕业而结束的观点，有以下原因。

41. It is commonly accepted that no college or university can teach its students all the knowledge by the time they graduate.

【译文】人们普遍认为高校是不可能在毕业的时候教会他们的学生所有知识的。

42. Even the best possible graduate needs to continue learning before she or he becomes an educated person.

【译文】即使最优秀的毕业生，要想成为一个博学的人也要不断地学习。

43. It is commonly thought that our society had dramatically changed by modern science and technology, and human had made extraordinary progress in science and technology over the recent decades.

【译文】人们普遍认为我们的现代科技使我们的社会发生了巨大的变化，近几十年人类在科技方面取得了惊人的进步。

44. Now people in growing numbers are beginning to believe that learning new skills and knowledge contributes directly to enhancing their job opportunities or promotion opportunities.

【译文】现在越来越多的人开始相信学习新的技术和知识能直接帮助他们获得工作机会或升职的机会。

45. An investigation shows that many older people express a strong desire to continue studying in university or college.

【译文】一项调查显示许多老人都有到大学继续学习的愿望。

46. For the majority of people, reading or learning a new skill has become the focus of their lives and the source of their happiness and contentment after their retirement.

【译文】对大多数人来讲，退休以后，阅读或学习一项新技术已成为他们生活的中心和快乐的来源。

47. For people who want to adopt a healthy and meaningful life style, it is important to find time to learn certain new knowledge. Just as an old saying goes, "it is never too late to learn."

【译文】对于那些想过上健康而有意义的生活的人们来说，找时间学习一些新知识是很重要的，正如那句老话："活到老，学到老。"

48. There is a general debate on campus today over the phenomenon of college or high school students doing a part-time job.

【译文】对于大学或高中生打工这一现象，校园里进行着广泛的争论。

49. By taking a major-related part-job, students can not only improve their academic studies, but gain much experience, which they will never be able to get from the textbooks.

【译文】通过做一份和专业相关的兼职工作，学生不仅能够提高他们的专业能力，而且能获得从课本上得不到的经验。

50. Although people's lives have been dramatically changed over the last decades, it must be admitted that, shortage of funds is still the one of the biggest questions that students nowadays have to face because that tuition fees and prices of books are soaring by the day.

【译文】近几十年，尽管人们的生活有了惊人的改变，但必须承认，由于学费和书费日益飞涨，资金短缺仍然是学生们面临的最大问题之一。

51. These days, people in growing numbers are beginning to complain that work is more stressful and less leisurely than in past. Many experts point out that, along with the development of modern society, it is an inevitable result and there is no way to avoid it.

【译文】现在，越来越多的人开始抱怨工作比以前更有压力。许多专家指出这是现代社会发展必然的结果，无法避免。

52. It is widely acknowledged that computer and other machines have become an indispensable part of our society, which makes our life and work more comfortable and less laborious.

【译文】人们普遍认为计算机和其他机器已经成为我们社会必不可少的一部分。它们使我们的生活更舒适，减少了大量劳动。

53. At the same time, along with the benefits of such machines, employees must study knowledge involved in such machines so that they are able to control them.

【译文】同时，除了这些机器带给我们的好处，员工们也必须要学习与之相关的知识以便使用它们。

54. No one can deny the basic fact that it is impossible for average workers to master those

high-technology skills easily.

【译文】没有人能否认这一基本事实：对于一般工人来讲，轻松掌握这些技术是不可能的。

55. In the second place, there seem to be too many people without job and no enough job position.

【译文】第二方面，失业的人似乎太多而又没有足够的工作岗位。

56. Millions of people have to spend more time and energy on studying new skills and technology so that they can keep a favorable position in job market.

【译文】成千上万的人们不得不花费更多的精力和时间学习新的技术和知识，以便他们在就业市场能保持优势。

57. According to a recent survey, a growing number of people express a strong desire to take another job or spend more time on their job in order to get more money to support their family.

【译文】根据最近的一项调查，越来越多的人表达了想从事另外的工作或加班以赚取更多的钱来补贴家用的强烈愿望。

58. From what has been discussed above, I am fully convinced that the leisure life-style is undergoing a decline with the progress of modern society, it is not necessary a bad thing.

【译文】通过以上讨论，我完全相信，随着现代社会的进步，悠闲的生活方式正在消失并不是件坏事。

59. The problem of international tourism has caused wide public concern over the recent years.

【译文】近些年，国际旅游的问题引起了广泛关注。

60. Many people believe that international tourism produce positive effects on economic growth and local government should be encouraged to promote international tourism.

【译文】许多人认为国际旅游对经济发展有积极作用，应鼓励地方政府发展国际旅游。

61. But what these people fail to see is that international tourism may bring about a disastrous

impact on our environment and local history.

【译文】但是这些人忽视了国际旅游可能会给当地环境和历史造成的灾难性的影响。

62. As for me, I'm firmly convinced that the number of foreign tourists should be limited, for the following reasons.

【译文】就我而言，我坚定地认为国外旅游者的数量应得到限制，理由如下。

63. In addition, in order to attract tourists, a lot of artificial facilities have been built, which have certain unfavorable effects on the environment.

【译文】另外，为了吸引旅游者，大量人工设施被修建，这对环境是不利的。

64. For lack of distinct culture, some places will not attract tourists any more. Consequently, the fast rise in number of foreign tourists may eventually lead to the decline of local tourism.

【译文】由于缺乏独特的文化，一些地方不再吸引旅游者。因此，国外旅游者数量的快速增加可能最终会导致当地旅游业的衰败。

65. There is a growing tendency for parents to ask their children to accept extra educational programs over the recent years.

【译文】近些年，父母要求他们的孩子接受额外的教育呈增长的势头。

66. This phenomenon has caused wide public concern in many places of the world.

【译文】这一现象在全世界许多地方已引起了广泛关注。

67. Many parents believe that additional educational activities enjoy obvious advantage. By extra studies, they maintain, their children are able to obtain many kinds of practical skills and useful knowledge, which will put them in a beneficial position in the future job markets when they grow up.

【译文】许多家长相信额外的教育活动有许多优点，通过学习，他们的孩子可以获得很多实践技能和有用的知识，当他们长大后，这些对他们就业是大有好处的。

68. In the first place, extra studies bring about unhealthy impacts on physical growth of children. Educational experts point out that, it is equally important to take some sport activities

instead of extra studies when children have spent the whole day in a boring classroom.

【译文】首先，额外的学习对孩子们的身体发育是不利的。教育专家指出，孩子们在枯燥的教室里待了一整天后，从事一些体育活动，而不是额外的学习，是非常重要的。

69. Children are undergoing fast physical development, lack of physical exercise may produce serious influence on their later life.

【译文】孩子们正处于身体快速发育时期，缺乏体育锻炼可能会对他们未来的生活造成严重的影响。

70. In the second place, from psychological aspect, the majority of children seem to tend to have an unfavorable attitude toward additional educational activities.

【译文】第二，从心理上讲，大部分孩子似乎对额外的学习没有什么好感。

71. It is hard to imagine a student focusing their energy on textbook while other children are playing.

【译文】当别的孩子在玩耍的时候，很难想象一个学生能集中精力在课本上。

72. Moreover, children will have less time to play and communicate with their peers due to extra studies, consequently, it is difficult to develop and cultivate their character and interpersonal skills. They may become more solitary and even suffer from certain mental illness.

【译文】而且，由于要额外地学习，孩子们没有多少时间和同龄的孩子玩耍和交流，很难培养他们的个性和交际能力。他们可能变得孤僻甚至产生某些心理疾病。

73. From what has been discussed above, we may safely draw the conclusion that, although extra studies indeed enjoy many obvious advantages, its disadvantages shouldn't be ignored and far outweigh its advantages. It is absurd to force children to take extra studies after school.

【译文】通过以上讨论，我们可以得出结论：尽管额外学习的确有很多优点，但它的缺点不可忽视，且远大于它的优点。因此，放学后强迫孩子额外学习是不明智的。

74. Any parents should place considerable emphasis on their children to keep the balance between play and study. As an old saying goes, "All work and no play makes Jack a dull boy."

【译文】任何家长都应非常重视保持孩子在学习与玩耍的平衡,正如那句老话:"只工作,不玩耍,聪明的孩子会变傻。"

75. There is a growing tendency for parent these days to stay at home to look after their children instead of returning to work earlier.

【译文】现在,父亲或母亲留在家里照顾他们的孩子而不愿过早返回工作岗位正呈日益增长的趋势。

76. Parents are firmly convinced that, to send their child to kindergartens or nursery schools will have an unfavorable influence on the growth of children.

【译文】父母们坚定地相信把孩子送到幼儿园或托儿所对他们的成长不利。

77. However, this idea is now being questioned by more and more experts, who point out that it is unhealthy for children who always stay with their parents at home.

【译文】然而,这一想法正遭受越来越多的专家的质疑,他们指出,孩子总是待在家里,和父母在一起,是不健康的。

78. Although parents would be able to devote much more time and energy to their children, it must be admitted that, parents have less experience and knowledge about how to educate and supervise children, when compared with professional teachers working in kindergartens or nursery schools.

【译文】尽管父母能在他们孩子身上投入更多时间和精力,但是必须承认,与工作在幼儿园或托儿所的专职教师相比,他们在如何管理教育孩子方面缺乏知识和经验。

79. From what has been discussed above, we may safely draw a conclusion that, although the parents' desire to look after children by themselves is understandable, its disadvantages far outweigh the advantages.

【译文】通过以上讨论,我们可以得出如下结论:尽管家长想亲自照看孩子的愿望是可以理解的,但是这样做的缺点远大于优点。

80. Parents should be encouraged to send their children to kindergartens, which will bring

about profound impacts on children and families, and even the society as a whole.

【译文】应该鼓励父母将他们的孩子送到幼儿园,这将对孩子、家庭甚至整个社会产生深远的影响。

81. Many leaders of government always go into raptures at the mere mention of artistic and cultural projects. They are forever talking about the nice parks, the smart sculptures in central city and the art galleries with various valuable rarities. Nothing, they maintain, is more essential than such projects in the economic growth.

【译文】只要一提起艺术和文化项目,一些政府领导就会兴奋不已,他们滔滔不绝地说着美丽的公园,城市中心漂亮的雕塑,还有满是稀世珍宝的艺术展览馆。他们认为在经济发展中,没有什么比这些艺术项目更重要了。

82. But is it really the case? The information I've collected over last few years leads me to believe that artistic and cultural projects may be less useful than many governments think. In fact, basic infrastructure projects are playing extremely important role and should be given priority.

【译文】这是真的吗?这些年我收集的信息让我相信这些文化、艺术项目并没有许多政府想象的那么重要。事实上,基础设施建设非常重要,应该放在首位。

83. Those who are in favor of artistic and cultural projects advocate that cultural environment will attract more tourists, which will bring huge profits to local residents. Some people even equate the build of such projects with the development of economy.

【译文】那些赞成建设文化艺术项目的人认为文化环境会吸引更多的游客,这将给当地居民带来巨大的利益。一些人甚至把建设文化艺术项目与发展经济等同起来。

84. Unfortunately, there is very few evidence that big companies are willing to invest a huge sums of money in a place without sufficient basic projects, such as supplies of electricity and water.

【译文】然而,很少有证据表明大公司愿意把巨额的资金投到一个连水电这些基础设施都不完善的地方去。

85. From what has been discussed above, it would be reasonable to believe that basic projects play far more important role than artistic and cultural projects in people's life and economic growth.

【译文】通过以上讨论，我们有理由相信在人们的生活和经济发展方面，基础建设比艺术文化项目发挥更大的作用。

86. Those urban planners who are blind to this point will pay a heavy price, which they cannot afford.

【译文】那些城市的规划者们如果忽视这一点，将会付出他们无法承受的代价。

87. There is a growing tendency these days for many people who live in rural areas to come into and work in city. This problem has caused wide public concern in most cities all over the world.

【译文】农民进城打工正成为增长的趋势，这一问题在世界上大部分城市已引起普遍关注。

88. An investigation shows that many migrant workers think that working at city provide them with not only a higher salary but also the opportunity of learning new skills.

【译文】一项调查显示许多民工认为在城市打工不仅有较高的收入，而且能学到一些新技术。

89. It must be noted that improvement in agriculture seems to not be able to catch up with the increase in population of rural areas and there are millions of peasants who still live a miserable life and have to face the dangers of exposure and starvation.

【译文】必须指出，农业的发展似乎赶不上农村人口的增加，并且仍有成千上万的农民过着缺衣挨饿的贫寒生活。

90. Although rural migrants contribute greatly to the economic growth of the cities, they may inevitably bring about many negative impacts.

【译文】尽管民工对城市的经济发展做出了巨大贡献，然而他们也不可避免地带来了一些负面影响。

91. Many sociologists point out that rural migrants are putting pressure on population control and social order; that they are threatening to take already scarce city jobs; and that they have worsened traffic and public health problems.

【译文】许多社会学家指出民工正给人口控制和社会治安带来压力。他们正在威胁着本已萧条的工作市场，他们恶化了交通和公共卫生状况。

92. It is suggested that governments ought to make efforts to reduce the increasing gap between cities and countryside. They ought to set aside an appropriate fund for improvement of the standard of peasants' lives. They ought to invite some experts in agriculture to share their experiences, information and knowledge with peasants, which will contribute directly to the economic growth of rural areas.

【译文】政府应该努力减少正在拉大的城乡差距，应该划拨适当的资金提高农民的生活水平，应该邀请农业专家向农民介绍他们的经验、知识和信息，这些将有助于发展农村经济。

93. In conclusion, we must take into account this problem rationally and place more emphases on peasants' lives. Any government that is blind to this point will pay a heavy price.

【译文】总之，我们应理智考虑这一问题，重视农民的生活。任何政府忽视这一点都将付出巨大的代价。

94. Although many experts from universities and institutes consistently maintain that it is an inevitable part of an independent life, parents in growing numbers are starting to realize that people, including teachers and experts in education, should pay considerable attention to this problem.

【译文】尽管来自高校和研究院的许多专家坚持认为这是独立生活不可避免的一部分，然而越来越多的家长开始意识到包括教师和教育专家在内的人们应该认真对待这一问题。

95. As for me, it is essential to know firstly, what kind of problems young students possibly

would encounter on campus.

【译文】我认为，首先应看看学生们在校园可能遇到哪些问题。

96. On the one hand, it is indisputable that boarding schools are exerting a growing important effect, especially in last few years.

【译文】一方面，寄宿学校正在发挥越来越重要的作用，尤其是最近几年，这是无可争辩的。

97. Students who attend a boarding school would cultivate their independence as apart from their parents.

【译文】离开父母上寄宿学校的学生将会培养他们的独立性。

98. What's more, living in school can save them a great deal of time on the way between home and school everyday, so they would be able to concentrate more time and energy on their academic work.

【译文】而且，生活在学校里能节省大量每天往返于学校和家的路上的时间，这会使他们有更多的时间和精力放在学习上。

99. It is more convenient for managing students.

【译文】更便于管理学生。

100. On the other hand, the contribution of day schools can't be ignored.

【译文】另一方面，日制学校的贡献是不能忽视的。

101. Due to high tuition fee, most of ordinary families cannot afford to send their children to boarding schools.

【译文】因为较高的学费，大部分普通家庭支付不起他们的孩子上寄宿学校的费用。

102. Since it is unnecessary to consider students' routine life, day school can lay stress on teaching instead of other aspects, such as management of dormitory and cafeteria.

【译文】由于无须考虑学生的日常生活，日制学校可以将重点放在教学上而不是放在像宿舍和食堂管理这些方面。

103. Furthermore, students living in their own home would have access to a comfortable life and have more opportunities to communicate with their parents, which have beneficial impact on development of their personal character.

【译文】而且,学生生活在自己家中,有舒适的生活,并有更多机会和父母交流,这对他们个性的培养是有利的。

104. From what has been discussed above, we may safely draw the conclusion that both of day schools and boarding schools are important to train young students for our society.

【译文】通过以上讨论,我们可以得出结论,寄宿学校和日制学校对我们社会培养年轻学生都是重要的。

105. There is much discussion over science and technology. One of the questions under debate is whether traditional technology and methods are bound to die out when a country begins to develop modern science and technology.

【译文】关于科学技术存在许多争论,其中一个问题是当国家发展现代科学技术时,传统的技术方法是否可能会消亡?

106. As for me, the declining of traditional technology and methods is not a bad thing; it is the natural result of progress of society.

【译文】我认为,传统技术方法的消亡不一定是坏事,这是社会进步的自然结果。

107. In the first place, some aspects of the traditional technology and methods are harmful and hampering the development of modern technology science.

【译文】首先,传统技术方法有些部分是有害的,并且会阻碍现代科技的发展。

108. Although modern science and technology have proved that such methods are absurd, there are still millions of people use such methods in many remote places nowadays.

【译文】尽管现代科学技术已经证明了这些方法是愚昧的,然而在许多偏僻的地方,仍有成千上万的人们在使用这些方法。

109. In the second place, many values of traditional technology are out of date and should be

replaced by modern science.

【译文】第二点,许多传统技术方法已经过时,应被现代科技所取代。

110. Although many people tend to live under the illusion that traditional technology and methods are still playing extremely important role in people's life, an increasing evidence shows that it is less useful than many people think.

【译文】尽管许多人保持着传统观念,认为传统技术方法在人们生活中仍发挥着重要作用,但是越来越多的证据显示它并没有人们想象的有用。

111. From what has been discussed above, I firmly believe that time will prove that traditional technology and methods would die out with the development of modern science and technology. The maintenance of the traditional technology and methods is futile.

【译文】通过以上讨论,我坚定地相信时间会证明传统技术方法将会随着现代技术的发展而消亡,坚持传统技术方法是徒劳的。

112. At the time when technology means ever more harmful gases in the air we breathe, we need these forests now more than ever.

【译文】当技术的发展意味着我们会吸入更多空气中的有害气体时,我们比任何时候更需要森林。

113. Nothing is more important than to receive education.

【译文】没有比接受教育更重要的事。

114. There is no denying that the qualities of our living have gone from bad to worse.

【译文】无可否认,我们的生活品质已经每况愈下。

115. It is universally acknowledged that trees are indispensable to us.

【译文】全世界都知道树木对我们而言是不可或缺的。

116. There is no doubt that our educational system leaves something to be desired.

【译文】毫无疑问,我们的教育制度令人不满意。

117. An advantage of using the solar energy is that it won't create any pollution.

【译文】使用太阳能的优点是它不会产生任何污染。

118. The reason why we have to grow trees is that they can supply fresh air for us.

【译文】我们必须种树的原因是它们能供应我们新鲜的空气。

119. So precious is time that we can't afford to waste it.

【译文】时间是如此珍贵,我们不能浪费它。

120. Rich as our country is, the qualities of our living are by no means satisfactory.

【译文】虽然我们的国家很富有,但是我们的生活质量却令人很不满意。

121. The harder you work, the more progress you make.

【译文】你越努力,你越进步。

122. The more books we read, the more learned we become.

【译文】我们书读得越多,我们越有学问。

123. To average people, they often tend to live under the illusion that English often means a good opportunity for one's career, is this really the case?

【译文】对于一般人来说,他们常常以为掌握英语就意味着一份好的工作,然而这是真的吗?

124. By taking exercise, we can always stay healthy.

【译文】通过体育锻炼,我们能够始终保持健康。

125. Listening to music enables us to feel relaxed.

【译文】听音乐能使我们放松。

126. On no account can we ignore the value of knowledge.

【译文】我们绝对不能忽视知识的价值。

127. It is time the authorities concerned took proper steps to solve the traffic problems.

【译文】该是有关当局采取适当的措施来解决交通问题的时候了。

128. Those who violate traffic regulations should be punished.

【译文】违反交通规则的人应该受到处罚。

129. There is no one but longs to go to college.

【译文】人们都希望上大学。

130. Since the examination is around the corner, I am compelled to give up doing sports.

【译文】既然考试迫在眉睫,我不得不放弃做运动。

131. It is conceivable that knowledge plays an important role in our life.

【译文】可想而知,知识在我们的一生中扮演一个重要的角色。

132. The progress of the society is based on harmony.

【译文】社会的进步是以和谐为基础的。

133. We should bring home to people the value of working hard.

【译文】我们应该让人们知道努力的价值。

134. Taking exercise is closely related to health.

【译文】做运动与健康息息相关。

135. We should get into the habit of keeping good hours.

【译文】我们应该养成早睡早起的习惯。

136. The condition of our traffic leaves much to be desired.

【译文】我们的交通状况令人不满意。

137. Smoking has a great influence on our health.

【译文】抽烟对我们的健康有很大的影响。

138. Reading does good to our mind.

【译文】读书对心灵有益。

139. Overwork does harm to health.

【译文】工作过度对健康有害。

140. Pollution poses a great threat to our existence.

【译文】污染对我们的生存造成巨大威胁。

141. We should do our best to achieve our goal in life.

【译文】我们应尽全力去达成我们的人生目标。

142. Whether a large family is a good thing or not is a very popular topic, which is often talked about not only by city residents but by farmers as well.

【译文】家庭人口多好还是家庭人口少好是一个非常普遍的话题，不仅是城里人，农民也经常讨论这个问题。

143. As is known to all, fake and inferior commodities harm the interests of consumers.

【译文】众所周知，假冒伪劣商品损害了消费者的利益。

144. Today an increasing number of people have realized that law education is of great importance, in order to keep law and order, every one of us is supposed to get a law education.

【译文】现在，愈来愈多的人认识到法制教育的重要性。为了维护社会治安，我们每人都应该接受法制教育。

145. From what I have mentioned above, we can see clearly that violence on TV has great influence on youngsters' behavior.

【译文】从上面我所提到的，我们可以清楚地看到，电视暴力对青少年的影响是极其深远的。

146. There are three reasons for the improvement in people's living conditions. In the first place, we have been carrying out the reform and opening-up policy. Secondly, there has been a rapid expansion of our national economy. Furthermore, the birth rate has been put under control.

【译文】人民生活状况的改善原因有三点。首先，我们一直在贯彻执行改革开放政策。其次，国民经济正在迅速发展。再者，出生率已经得到控制。

147. My suggestions to deal with the problem are as follows. To begin with, it is urgent to create nature reserves. Secondly, certain rare wild animals that are going to be extinct should be collected, fed and reproduced artificially. Finally, those who hunter them must be punished severely.

【译文】我对解决这个问题的建议如下：首先，迫在眉睫的是建立自然保护区。其次，有些濒临灭绝的珍稀野生动物应该被收捕、人工喂养并繁殖。最后，对于捕猎珍稀野生动物的人必须严惩。

148. People differ in their attitudes towards failure. Faced with it, some of them can stand up to it, draw useful lessons from it and try hard to fulfill what they are determined to do. Others, however, lose heart and give in.

【译文】人们对失败持有不同的态度。面对失败，有人能够经得起考验，从失败中吸取教训，并努力去完成他们下定决心要做的事情。然而，另一些人却丧失信心并退却了。

149. It is desirable to build more hospitals, shopping centers, recreation centers, cinemas and other public facilities to meet the growing needs of people.

【译文】人们希望建立更多的医院、购物中心、娱乐中心、电影院和其他公用设施来满足人们日益增长的需求。

150. As a popular saying goes, "everything has two sides." Now the public are benefiting more and more from scientific and technological inventions. On the other hand, the progress of science and technology is bringing us a lot of trouble. People in many countries are suffering from public hazards.

【译文】常言道："事情总是一分为二的。"如今人们从科技发明中得到越来越多的好处。另一方面，科技进步也给我们带来了许多麻烦。许多国家的人民正在饱受公害之苦。

十五、分类词汇、短语

（一）经济

economic globalization（经济全球化）

sustainable development（可持续发展）

unfair competition（不正当竞争）

crack down on fake commodities（打假）

booming（繁荣的）

fierce competition（激烈竞争）

credit crisis（信用危机）

stabilize prices（稳定物价）

（二）文化

great and profound（博大精深的）

integration and interaction（融合交汇）

crash（碰撞）

charming（极具魅力的）

splendid（壮丽辉煌的）

English fever（英语热）

（三）环保

environmental-friendly（生态型的，环保的）

threat of global warming（全球变暖的威胁）

promote fundamental shifts in the economic system and mode of economic growth（促进经济体制和经济增长方式的转变）

curb environmental pollution/ bring the pollution under control（治理环境污染）

develop renewable resources（开发可再生资源）

a low-carbon economy（低碳经济）

（四）科技

science and technology（科学技术）

web-addiction（沉迷网络）

computer crime（电脑犯罪）

e-commerce（电子商务）

virtual life（虚拟生活）

information era（信息时代）

cyber romance（网恋）

surf the Internet（网上冲浪）

（五）就业

applicant（申请人）

position available/ vacant position（空缺职位）

competent（能胜任的）

be qualified for（合格的）

proficiency（熟练程度）

job arrangement and benefit（工作待遇和福利）

promotion（晋升）

（六）大学生活／教育

cultivate（培养）

further one's study（深造）

quality education（素质教育）

foster abilities（培养能力）

relieve the burden on students（减轻学生负担）

be occupied with so much schoolwork（忙于功课）

place emphasis on...（以……为重心）

comprehensive（全面的，广泛的）

practical capability（实际能力）

duck-stuffing（填鸭式）

（七）社会现象

enlightening（富有启发的）

cause alarm and attention（引起了警惕和重视）

set good example for...（为……树立榜样）

dedicate（做贡献）

take action（采取行动）

ensure implementing activities（确保执行）

vulnerable（易诱惑的，易受影响的）

be supposed to（应该）

（八）人物特征、情感描写

strong-minded（坚强的）

industrious（勤奋的）

promising（有前途的）

dynamic（有生机的；有活力的）

responsible（有责任心的）

influential（有影响力的）

profound（渊博精深的）

devoted（忠实的；投入的）

warm-hearted（热心的）

十六、高频替换表达

保护：protect, preserve, conserve

确保：assure, ensure, guarantee

要求：request, demand, need

消除：eliminate, remove, get rid of, erase

导致：cause, lead to, result in, account for, give rise to, bring about

显示：show, reveal, illustrate, indicate

对手：competitor, rival, opponent

观点：idea, belief, opinion, view, perspective

改变：change, convert, alter, modify

人：people, person, individual, character, folks

事情：affair, business, matter, thing

顾客：shopper, client, consumer, purchaser, customer

非常：overwhelmingly, exceedingly, extremely, intensely, very

拥有：enjoy, possess, have

比如：to name only a few, as an example, for example, for instance

关于：regarding, concerning, about

总是：invariably, always, constantly

解决：solve, deal with, cope with, handle, resolve, address, tackle

损害：damage, hurt, harm, impair, undermine, jeopardize

给予：give, offer, render, impart, provide, supply, afford

培养：develop, cultivate, foster

优势：advantage, merit, virtue, benefit, upside, strength

缺陷：disadvantage, demerit, drawback, downside, weakness

重要的：key, crucial, critical, important, significant, vital, substantial, indispensable, imperative

认为：think, believe, insist, maintain, assert, conclude, deem, hold, argue, be convinced

因此：so, therefore, thus, hence, consequently, as a consequence, accordingly, as a result, because of, as a result of

增长至：grow to, rise to, increase to, go up to, climb to, ascend to, jump to, shoot to

降低至：dip to, fall to, decline to, decrease to, drop to, go down to, reduce to, slump to, descend to, sink to, slide to

保持稳定：level out, remain stable, remain still, remain steady, be stable, maintain the same level, remain unchanged, be still, remain the same level, stay constant, keep at the same level, level off, stabilize

急剧地：dramatically, drastically, sharply, hugely, enormously, steeply, substantially, considerably, significantly, markedly, surprisingly, strikingly, radically, remarkably, vastly, noticeably

平稳地：steadily, smoothly, slightly, slowly, marginally, gradually, moderately, mildly.

有益的：useful, helpful, beneficial, profitable, rewarding, advantageous

明显的：clear, obvious, evident, self-evident, manifest, apparent, crystal-clear

占（份额/比例）：take up, account for, constitute, consist of, make up, occupy, hold, compose

与……相比：compared with..., in comparison with...

相反：by contrast, in contrast, on the other hand, on the contrary, conversely

展示：show, reveal, illustrate, demonstrate, depict, present, represent, describe

大约：approximately, almost, about, around, nearly, roughly

波动：fluctuate, go ups and downs, display a fluctuation, demonstrate a fluctuation

事实上：practically, in practice, essentially, in essence, in reality, in effect, in fact, as a matter of fact, it is a fact that

换言之：namely, that is to say, in other words, to put it differently, to put it another way, to put it from another angle

第七节 作文修改

下面附上学员的小作文和大作文各两篇,原稿有一些错误,改进稿进行了修订,用下划线表示。通过对比,希望大家能够对英文写作的基本要求达到更深的理解和掌握,真正做到得心应手,信手拈来。

小作文原稿 1:

Dear boss:

I am writing to ask for five days leave because of my mother's illness. Yesterday, she called me that she fell sick and have hard headache, I have to spend several days to take her go to hospital. So I want ask for my annual leave to take care of her.

Before I leave, I will try my best to accomplish the work in my hand currently. If there was

some important task need me to complete in the time when I am absent, I will work overtime to finish it when I come back. In these days that I am leaving, you can call me immediately when you need ask me something.

Thank you for your assistance in this matter. I look forward to hearing from you soon.

Yours sincerely,

Jack Cheng

改进稿:

Dear boss,

I am writing to ask for five days leave because of my mother's illness. Yesterday, she called me that she fell sick and got a serious headache. So I want to ask for my annual leave to take care of her in hospital for several days. Before my departure, I will fulfill the work in hand. In case there were any important task during my absence, I will work overtime to finish it late on. In these days when I am out, please feel free to call me.

Thank you for your assistance in this matter. I look forward to your early reply.

Yours sincerely,

Jack Cheng

小作文原稿 2:

Mr. Bob,

We have arrived in Beijing, China at 7 o'clock. While I feel tired, I find something in my luggage—your favorite music CD, that I borrowed from you last week. Please let me make an apology to you for my forgetting to return to you. How can you get it as soon as possible? I have an idea that I can send it to you by post. Of course, you know, you are my landlord, so I shall post it according to your room address. When you receive my package, please no hesitate to let me know by telephone or email.

Finally, please let me to apology to you for the my mistakes, and I am regretful for some trouble from the faulty. This is all, and I am looking forward to your reply.

　　Yours sincerely,
　　Li Ming

改进稿:

Mr. Bob,

We arrived in Beijing, China at 7 o'clock. Then I **found** something else in my luggage besides my own belongings—your favorite music CD, which I borrowed from you last week. Please let me make an apology for forgetting to return it to you. How can you get it as soon as possible? To send it by post may be the best choice. So, for the convenience of posting, please give me your room address. When you receive my package, please feel no hesitation to let me know by telephone or email.

Finally, please let me apologize for my mistakes, and I am regretful for the trouble.

Look forward to your reply.

　　　　　　　　Yours Sincerely,
　　　　　　　　Li Ming

大作文原稿 1:

It is well-known that there is so much white pollution around us that our life is under their trouble. Maybe some people will ask me what is so called white pollution. In brief, it is something unbreakable, such as some plastic products. And now more and more people is concerned about this serious matter.

Why this trouble is so serious? I argue that it is mainly due to the shortage of the

改进稿:

It is clear that there is so much white pollution around us that our life is under great trouble. Maybe some people will ask what is so-called white pollution. In brief, it is something unbreakable, such as some plastic products. And now more and more people are concerned about this serious matter.

Why this trouble is so serious? I argue that it is mainly due to the shortage of the environmental protection knowledge. And we are not paying attention enough to the environmental protection which is not rooted in our environmental consciousness.

In order to avoid the further environment deterioration, I suggest that we can train our environmental consciousness by all kinds of meaning, such as TV, broadcast, and other media. But first of all, it is important for us to reinforce the environmental consciousness of our students. Because they are on behalf of our future. We can add some lecture of the environmental protection and launch some public benefit activities to let everybody know further the environmental protection knowledge.

All in one word, I believe in that our world will be more and more beautiful if everyone can do it well by ourselves.

environmental protection knowledge. And we are not paying <u>enough</u> attention to environmental <u>issues</u>.

In order to avoid the further environment deterioration, we can <u>develop</u> our environ-mental consciousness by all kinds of means, such as TV, broadcast, and other media. But first of all, it is important for us to <u>raise</u> environmental <u>consciousness</u> of our students, <u>because they are our future</u>. We can give lectures on environmental protection and <u>launch some charity activities</u> to let everybody further know environmental protection.

<u>In one word</u>, I believe in that our world will be more and more beautiful if everyone can do it well by ourselves.

大作文原稿 2：

Nowadays, there are more and more people thinking that it is important to create a green campus. It is estimated that about 80 percent of university is driving away at it in entire country. The reason can be listed as follows.

The first one is everyone wish to live and study in beautiful circumstance rather than disgraceful one. Beside, we can improve our learning efficiency in pleasing surrounding. The last reason is the earth need more and more green, creating a green campus is involved of protecting our environment.

改进稿：

Nowadays, <u>more and more people think</u> that it is important to create a green campus. It is estimated that about 80 percent of <u>universities are</u> driving away at it in <u>the</u> entire country. The reasons can be listed as follows.

<u>First</u>, everyone wishes to live and study in beautiful rather than disgraceful <u>circumstances</u>. Besides, <u>learning efficiency can be improved in pleasing surroundings</u>. Last but not the least, the earth <u>needs</u> more <u>greenness</u>. So, to create a green campus is to protect our environment.

In addition, green campus includes not only the green environment, but also green culture and green behavior. It is high time something were done upon it. We should realize the importance and necessity of creating it. Everyone should make effort to protect our environment, obey the society rules, and create healthy circumstance and culture. All the measures will certainly to create more and more green campuses.

In addition, a green campus includes not only the green environment, but also a green culture and green behaviors. It is high time something were done upon it. We should realize its importance and necessity. Everyone should make an effort to protect our environment, follow the social rules, and create healthy circumstances and culture. All the measures will be beneficial to creating more green campuses.

Part C 真题实战篇

- 2018 年全国硕士研究生招生考试 英语（二）试题
- 2018 年全国硕士研究生招生考试 英语（二）参考答案
- 2019 年全国硕士研究生招生考试 英语（二）试题
- 2019 年全国硕士研究生招生考试 英语（二）参考答案
- 2020 年全国硕士研究生招生考试 英语（二）试题
- 2020 年全国硕士研究生招生考试 英语（二）参考答案

2018年全国硕士研究生招生考试英语（二）试题

Section I   Use of English

Directions: Read the following text. Choose the best word(s) for each numbered blank and mark A, B, C or D on the ANSWER SHEET. (10 points)

Why do people read negative Internet comments and do other things that will obviously be painful? Because humans have an inherent need to __1__ uncertainty, according to a recent study in *Psychological Science*. The new research reveals that the need to know is so strong that people will __2__ to satisfy their curiosity even when it is clear the answer will __3__.

In a series of four experiments, behavioral scientists at the University of Chicago and the Wisconsin School of Business tested students' willingness to __4__ themselves to unpleasant stimuli in an effort to satisfy curiosity. For one __5__, each participant was shown a pile of pens that the researcher claimed were from a previous experiment. The twist? Half of the pens would __6__ an electric shock when clicked.

Twenty-seven students were told which pens were electrified; another twenty-seven were told only that some were electrified. __7__ left alone in the room, the students who did not know which ones would shock them clicked more pens and incurred more shocks than the students who knew what would __8__. Subsequent experiments reproduced this effect with other stimuli, __9__ the sound of fingernails on a chalkboard and photographs of disgusting insects.

The drive to __10__ is deeply rooted in humans, much the same as the basic drives for __11__ or shelter, says Christopher Hsee of the University of Chicago. Curiosity is often considered a good instinct—it can __12__ new scientific advances, for instance—but sometimes such __13__ can backfire. The insight that curiosity can drive you to do __14__ things is a profound one.

Unhealthy curiosity is possible to __15__, however. In a final experiment, participants who were encouraged to __16__ how they would feel after viewing an unpleasant picture were less likely to __17__ to see such an image. These results suggest that imagining the __18__ of following through on one's curiosity ahead of time can help determine __19__ it is worth the endeavor. "Thinking about long-term __20__ is key to reducing the possible negative effects of curiosity," Hsee says. In other words, don't read online comments.

1. [A] resolve   [B] protect   [C] discuss   [D] ignore
2. [A] refuse   [B] wait   [C] seek   [D] regret
3. [A] rise   [B] last   [C] mislead   [D] hurt
4. [A] alert   [B] tie   [C] expose   [D] treat
5. [A] message   [B] trial   [C] review   [D] concept
6. [A] remove   [B] weaken   [C] deliver   [D] interrupt
7. [A] Unless   [B] If   [C] Though   [D] When
8. [A] happen   [B] continue   [C] disappear   [D] change
9. [A] rather than   [B] such as   [C] regardless of   [D] owing to
10. [A] disagree   [B] forgive   [C] forget   [D] discover
11. [A] pay   [B] marriage   [C] food   [D] schooling
12. [A] begin with   [B] rest on   [C] learn from   [D] lead to
13. [A] withdrawal   [B] inquiry   [C] persistence   [D] diligence
14. [A] self-destructive [B] self-reliant [C] self-evident   [D] self-deceptive
15. [A] resist   [B] define   [C] replace   [D] trace
16. [A] predict   [B] overlook   [C] design   [D] conceal
17. [A] remember   [B] choose   [C] promise   [D] pretend

18. [A] relief   [B] plan   [C] outcome   [D] duty

19. [A] whether   [B] why   [C] where   [D] how

20. [A] limitations [B] investments [C] strategies [D] consequences

Section II Reading Comprehension

Part A

Directions: Read the following four texts. Answer the questions after each text by choosing A, B, C or D. Mark your answers on the ANSWER SHEET. (40 points)

Text 1

It is curious that Stephen Koziatek feels almost as though he has to justify his efforts to give his students a better future.

Mr. Koziatek is part of something pioneering. He is a teacher at a New Hampshire high school where learning is not something of books and tests and mechanical memorization, but practical. When did it become accepted wisdom that students should be able to name the 13th president of the United States but be utterly overwhelmed by a broken bike chain?

As Koziatek knows, there is learning in just about everything. Nothing is necessarily gained by forcing students to learn geometry at a graffitied desk stuck with generations of discarded chewing gum. They can also learn geometry by assembling a bicycle.

But he's also found a kind of insidious prejudice. Working with your hands is seen as almost a mark of inferiority. Schools in the family of vocational education "have that stereotype... that it's for kids who can't make it academically," he says.

On one hand, that viewpoint is a logical product of America's evolution. Manufacturing is not the economic engine that it once was. The job security that the US economy once offered to high school graduates has largely evaporated. More education is the new principle. We want more for our kids, and rightfully so.

But the headlong push into bachelor's degrees for all—and the subtle devaluing of anything less—misses an important point: That's not the only thing the American economy needs. Yes, a bachelor's degree opens more doors. But even now, 54 percent of the jobs in the country are middle-skill jobs, such as construction and high-skill manufacturing. But only 44 percent of workers are adequately trained.

In other words, at a time when the working class has turned the country on its political head, frustrated that the opportunity that once defined America is vanishing, one obvious solution is staring us in the face. There is a gap in working-class jobs, but the workers who need those jobs most aren't equipped to do them. Koziatek's Manchester School of Technology High School is trying to fill that gap.

Koziatek's school is a wake-up call. When education becomes one-size-fits-all, it risks overlooking a nation's diversity of gifts.

21. A broken bike chain is mentioned to show students' lack of _____.

   [A] mechanical memorization   [B] academic training

   [C] practical ability   [D] pioneering spirit

22. There exists the prejudice that vocational education is for kids who _____.

   [A] are financially disadvantaged   [B] are not academically successful

   [C] have a stereotyped mind   [D] have no career motivation

23. We can infer from Paragraph 5 that high school graduates _____.

   [A] are entitled to more educational privileges

   [B] are reluctant to work in manufacturing

   [C] used to have more job opportunities

   [D] used to have big financial concerns

24. The headlong push into bachelor's degrees for all _____.

[A] helps create a lot of middle-skill jobs

[B] may narrow the gap in working-class jobs

[C] is expected to yield a better-trained workforce

[D] indicates the overvaluing of higher education

25. The author's attitude toward Koziatek's school can be described as _____.

[A] supportive   [B] disappointed   [C] tolerant   [D] cautious

Text 2

While fossil fuels—coal, oil, gas—still generate roughly 85 percent of the world's energy supply, it's clearer than ever that the future belongs to renewable sources such as wind and solar. The move to renewables is picking up momentum around the world: They now account for more than half of new power sources going on line.

Some growth stems from a commitment by governments and farsighted businesses to fund cleaner energy sources. But increasingly the story is about the plummeting prices of renewables, especially wind and solar. The cost of solar panels has dropped by 80 percent and the cost of wind turbines by close to one-third in the past eight years.

In many parts of the world renewable energy is already a principal energy source. In Scotland, for example, wind turbines provide enough electricity to power 95 percent of homes. While the rest of the world takes the lead, notably China and Europe, the United States is also seeing a remarkable shift. In March, for the first time, wind and solar power accounted for more than 10 percent of the power generated in the US, reported the US Energy Information Administration.

President Trump has underlined fossil fuels—especially coal—as the path to economic growth. In a recent speech in Iowa, he dismissed wind power as an unreliable energy source. But that message did not play well with many in Iowa, where wind turbines dot the fields and provide 36 percent of the state's electricity generation and where tech giants like Microsoft are being attracted by the availability of clean energy to power their data centers.

The question "what happens when the wind doesn't blow or the sun doesn't shine?" has provided a quick put-down for skeptics. But a boost in the storage capacity of batteries is making their ability to keep power flowing around the clock more likely.

The advance is driven in part by vehicle manufacturers, who are placing big bets on battery-powered electric vehicles. Although electric cars are still a rarity on roads now, this massive investment could change the picture rapidly in coming years.

While there's a long way to go, the trend lines for renewables are spiking. The pace of change in energy sources appears to be speeding up—perhaps just in time to have a meaningful effect in slowing climate change. What Washington does—or doesn't do—to promote alternative energy may mean less and less at a time of a global shift in thought.

26. The word "plummeting" (Line 2, Para.2) is closest in meaning to _____.

[A] changing [B] stabilizing [C] rising [D] falling

27. According to Paragraph 3, the use of renewable energy in America _____.

[A] has proved to be impractical [B] is as extensive as in Europe
[C] faces many challenges [D] is progressing notably

28. It can be learned that in Iowa, _____.

[A] wind energy has replaced fossil fuels [B] wind is a widely used energy source
[C] tech giants are investing in clean energy [D] there is a shortage of clean energy supply

29. Which of the following is true about clean energy according to Paragraphs 5&6?

[A] Its continuous supply is becoming a reality.

[B] It is commonly used in car manufacturing.

[C] Its sustainable exploitation will remain difficult.

[D] Its application has boosted battery storage.

30. It can be inferred from the last paragraph that renewable energy _____.

[A] will bring the US closer to other countries

[B] will accelerate global environmental change

[C] is not really encouraged by the US government

[D] is not competitive enough with regard to its cost

Text 3

The power and ambition of the giants of the digital economy is astonishing—Amazon has just announced the purchase of the upmarket grocery chain Whole Foods for $13.5 bn, but two years ago Facebook paid even more than that to acquire the WhatsApp messaging service, which doesn't have any physical product at all. What WhatsApp offered Facebook was an intricate and finely detailed web of its users' friendships and social lives.

Facebook promised the European commission then that it would not link phone numbers to Facebook identities, but it broke the promise almost as soon as the deal went through. Even without knowing what was in the messages, the knowledge of who sent them and to whom was enormously revealing and still could be. What political journalist, what party whip, would not want to know the makeup of the WhatsApp groups in which Theresa May's enemies are currently plotting? It may be that the value of Whole Foods to Amazon is not so much the 460 shops it owns, but the records of which customers have purchased what.

Competition law appears to be the only way to address these imbalances of power. But it is clumsy. For one thing, it is very slow compared to the pace of change within the digital economy. By the time a problem has been addressed and remedied it may have vanished in the marketplace, to be replaced by new abuses of power. But there is a deeper conceptual problem, too. Competition law as presently interpreted deals with financial disadvantage to consumers and this is not obvious when the users of these services don't pay for them. The users of their services are not their customers. That would be the people who buy advertising from them—and Facebook and Google, the two virtual giants, dominate digital advertising to the disadvantage of all other media and entertainment companies.

The product they're selling is data, and we, the users, convert our lives to data for the benefit of the digital giants. Just as some ants farm the bugs called aphids for the honeydew they produce when they feed, so Google farms us for the data that our digital lives yield. Ants keep predatory insects away from where their aphids feed; Gmail keeps the spammers out of our inboxes. It doesn't feel like a human or democratic relationship, even if both sides benefit.

31. According to Paragraph 1, Facebook acquired WhatsApp for its _____.

    [A] digital products   [B] physical assets

    [C] user information   [D] quality service

32. Linking phone numbers to Facebook identities may _____.

    [A] worsen political disputes   [B] pose a risk to Facebook users

    [C] mess up customer records   [D] mislead the European commission

33. According to the author, competition law _____.

    [A] should serve the new market powers   [B] may worsen the economic imbalance

    [C] should not provide just one legal solution   [D] cannot keep pace with the changing market

34. Competition law as presently interpreted can hardly protect Facebook users because ____.

    [A] the services are generally digital   [B] the services are paid for by advertisers

    [C] they are not defined as customers   [D] they are not financially reliable

35. The ants analogy is used to illustrate _____.

    [A] the relationship between digital giants and their users

    [B] a typical competition pattern among digital giants

    [C] the benefits provided for digital giants' customers

    [D] a win-win business model between digital giant

Text 4

To combat the trap of putting a premium on being busy, Cal Newport, author of *Deep Work: Rules for Focused Success in a Distracted World*, recommends building a habit of "deep work"—the ability to focus without distraction.

There are a number of approaches to mastering the art of deep work—be it lengthy retreats dedicated to a specific task; developing a daily ritual; or taking a "journalistic" approach to seizing moments of deep work when you can throughout the day. Whichever approach, the key is to determine your length of focus time and stick to it.

Newport also recommends "deep scheduling" to combat constant interruptions and get more done in less time. "At any given point, I should have deep work scheduled for roughly the next month. Once on the calendar, I protect this time like I would a doctor's appointment or important meeting," he writes.

Another approach to getting more done in less time is to rethink how you prioritise your day—in particular how we craft our to-do lists. Tim Harford, author of *Messy: The Power of Disorder to Transform Our Lives*, points to a study in the early 1980s that divided undergraduates into two groups: some were advised to set out monthly goals and study activities; others were told to plan activities and goals in much more detail, day by day.

While the researchers assumed that the well-structured daily plans would be most effective when it came to the execution of tasks, they were wrong: the detailed daily plans demotivated students. Harford argues that inevitable distractions often render the daily to-do list ineffective, while leaving room for improvisation in such a list can reap the best results.

In order to make the most of our focus and energy, we also need to embrace downtime, or as Newport suggests, "be lazy."

"Idleness is not just a vacation, an indulgence or a vice; it is as indispensable to the brain as vitamin D is to the body...[idleness] is, paradoxically, necessary to getting any work done," he argues.

Srini Pillay, an assistant professor of psychiatry at Harvard Medical School, believes this counterintuitive link between downtime and productivity may be due to the way our brains operate. When our brains switch between being focused and unfocused on a task, they tend to be more efficient.

"What people don't realise is that in order to complete these tasks they need to use both the focus and unfocus circuits in their brain," says Pillar.

36. The key to mastering the art of deep work is to _____.

   [A] seize every minute to work   [B] list your immediate tasks

   [C] make specific daily plans   [D] keep to your focus time

37. The study in the early 1980s cited by Harford shows that _____.

   [A] students are hardly motivated by monthly goals

   [B] detailed plans may not be as fruitful as expected

   [C] distractions may actually increase efficiency

   [D] daily schedules are indispensable to studying

38. According to Newport, idleness is _____.

   [A] a desirable mental state for busy people

   [B] a major contributor to physical health

   [C] an effective way to save time and energy

   [D] an essential factor in accomplishing any work

39. Pillay believes that our brains' shift between being focused and unfocused _____.

   [A] can bring about greater efficiency   [B] can result in psychological well-being

   [C] is driven by task urgency   [D] is aimed at better balance in work

40. This text is mainly about _____.

   [A] approaches to getting more done in less time

   [B] ways to relieve the tension of busy life

[C] the key to eliminating distractions

[D] the cause of the lack of focus time

Part B

Directions: Read the following text and answer the questions by choosing the most suitable subheading from the list A–G for each of the numbered paragraphs (41–45). There are two extra subheadings which you do not need to use. Mark your answers on the ANSWER SHEET. (10 points)

[A] Be present

[B] Just say it

[C] Ask for an opinion

[D] Find the "me too" s

[E] Name, places, things

[F] Skip the small talk

[G] Pay a unique compliment

Five ways to make conversation with anyone

Conversations are links, which means when you have a conversation with a new person a link gets formed and every conversation you have after that moment will strengthen the link.

You meet new people every day: the grocery worker, the cab driver, new people at work or the security guard at the door. Simply starting a conversation with them will form a link.

Here are five simple ways that you can make the first move and start a conversation with strangers.

41. _____

Suppose you are in a room with someone you don't know and something within you says "I want to talk with this person"—this is something that mostly happens with all of us. You wanted to say something—the first word—but it just won't come out, it feels like it is stuck somewhere. I know the feeling and here is my advice: just get it out.

Just think: what is the worst that could happen? They won't talk with you? Well, they are not talking with you now!

I truly believe that once you get that first word out everything else will just flow. So keep it simple: "Hi", "Hey" or "Hello"—do the best you can to gather all of the enthusiasm and energy you can, put on a big smile and say "Hi."

42. _____

It's a problem all of us face; you have limited time with the person that you want to talk with and you want to make this talk memorable.

Honestly, if we got stuck in the rut of "hi", "hello", "how are you?" and "what's going on?", you will fail to give the initial jolt to the conversation that can make it so memorable.

So don't be afraid to ask more personal questions. Trust me, you'll be surprised to see how much people are willing to share if you just ask.

43. _____

When you meet a person for the first time, make an effort to find the things which you and that person have in common so that you can build the conversation from that point. When you start conversation from there and then move outwards, you'll find all of a sudden that the conversation becomes a lot easier.

44. _____

Imagine you are pouring your heart out to someone and they are just busy on their phone, and if you ask for their attention you get the response "I can multitask".

So when someone tries to communicate with you, just be in that communication wholeheartedly. Make eye contact. Trust me, eye contact is where all the magic happens. When you make eye contact, you can feel the conversation.

45. _____

You all came into a conversation where you first met the person, but after some time you may have met again and have forgotten their name. Isn't that awkward?

So, remember the little details of the people you met or you talked with; perhaps the places they have been to, the places they want to go, the things they like, the things they hate—whatever you talk about.

When you remember such things you can automatically become investor in their wellbeing. So they feel a responsibility to you to keep that relationship going.

That's it. Five amazing ways that you can make conversation with almost anyone. Every person is a really good book to read, or to have a conversation with!

Section III   Translation

46. **Directions:** Translate the following text into Chinese. Write your translation on the ANSWER SHEET. (15 points)

A fifth grader gets a homework assignment to select his future career path from a list of occupations. He ticks "astronaut" but quickly adds "scientist" to the list and selects it as well. The boy is convinced that if he reads enough, he can explore as many career paths as he likes. And so he reads—everything from encyclopedias to science fiction novels. He reads so passionately that his parents have to institute a "no reading policy" at the dinner table.

That boy was Bill Gates, and he hasn't stopped reading yet—not even after becoming one of the most successful people on the planet. Nowadays, his reading material has changed from science fiction and reference books: recently, he revealed that he reads at least 50 nonfiction books a year. Gates chooses nonfiction titles because they explain how the world works. "Each book opens up new avenues of knowledge to explore," Gates says.

Section IV Writing

Part A

47. Directions:

Suppose you have to cancel your travel plan and will not be able to visit Professor Smith. Write him an email to

1) apologize and explain the situation, and

2) suggest a future meeting.

You should write about 100 words on the ANSWER SHEET.

Do not use your own name. Use "Li Ming" instead.

Do not write your address. (10 points)

Part B

48. Directions:

Write an essay based on the chart below. In your writing, you should

1) interpret the chart, and

2) give your comments.

You should write about 150 words on the ANSWER SHEET. (15 points)

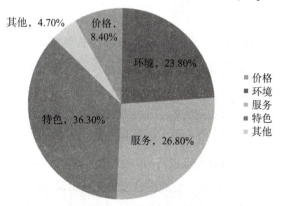

2017年某市消费者选择餐厅时的关注因素

2018 年全国硕士研究生招生考试 英语（二）参考答案

Section I Use of English

1. A   2. C   3. D   4. C   5. B   6. C   7. D   8. A   9. B   10. D
11. C   12. D   13. B   14. A   15. A   16. A   17. B   18. C   19. A   20. D

Section II Reading Comprehension

Part A

21. C   22. B   23. C   24. D   25. A   26. D   27. D   28. B   29. A   30. C
31. C   32. B   33. D   34. C   35. A   36. D   37. B   38. B   39. A   40. A

Part B

41. B   42. F   43. D   44. A   45. E

Section III Translation

46.【参考译文】

　　一个五年级的学生得到一份家庭作业，作业要求是从一系列职业中选择自己未来的职业道路。他在"宇航员"那一项后面画了勾，但很快自己给名单增加了"科学家"这一项，然后也打了个勾。男孩相信，只要他读的书够多，他就可以探索各种自己喜欢的职业道路。于是他真的读了很多书，从百科全书到科幻小说，各种书读了个遍。他对读书是如此有激情（痴迷），以至于他的父母不得不制定"吃饭时不许读书"的规矩。

　　那个男孩就是比尔·盖茨，时至今日，他依然没有停下读书的脚步，甚至在他已经成为这个地球上最成功的人士之一后，也依然如此。现如今，他读的书已不再是科幻小说和参考书：最近，他透露自己每年至少要阅读50本非小说类书籍。盖茨之所以选择非小说类作品，是因为这些书诠释了这个世界是如何运作的（这个世界的运作方式）。盖茨说："每本书都为我推开了一扇通向新知的大门。"

扫码查看2018年英语真题解析

2019年全国硕士研究生招生考试英语（二）试题

Section I   Use of English

Directions: Read the following text. Choose the best word(s) for each numbered blank and mark A, B, C or D on the ANSWER SHEET. (10 points)

Weighing yourself regularly is a wonderful way to stay aware of any significant weight fluctuations. __1__, when done too often, this habit can sometimes hurt more than it __2__.

As for me, weighing myself every day caused me to shift my focus from being generally healthy and physically active to focusing __3__ on the scale. That was bad to my overall fitness goals. I had gained weight in the form of muscle mass, but thinking only of __4__ the number on the scale, I altered my training program. That conflicted with how I needed to train to __5__ my goals.

I also found that weighing myself daily did not provide an accurate __6__ of the hard work and progress I was making in the gym. It takes about three weeks to a month to notice any significant changes in your weight __7__ altering your training program. The most __8__ changes will be observed in skill level, strength and inches lost.

For these __9__, I stopped weighing myself every day and switched to a bimonthly weighing schedule __10__. Since weight loss is not my goal, it is less important for me to __11__ my weight each week. Weighing every other week allows me to observe and __12__ any significant weight changes. That tells me whether I need to __13__ my training program.

I use my bimonthly weigh-in __14__ to get information about my nutrition as well. If my training intensity remains the same, but I'm constantly __15__ and dropping weight, this is a __16__ that I need to increase my daily caloric intake.

The __17__ to stop weighing myself every day has done wonders for my overall health, fitness and well-being. I'm experiencing increased zeal for working out since I no longer carry the burden of a __18__ morning weigh-in. I've also experienced greater success in achieving my specific fitness goals, __19__ I'm training according to those goals, not the numbers on a scale.

Rather than __20__ over the scale, turn your focus to how you look, feel, how your clothes fit and your overall energy level.

1. [A] Therefore   [B] Otherwise   [C] However   [D] Besides
2. [A] cares   [B] warns   [C] reduces   [D] helps
3. [A] solely   [B] occasionally   [C] formally   [D] initially
4. [A] lowering   [B] explaining   [C] accepting   [D] recording
5. [A] set   [B] review   [C] reach   [D] modify
6. [A] depiction   [B] distribution   [C] prediction   [D] definition
7. [A] regardless of [B] aside from   [C] along with   [D] due to
8. [A] rigid   [B] precise   [C] immediate   [D] orderly
9. [A] judgments   [B] reasons   [C] methods   [D] claims
10. [A] though   [B] again   [C] indeed   [D] instead
11. [A] track   [B] overlook   [C] conceal   [D] report
12. [A] approve of   [B] hold onto   [C] account for   D] depend on
13. [A] share   [B] adjust   [C] confirm   [D] prepare
14. [A] features   [B] rules   [C] tests   [D] results
15. [A] anxious   [B] hungry   [C] sick   [D] bored
16. [A] secret   [B] belief   [C] sign   [D] principle
17. [A] necessity   [B] decision   [C] wish   [D] request

18. [A] surprising   [B] restricting   [C] consuming   [D] disappointing
19. [A] because   [B] unless   [C] until   [D] if
20. [A] dominating   [B] puzzling   [C] triumphing   [D] obsessing

Section II Reading Comprehension

Part A

Directions: Read the following four texts. Answer the questions after each text by choosing A, B, C or D. Mark your answers on the ANSWER SHEET. (40 points)

Text 1

Unlike so-called basic emotions such as sadness, fear, and anger, guilt emerges a little later, in conjunction with a child's growing grasp of social and moral norms. Children aren't born knowing how to say "I'm sorry"; rather, they learn over time that such statements appease parents and friends—and their own consciences. This is why researchers generally regard so-called moral guilt, in the right amount, to be a good thing.

In the popular imagination, of course, guilt still gets a bad rap. It is deeply uncomfortable—it's the emotional equivalent of wearing a jacket weighted with stones. Yet this understanding is outdated. "There has been a kind of revival or a rethinking about what guilt is and what role guilt can serve," says Amrisha Vaish, a psychology researcher at the University of Virginia, adding that this revival is part of a larger recognition that emotions aren't binary—feelings that may be advantageous in one context may be harmful in another. Jealousy and anger, for example, may have evolved to alert us to important inequalities. Too much happiness can be destructive.

And guilt, by prompting us to think more deeply about our goodness, can encourage humans to make up for errors and fix relationships. Guilt, in other words, can help hold a cooperative species together. It is a kind of social glue.

Viewed in this light, guilt is an opportunity. Work by Tina Malti, a psychology professor at the University of Toronto, suggests that guilt may compensate for an emotional deficiency. In a number of studies, Malti and others have shown that guilt and sympathy may represent different pathways to cooperation and sharing. Some kids who are low in sympathy may make up for that shortfall by experiencing more guilt, which can rein in their nastier impulses. And vice versa: High sympathy can substitute for low guilt.

In a 2014 study, for example, Malti looked at 244 children. Using caregiver assessments and the children's self-observations, she rated each child's overall sympathy level and his or her tendency to feel negative emotions after moral transgressions. Then the kids were handed chocolate coins, and given a chance to share them with an anonymous child. For the low-sympathy kids, how much they shared appeared to turn on how inclined they were to feel guilty. The guilt-prone ones shared more, even though they hadn't magically become more sympathetic to the other child's deprivation.

"That's good news," Malti says. "We can be prosocial because we caused harm and we feel regret."

21. Researchers think that guilt can be a good thing because it may help _____.

   [A] regulate a child's basic emotions   [B] improve a child's intellectual ability
   [C] intensify a child's positive feelings   [D] foster a child's moral development

22. According to Paragraph 2, many people still consider guilt to be _____.

   [A] deceptive   [B] addictive   [C] burdensome   [D] inexcusable

23. Vaish holds that the rethinking about guilt comes from an awareness that _____.

   [A] an emotion can play opposing roles   [B] emotions are socially constructive
   [C] emotional stability can benefit health   [D] emotions are context-independent

24. Malti and others have shown that cooperation and sharing _____.

   [A] may help correct emotional deficiencies   [B] can bring about emotional satisfaction

[C] can result from either sympathy or guilt [D] may be the outcome of impulsive acts

25. The word "transgressions" (Para. 5) is closest in meaning to _____.

   [A] wrongdoings   [B] discussions   [C] restrictions   [D] teachings

Text 2

Forests give us shade, quiet and one of the harder challenges in the fight against climate change. Even as we humans count on forests to soak up a good share of the carbon dioxide we produce, we are threatening their ability to do so. The climate change we are hastening could one day leave us with forests that emit more carbon than they absorb.

Thankfully, there is a way out of this trap—but it involves striking a subtle balance. Helping forests flourish as valuable "carbon sinks" long into the future may require reducing their capacity to absorb carbon now. California is leading the way, as it does on so many climate efforts, in figuring out the details.

The state's proposed Forest Carbon Plan aims to double efforts to thin out young trees and clear brush in parts of the forest. This temporarily lowers carbon-carrying capacity. But the remaining trees draw a greater share of the available moisture, so they grow and thrive, restoring the forest's capacity to pull carbon from the air. Healthy trees are also better able to fend off insects. The landscape is rendered less easily burnable. Even in the event of a fire, fewer trees are consumed.

The need for such planning is increasingly urgent. Already, since 2010, drought and insects have killed over 100 million trees in California, most of them in 2016 alone, and wildfires have burn hundreds of thousands of acres.

California plans to treat 35,000 acres of forest a year by 2020, and 60,000 by 2030—financed from the proceeds of the state's emissions-permit auctions. That's only a small share of the total acreage that could benefit, about half a million acres in all, so it will be vital to prioritize areas at greatest risk of fire or drought.

The strategy also aims to ensure that carbon in woody material removed from the forests is locked away in the form of solid lumber or burned as biofuel in vehicles that would otherwise run on fossil fuels. New research on transportation biofuels is already under way.

State governments are well accustomed to managing forests, but traditionally they've focused on wildlife, watersheds and opportunities for recreation. Only recently have they come to see the vital part forests will have to play in storing carbon. California's plan, which is expected to be finalized by the governor next year, should serve as a model.

26. By saying "one of the harder challenges," the author implies that _____.

 [A] forests may become a potential threat

 [B] people may misunderstand global warming

 [C] extreme weather conditions may arise

 [D] global climate change may get out of control

27. To maintain forests as valuable "carbon sinks," we may need to _____.

 [A] lower their present carbon-absorbing capacity

 [B] strike a balance among different plants

 [C] accelerate the growth of young trees

 [D] preserve the diversity of species in them

28. California's Forest Carbon Plan endeavors to _____.

 [A] cultivate more drought-resistant trees

 [B] find more effective ways to kill insects

 [C] reduce the density of some of its forests

 [D] restore its forests quickly after wildfires

29. What is essential to California's plan according to Paragraph 5?

 [A] To carry it out before the year of 2020.   [B] To handle the areas in serious danger first.

[C] To perfect the emissions-permit auctions.   [D] To obtain enough financial support.

30. The author's attitude to California's plan can best be described as _____.

    [A] ambiguous   [B] tolerant   [C] cautious   [D] supportive

Text 3

American farmers have been complaining of labor shortages for several years. The complaints are unlikely to stop without an overhaul of immigration rules for farm workers.

Congress has obstructed efforts to create a more straightforward visa for agricultural workers that would let foreign workers stay longer in the U.S. and change jobs within the industry. If this doesn't change, American businesses, communities and consumers will be the losers.

Perhaps half of U.S. farm laborers are undocumented immigrants. As fewer such workers enter the country, the characteristics of the agricultural workforce are changing. Today's farm laborers, while still predominantly born in Mexico, are more likely to be settled rather than migrating and more likely to be married than single. They're also aging. At the start of this century, about one-third of crop workers were over the age of 35. Now more than half are. And picking crops is hard on older bodies. One oft-debated cure for this labor shortage remains as implausible as it's been all along: Native U.S. workers won't be returning to the farm.

Mechanization isn't the answer, either—not yet, at least. Production of corn, cotton, rice, soybeans, and wheat has been largely mechanized, but many high-value, labor-intensive crops, such as strawberries, need labor. Even dairy farms, where robots do a small share of milking, have a long way to go before they're automated.

As a result, farms have grown increasingly reliant on temporary guest workers using the H-2A visa to fill the gaps in the workforce. Starting around 2012, requests for the visas rose sharply; from 2011 to 2016 the number of visas issued more than doubled.

The H-2A visa has no numerical cap, unlike the H-2B visa for nonagricultural work, which is limited to 66,000 a year. Even so, employers complain they aren't given all the workers they need. The process is cumbersome, expensive, and unreliable. One survey found that bureaucratic delays led the average H-2A worker to arrive on the job 22 days late. The shortage is compounded by federal immigration raids, which remove some workers and drive others underground.

In a 2012 survey, 71 percent of tree-fruit growers and almost 80 percent of raisin and berry growers said they were short of labor. Some western farmers have responded by moving operations to Mexico. From 1998 to 2000, 14.5 percent of the fruit Americans consumed was imported. Little more than a decade later, the share of imports was 25.8 percent.

In effect, the U.S. can import food or it can import the workers who pick it.

31. What problem should be addressed according to the first two paragraphs?

[A] Discrimination against foreign workers in the U.S.

[B] Biased laws in favor of some American businesses.

[C] Flaws in U.S. immigration rules for farm workers.

[D] Decline of job opportunities in U.S. agriculture.

32. One trouble with U.S. agricultural workforce is _____.

[A] the rising number of illegal immigrants   [B] the high mobility of crop workers

[C] the lack of experienced laborers   [D] the aging of immigrant farm workers

33. What is the much-argued solution to the labor shortage in U.S. farming?

[A] To attract younger laborers to farm work.

[B] To get native U.S. workers back to farming.

[C] To use more robots to grow high-value crops.

[D] To strengthen financial support for farmers.

34. Agricultural employers complain about the H-2A visa for its _____.

[A] slow granting procedures   [B] limit on duration of stay

[C] tightened requirements   [D] control of annual admissions

35. Which of the following could be the best title for this text?

[A] U.S. Agriculture in Decline?

[B] Import Food or Labor?

[C] America Saved by Mexico?

[D] Manpower vs. Automation?

Text 4

Arnold Schwarzenegger, Dia Mirza and Adrian Grenier have a message for you: It's easy to beat plastic. They're part of a bunch of celebrities starring in a new video for World Environment Day—encouraging you, the consumer, to swap out your single-use plastic staples to combat the plastic crisis.

The key messages that have been put together for World Environment Day do include a call for governments to enact legislation to curb single-use plastics. But the overarching message is directed at individuals.

My concern with leaving it up to the individual, however, is our limited sense of what needs to be achieved. On their own, taking our own bags to the grocery store or quitting plastic straws, for example, will accomplish little and require very little of us. They could even be harmful, satisfying a need to have "done our bit" without ever progressing onto bigger, bolder, more effective actions—a kind of "moral licensing" that eases our concerns and stops us doing more and asking more of those in charge.

While the conversation around our environment and our responsibility toward it remains centered on shopping bags and straws, we're ignoring the balance of power that implies that as "consumers" we must shop sustainably, rather than as "citizens" hold our governments and industries to account to push for real systemic change.

It's important to acknowledge that the environment isn't everyone's priority—or even most people's. We shouldn't expect it to be. In her latest book, *Why Good People Do Bad Environmental Things*, Elizabeth R. DeSombre argues that the best way to collectively change the behavior of large numbers of people is for the change to be structural.

This might mean implementing policy such as a plastic tax that adds a cost to environmentally problematic action, or banning single-use plastics altogether. India has just announced it will "eliminate all single-use plastic in the country by 2022." There are also incentive-based ways of making better environmental choices easier, such as ensuring recycling is at least as easy as trash disposal.

DeSombre isn't saying people should stop caring about the environment. It's just that individual actions are too slow, she says, for that to be the only, or even primary, approach to changing widespread behavior.

None of this is about writing off the individual. It's just about putting things into perspective. We don't have time to wait. We need progressive policies that shape collective action, alongside engaged citizens pushing for change.

36. Some celebrities star in a new video to _____.

   [A] demand new laws on the use of plastics   [B] urge consumers to cut the use of plastics

   [C] invite public opinion on the plastics crisis   [D] disclose the causes of the plastics crisis

37. The author is concerned that "moral licensing" may _____.

   [A] mislead us into doing worthless things   [B] prevent us from making further efforts

   [C] weaken our sense of accomplishment   [D] suppress our desire for success

38. By pointing out our identity as "citizens," the author indicates that _____.

   [A] our focus should be shifted to community welfare

   [B] our relationship with local industries is improving

   [C] we have been actively exercising our civil rights

   [D] we should press our governments to lead the combat

39. DeSombre argues that the best way for a collective change should be _____.

   [A] a win-win arrangement   [B] a self-driven mechanism

[C] a cost-effective approach [D] a top-down process

40. The author concludes that individual efforts _____.

[A] can be too aggressive [B] are far from sufficient

[C] can be too inconsistent [D] are far from rational

Part B

Directions: Read the following text and match each of the numbered items in the left column to its corresponding information in the right column. There are two extra choices in the right column. Mark your answers on the ANSWER SHEET. (10 points)

How seriously should parents take kids' opinions when searching for a home?

In choosing a new home, Camille McClain's kids have a single demand: a backyard.

McClain's little ones aren't the only kids who have an opinion when it comes to housing, and in many cases youngsters' views weigh heavily on parents' real estate decisions, according to a 2018 Harris Poll survey of more than 2,000 U.S. adults.

While more families buck an older-generation proclivity to leave kids in the dark about real estate decisions, realty agents and psychologists have mixed views about the financial, personal and long-term effects kids' opinions may have.

The idea of involving children in a big decision is a great idea because it can help them feel a sense of control and ownership in what can be an overwhelming process, said Ryan Hooper, a clinical psychologist in Chicago.

"Children may face serious difficulties in coping with significant moves, especially if it removes them from their current school or support system," he said.

Greg Jaroszewski, a real estate broker with Gagliardo Realty Associates, said he's not convinced that kids should be involved in selecting a home—but their opinions should be considered in regards to proximity to friends and social activities, if possible.

Younger children should feel like they're choosing their home—without actually getting a choice in the matter, said Adam Bailey, a real estate attorney based in New York.

Asking them questions about what they like about the backyard of a potential home will make them feel like they're being included in the decision-making process, Bailey said.

Many of the aspects of homebuying aren't a consideration for children, said Tracey Hampson, a real estate agent based in Santa Clarita, Calif. And placing too much emphasis on their opinions can ruin a fantastic home purchase.

"Speaking with your children before you make a real estate decision is wise, but I wouldn't base the purchasing decision solely on their opinions," Hampson said.

The other issue is that many children—especially older ones—may base their real estate knowledge on HGTV shows, said Aaron Norris of The Norris Group in Riverside, Calif.

"They love Chip and Joanna Gaines just as much as the rest of us," he said. "HGTV has seriously changed how people view real estate. It's not shelter; it's a lifestyle. With that mindset change come some serious money consequences."

Kids tend to get stuck in the features and the immediate benefits to them personally, Norris said.

Parents need to remind their children that their needs and desires may change over time, said Julie Gurner, a real estate analyst with FitSmallBusiness.com.

"Their opinions can change tomorrow," Gurner said. "Harsh as it may be to say, that decision should likely not be made contingent on a child's opinions, but rather made for them with great consideration into what home can meet their needs best—and give them an opportunity to customize it a bit and make it their own."

This advice is more relevant now than ever before, even as more parents want to embrace the ideas of their children, despite the current housing crunch.

	[A] notes that aspects like children's friends and social activities should be considered upon homebuying.
41. Ryan Hooper	[B] believes that homebuying decisions should be based on children's needs rather than their opinions.
42. Adam Bailey	[C] assumes that many children's views on real estate are influenced by the media.
43. Tracey Hampson	[D] remarks that significant moves may pose challenges to children.
44. Aaron Norris	[E] says that it is wise to leave kids in the dark about real estate decisions.
45. Julie Gurner	[F] advises that home purchases should not be based only on children's opinions.
	[G] thinks that children should be given a sense of involvement in homebuying decisions.

Section III Translation

46. **Directions:** Translate the following text into Chinese. Write your translation on the ANSWER SHEET. (15 points)

It is easy to underestimate English writer James Herriot. He had such a pleasant, readable style that one might think that anyone could imitate it. How many times have I heard people say, "I could write a book. I just haven't the time." Easily said. Not so easily done. James Herriot, contrary to popular opinion, did not find it easy in his early days of, as he put it, "having a go at the writing game". While he obviously had an abundance of natural talent, the final, polished work that he gave to the world was the result of years of practising, re-writing and reading. Like the majority of authors, he had to suffer many disappointments and rejections along the way, but these made him all the more determined to succeed. Everything he achieved in life was earned the hard way and his success in the literary field was no exception.

Section IV Writing

Part A

47. **Directions:**

Suppose Professor Smith asked you to plan a debate on the theme of city traffic. Write him an email to

1) suggest a specific topic with your reasons, and

2) tell him about your arrangements.

You should write about 100 words on the ANSWER SHEET.

Do not use your own name. Use "Li Ming" instead. (10 points)

Part B

48. Directions:

Write an essay based on the chart below. In your writing, you should

1) interpret the chart, and

2) give your comments.

You should write about 150 words on the ANSWER SHEET. (15 points)

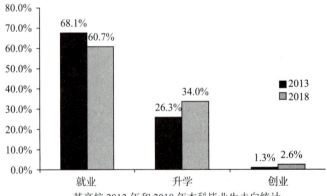

某高校 2013 年和 2018 年本科毕业生去向统计

2019年全国硕士研究生招生考试

英语（二）参考答案

Section I Use of English

1. C   2. D   3. A   4. A   5. C   6. A   7. D   8. C   9. B   10. D
11. A 12. C 13. B 14. D 15. B 16. C 17. B 18. D 19. A 20. D

Section II Reading Comprehension

Part A

21. D 22. C 23. A 24. C 25. A 26. A 27. A 28. C 29. B 30. D
31. C 32. D 33. B 34. A 35. B 36. B 37. B 38. D 39. D 40. B

Part B

41. D 42. G 43. F 44. C 45. B

Section III Translation

46. 【参考译文】

对于英国作家詹姆斯·赫里奥特，人们往往不甚重视。其创作风格明快自如、朗朗上口，以至于令人感觉极易模仿。我不止三番五次地听人说："我也能写书，只是没时间。"说来容易做来难。与大众观点相反，詹姆斯·赫里奥特在如他所言的"尝试写作"的早期并未感觉轻而易举。尽管赫里奥特天赋异禀，他呈递给世人的精雕细琢的作品皆是数年练习、重写和阅读的结果。和大多数作家一样，他在创作的道路上也屡屡经历失意和遭遇拒绝。但这一切更令他义无反顾地走向成功。其一生所获皆是筚路蓝缕，文学成就也概莫能外。

2020年全国硕士研究生招生考试英语（二）试题

Section I Use of English

Directions: Read the following text. Choose the best word(s) for each numbered blank and mark A, B, C or D on the ANSWER SHEET. (10 points)

Being a good parent is what every parent would like to be. But defining what it means to be a good parent is undoubtedly very __1__, particularly since children respond differently to the same style of parenting. A calm, rule-following child might respond better to a different sort of parenting than, __2__, a younger one.

__3__, there's another sort of parent that's easier to __4__: a patient parent. Children of every age benefit from patient parenting. Still, __5__ every parent would like to be patient, this is no easy __6__. Sometimes parents get exhausted and are unable to maintain a __7__ style with their kids. I understand this.

You're only human, and sometimes your kids can __8__ you just a little too far. And then the __9__ happens: You lose your patience and either scream at your kids or say something that was too __10__ and does nobody any good. You wish that you could __11__ the clock and start over. We've all been there.

__12__, even though it's common, it's vital to keep in mind that in a single moment of fatigue, you can say something to your child that you may __13__ for a long time. This may not only do damage to your relationship with your child but also __14__ your child's self-esteem.

If you consistently lose your __15__ with your kids, then you are modeling a lack of emotional control for your kids. We are all becoming increasingly aware of the __16__ of modeling patience for the younger generation. This is a skill that will help them throughout life. In fact, the ability to maintain emotional control when __17__ by stress is one of the most significant of all life's skills.

Certainly, it's __18__ to maintain patience at all times with your kids. A more practical goal is to try to be as calm as you can when faced with __19__ situations involving your children. I can promise you this: As a result of working toward this goal, you and your children will benefit and __20__ from stressful moments feeling better physically and emotionally.

1. [A] tedious   [B] pleasant   [C] instructive   [D] tricky
2. [A] in addition [B] for example   [C] at once   [D] by accident
3. [A] Fortunately [B] Occasionally   [C] Accordingly   [D] Eventually
4. [A] amuse   [B] assist   [C] describe   [D] train
5. [A] while   [B] because   [C] unless   [D] once
6. [A] answer   [B] task   [C] choice   [D] access
7. [A] tolerant   [B] formal   [C] rigid   [D] critical
8. [A] move   [B] drag   [C] push   [D] send
9. [A] mysterious   [B] illogical   [C] suspicious   [D] inevitable
10. [A] boring   [B] naive   [C] harsh   [D] vague
11. [A] turn back   [B] take apart   [C] set aside   [D] cover up
12. [A] Overall   [B] Instead   [C] However   [D] Otherwise
13. [A] like   [B] miss   [C] believe   [D] regret
14. [A] raise   [B] affect   [C] justify   [D] reflect
15. [A] time   [B] bond   [C] race   [D] cool
16. [A] nature   [B] secret   [C] importance   [D] context
17. [A] cheated   [B] defeated   [C] confused   [D] confronted
18. [A] terrible   [B] hard   [C] strange   [D] wrong

19. [A] trying   [B] changing   [C] exciting   [D] surprising

20. [A] hide   [B] emerge   [C] withdraw   [D] escape

Section II Reading Comprehension

Part A

Directions: Read the following four texts. Answer the questions after each text by choosing A, B, C or D. Mark your answers on the ANSWER SHEET. (40 points)

Text 1

Rats and other animals need to be highly attuned to social signals from others so they can identify friends to cooperate with and enemies to avoid. To find out if this extends to non-living beings, Laleh Quinn at the University of California, San Diego, and her colleagues tested whether rats can detect social signals from robotic rats.

They housed eight adult rats with two types of robotic rat—one social and one asocial—for four days. The robot rats were quite minimalist, resembling a chunkier version of a computer mouse with wheels to move around and colourful markings.

During the experiment, the social robot rat followed the living rats around, played with the same toys, and opened cage doors to let trapped rats escape. Meanwhile, the asocial robot simply moved forwards and backwards and side to side.

Next, the researchers trapped the robots in cages and gave the rats the opportunity to release them by pressing a lever. Across 18 trials each, the living rats were 52 per cent more likely on average to set the social robot free than the asocial one. This suggests that the rats perceived the social robot as a genuine social being. They may have bonded more with the social robot because it displayed behaviors like communal exploring and playing. This could lead to the rats better remembering having freed it earlier, and wanting the robot to return the favour when they get trapped, says Quinn.

"Rats have been shown to engage in multiple forms of reciprocal help and cooperation, including what is referred to as direct reciprocity—where a rat will help another rat that has previously helped them," says Quinn.

The readiness of the rats to befriend the social robot was surprising given its minimal design. The robot was the same size as a regular rat but resembled a simple plastic box on wheels. "We'd assumed we'd have to give it a moving head and tail, facial features, and put a scent on it to make it smell like a real rat, but that wasn't necessary," says Janet Wiles at the University of Queensland in Australia, who helped with the research.

The finding shows how sensitive rats are to social cues, even when they come from basic robots. Similarly, children tend to treat robots as if they are fellow beings, even when they display only simple social signals. "We humans seem to be fascinated by robots, and it turns out other animals are too," says Wiles.

21. Quinn and her colleagues conducted a test to see if rats can _____.

    [A] distinguish a friendly rat from a hostile one

    [B] pick up social signals from non-living rats

    [C] attain sociable traits through special training

    [D] send out warning messages to their fellows

22. What did the asocial robot do during the experiment?

    [A] It played with some toys.   [B] It set the trapped rats free.

    [C] It moved around alone.   [D] It followed the social robot.

23. According to Quinn, the rats released the social robot because they _____.

    [A] expected it to do the same in return   [B] considered that an interesting game

    [C] wanted to display their intelligence   [D] tried to practise a means of escape

24. Janet Wiles notes that rats _____.

[A] respond more to actions than to looks

[B] differentiate smells better than sizes

[C] can be scared by a plastic box on wheels

[D] can remember other rats' facial features

25. It can be learned from the text that rats _____.

[A] appear to be adaptable to new surroundings

[B] are more socially active than other animals

[C] are more sensitive to social cues than expected

[D] behave differently from children in socializing

Text 2

It is true that CEO pay has gone up—top ones may make 300 times the pay of typical workers on average, and since the mid-1970s, CEO pay for large publicly traded American corporations has, by varying estimates, gone up by about 500%. The typical CEO of a top American corporation now makes about $18.9 million a year.

The best model for understanding the growth of CEO pay is that of limited CEO talent in a world where business opportunities for the top firms are growing rapidly. The efforts of America's highest-earning 1% have been one of the most dynamic elements of the global economy. It's not popular to say, but one reason their pay has gone up so much is that CEOs really have upped their game relative to many other workers in the U.S. economy.

Today's CEO, at least for major American firms, must have many more skills than simply being able to "run the company." CEOs must have a good sense of financial markets and maybe even how the company should trade in them. They also need better public relations skills than their predecessors, as the costs of even a minor slip-up can be significant. Then there's the fact that large American companies are much more globalized than ever before, with supply chains spread across a larger number of countries. To lead in that system requires knowledge that is fairly mind-boggling. Plus, virtually all major American companies are becoming tech companies, often with their own research and development. And beyond this, major CEOs still have to do all the day-to-day work they have always done.

The common idea that high CEO pay is mainly about ripping people off doesn't explain history very well. By most measures, corporate governance has become a lot tighter and more rigorous since the 1970s. Yet it is principally during this period of stronger governance that CEO pay has been high and rising. That suggests it is in the broader corporate interest to recruit top candidates for increasingly tough jobs.

Furthermore, the highest CEO salaries are paid to outside candidates, not to the cozy insider picks, another sign that high CEO pay is not some kind of depredation at the expense of the rest of the company. And the stock market reacts positively when companies tie CEO pay to, say, stock prices, a sign that those practices build up corporate value not just for the CEO.

26. Which of the following has contributed to CEO pay rise?

   [A] Increased business opportunities for top firms.

   [B] Close cooperation among leading economies.

   [C] The general pay rise with a better economy.

   [D] The growth in the number of corporations.

27. Compared with their predecessors, today's CEOs are required to _____.

   [A] establish closer ties with tech companies   [B] operate more globalized companies

   [C] finance more research and development   [D] foster a stronger sense of teamwork

28. CEO pay has been rising since the 1970s despite _____.

   [A] continual internal opposition   [B] conservative business strategies

   [C] repeated government warnings   [D] strict corporate governance

29. High CEO pay can be justified by the fact that it helps _____.

   [A] confirm the status of CEOs   [B] increase corporate value

   [C] boost the efficiency of CEOs   [D] motivate inside candidates

30. The most suitable title for this text would be _____.

[A] CEO Traits: Not Easy to Define

[B] CEO Pay: Past and Present

[C] CEOs Are Not Overpaid

[D] CEOs' Challenges of Today

Text 3

Madrid was hailed as a public health guiding light last November when it rolled out ambitious restrictions on the most polluting cars. Seven months and one election day later, a new conservative city council suspended enforcement of the clean air zone, a first step toward its possible termination. Mayor José Luis Martínez-Almeida made opposition to the zone a centrepiece of his election campaign, despite its success in improving air quality. A judge has now overruled the city's decision to stop levying fines, ordering them restored. But with legal battles ahead, the zone's future looks uncertain at best.

Madrid's back and forth on clean air is a pointed reminder of the limits to the patchwork, city-by-city approach that characterises efforts on air pollution across Europe, Britain very much included.

Among other weaknesses, the measures cities must employ when left to tackle dirty air on their own are politically controversial, and therefore vulnerable. That's because they inevitably put the costs of cleaning the air on to individual drivers—who must pay fees or buy better vehicles—rather than on to the car manufacturers whose cheating is the real cause of our toxic pollution. It's not hard to imagine a similar reversal happening in London. The new ultra-low emission zone (Ulez) is likely to be a big issue in next year's mayoral election. And if Sadiq Khan wins and extends it to the North and South Circular roads in 2021 as he intends, it is sure to spark intense opposition from the far larger number of motorists who will then be affected.

It's not that measures such as London's Ulez are useless. Far from it. Local officials are using the levers that are available to them to safeguard residents' health in the face of a serious threat.

The zones do deliver some improvements to air quality, and the science tells us that means real health benefits.

But mayors and councillors can only do so much about a problem that is far bigger than any one city or town. They are acting because national governments—Britain's and others across Europe—have failed to do so.

Restrictions that keep highly polluting cars out of certain areas—city centres, "school streets", even individual roads—are a response to the absence of a larger effort to properly enforce existing regulations and require auto companies to bring their vehicles into compliance. Wales has introduced special low speed limits to minimise pollution. We're doing everything but insist that manufacturers clean up their cars.

31. Which of the following is true about Madrid's clean air zone?

   [A] Its effects are questionable.   [B] Its fate is yet to be decided.

   [C] It needs tougher enforcement.   [D] It has been opposed by a judge.

32. Which is considered a weakness of the city-level measures to tackle dirty air?

   [A] They are biased against car manufacturers.

   [B] They prove impractical for city councils.

   [C] They are deemed too mild by politicians.

   [D] They put the burden on individual motorists.

33. The author believes that the extension of London's Ulez will _____.

   [A] arouse strong resistance   [B] ensure Khan's electoral success

   [C] improve the city's traffic   [D] discourage car manufacturing

34. Who does the author think should have addressed the problem?

   [A] Local residents.   [B] Mayors.

   [C] Councillors.   [D] National governments.

35. It can be learned from the last paragraph that auto companies _____.

[A] will raise low-emission car production

[B] should be forced to follow regulations

[C] will upgrade the design of their vehicles

[D] should be put under public supervision

Text 4

Now that members of Generation Z are graduating college this spring—the most commonly-accepted definition says this generation was born after 1995, give or take a year—the attention has been rising steadily in recent weeks. Gen Zs are about to hit the streets looking for work in a labor market tha's tighter than it's been in decades. And employers are planning on hiring about 17 percent more new graduates for jobs in the U.S. this year than last, according to a survey conducted by the National Association of Colleges and Employers. Everybody wants to know how the people who will soon inhabit those empty office cubicles will differ from those who came before them.

If "entitled" is the most common adjective, fairly or not, applied to millennials (those born between 1981 and 1995), the catchwords for Generation Z are practical and cautious. According to the career counselors and experts who study them, Generation Zs are clear-eyed, economic pragmatists. Despite graduating into the best economy in the past 50 years, Generation Zs know what an economic train wreck looks like. They were impressionable kids during the crash of 2008, when many of their parents lost their jobs or their life savings or both. They aren't interested in taking any chances. The booming economy seems to have done little to assuage this underlying generational sense of anxious urgency, especially for those who have college debt. College loan balances in the U.S. now stand at a record $1.5 trillion, according to the Federal Reserve.

One survey from Accenture found that 88 percent of graduating seniors this year chose their major with a job in mind. In a 2019 survey of University of Georgia students, meanwhile, the career office found the most desirable trait in a future employer was the ability to offer secure employment (followed by professional development and training, and then inspiring purpose). Job security or stability was the second most important career goal (work-life balance was number one), followed by a sense of being dedicated to a cause or to feel good about serving the greater good.

That's a big change from the previous generation. "Millennials wanted more flexibility in their lives," notes Tanya Michelsen, Associate Director of YouthSight, a UK-based brand manager that conducts regular 60-day surveys of British youth, in findings that might just as well apply to American youth. "Generation Zs are looking for more certainty and stability, because of the rise of the gig economy. They have trouble seeing a financial future and they are quite risk averse."

36. Generation Zs graduating college this spring _____.

   [A] are recognized for their abilities   [B] are optimistic about the labor market

   [C] are in favor of job offers   [D] are drawing growing public attention

37. Generation Zs are keenly aware _____.

   [A] what their parents expect of them   [B] how they differ from past generations

   [C] what a tough economic situation is like   [D] how valuable a counselor's advice is

38. The word "assuage" (Para. 2) is closest in meaning to _____.

   [A] maintain   [B] define

   [C] deepen   [D] relieve

39. It can be learned from Paragraph 3 that Generation Zs _____.

   [A] care little about their job performance

   [B] have a clear idea about their future jobs

   [C] give top priority to professional training

   [D] think it hard to achieve work-life balance

40. Michelsen thinks that compared with millennials, Generation Zs are _____.

   [A] more diligent   [B] more generous

   [C] less realistic   [D] less adventurous

Part B

Directions: Read the following text and answer the questions by choosing the most suitable subheading from the list A-G for each numbered paragraph (41-45). There are two extra subheadings which you do not need to use. Mark your answers on the ANSWER SHEET. (10 points)

[A] Slow down and listen.

[B] Put on a good face, always.

[C] Give compliments, just not too many.

[D] Put yourselves in others' shoes.

[E] Tailor your interactions.

[F] Spend time with everyone.

[G] Reveal, don't hide information.

Five Ways to Win Over Everyone in the Office

Is it possible to like everyone in your office? Think about how tough it is to get together 15 people, much less 50, who all get along perfectly. But unlike in friendships, you need coworkers. You work with them every day and you depend on them just as they depend on you. Here are some ways that you can get the whole office on your side.

41._____

If you have a bone to pick with someone in your workplace, you may try to stay tight-lipped around them. But you won't be helping either one of you. A Harvard Business School study found that observers consistently rated those who were frank about themselves more highly, while those who hid lost trustworthiness. The lesson is not that you should make your personal life an open book, but rather, when given the option to offer up details about yourself or painstakingly conceal them, you should just be honest.

42._____

Just as important as being honest about yourself is being receptive to others. We often feel the need to tell others how we feel, whether it's a concern about a project, a stray thought, or a compliment. Those are all valid, but you need to take time to hear out your coworkers, too. In fact, rushing to get your own ideas out there can cause colleagues to feel you don't value their opinions. Do your best to engage coworkers in a genuine, back-and-forth conversation, rather than prioritizing your own thoughts.

43. _____

It's common to have a "cubicle mate" or special confidant in a work setting. But in addition to those trusted coworkers, you should expand your horizons and find out about all the people around you. Use your lunch and coffee breaks to meet up with colleagues you don't always see. Find out about their lives and interests beyond the job. It requires minimal effort and goes a long way. This will help to grow your internal network, in addition to being a nice break in the work day.

44. _____

Positive feedback is important for anyone to hear. And you don't have to be someone's boss to tell them they did an exceptional job on a particular project. This will help engender good will in others. But don't overdo it or be fake about it. One study found that people responded best to comments that shifted from negative to positive, possibly because it suggested they had won somebody over.

45. _____

This one may be a bit more difficult to pull off, but it can go a long way to achieving results. Remember in dealing with any coworker what they appreciate from an interaction. Watch out for how they verbalize with others. Some people like small talk in a meeting before digging into important matters, while others are more straightforward. Jokes that work on one person won't necessarily land with another. So, adapt your style accordingly to type. Consider the person that you're dealing with in advance and what will get you to your desired outcome.

Section III　Translation

46. Directions: Translate the following text from English into Chinese. Write your translation on the ANSWER SHEET. (15 points)

It's almost impossible to go through life without experiencing some kind of failure. But, the wonderful thing about failure is that it's entirely up to us to decide how to look at it.

We can choose to see failure as "the end of the world". Or, we can look at failure as the incredible learning experience that it often is. Every time we fail at something, we can choose to look for the same lesson we're meant to learn. These lessons are very important; they're how we grow, and how we keep from making that same mistake again. Failures stop us only if we let them.

Failure can also teach us things about ourselves that we would never have learned otherwise. For instance, failure can help you discover how strong a person you are. Failing at something can help you discover your truest friends, or help you find unexpected motivation to succeed.

Section IV　Writing

Part A

47. Directions:

Suppose you are planning a tour of a historical site for a group of international students. Write them an email to

1) tell them about the site, and

2) give them some tips for the tour.

You should write about 100 words on the ANSWER SHEET.

Do not sign your own name. Use "Li Ming" instead.

Do not write your address. (10 points)

Part B

48. Directions:

Write an essay based on the following chart. In your writing, you should

1) interpret the chart, and

2) give your comments.

You should write about 150 words. Write your essay on the ANSWER SHEET. (15 points)

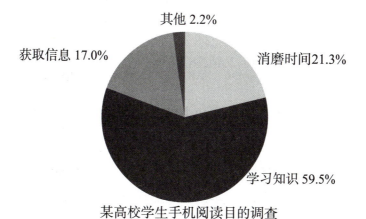

某高校学生手机阅读目的调查

2020年全国硕士研究生招生考试

英语（二）参考答案

Section I Use of English

1. D 2. B 3. A 4. C 5. A 6. B 7. A 8. C 9. D 10. C
11. A 12. C 13. D 14. B 15. D 16. C 17. D 18. B 19. A 20. B

Section II Reading Comprehension

Part A

21. B 22. C 23. A 24. A 25. C 26. A 27. B 28. D 29. B 30. C
31. B 32. D 33. A 34. D 35. B 36. D 37. C 38. D 39. B 40. D

Part B

41. G 42. A 43. F 44. C 45. E

Section III Translation

46.【参考译文】

人的一生几乎不可能没有经历过某种失败。但失败的奥妙之处在于它完全取决于一个人自身如何看待它。

我们可以选择把失败视为"世界末日"。又或者，我们也可以把失败看作是一种难以置信的成长经历。每当我们在某件事上失败时，我们可以选择寻找我们本应学习的经验。这些经验非常重要。它们既是我们成长的方式，又是我们避免再犯同样错误的方法。失败无法阻挡我们前进，除非我们自己放弃。

失败也可以教会我们一些关于我们自己的东西。如果没有失败，我们永远也学不到这些东西。例如，失败可以帮助你发现自己到底有多强大。通过某些事情的失败，你还可以找到真正的朋友，或者获得一些意想不到的促使成功的动力。

扫码查看2020年英语真题解析

附录

➡ 全国专业硕士培养单位

全国专业硕士培养单位

  国内一流商学院门户网站 MBAChina 为全国 MBA、EMBA、MPAcc、MPA、MEM 等管理类联考专业的考生提供了一款商学院信息检索和信息查询工具，非常适合择校阶段的考生使用。考生可以按照地区、学费预算、分数线、认证、项目特色等要素对国内商学院进行检索。考生扫描下方二维码，即可关注最前沿的管理类联考院校信息。

MBA 院校库

网址：http://mba.mbachina.com

MPAcc 院校库

网址：http://mpacc.mbachina.com

EMBA 院校库

网址：http://emba.mbachina.com

MPA 院校库

网址：http://mpa.mbachina.com

MEM 院校库

网址：http://mem.mbachina.com